c o n t e n t s

Chapter 1
Adolte and Adalte

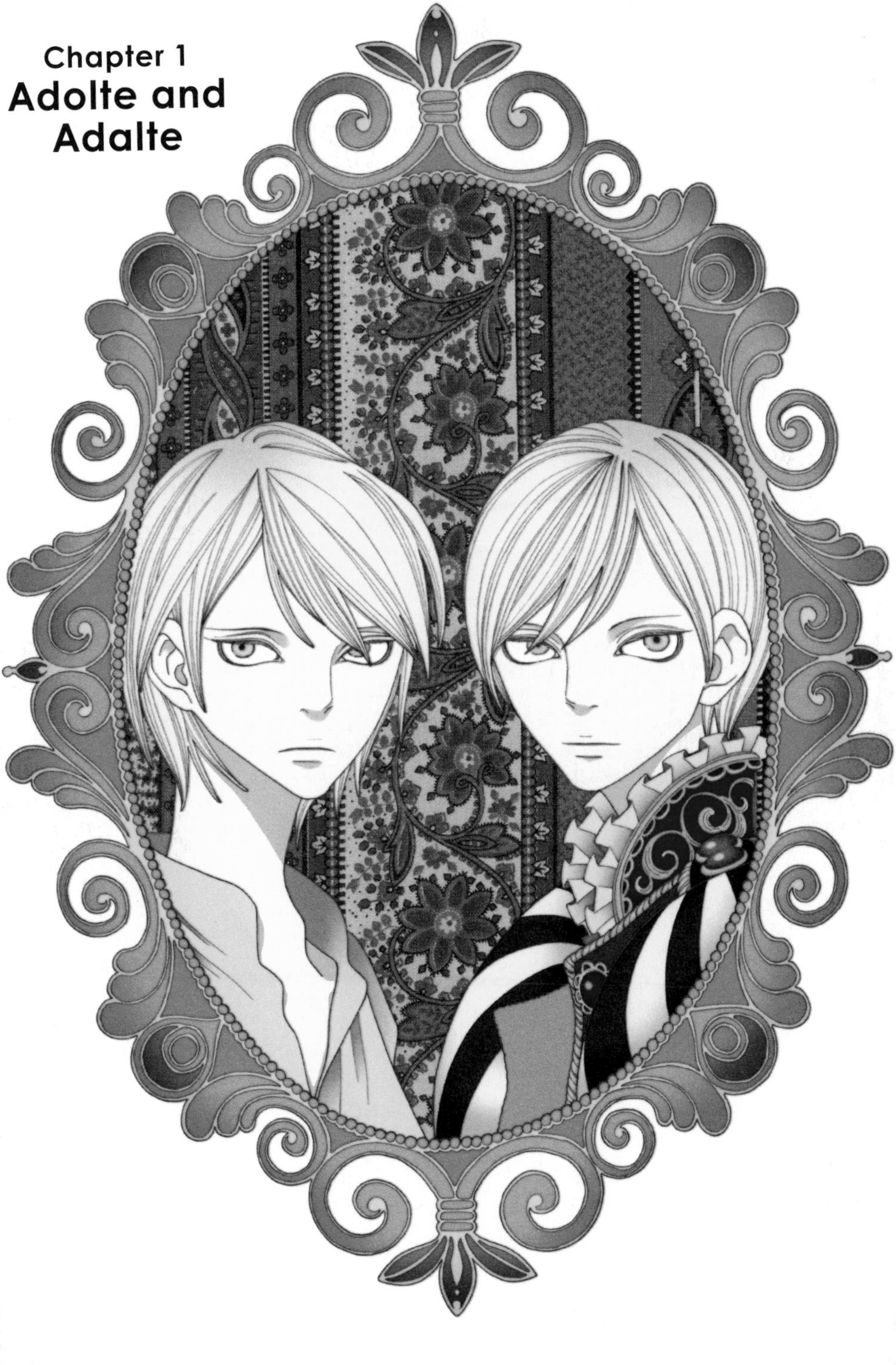

Tales
of the
Kingdom

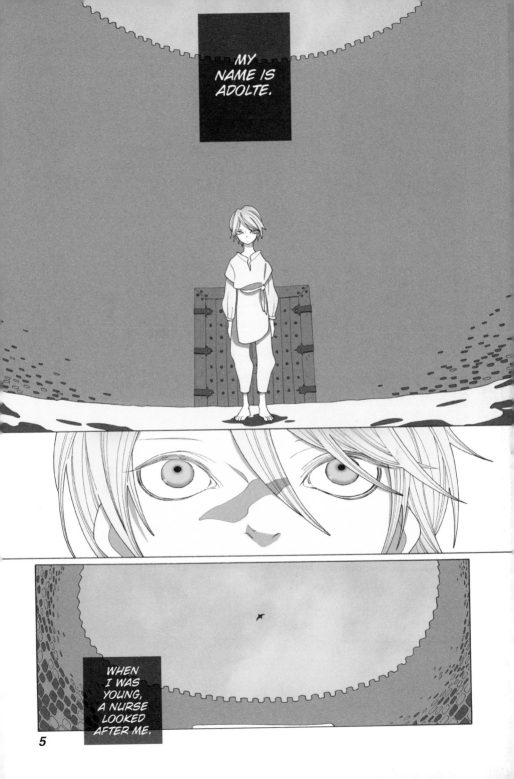

MY NAME IS ADOLTE.

WHEN I WAS YOUNG, A NURSE LOOKED AFTER ME.

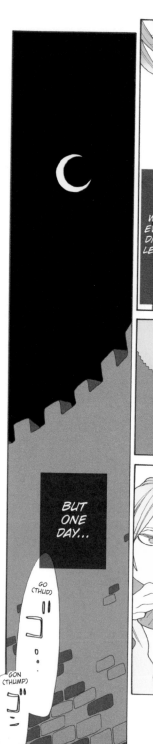

SHE FED ME THREE TIMES A DAY, AND WHEN SHE PUT ME TO BED...

...SHE WOULD CRY FOR ME OUT OF PITY.

WHEN SHE EVENTUALLY DIED, I WAS LEFT ALONE.

BUT ONE DAY...

GO
(THUD)

GON
(THUMP)

6

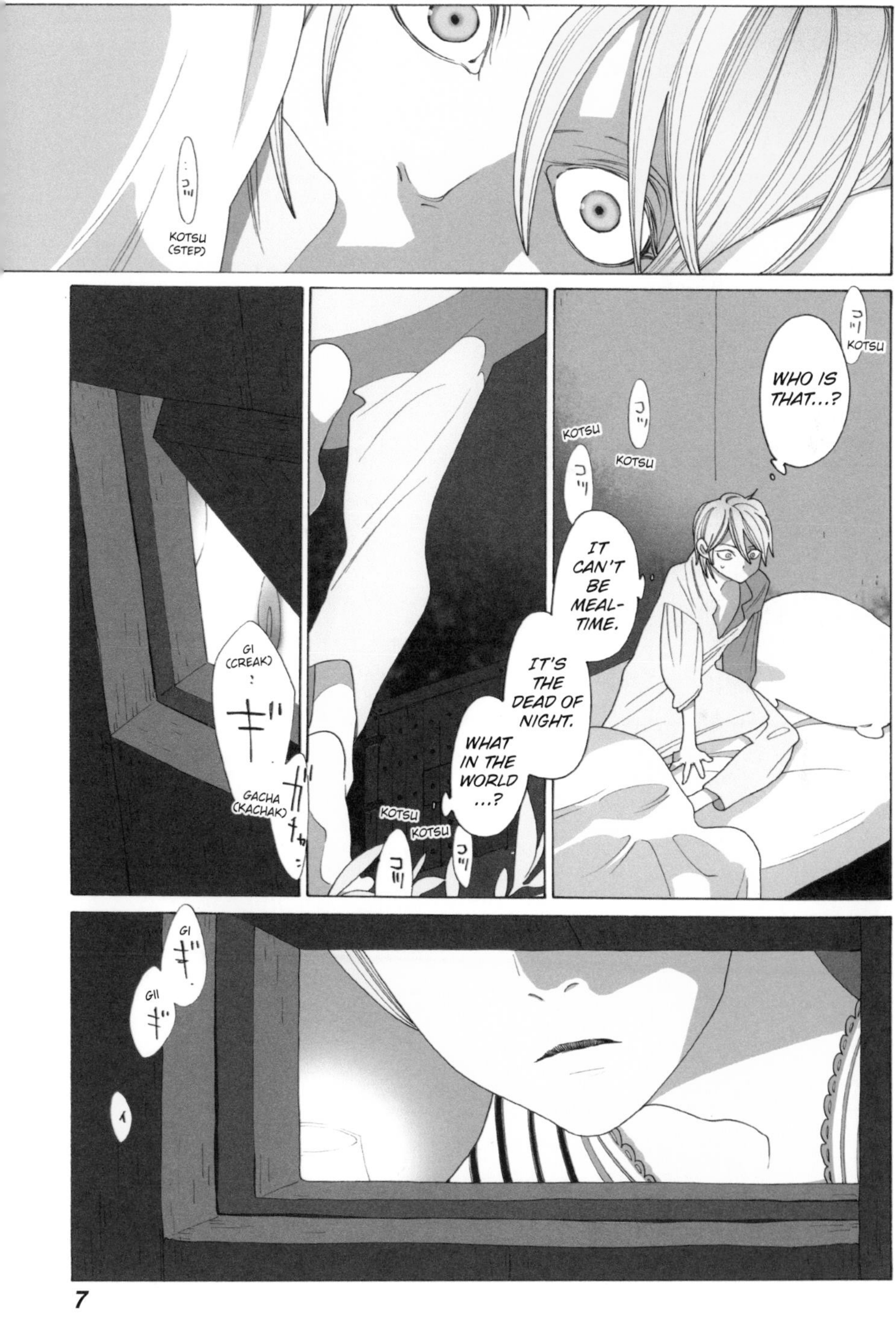
KOTSU (STEP)
KOTSU
WHO IS THAT...?
KOTSU
KOTSU
IT CAN'T BE MEAL-TIME.
IT'S THE DEAD OF NIGHT.
WHAT IN THE WORLD ...?
KOTSU
KOTSU
GI (CREAK)
GACHA (KACHAK)
GI
GII

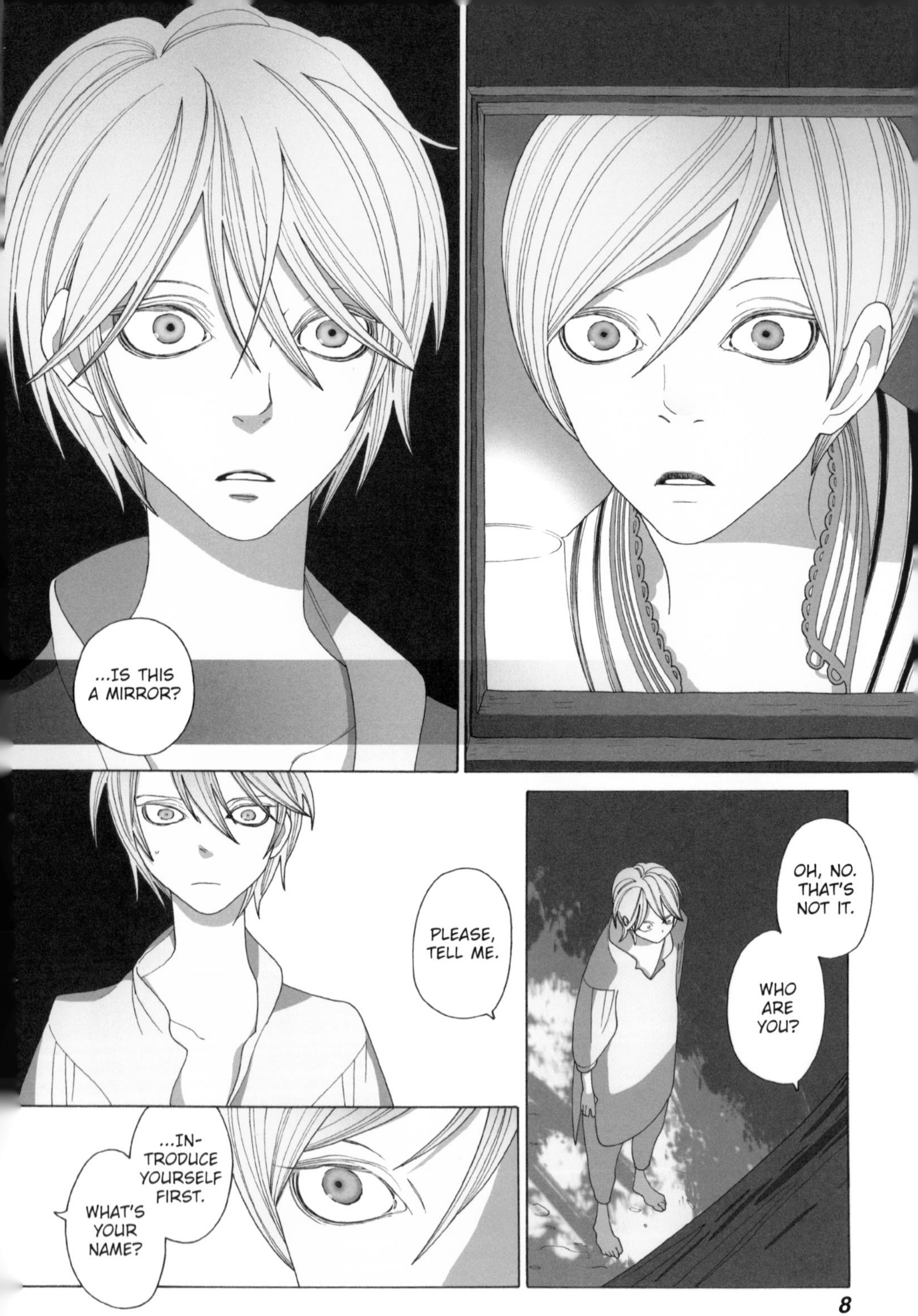
...IS THIS A MIRROR?
OH, NO. THAT'S NOT IT.
WHO ARE YOU?
PLEASE, TELL ME.
...IN-TRODUCE YOURSELF FIRST.
WHAT'S YOUR NAME?

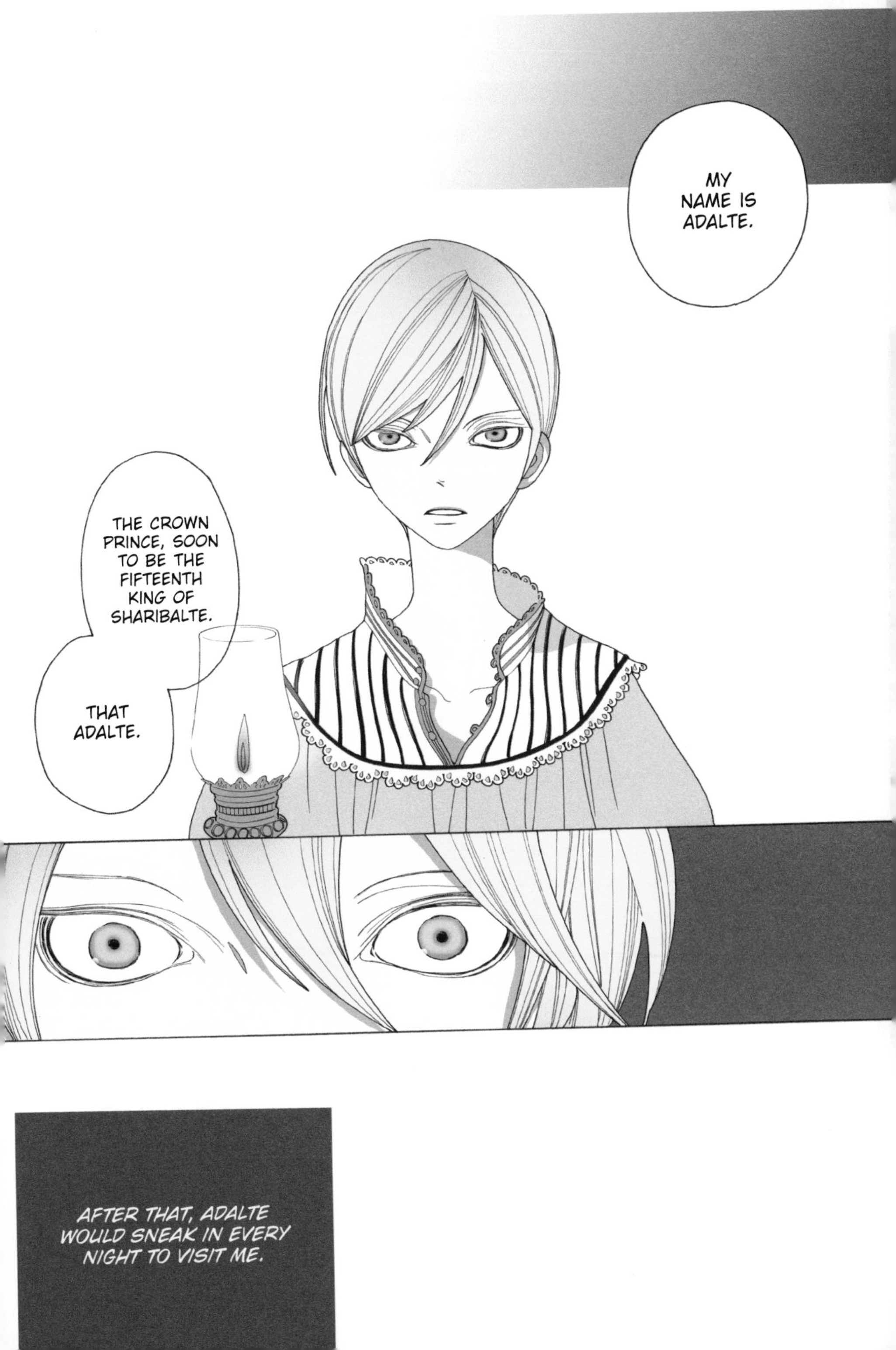
MY NAME IS ADALTE.
THE CROWN PRINCE, SOON TO BE THE FIFTEENTH KING OF SHARIBALTE.
THAT ADALTE.
AFTER THAT, ADALTE WOULD SNEAK IN EVERY NIGHT TO VISIT ME.

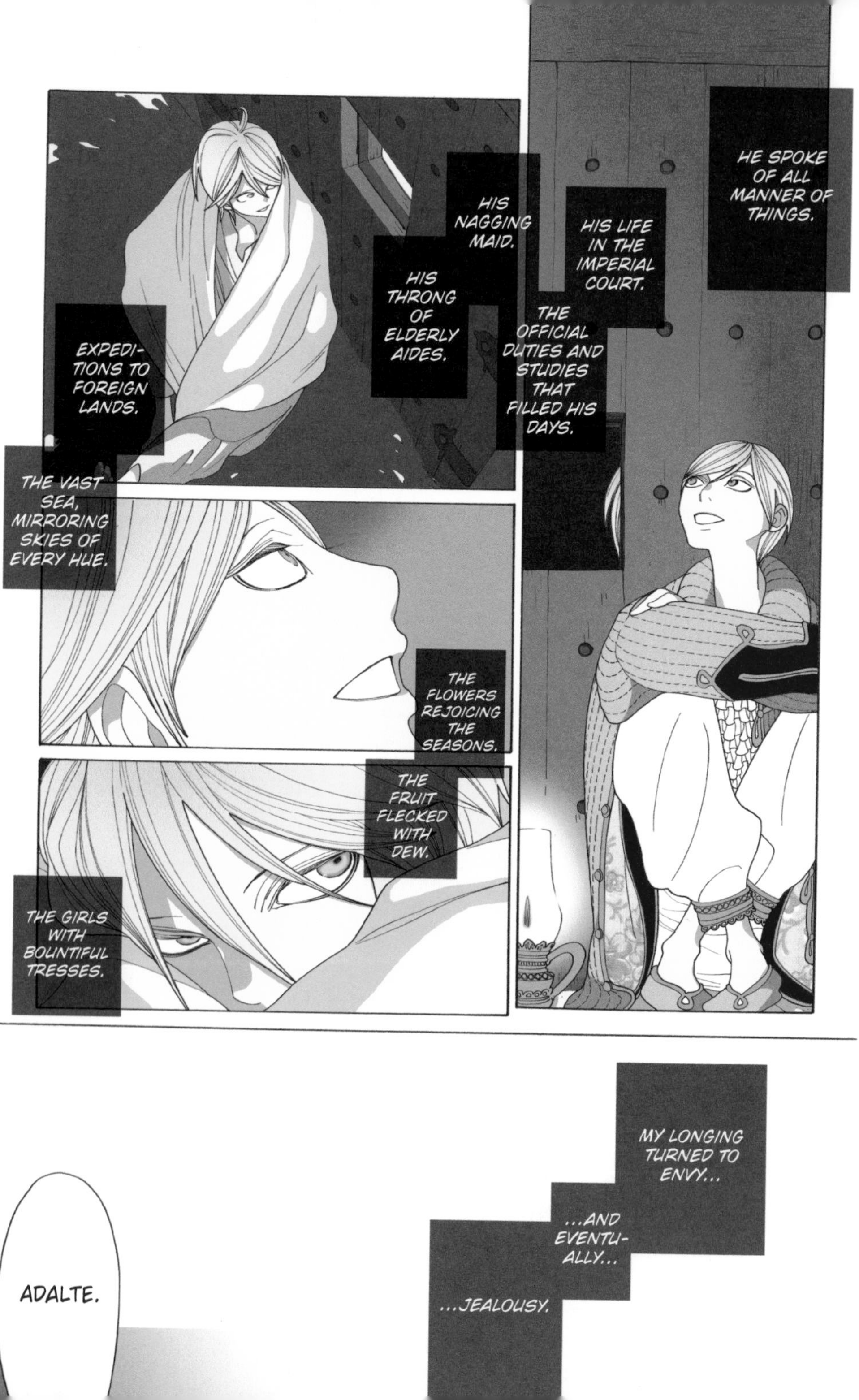
HE SPOKE OF ALL MANNER OF THINGS.
HIS LIFE IN THE IMPERIAL COURT.
HIS NAGGING MAID.
HIS THRONG OF ELDERLY AIDES.
THE OFFICIAL DUTIES AND STUDIES THAT FILLED HIS DAYS.
EXPEDITIONS TO FOREIGN LANDS.
THE VAST SEA, MIRRORING SKIES OF EVERY HUE.
THE FLOWERS REJOICING THE SEASONS.
THE FRUIT FLECKED WITH DEW.
THE GIRLS WITH BOUNTIFUL TRESSES.
MY LONGING TURNED TO ENVY...
...AND EVENTU-ALLY...
...JEALOUSY.
ADALTE.

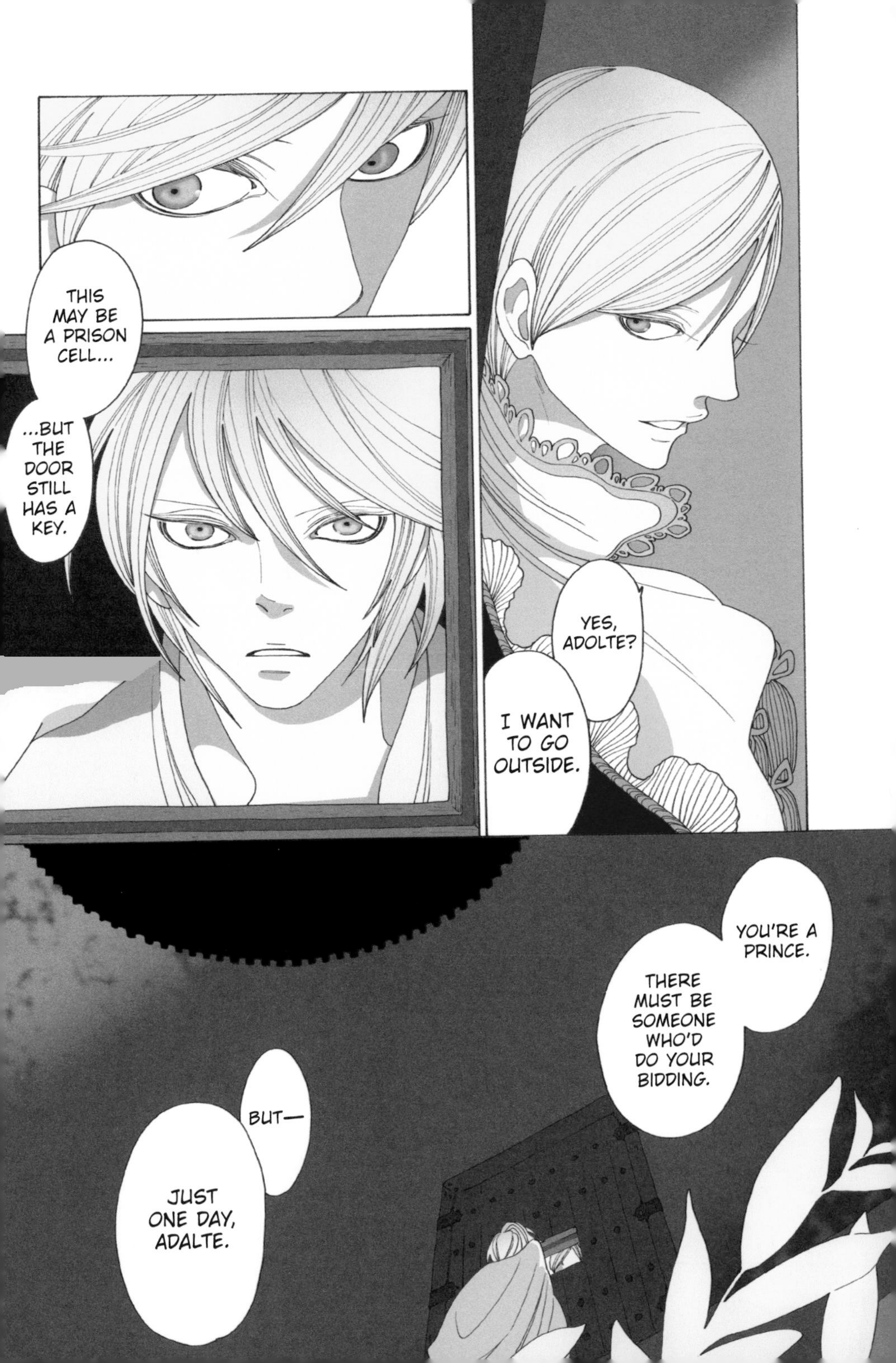
YES, ADOLTE?
I WANT TO GO OUTSIDE.
THIS MAY BE A PRISON CELL...
...BUT THE DOOR STILL HAS A KEY.
YOU'RE A PRINCE.
THERE MUST BE SOMEONE WHO'D DO YOUR BIDDING.
BUT—
JUST ONE DAY, ADALTE.

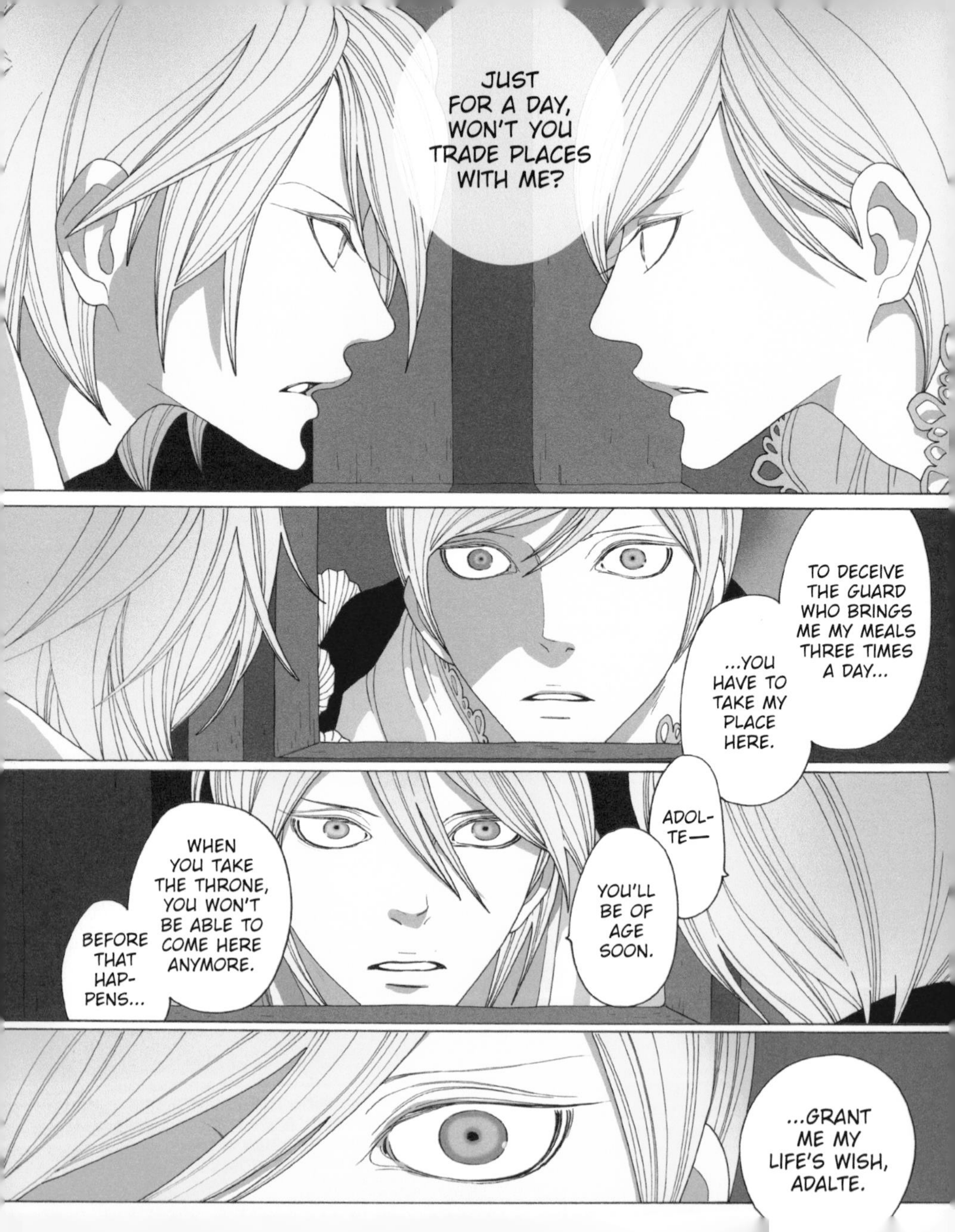
JUST FOR A DAY, WON'T YOU TRADE PLACES WITH ME?
TO DECEIVE THE GUARD WHO BRINGS ME MY MEALS THREE TIMES A DAY...
...YOU HAVE TO TAKE MY PLACE HERE.
ADOL-TE—
YOU'LL BE OF AGE SOON.
WHEN YOU TAKE THE THRONE, YOU WON'T BE ABLE TO COME HERE ANYMORE.
BEFORE THAT HAP-PENS...
...GRANT ME MY LIFE'S WISH, ADALTE.

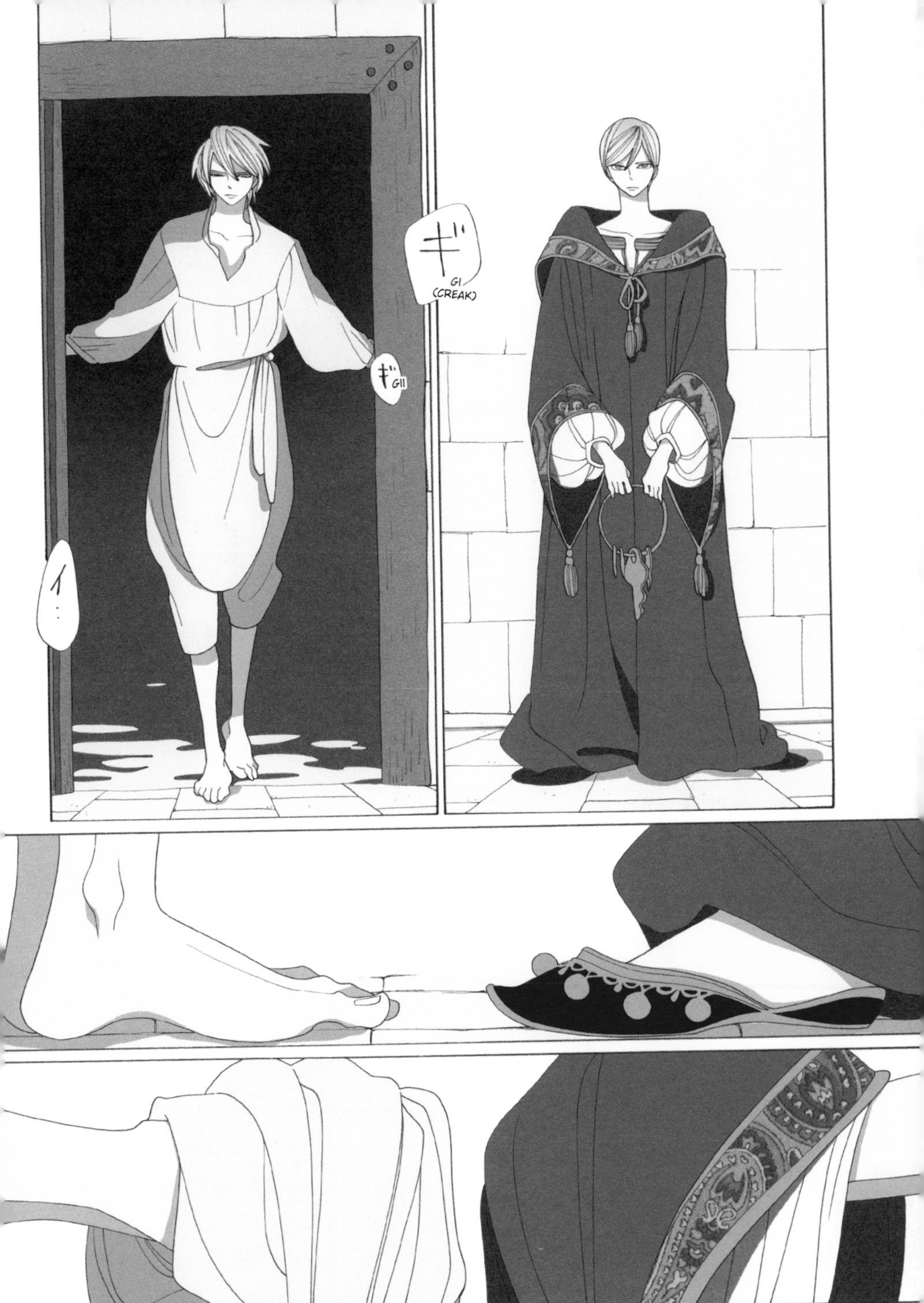
ギ
GI
(CREAK)
ギ GII
イ…

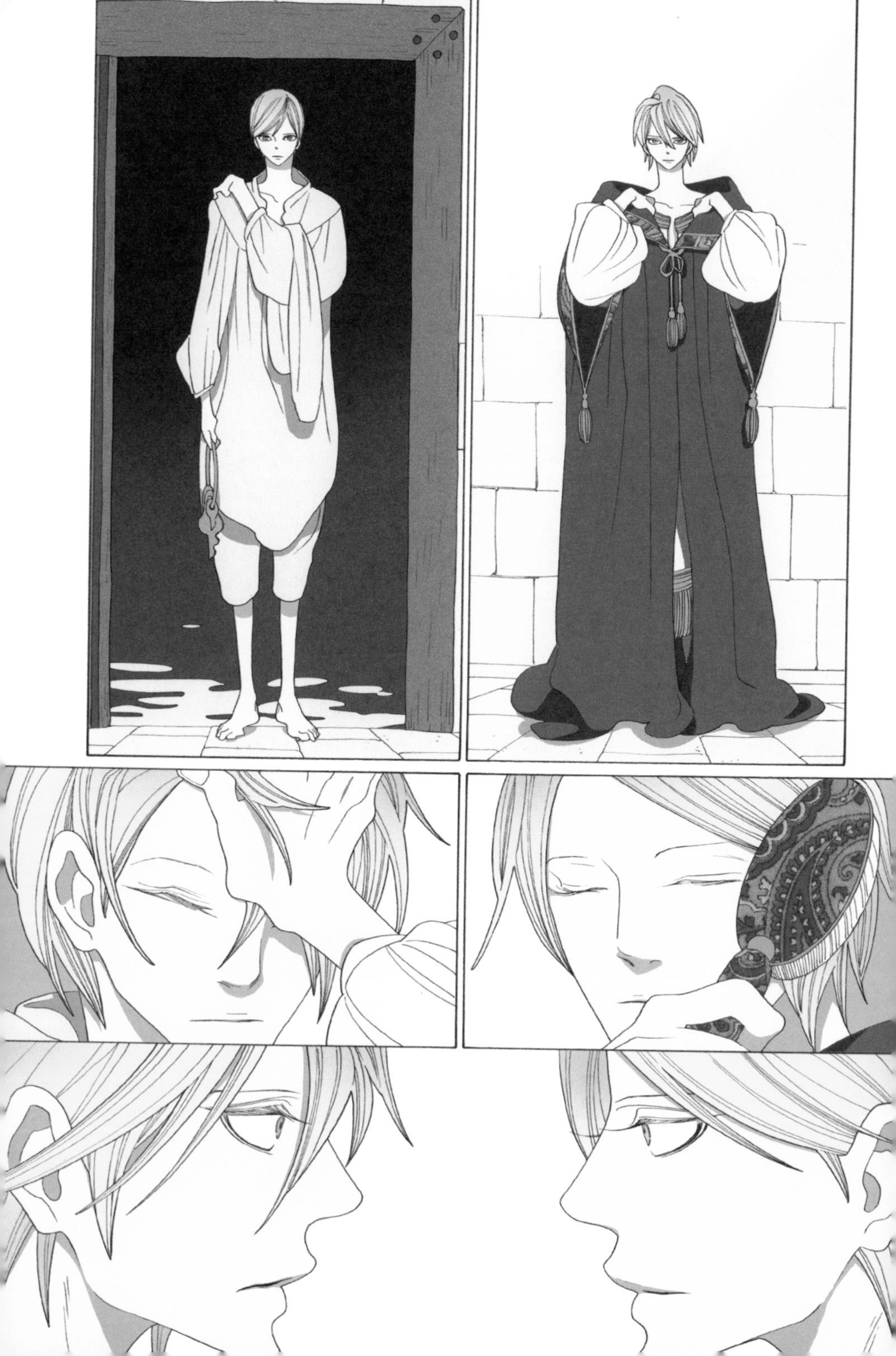

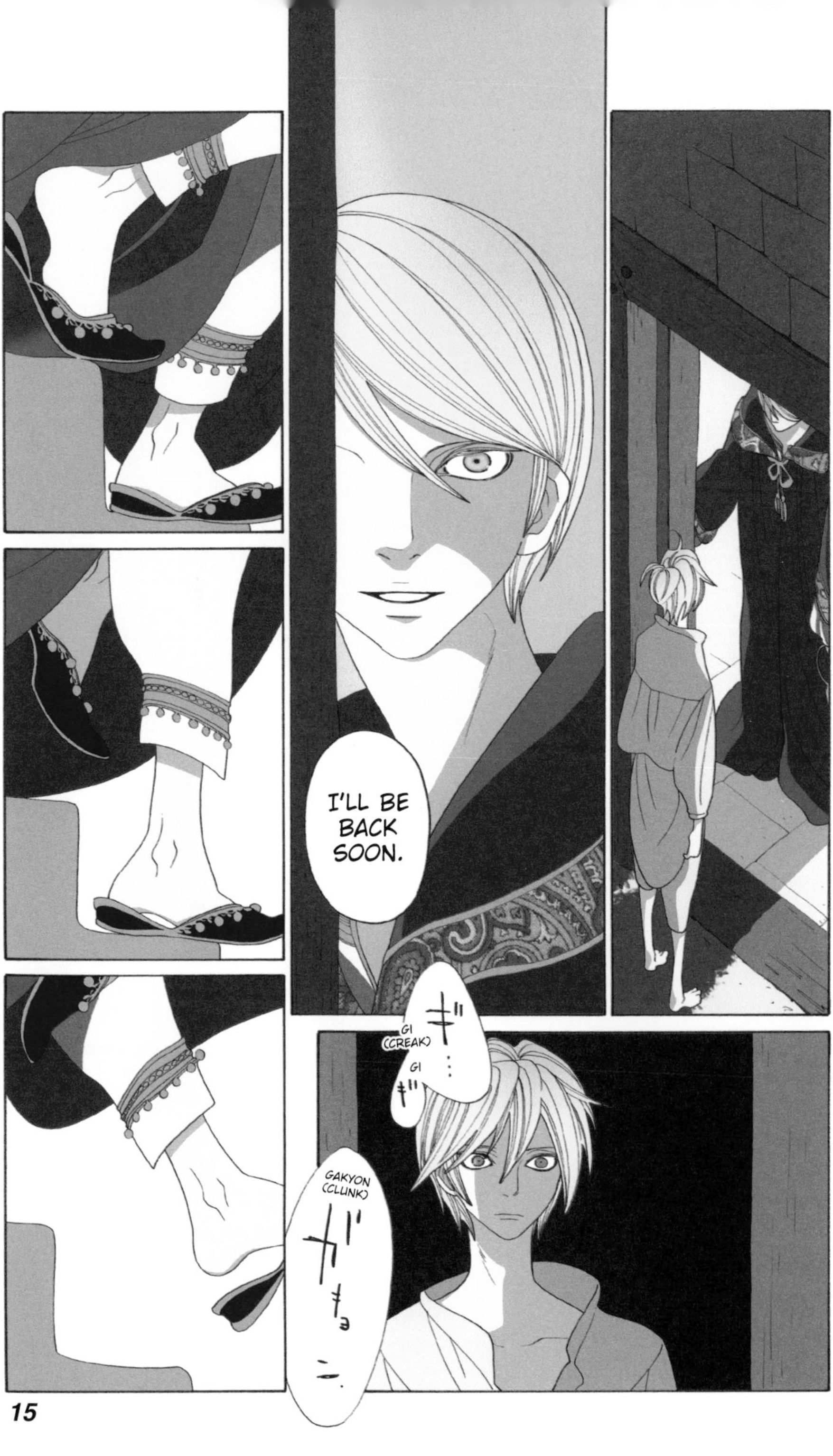

I'LL BE BACK SOON.
GI (CREAK)
GI
ギ…
ギ
GAKYON (CLUNK)
ガキョン…

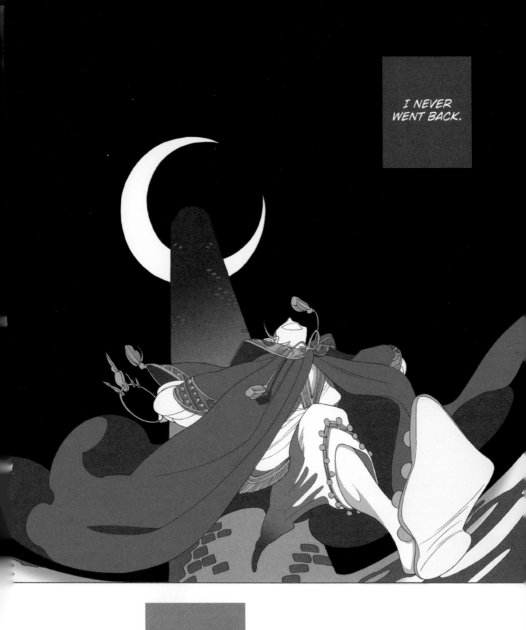

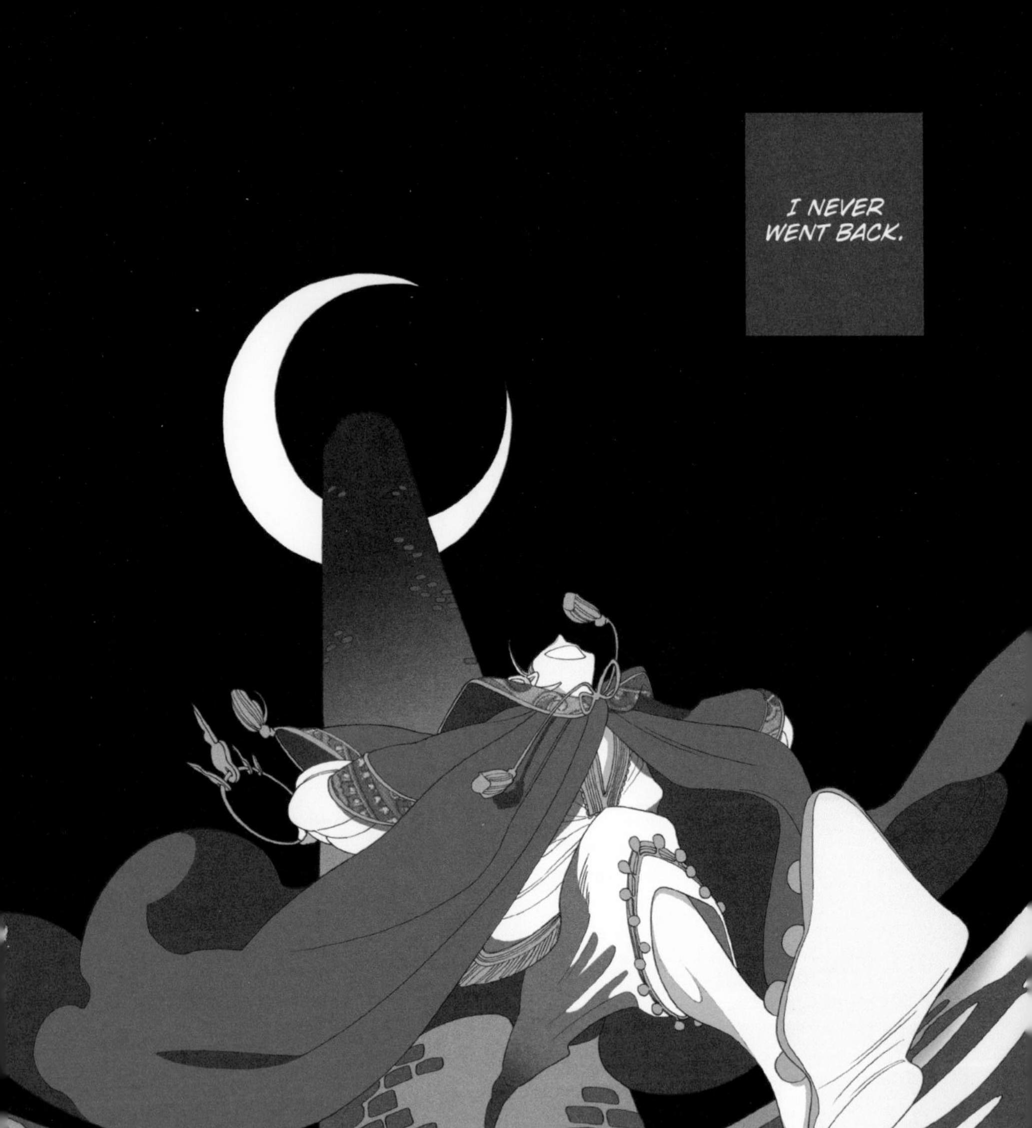
I NEVER WENT BACK.

YEARS PASSED.

YOUR HIGHNESS.

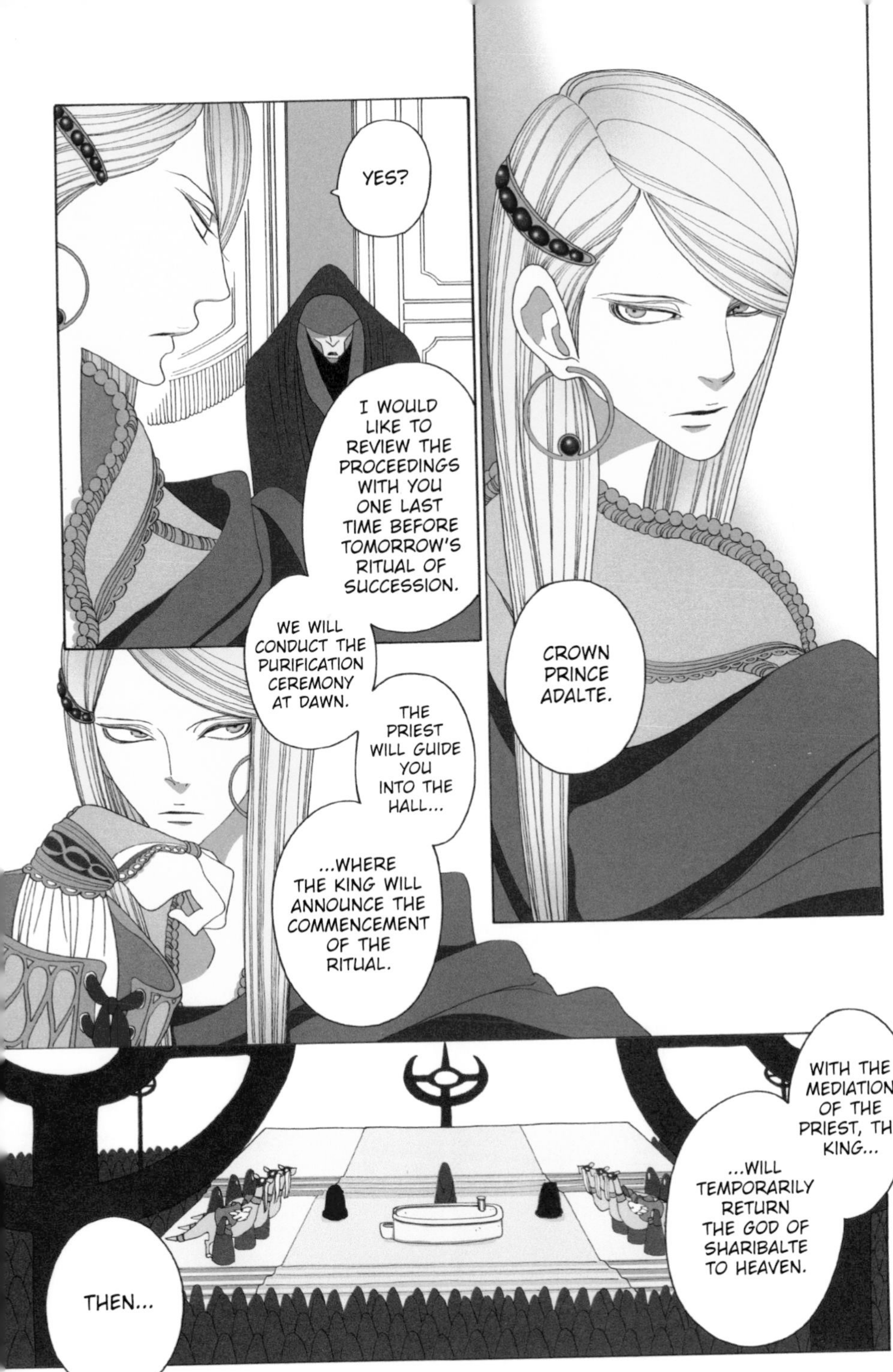
CROWN PRINCE ADALTE.
YES?
I WOULD LIKE TO REVIEW THE PROCEEDINGS WITH YOU ONE LAST TIME BEFORE TOMORROW'S RITUAL OF SUCCESSION.
WE WILL CONDUCT THE PURIFICATION CEREMONY AT DAWN.
THE PRIEST WILL GUIDE YOU INTO THE HALL...
...WHERE THE KING WILL ANNOUNCE THE COMMENCEMENT OF THE RITUAL.
WITH THE MEDIATION OF THE PRIEST, THE KING...
...WILL TEMPORARILY RETURN THE GOD OF SHARIBALTE TO HEAVEN.
THEN...

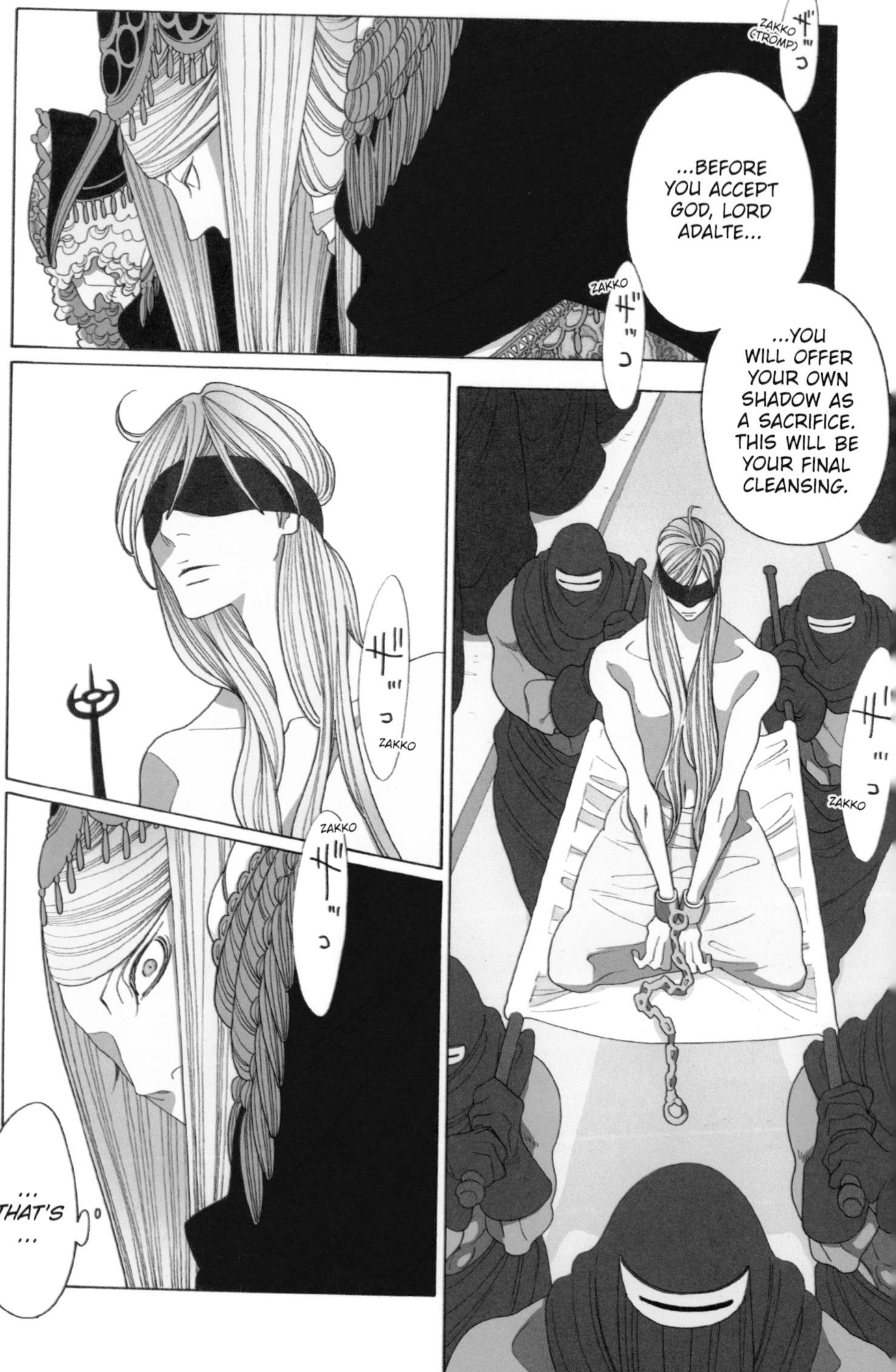
ザッ
ZAKKO (TROMP)
...BEFORE YOU ACCEPT GOD, LORD ADALTE...
ザッ
ZAKKO
...YOU WILL OFFER YOUR OWN SHADOW AS A SACRIFICE. THIS WILL BE YOUR FINAL CLEANSING.
ザッ
ZAKKO
ザッ
ZAKKO
ザッ
ZAKKO
...THAT'S...

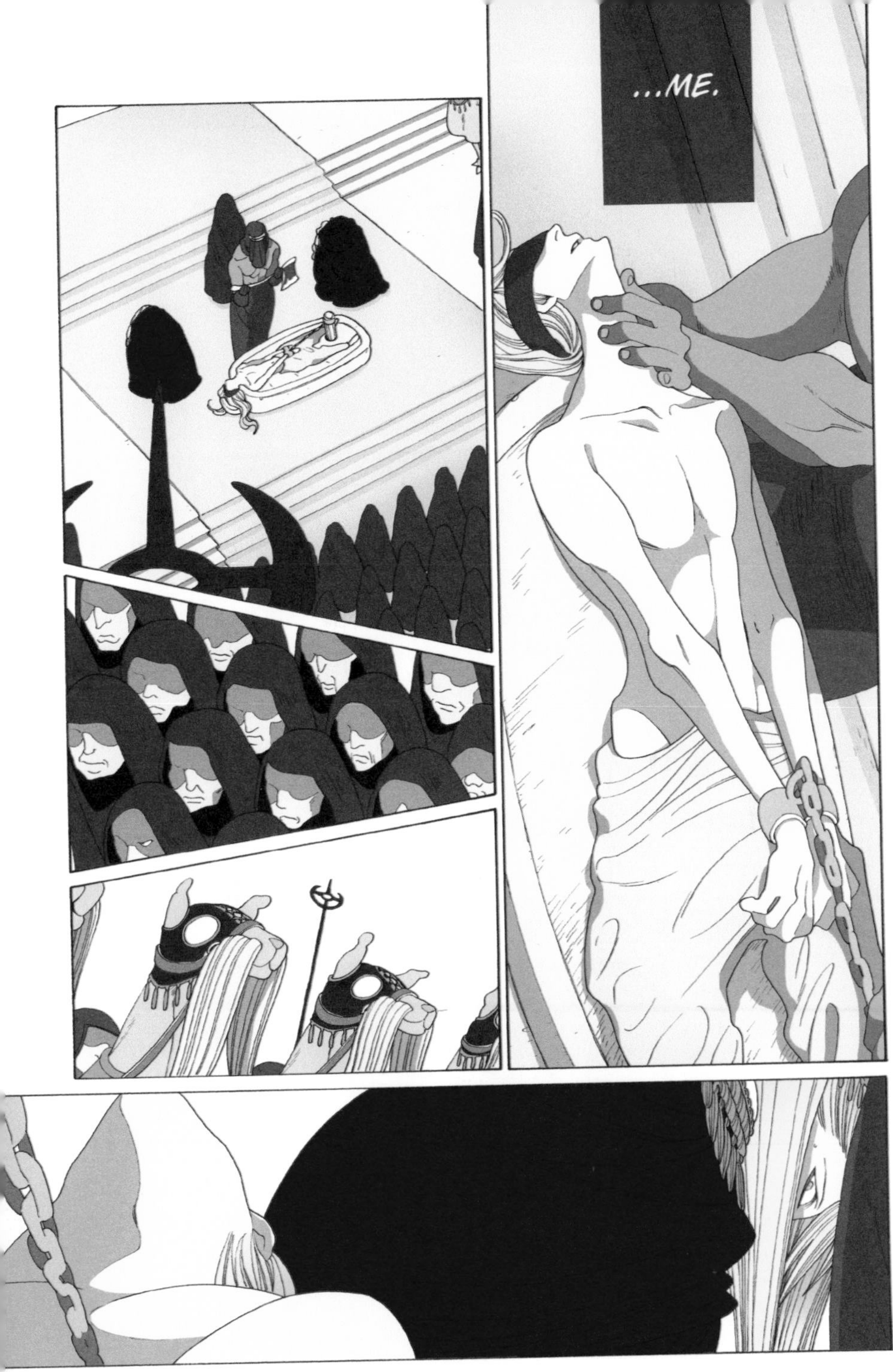
...ME.

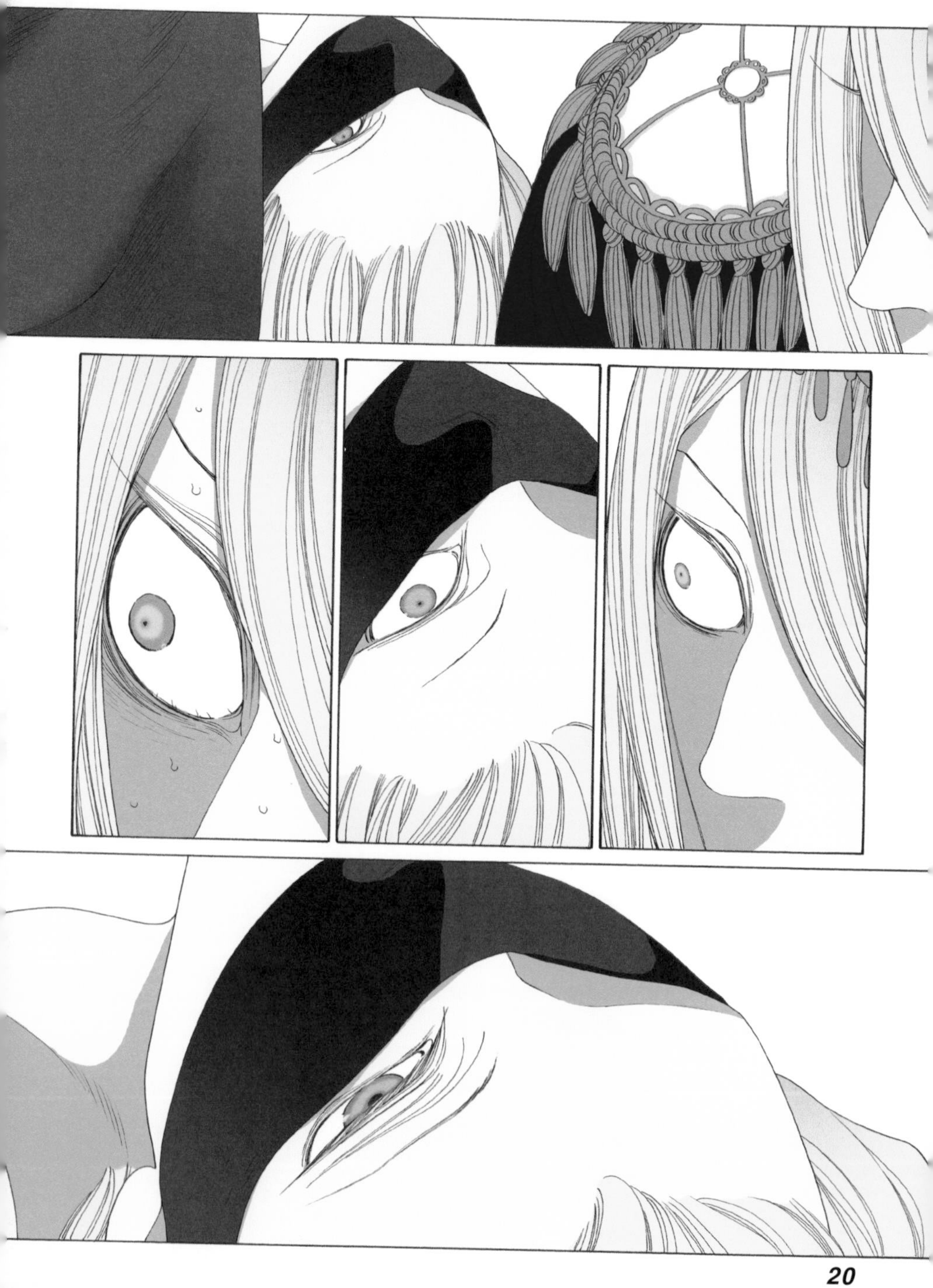

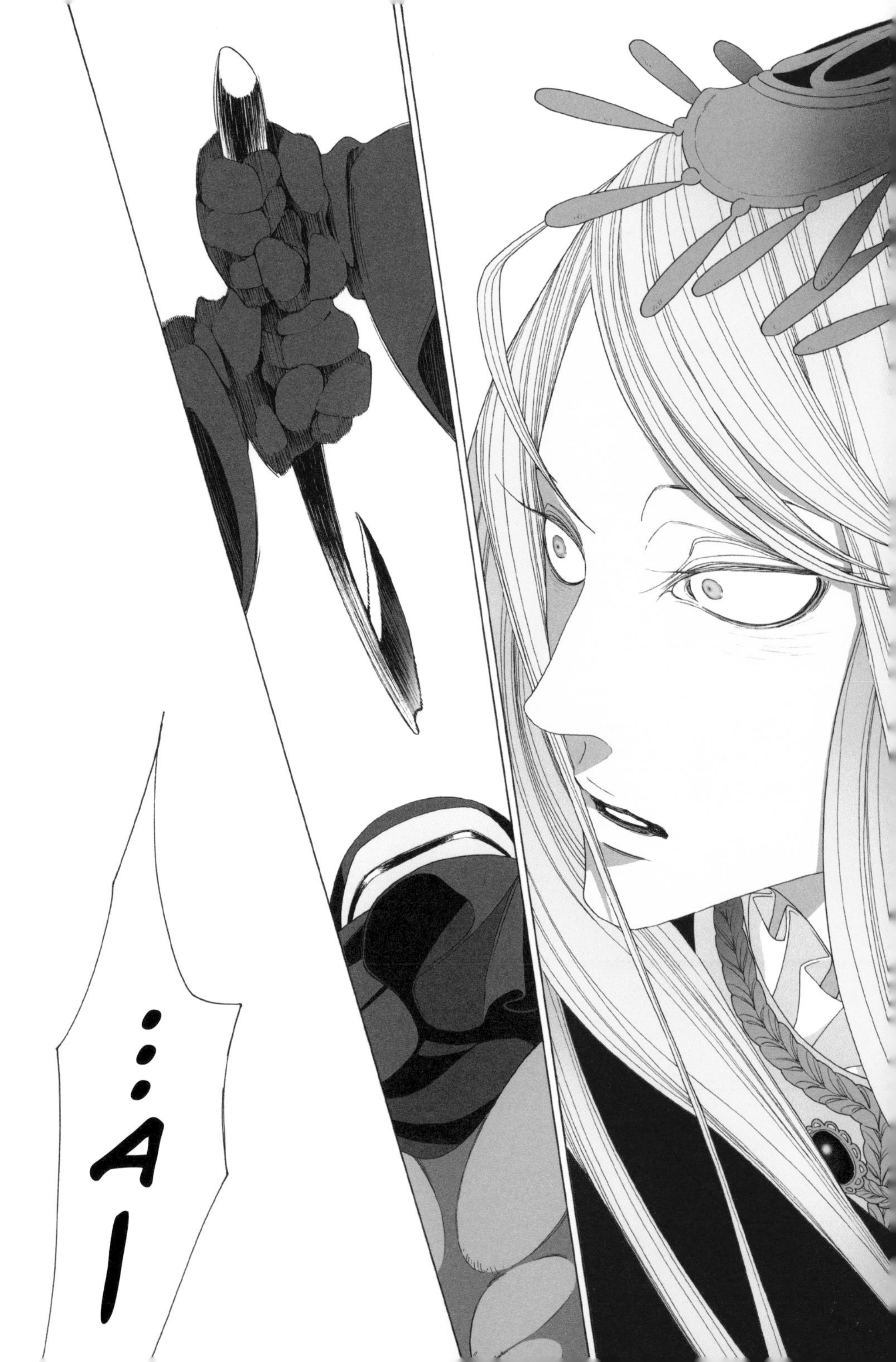
...AH

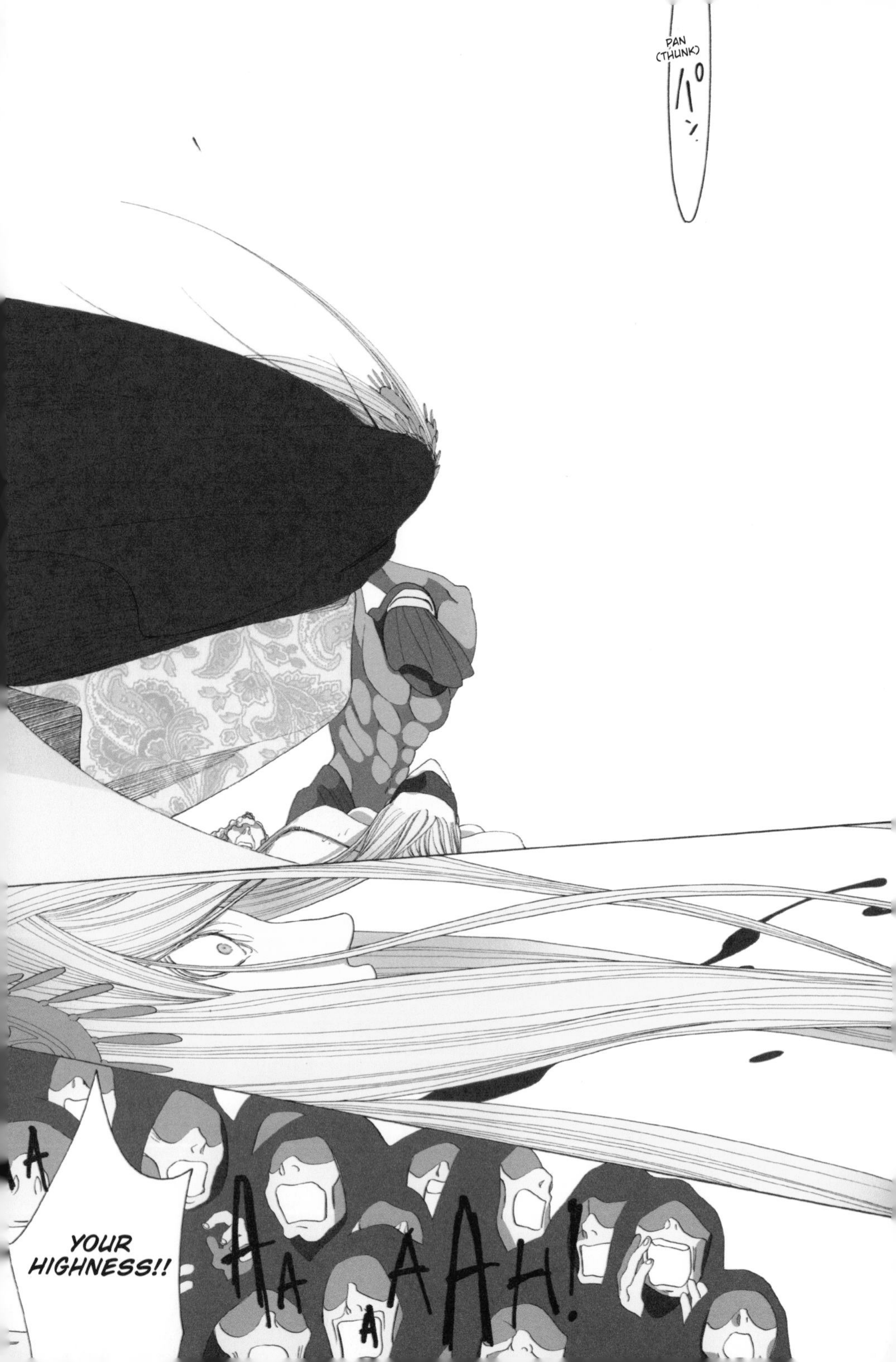
PAN
(THUNK)
YOUR HIGHNESS!!
AAAAAH!

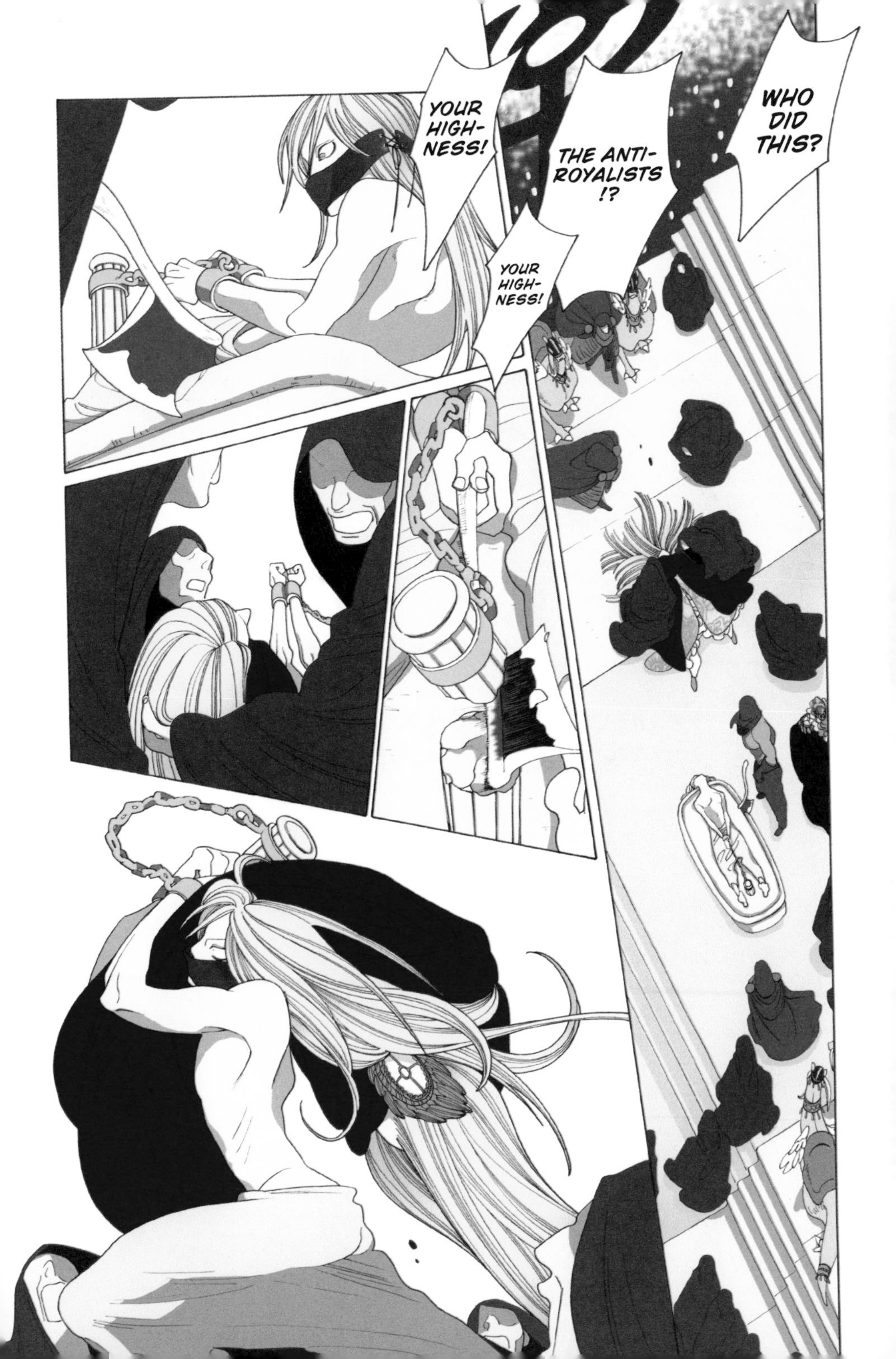
WHO DID THIS?
THE ANTI-ROYALISTS !?
YOUR HIGH-NESS!
YOUR HIGH-NESS!

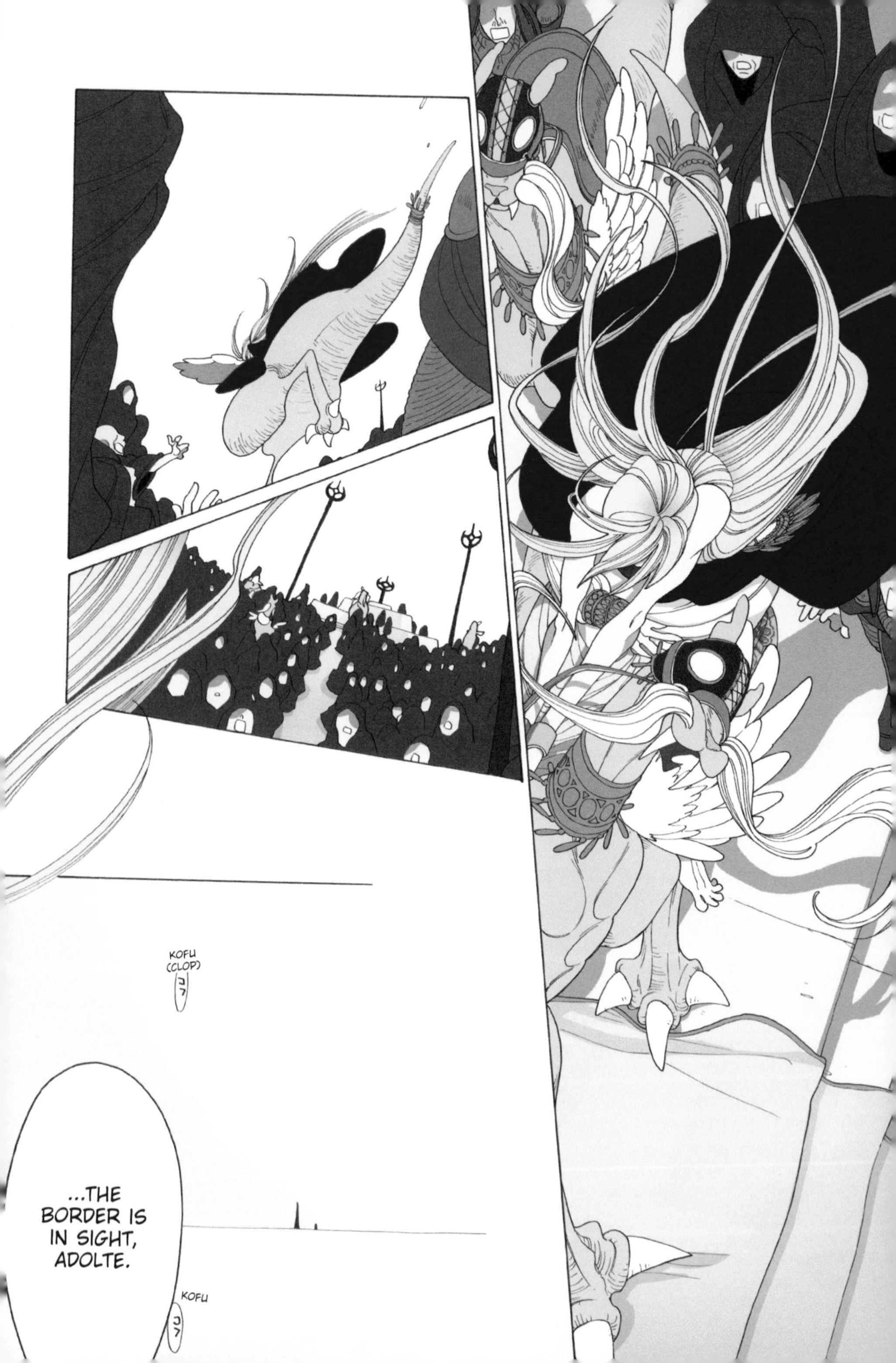
KOFU (CLOP)
コフ
...THE BORDER IS IN SIGHT, ADOLTE.
KOFU
コフ

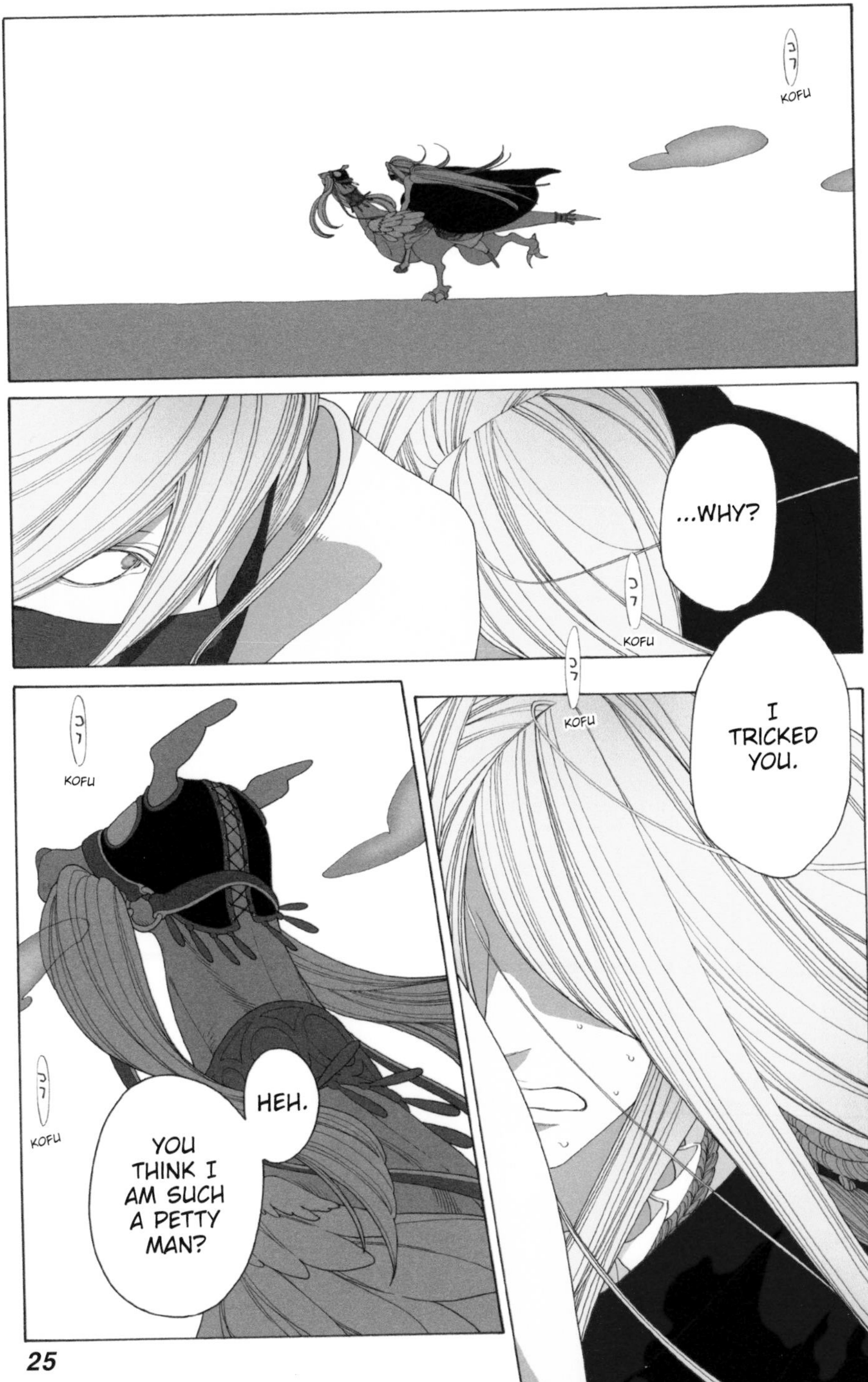

コフ
KOFU
...WHY?
コフ
KOFU
コフ
KOFU
I TRICKED YOU.
コフ
KOFU
HEH.
YOU THINK I AM SUCH A PETTY MAN?
コフ
KOFU

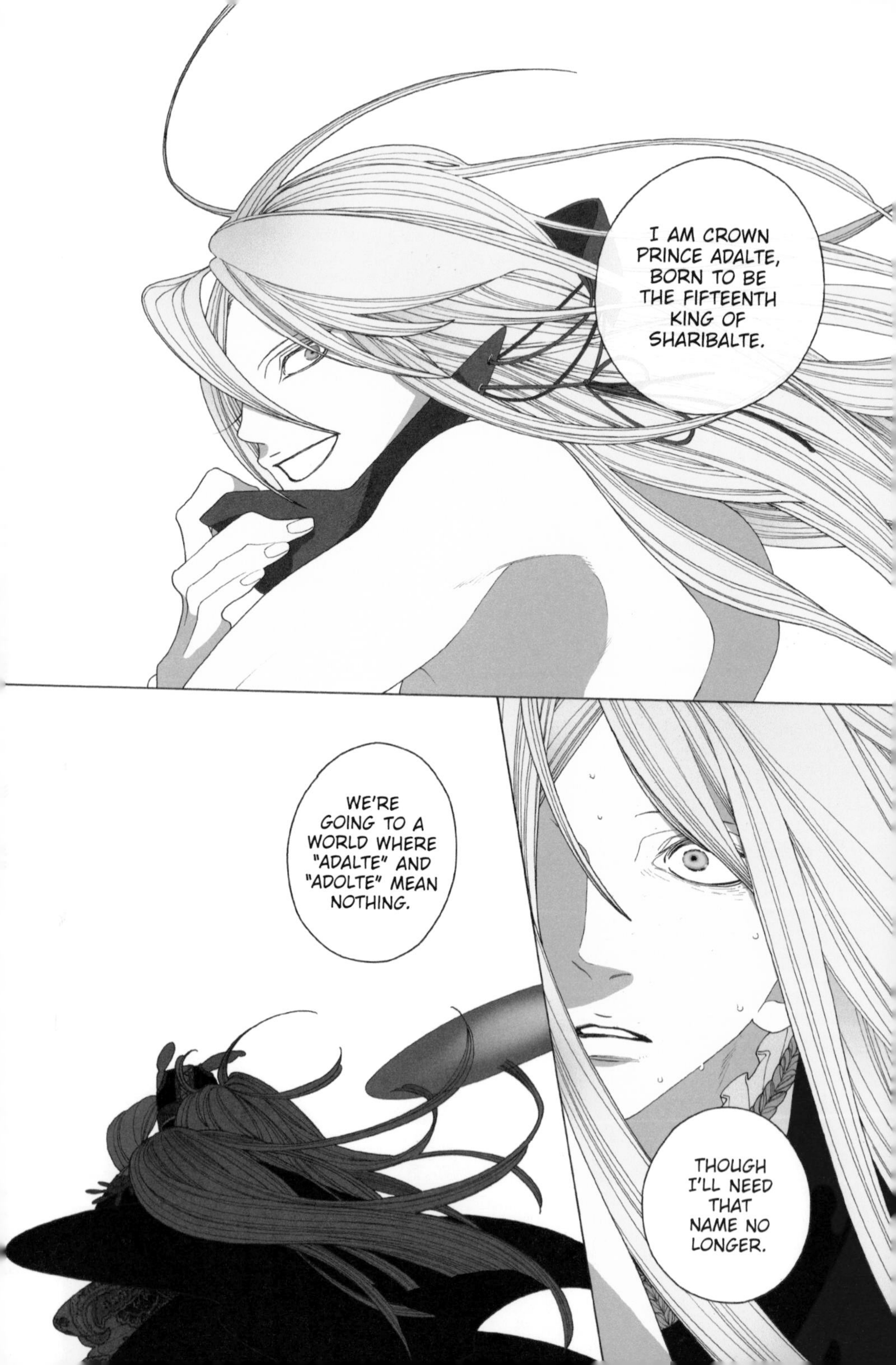
I AM CROWN PRINCE ADALTE, BORN TO BE THE FIFTEENTH KING OF SHARIBALTE.
THOUGH I'LL NEED THAT NAME NO LONGER.
WE'RE GOING TO A WORLD WHERE "ADALTE" AND "ADOLTE" MEAN NOTHING.

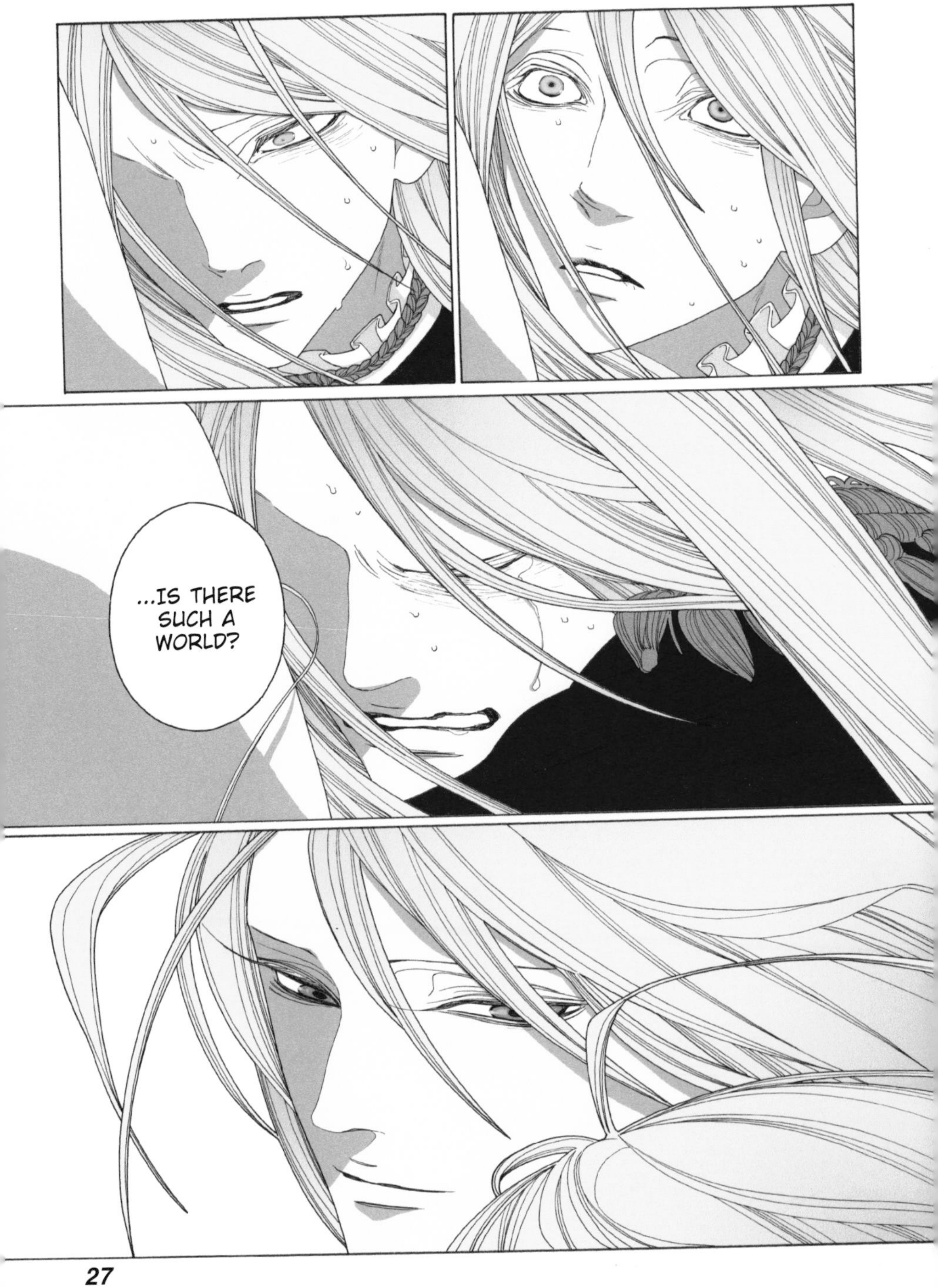
...IS THERE SUCH A WORLD?

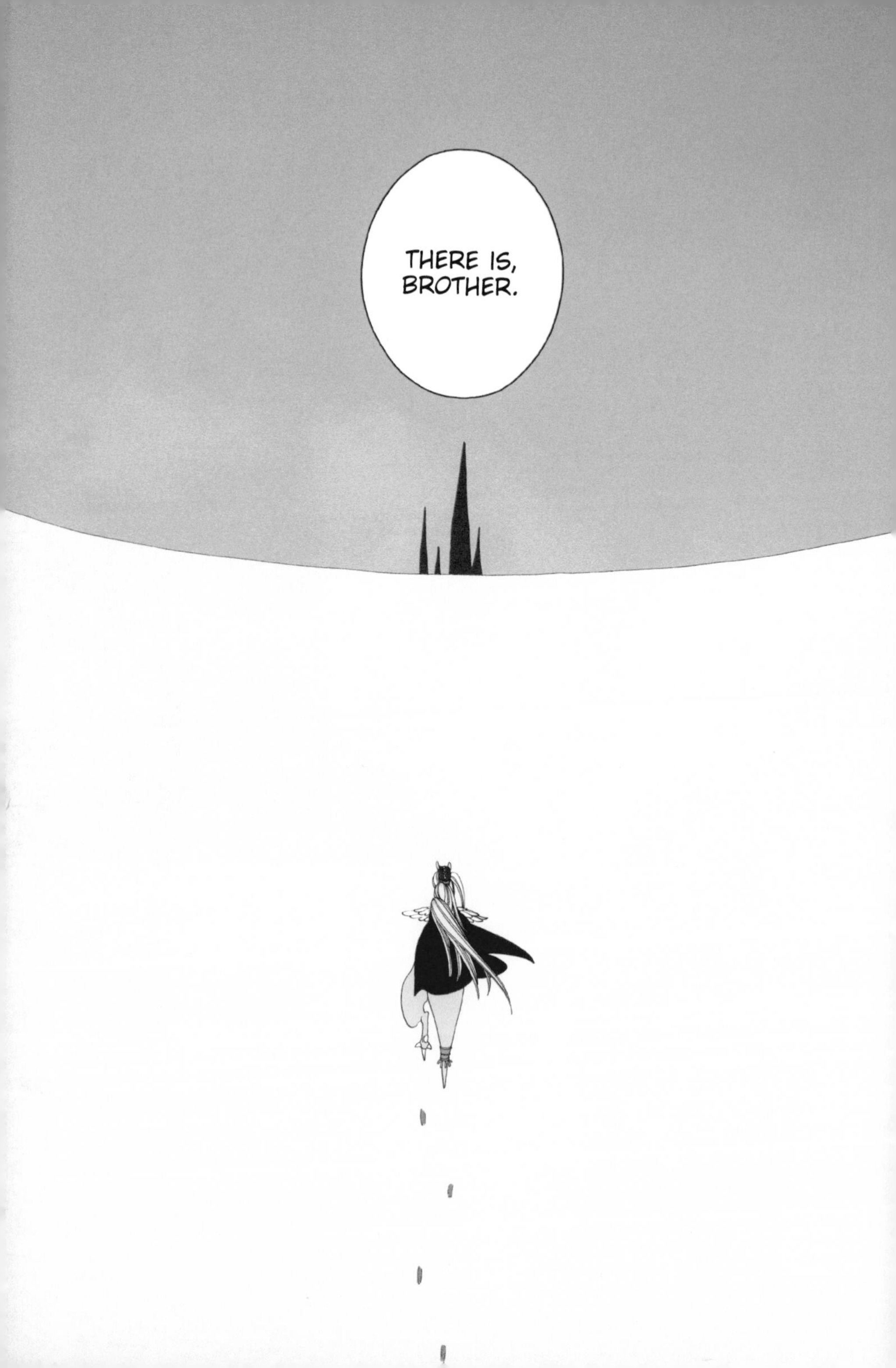
THERE IS, BROTHER.

Chapter 2

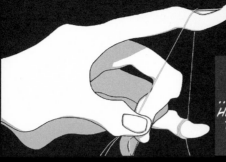

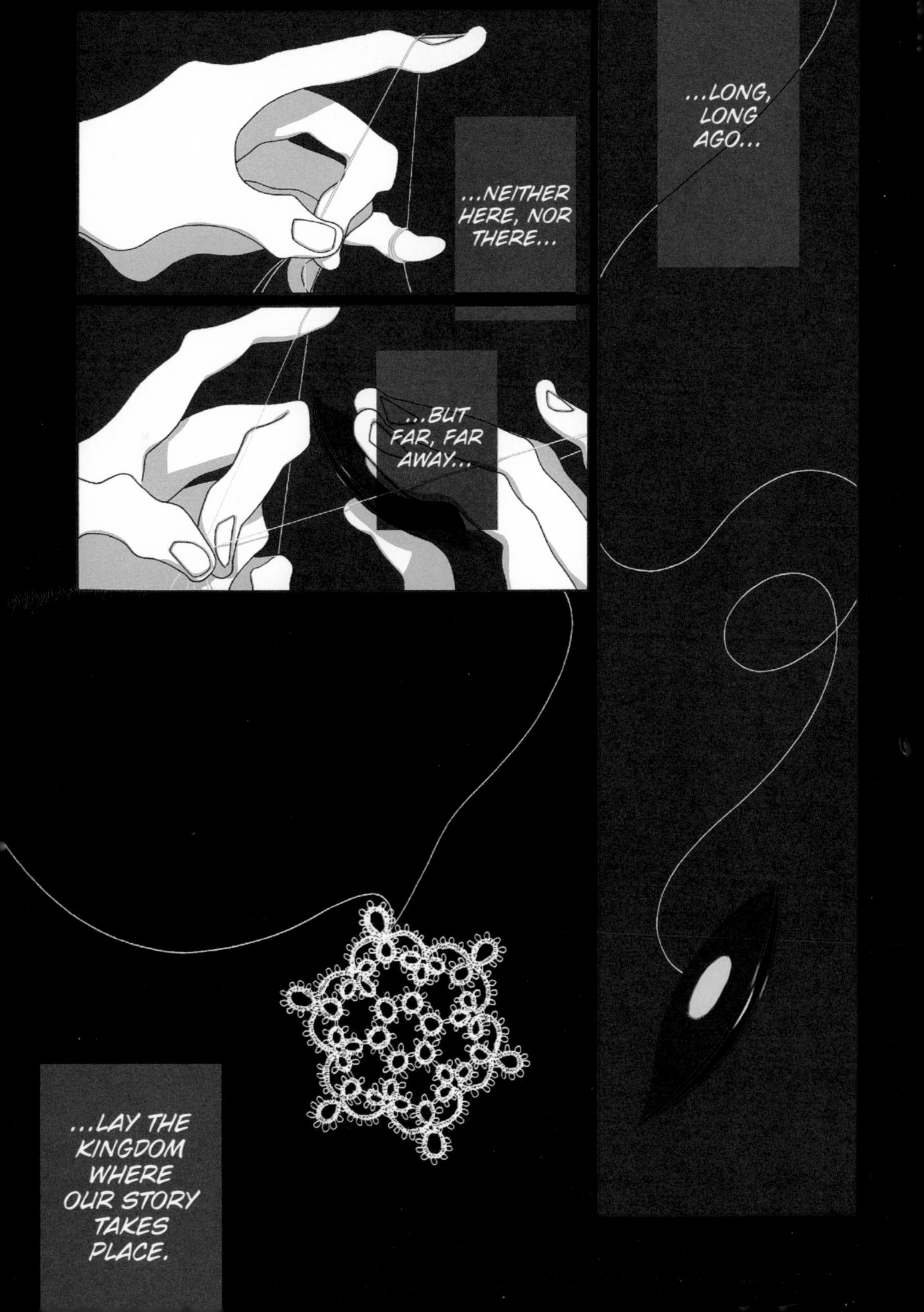

...NEITHER HERE, NOR THERE...

...LONG, LONG AGO...

...BUT FAR, FAR AWAY...

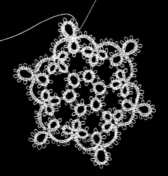

...LAY THE KINGDOM WHERE OUR STORY TAKES PLACE.

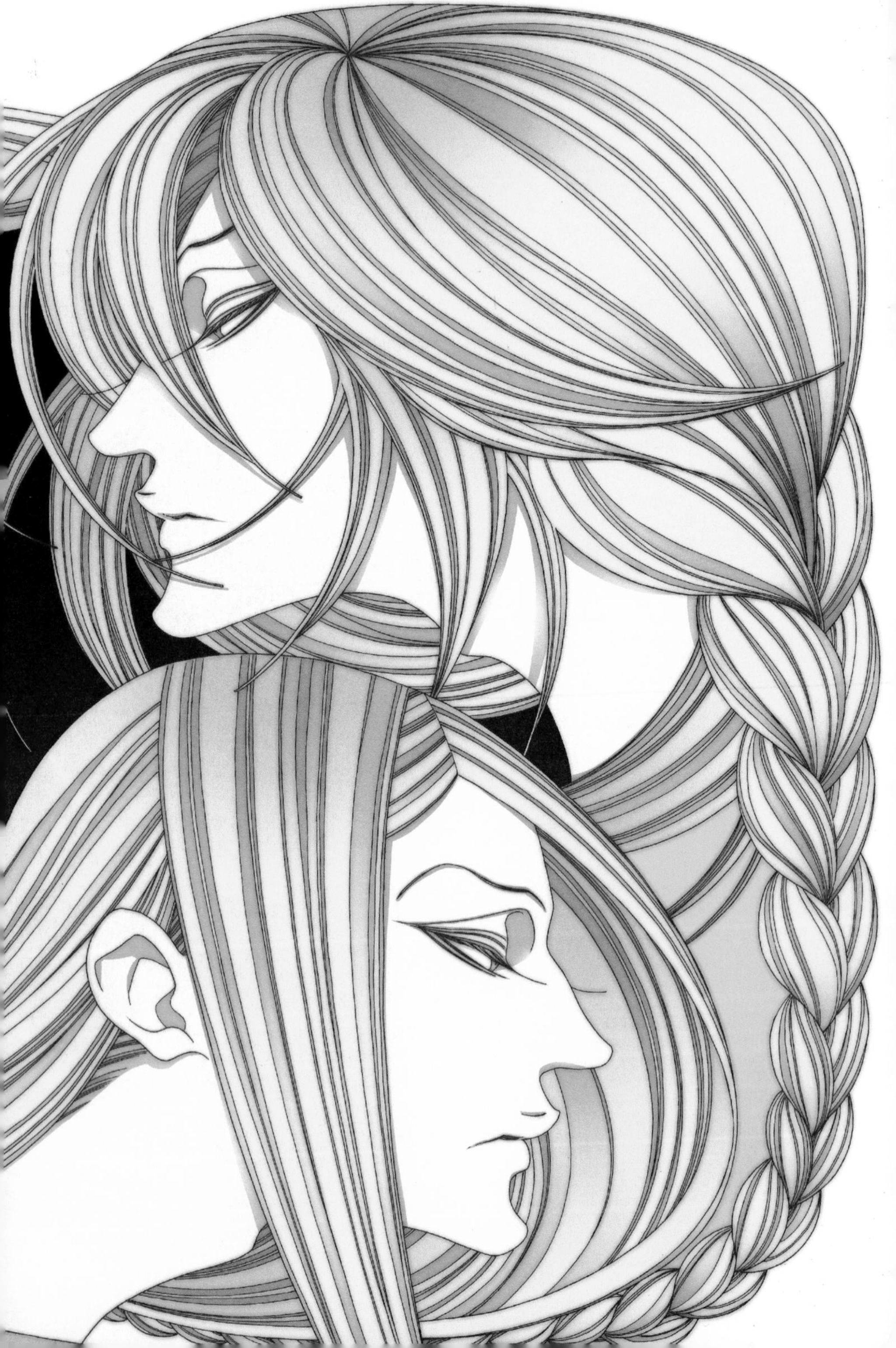

Chapter 2
Adalte and Adolte

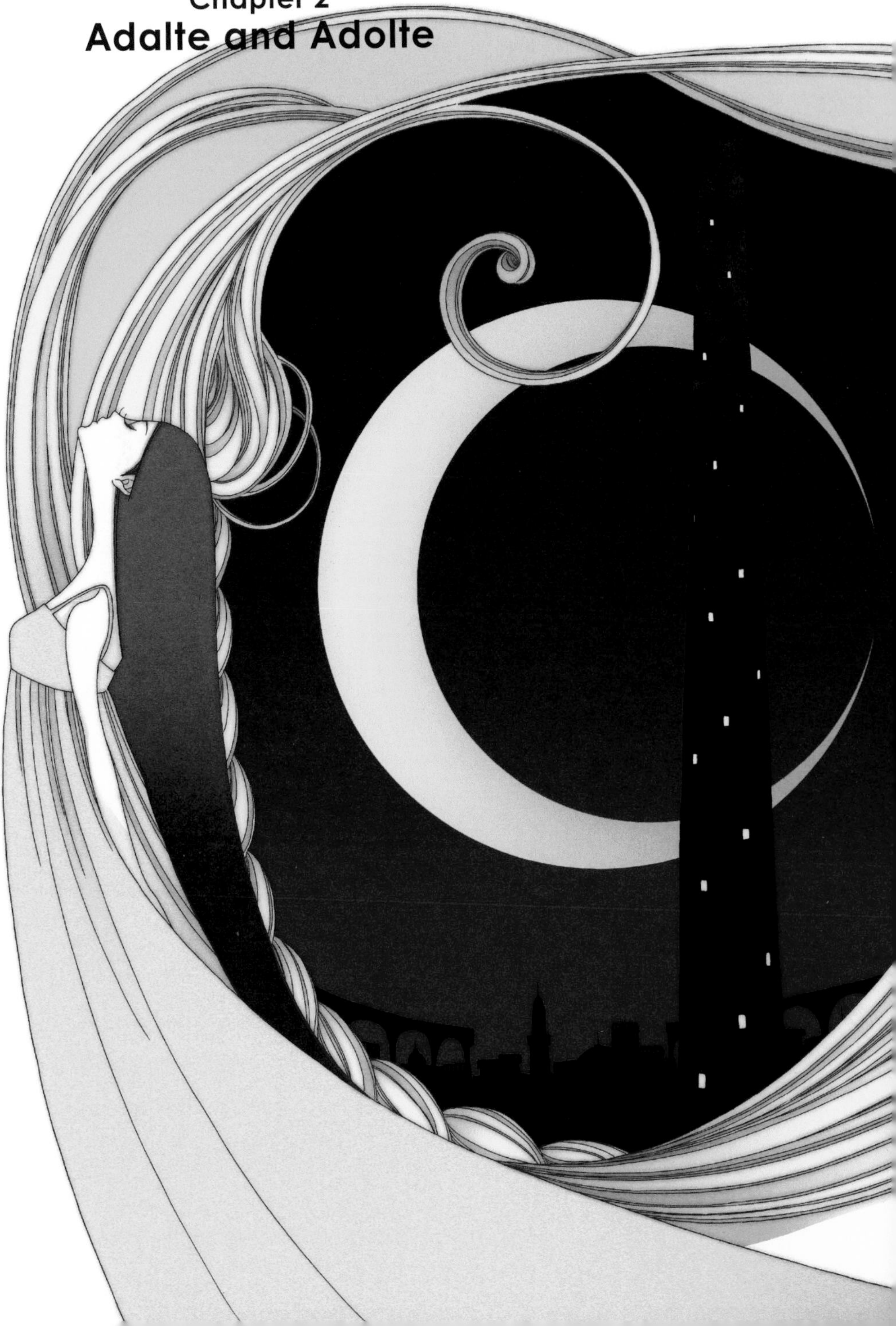

*Tales
of the
Kingdom*

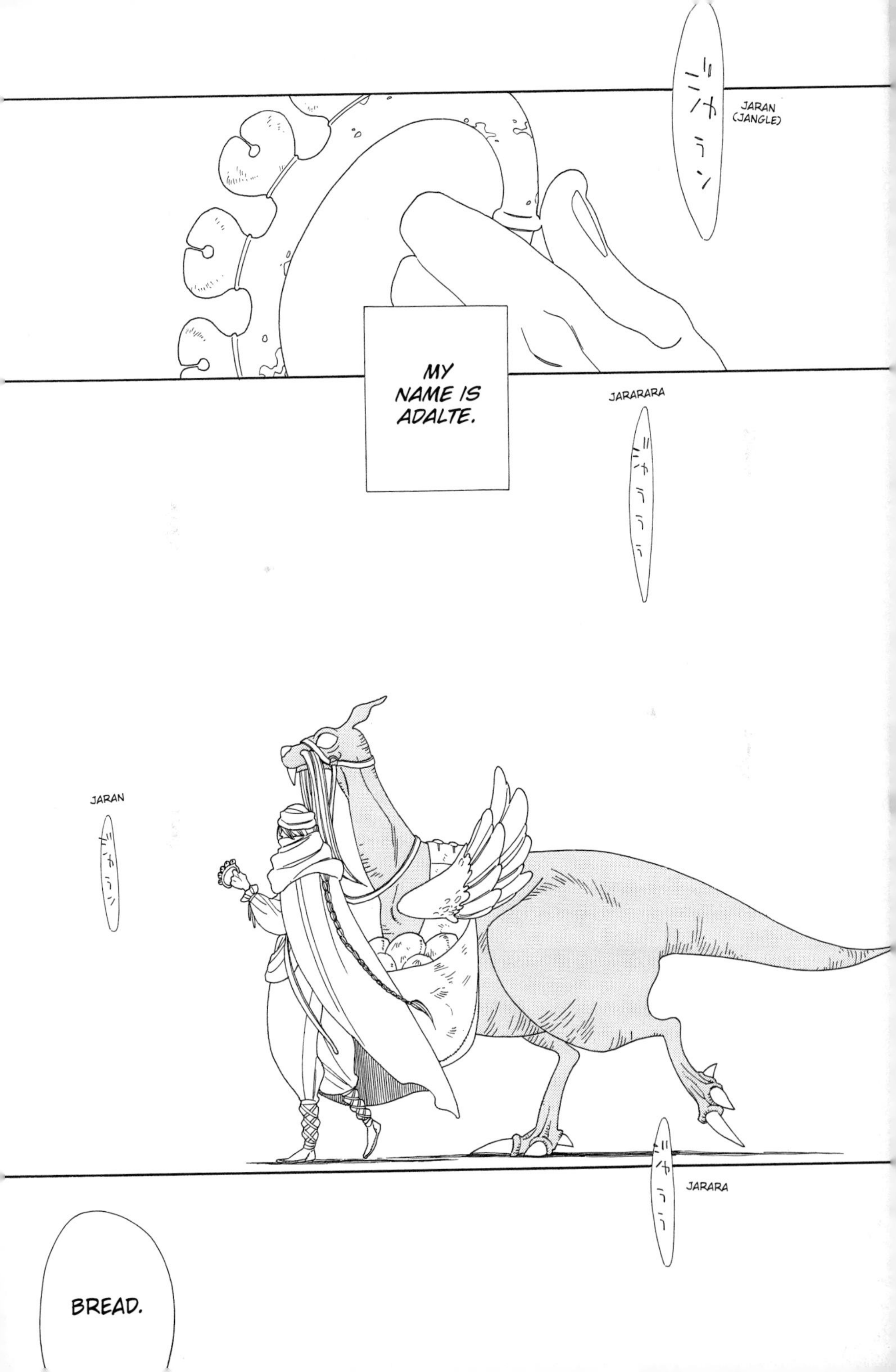
ジャラン
JARAN (JANGLE)
MY NAME IS ADALTE.
ジャラララ
JARARARA
ジャラン
JARAN
ジャララ
JARARA
BREAD.

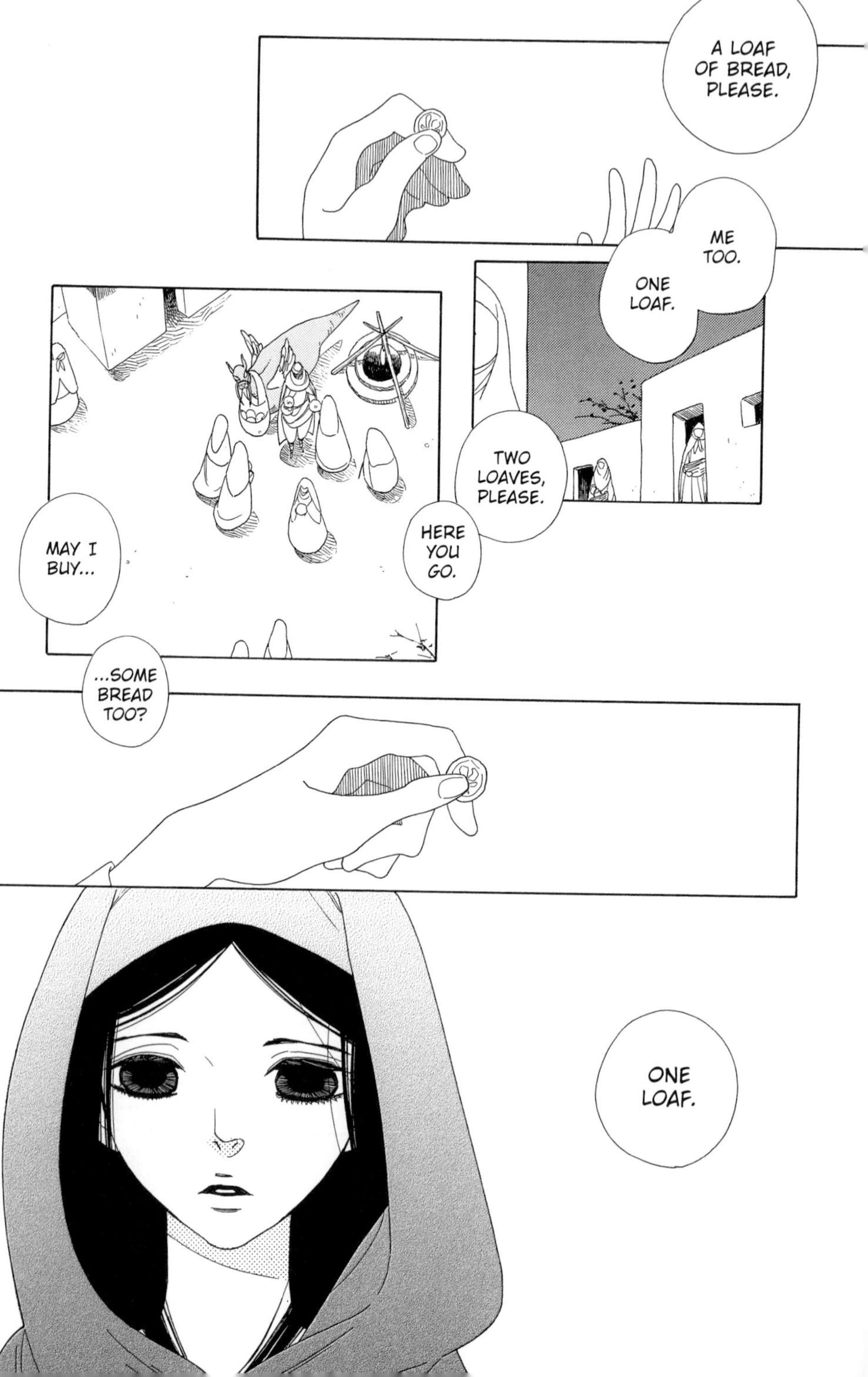
A LOAF OF BREAD, PLEASE.
ME TOO.
ONE LOAF.
TWO LOAVES, PLEASE.
HERE YOU GO.
MAY I BUY...
...SOME BREAD TOO?
ONE LOAF.

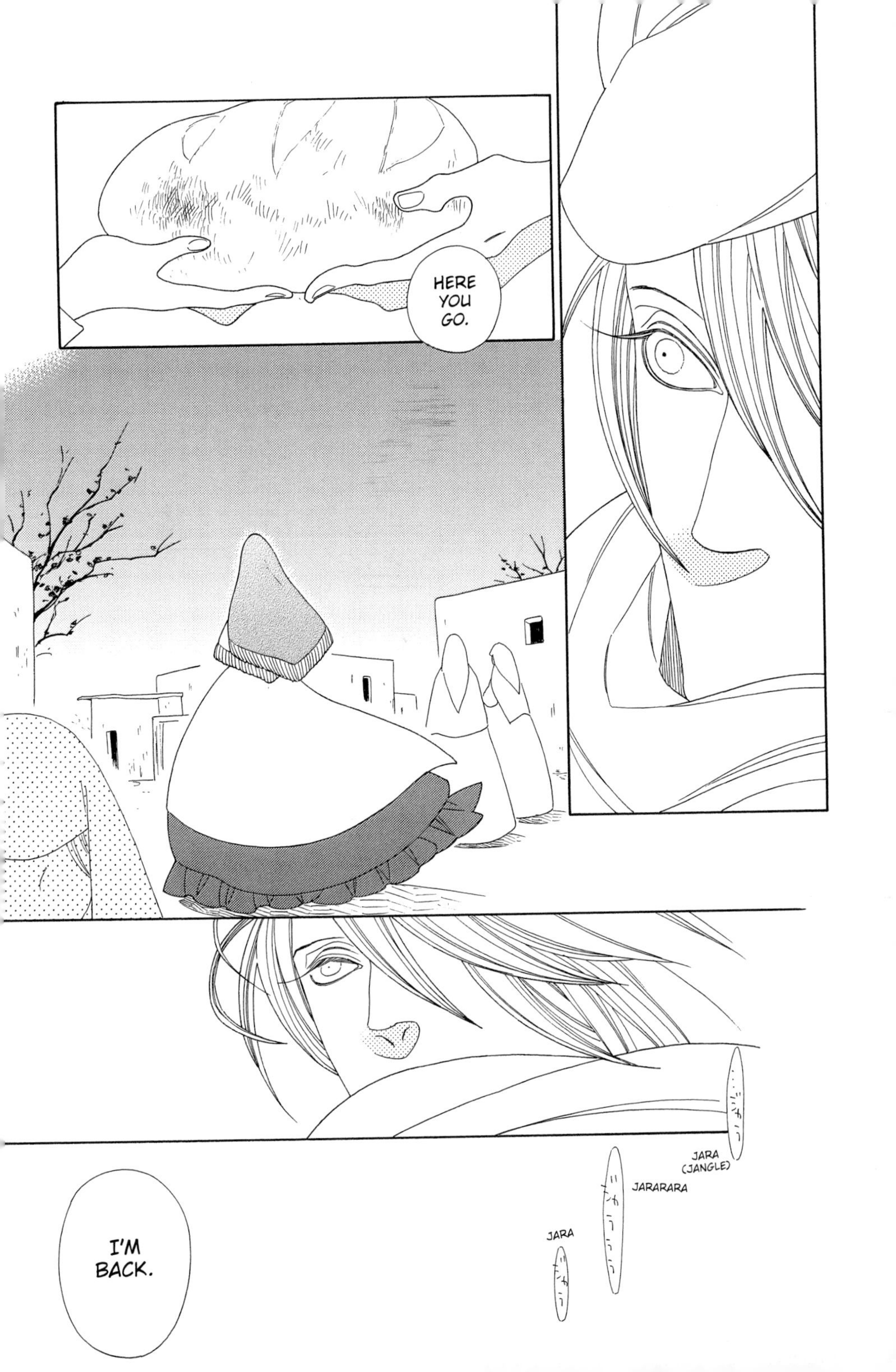
HERE YOU GO.
JARA (JANGLE)
JARARARA
JARA
I'M BACK.

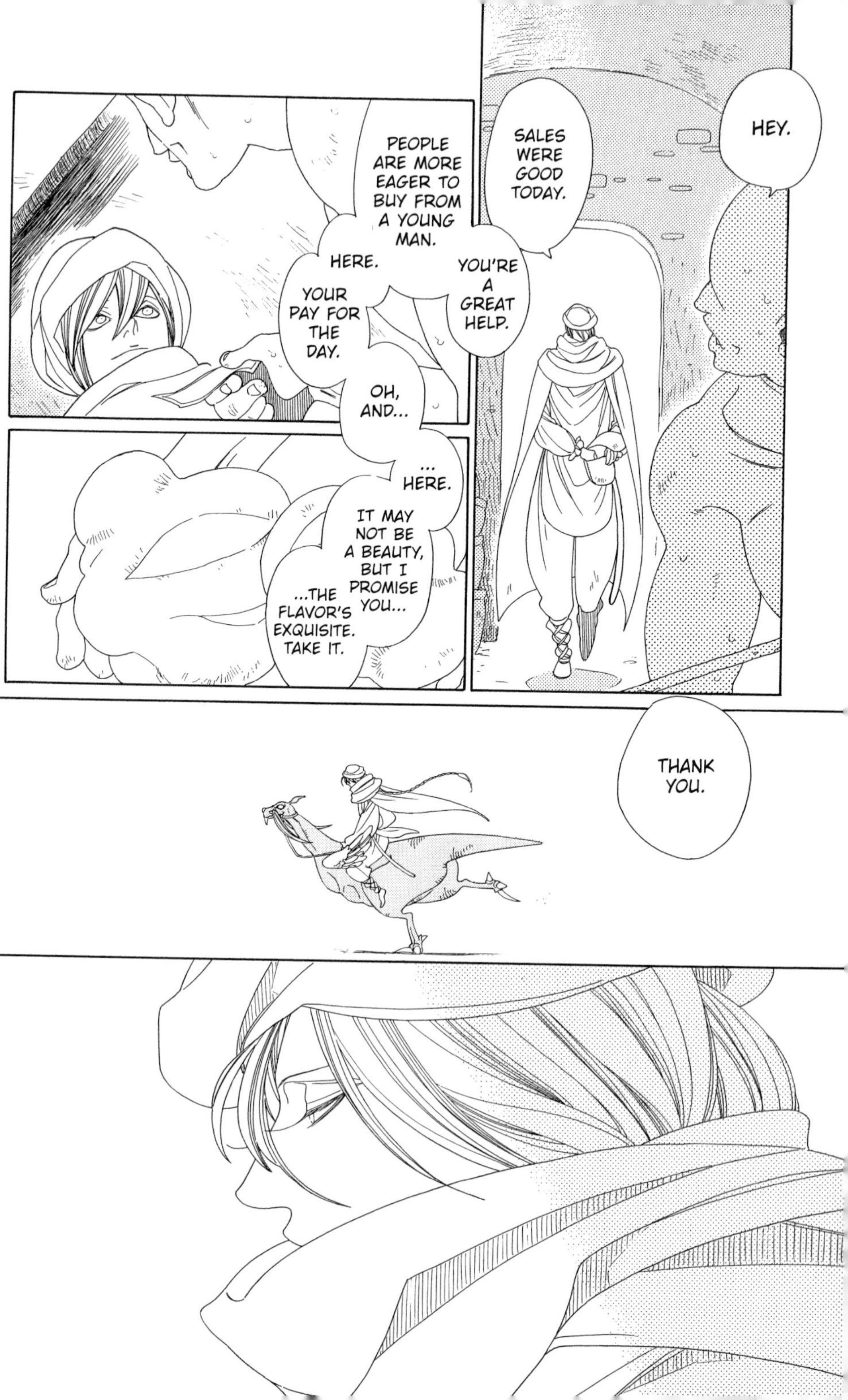
HEY.
SALES WERE GOOD TODAY.
YOU'RE A GREAT HELP.
PEOPLE ARE MORE EAGER TO BUY FROM A YOUNG MAN.
HERE.
YOUR PAY FOR THE DAY.
OH, AND...
...HERE.
IT MAY NOT BE A BEAUTY, BUT I PROMISE YOU...
...THE FLAVOR'S EXQUISITE. TAKE IT.
THANK YOU.

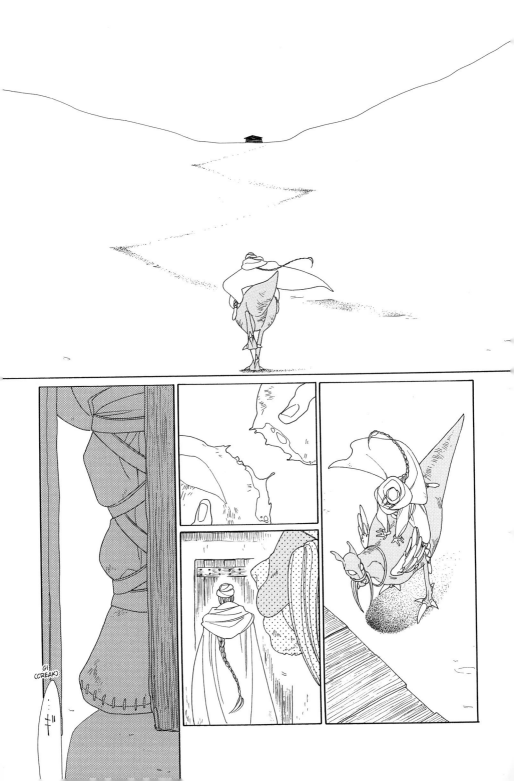

GI
(CREAK)

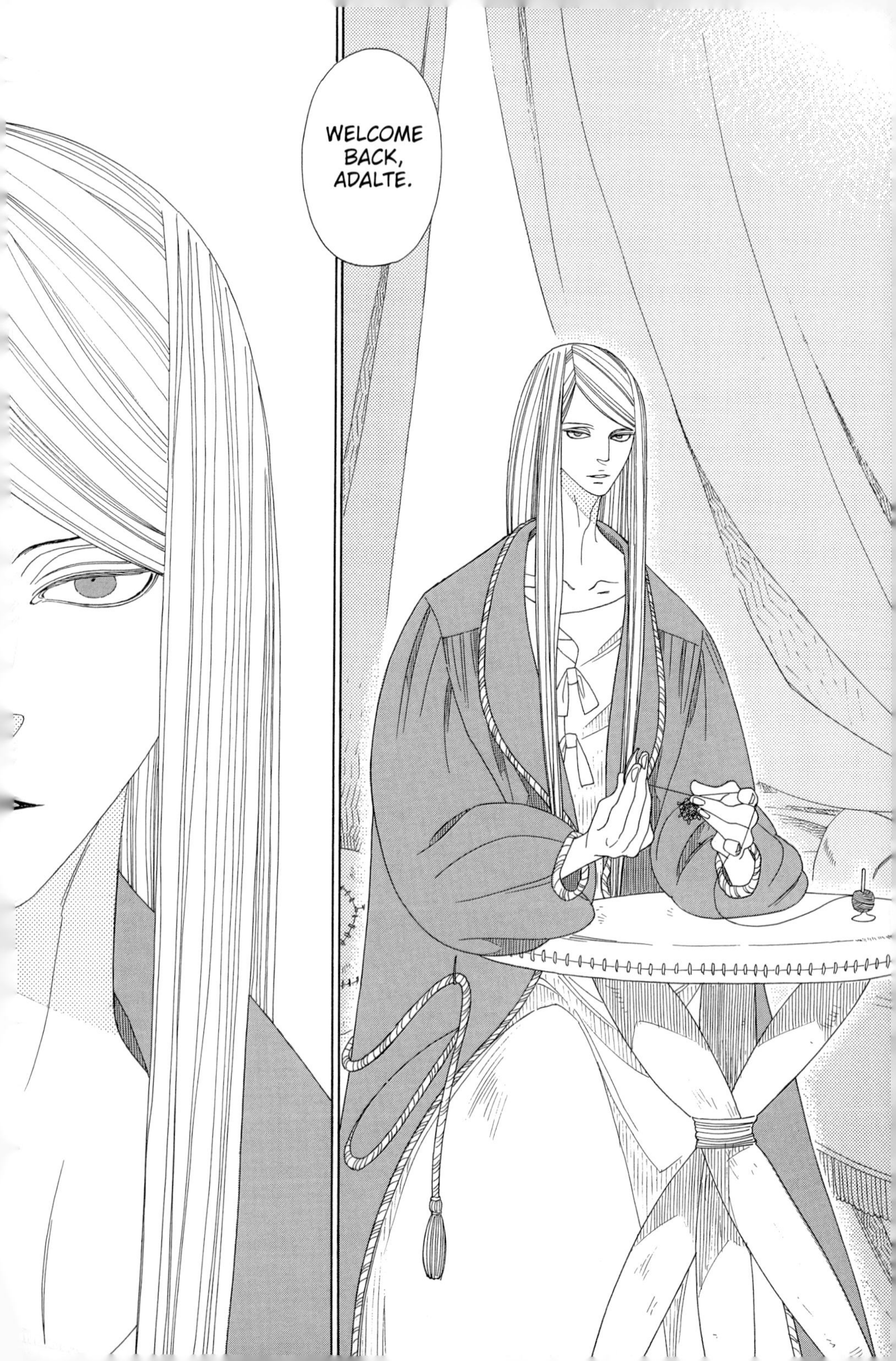
WELCOME BACK, ADALTE.

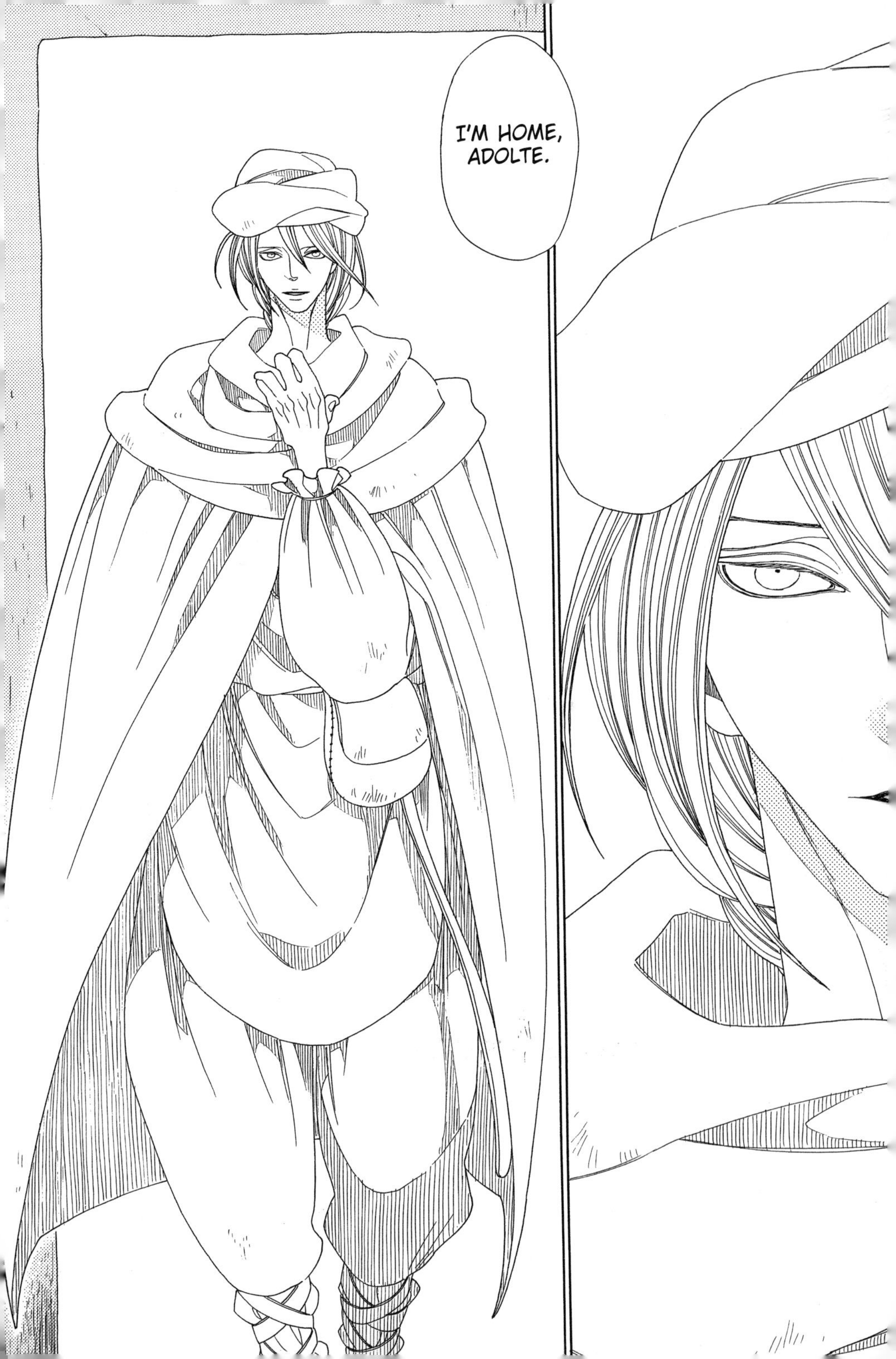
I'M HOME, ADOLTE.

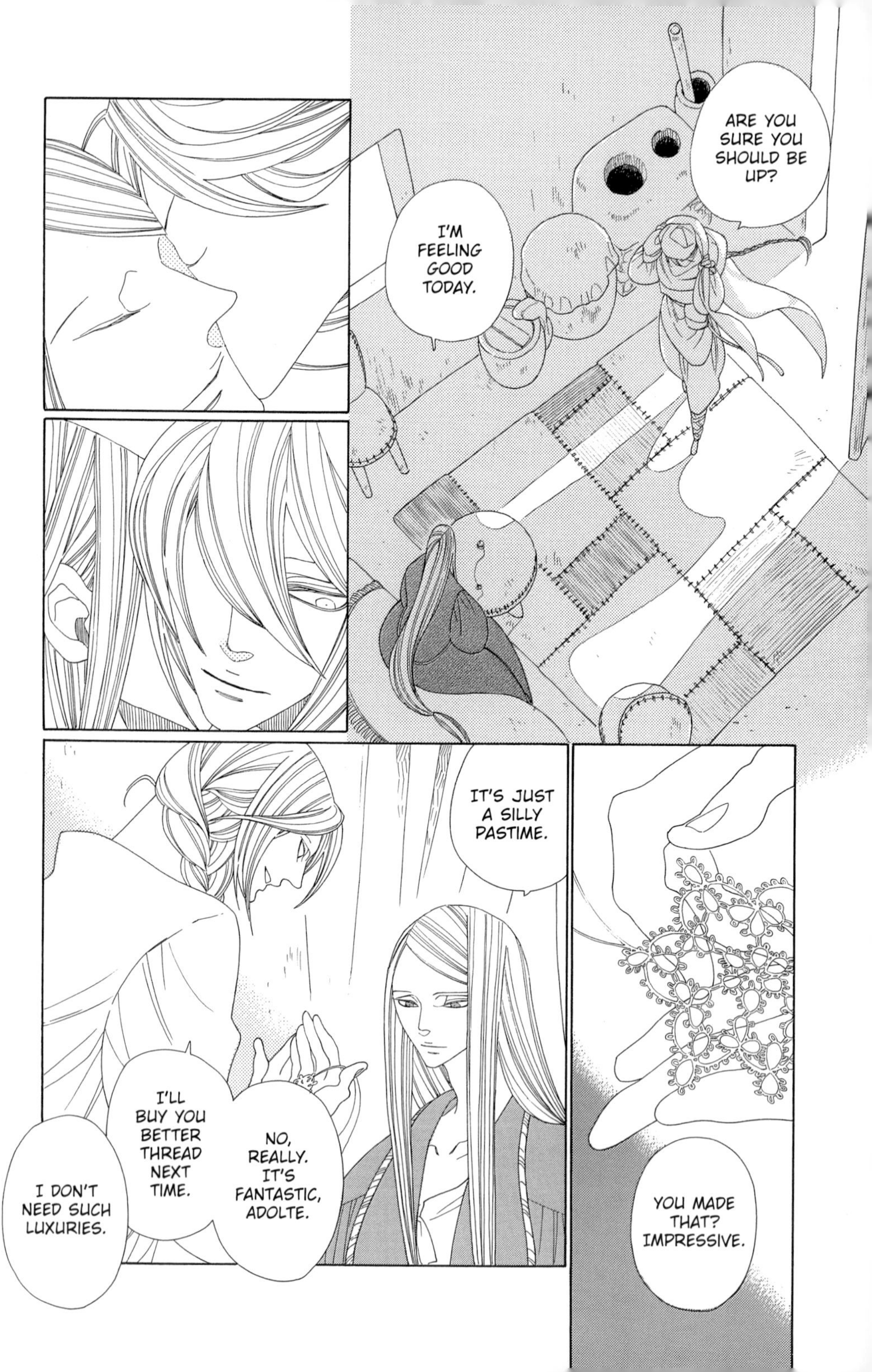
ARE YOU SURE YOU SHOULD BE UP?
I'M FEELING GOOD TODAY.
YOU MADE THAT? IMPRESSIVE.
IT'S JUST A SILLY PASTIME.
NO, REALLY. IT'S FANTASTIC, ADOLTE.
I'LL BUY YOU BETTER THREAD NEXT TIME.
I DON'T NEED SUCH LUXURIES.

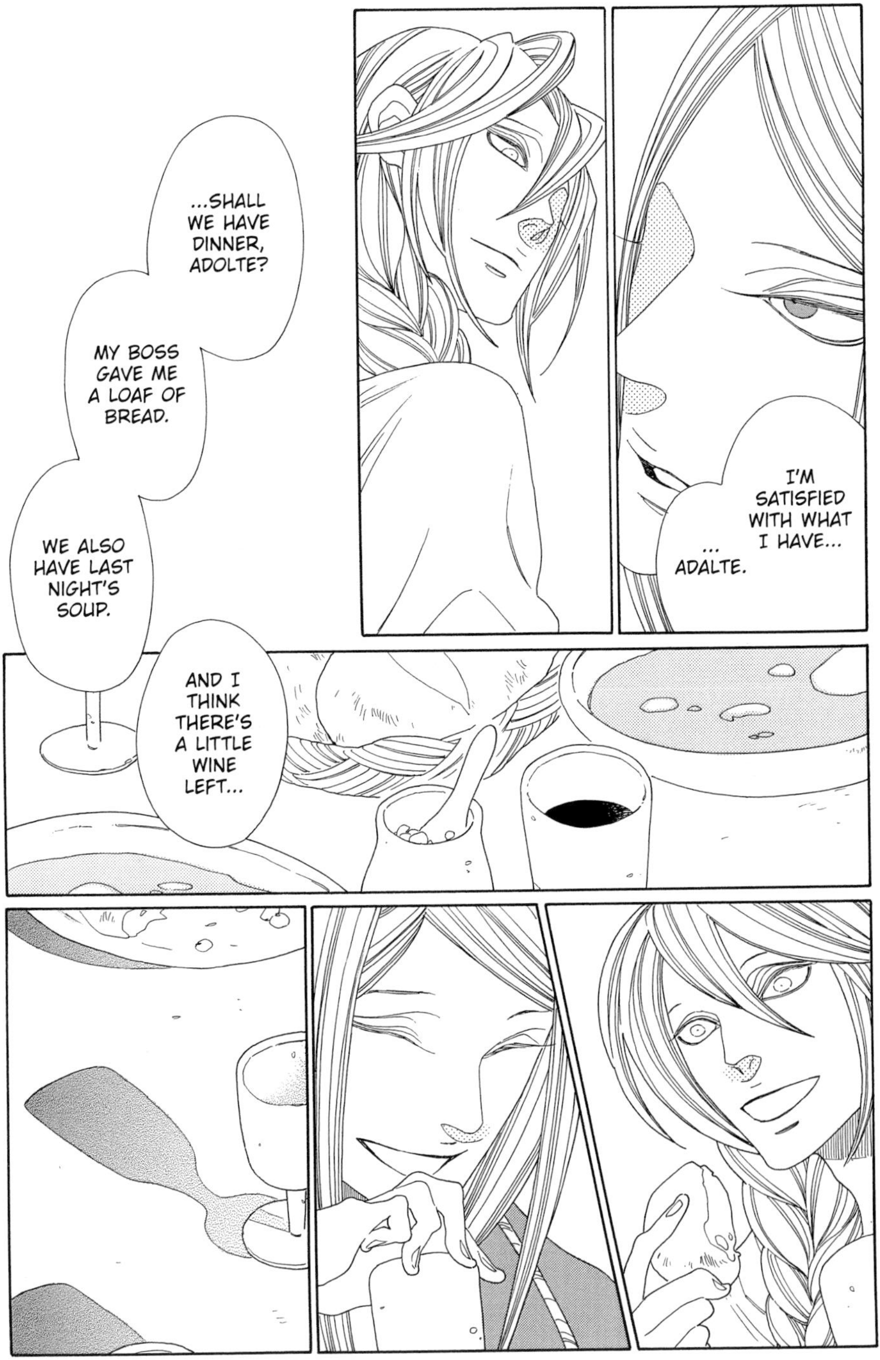
I'M SATISFIED WITH WHAT I HAVE... ...ADALTE.
...SHALL WE HAVE DINNER, ADOLTE?
MY BOSS GAVE ME A LOAF OF BREAD.
WE ALSO HAVE LAST NIGHT'S SOUP.
AND I THINK THERE'S A LITTLE WINE LEFT...

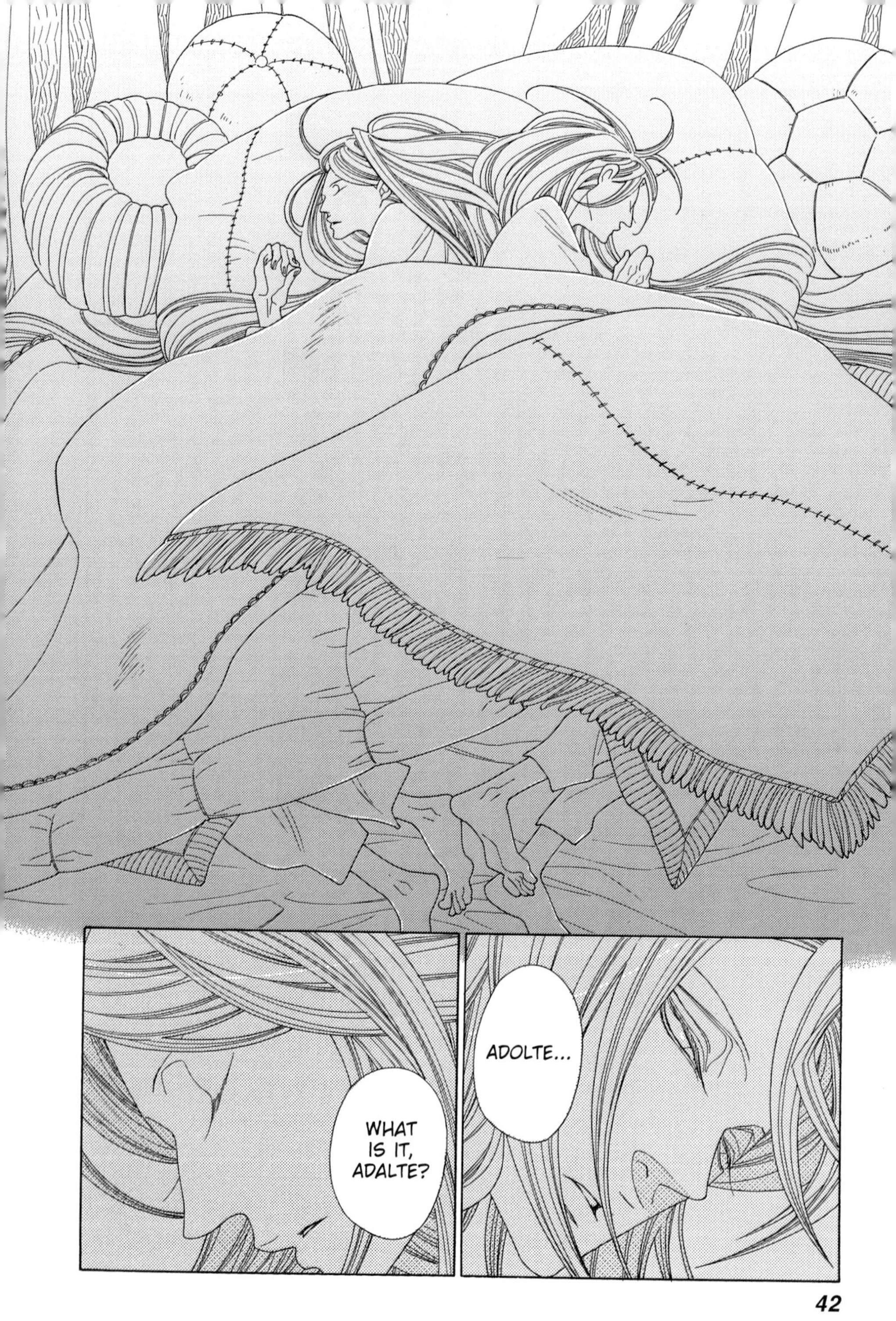
ADOLTE...
WHAT IS IT, ADALTE?

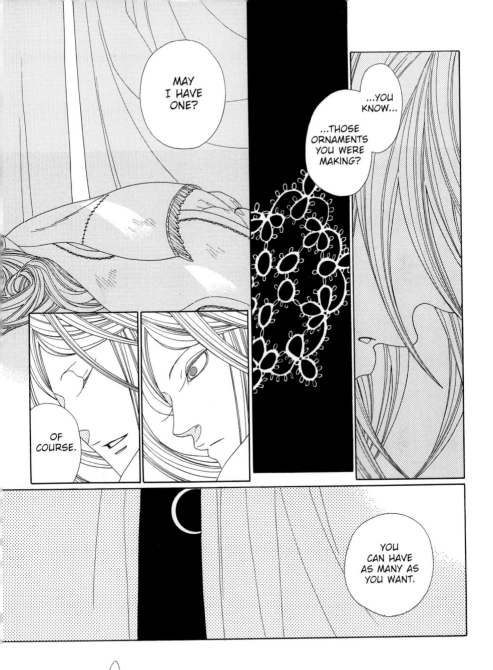

MAY I HAVE ONE?

...YOU KNOW...

...THOSE ORNAMENTS YOU WERE MAKING?

OF COURSE.

YOU CAN HAVE AS MANY AS YOU WANT.

JARA
(JANGLE)

JARARA

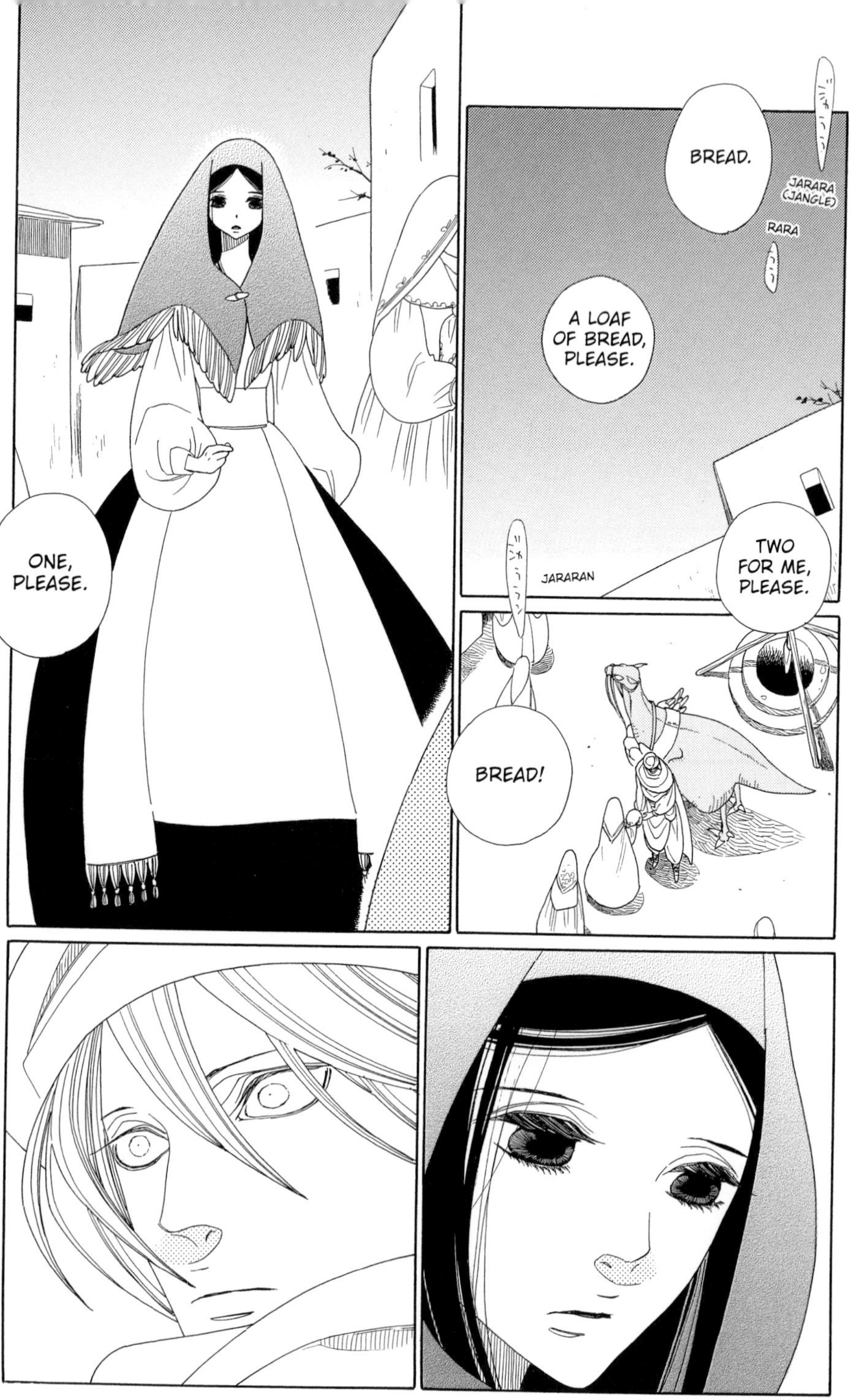

BREAD.
JARARA (JANGLE)
RARA
A LOAF OF BREAD, PLEASE.
JARARAN
TWO FOR ME, PLEASE.
BREAD!
ONE, PLEASE.

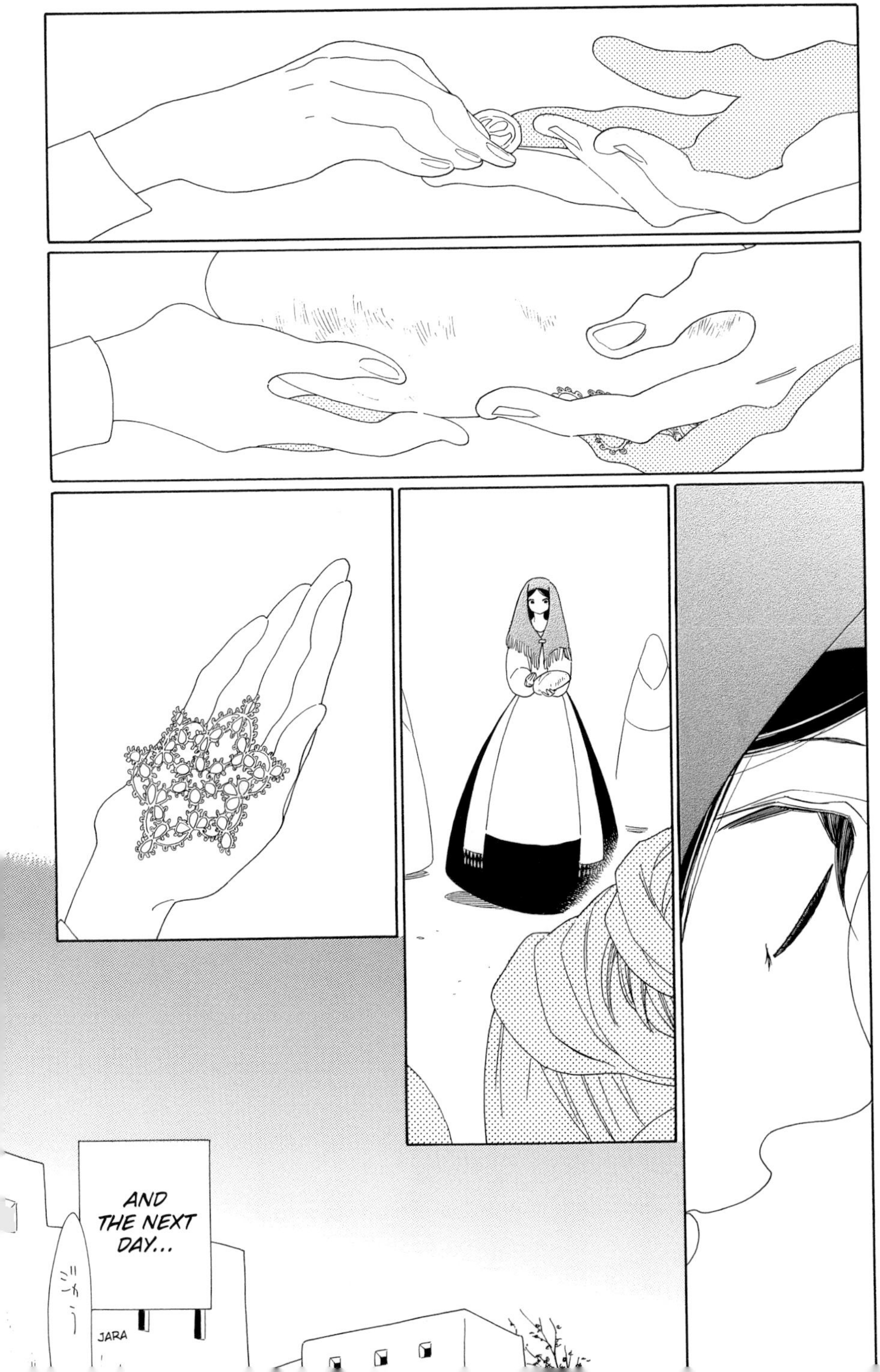
AND THE NEXT DAY...
ジャラ
JARA

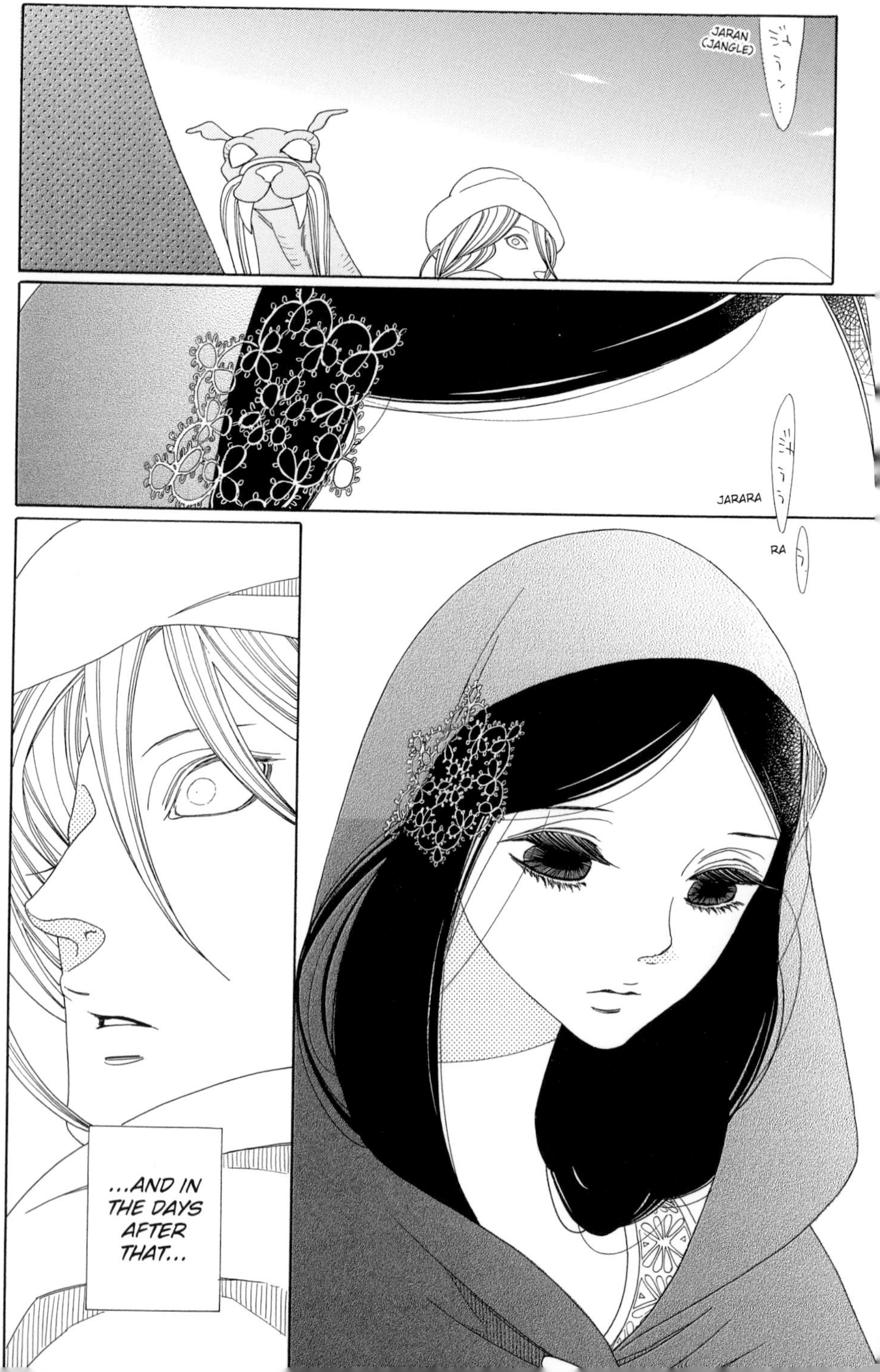

JARAN (JANGLE)
ジャラン…
JARARA
ジャララ
RA
ラ
...AND IN THE DAYS AFTER THAT...

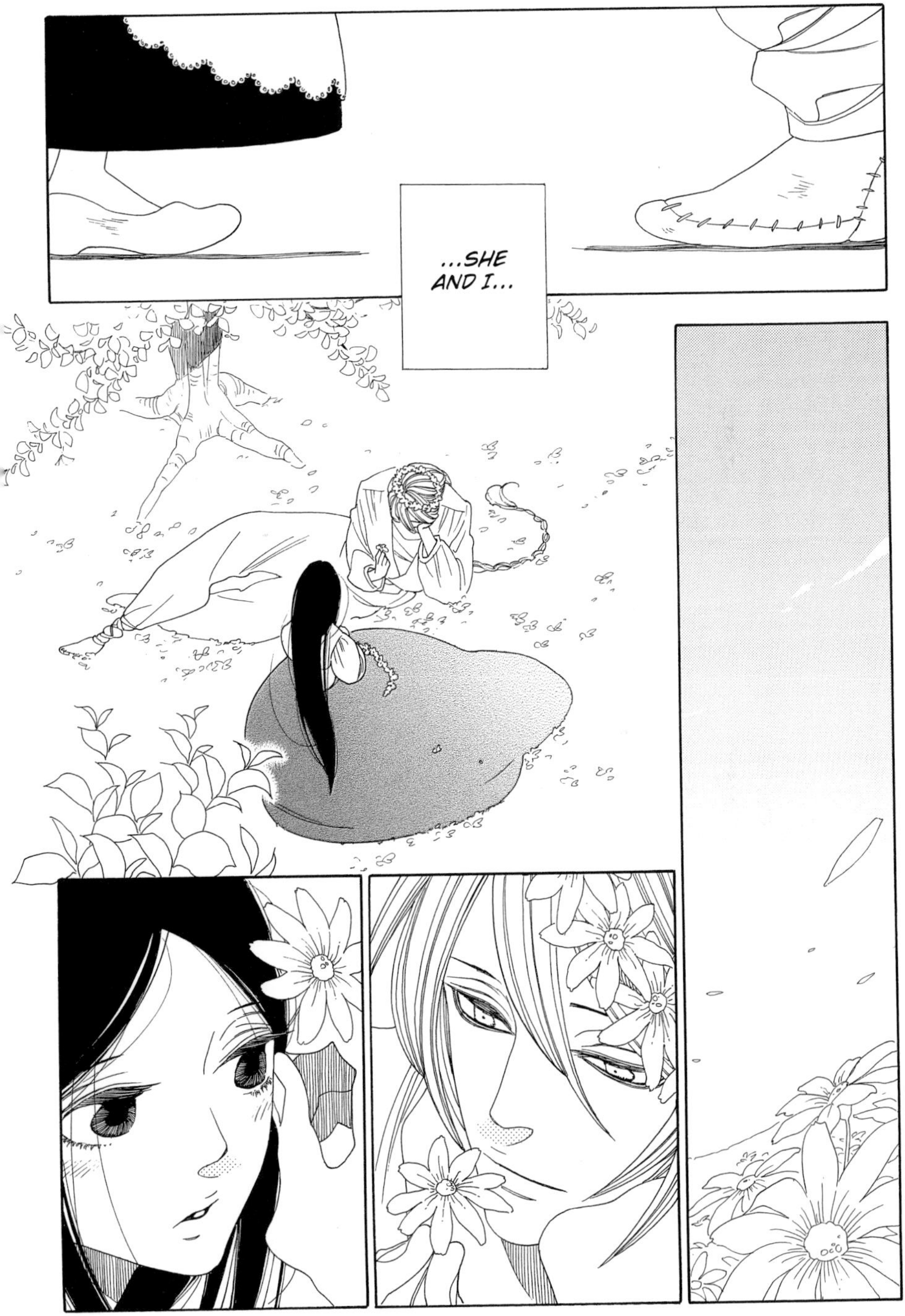
...SHE AND I...

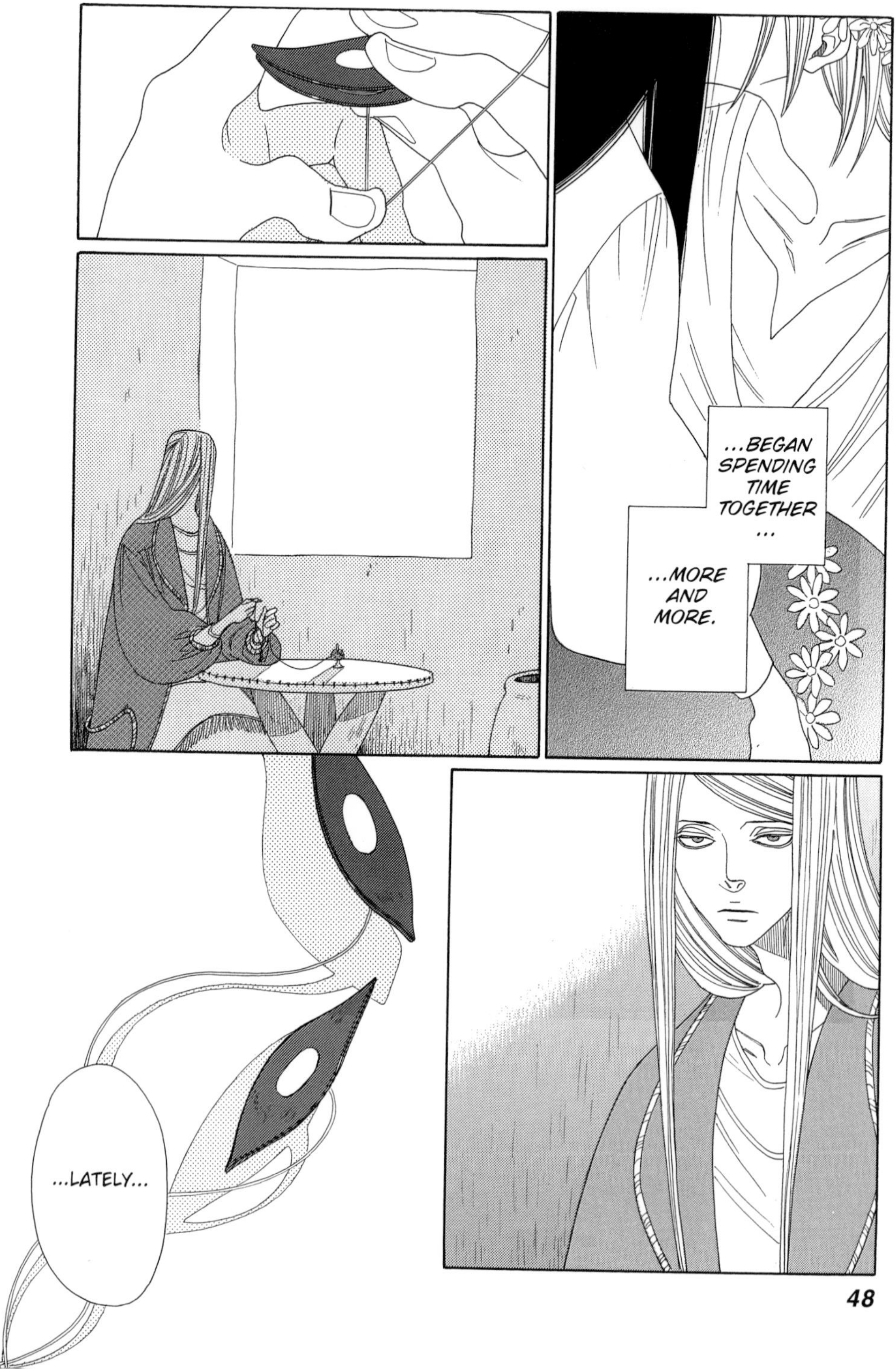
...BEGAN SPENDING TIME TOGETHER ...
...MORE AND MORE.
...LATELY...

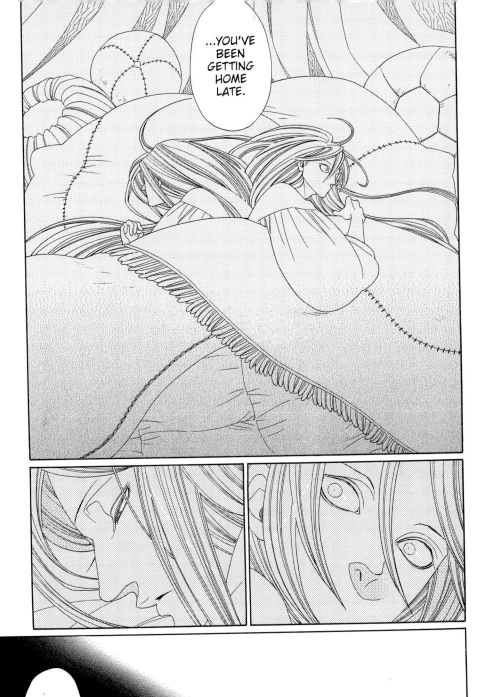

...YOU'VE
BEEN
GETTING
HOME
LATE.

...NEVER
MIND.

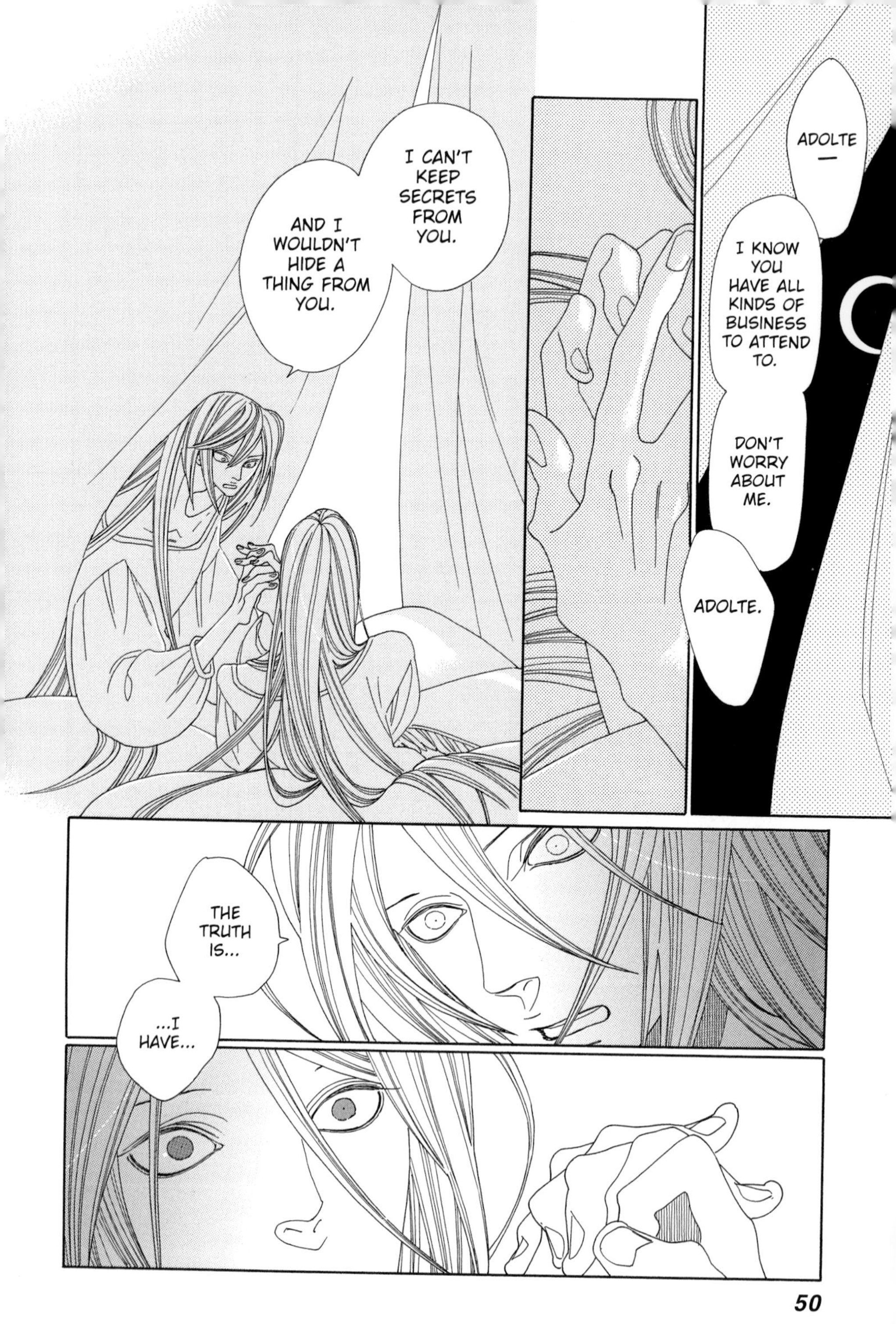
ADOLTE —
I KNOW YOU HAVE ALL KINDS OF BUSINESS TO ATTEND TO.
DON'T WORRY ABOUT ME.
ADOLTE.
I CAN'T KEEP SECRETS FROM YOU.
AND I WOULDN'T HIDE A THING FROM YOU.
THE TRUTH IS...
...I HAVE...

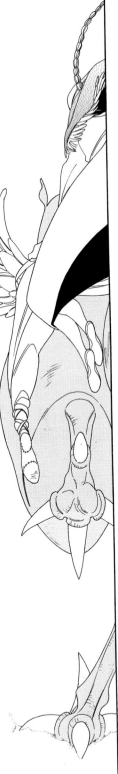

...I'M...

...A LITTLE SCARED.

WHY?

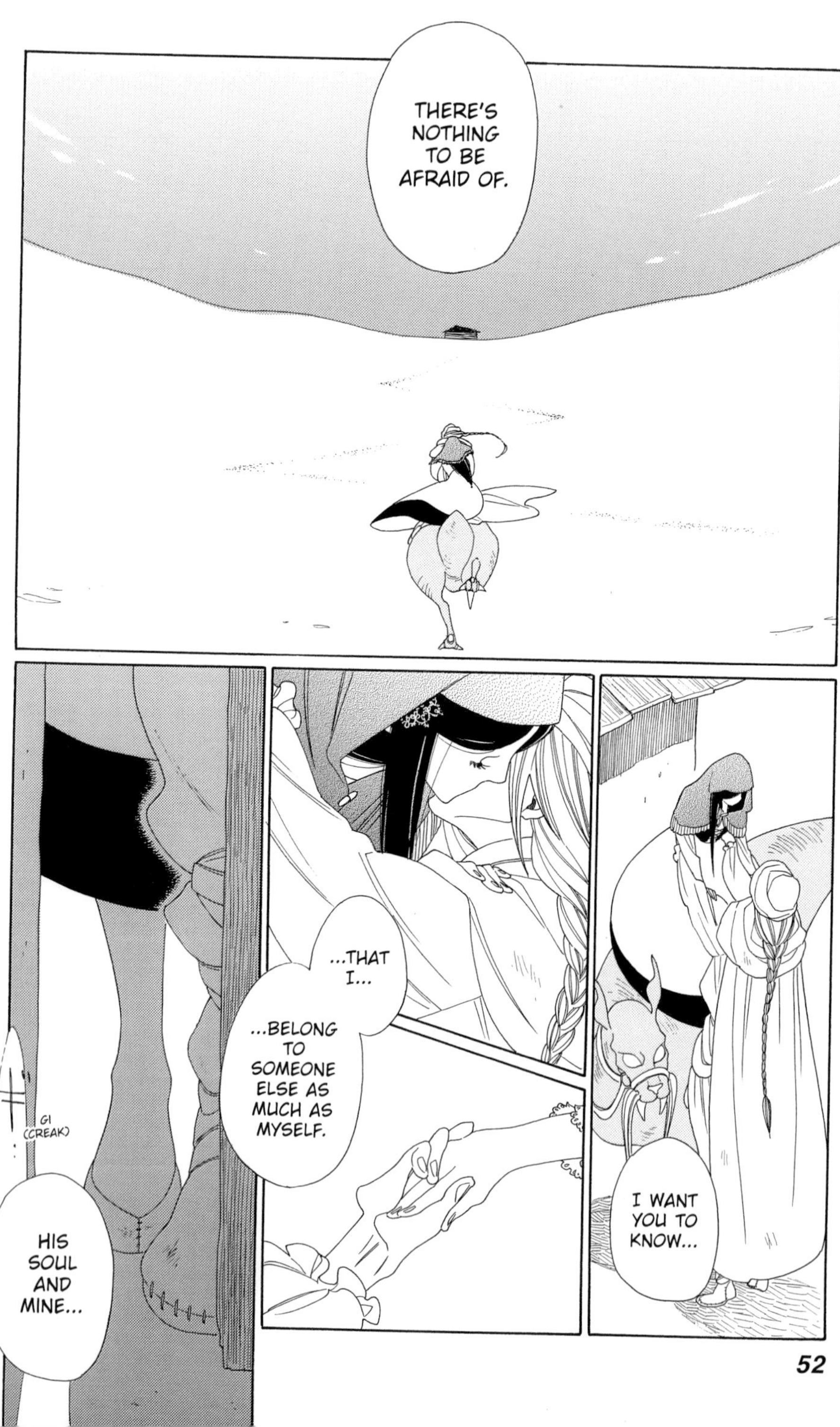
THERE'S NOTHING TO BE AFRAID OF.
I WANT YOU TO KNOW...
...THAT I...
...BELONG TO SOMEONE ELSE AS MUCH AS MYSELF.
GI (CREAK)
HIS SOUL AND MINE...

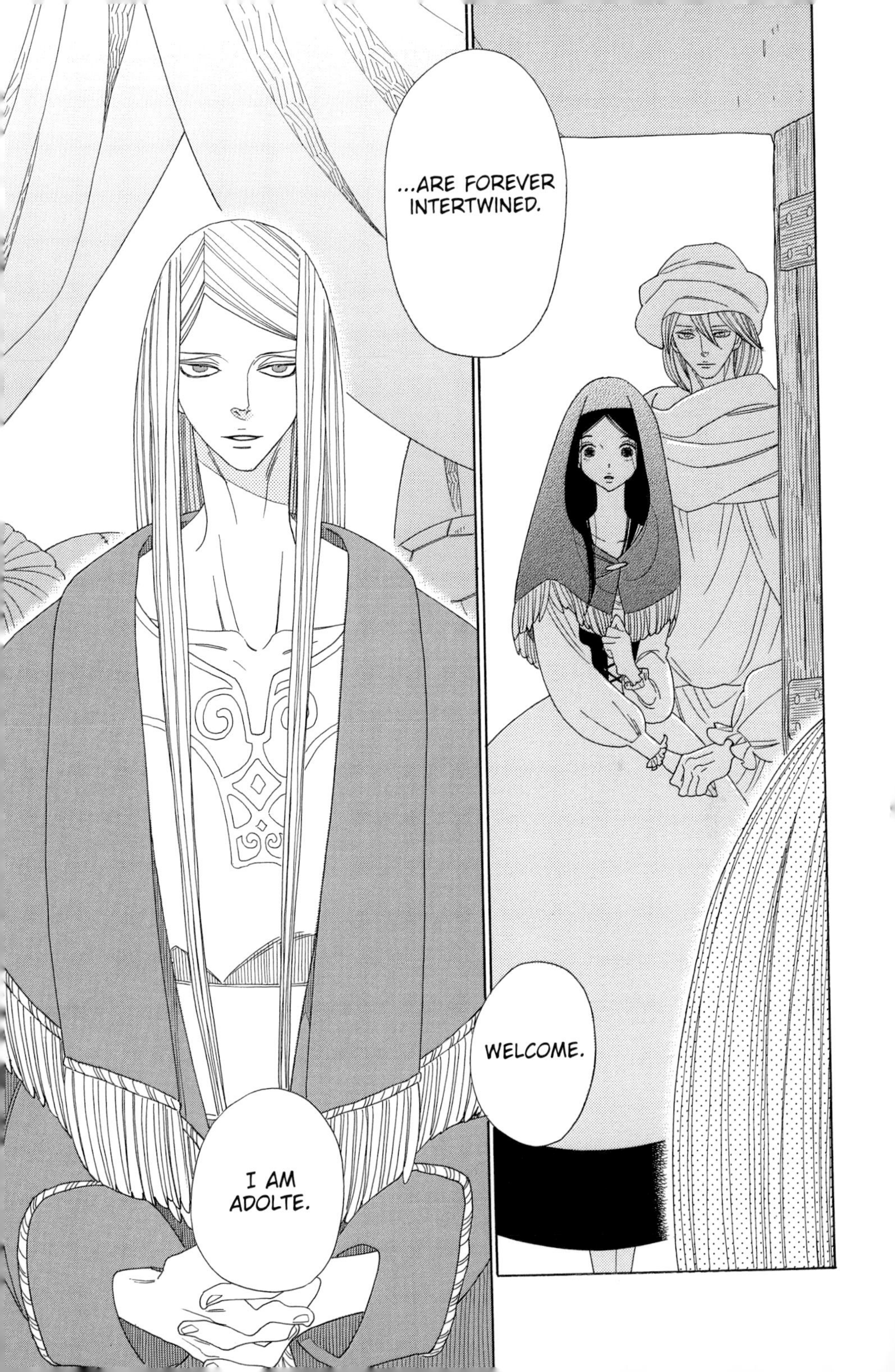
...ARE FOREVER INTERTWINED.
WELCOME.
I AM ADOLTE.

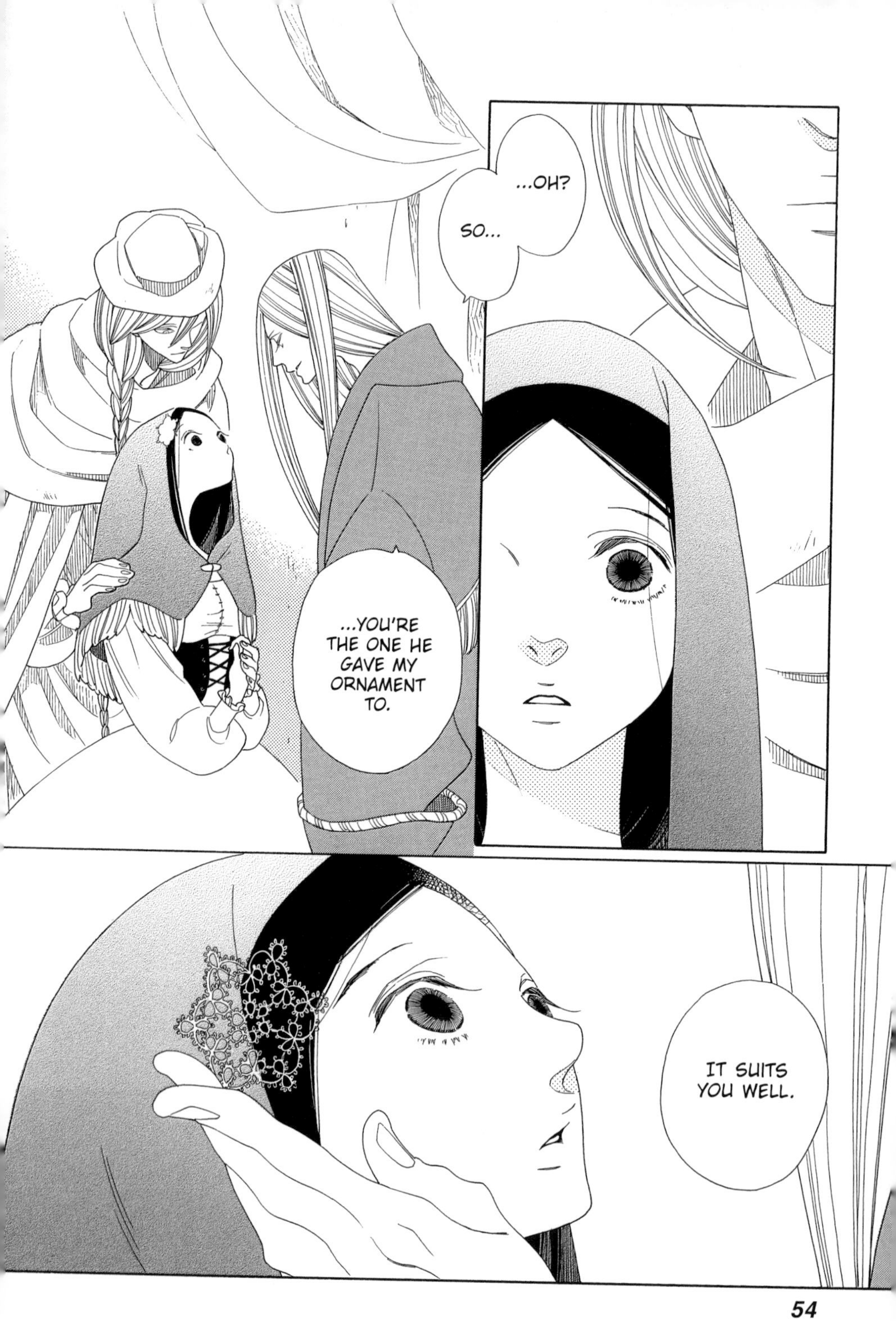
...OH? SO...
...YOU'RE THE ONE HE GAVE MY ORNAMENT TO.
IT SUITS YOU WELL.

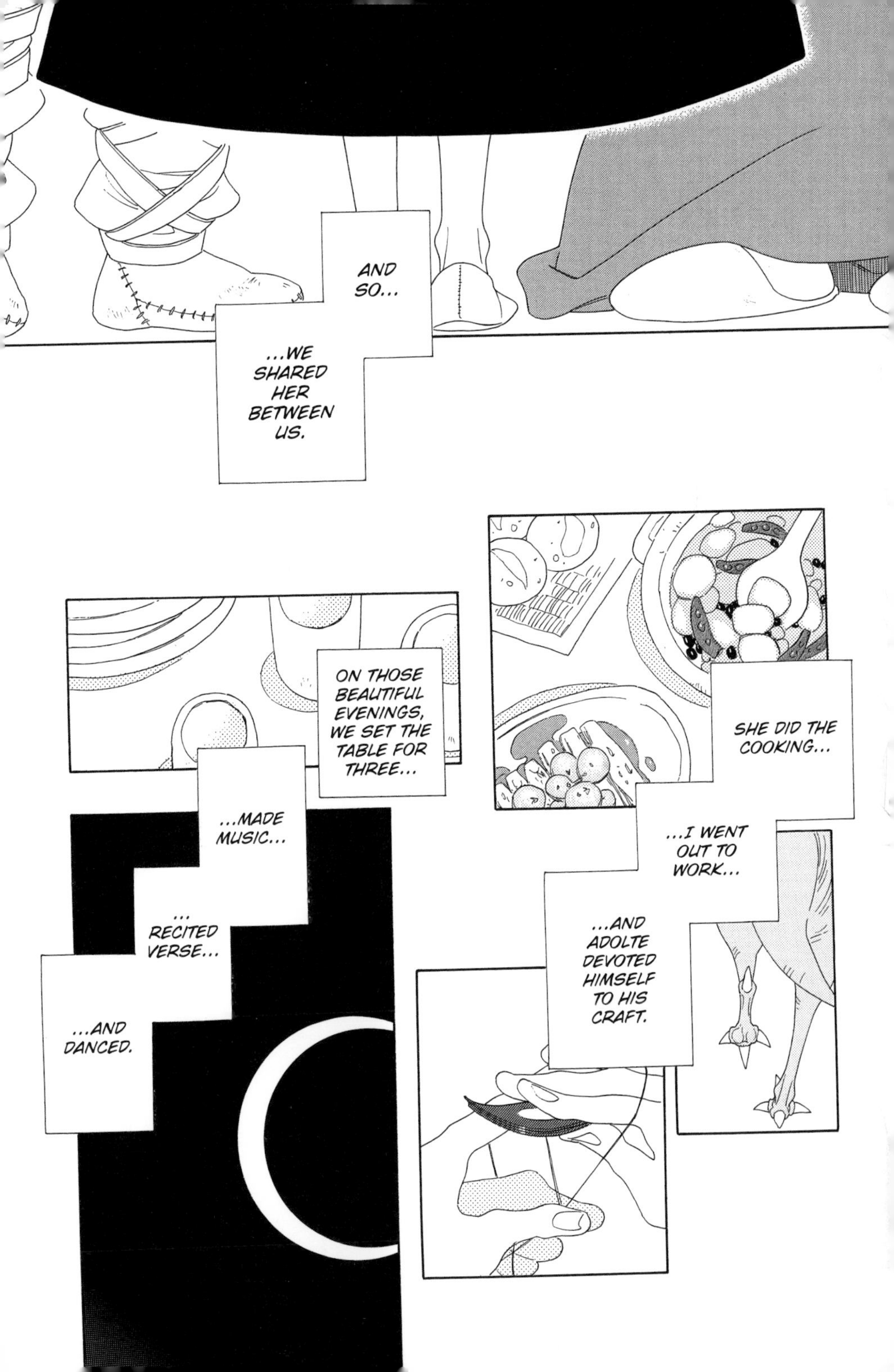
AND SO...
...WE SHARED HER BETWEEN US.
SHE DID THE COOKING...
...I WENT OUT TO WORK...
...AND ADOLTE DEVOTED HIMSELF TO HIS CRAFT.
ON THOSE BEAUTIFUL EVENINGS, WE SET THE TABLE FOR THREE...
...MADE MUSIC...
...RECITED VERSE...
...AND DANCED.

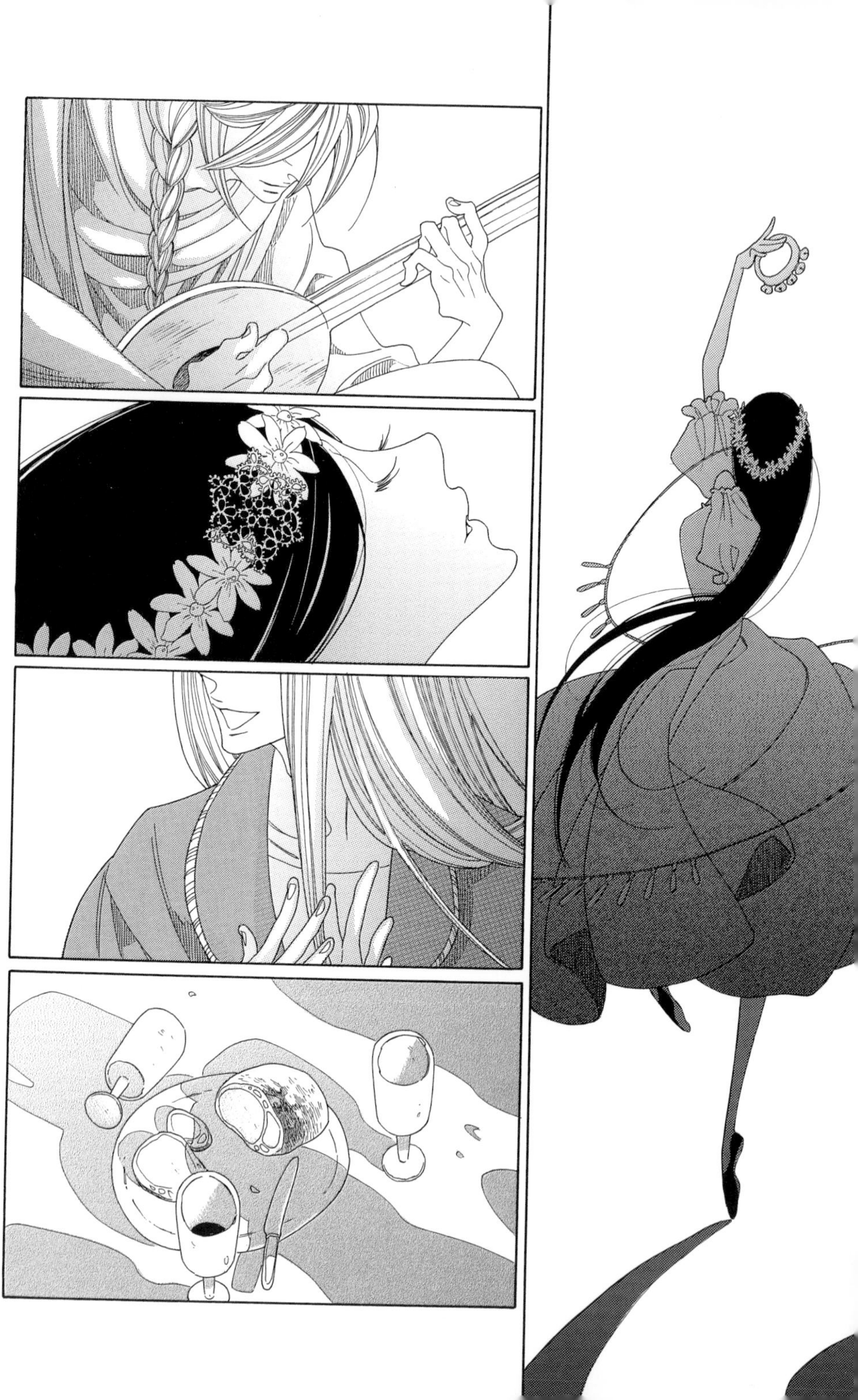

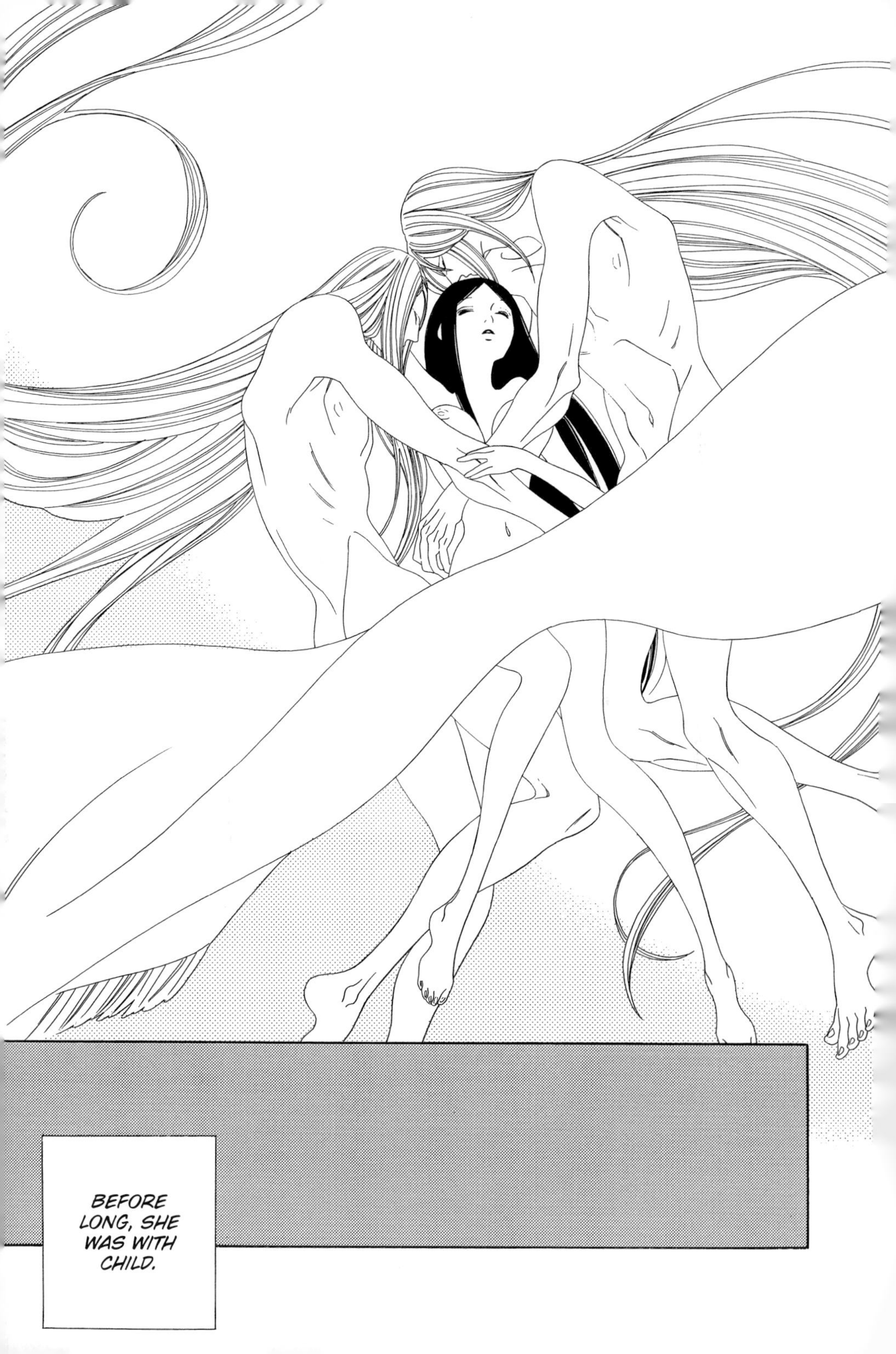
BEFORE LONG, SHE WAS WITH CHILD.

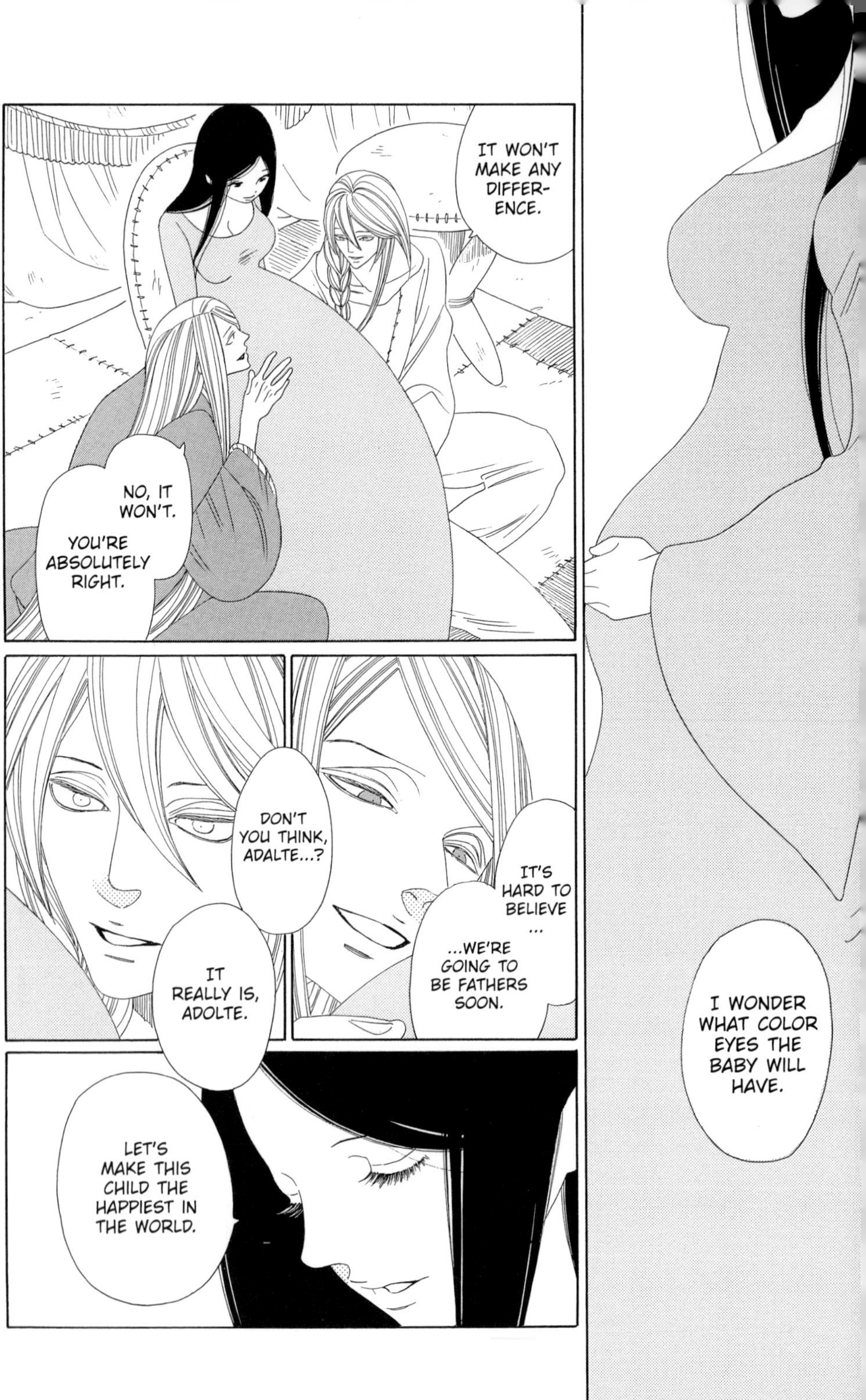
I WONDER WHAT COLOR EYES THE BABY WILL HAVE.
IT WON'T MAKE ANY DIFFER-ENCE.
NO, IT WON'T.
YOU'RE ABSOLUTELY RIGHT.
IT'S HARD TO BELIEVE ...
...WE'RE GOING TO BE FATHERS SOON.
DON'T YOU THINK, ADALTE...?
IT REALLY IS, ADOLTE.
LET'S MAKE THIS CHILD THE HAPPIEST IN THE WORLD.

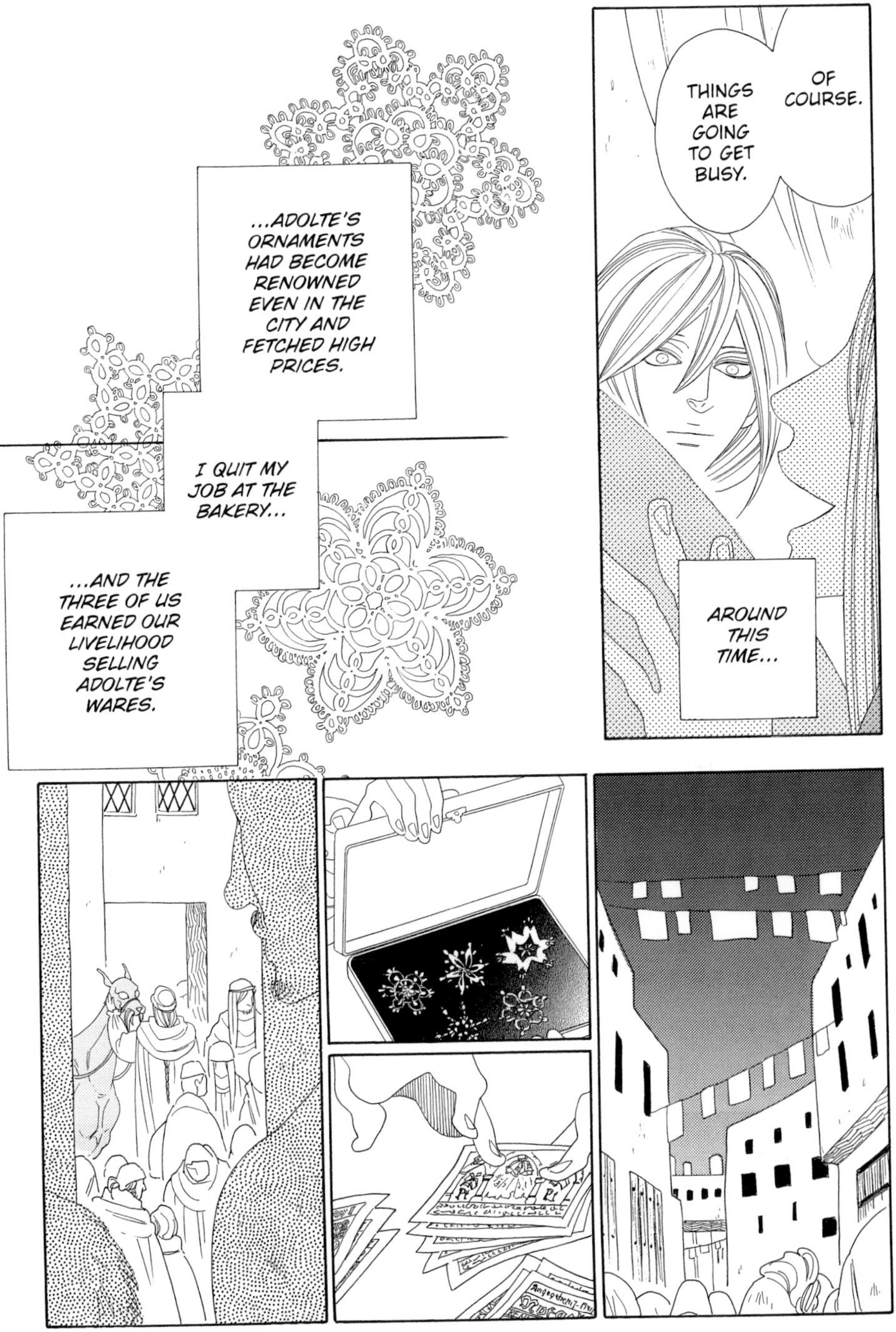

OF COURSE.
THINGS ARE GOING TO GET BUSY.
AROUND THIS TIME...
...ADOLTE'S ORNAMENTS HAD BECOME RENOWNED EVEN IN THE CITY AND FETCHED HIGH PRICES.
I QUIT MY JOB AT THE BAKERY...
...AND THE THREE OF US EARNED OUR LIVELIHOOD SELLING ADOLTE'S WARES.

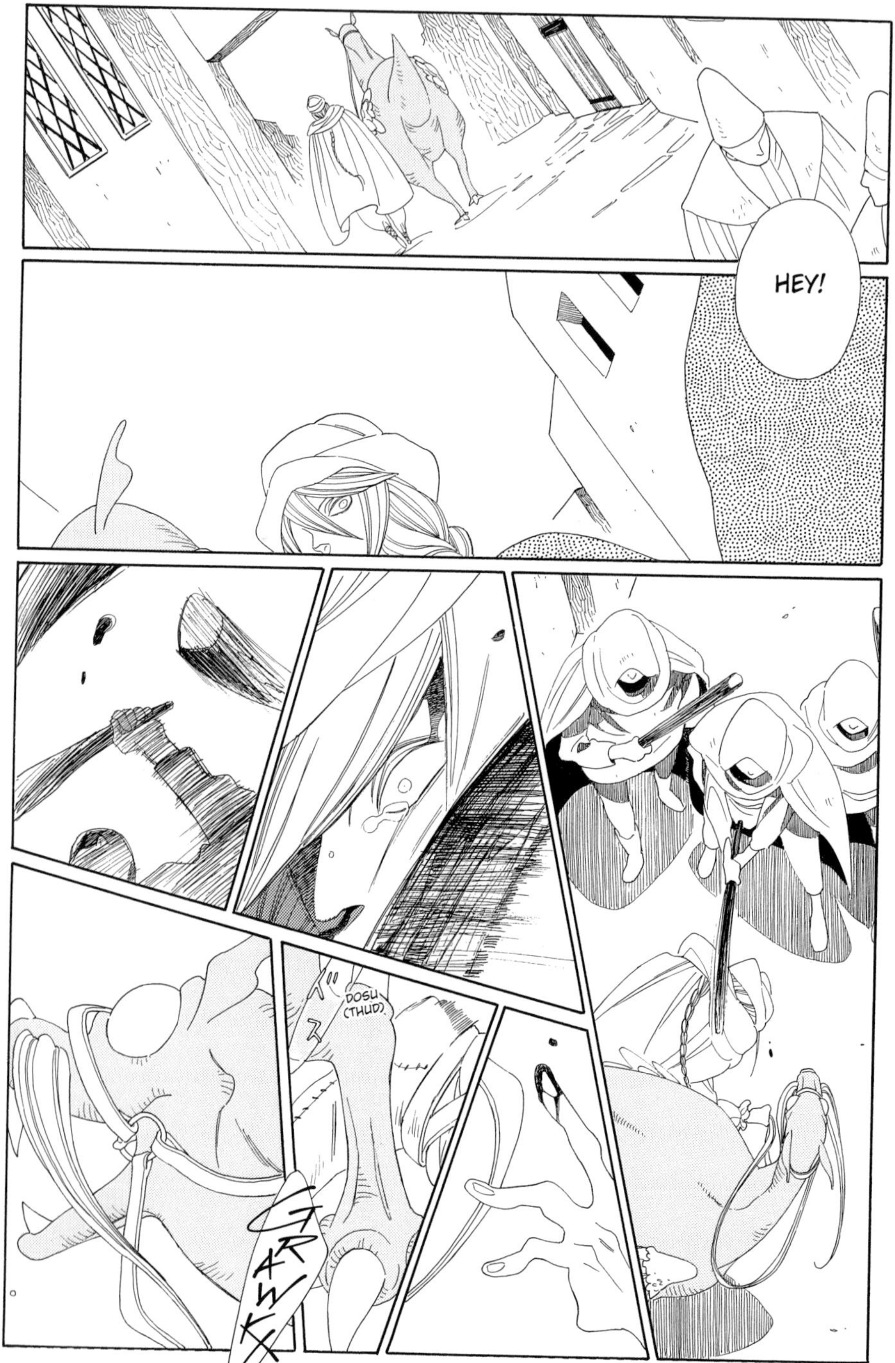
HEY!
DOSU (THUD)
GRAWK

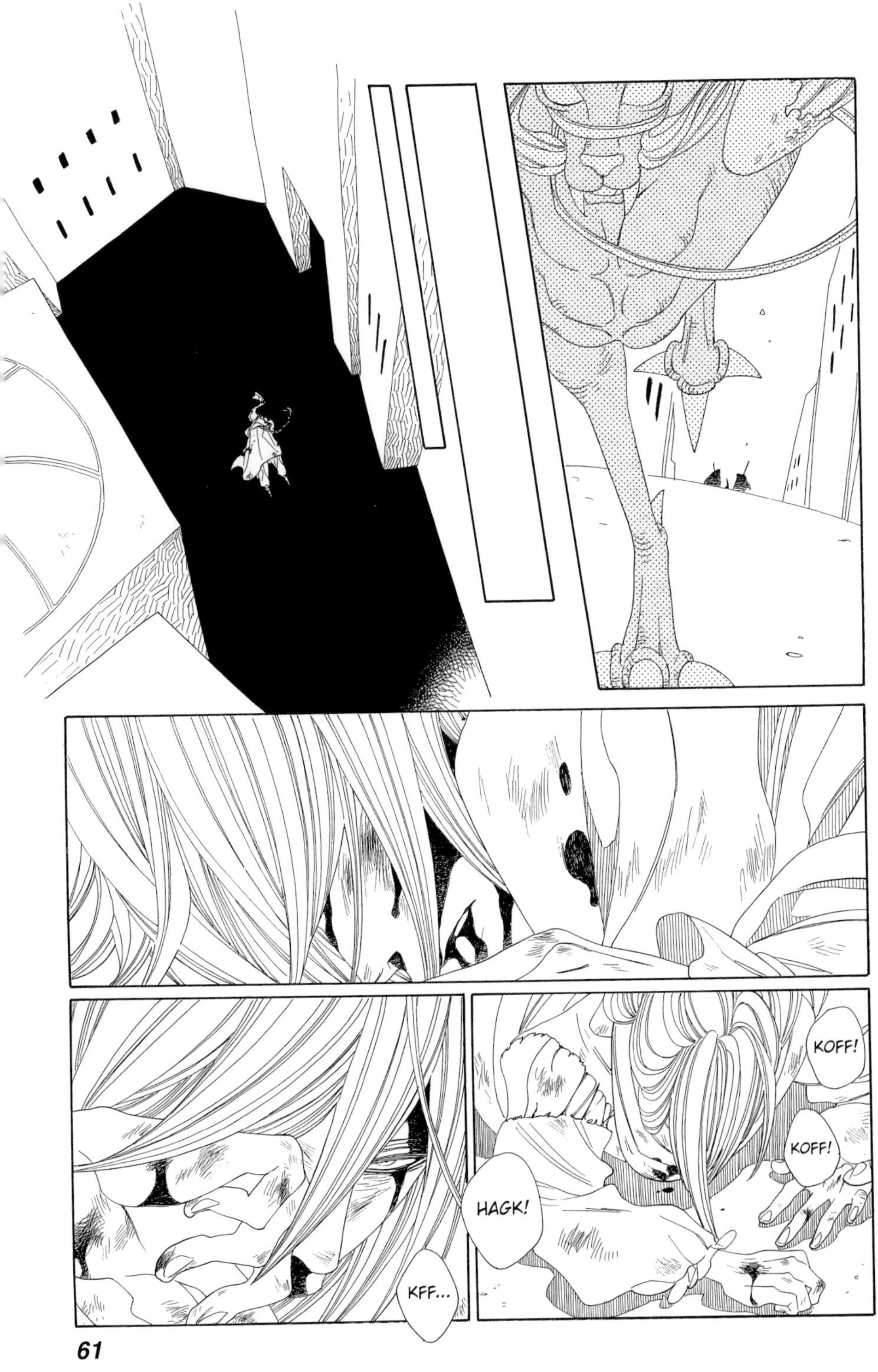
KOFF!
KOFF!
HAGK!
KFF...

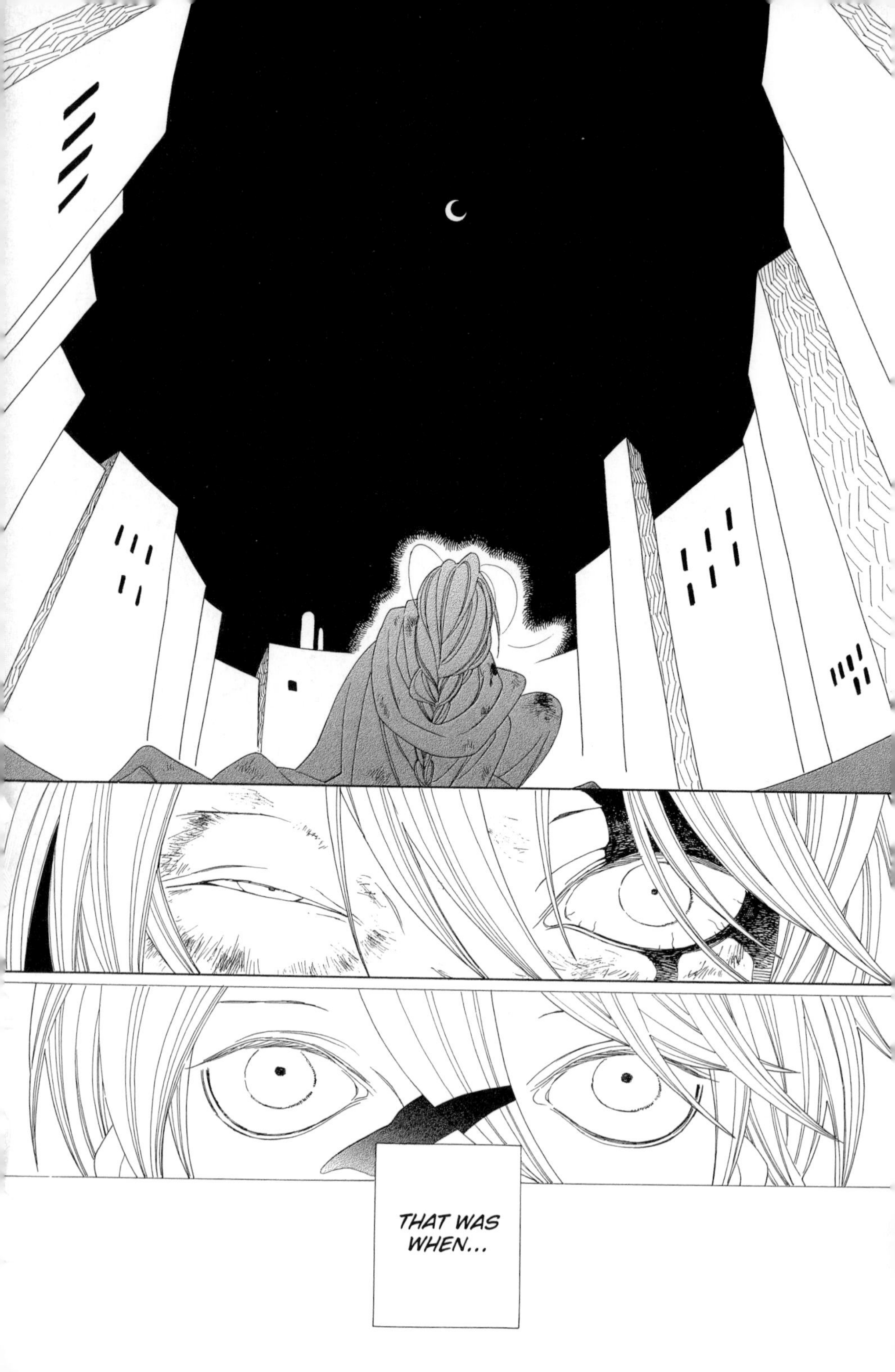
THAT WAS WHEN...

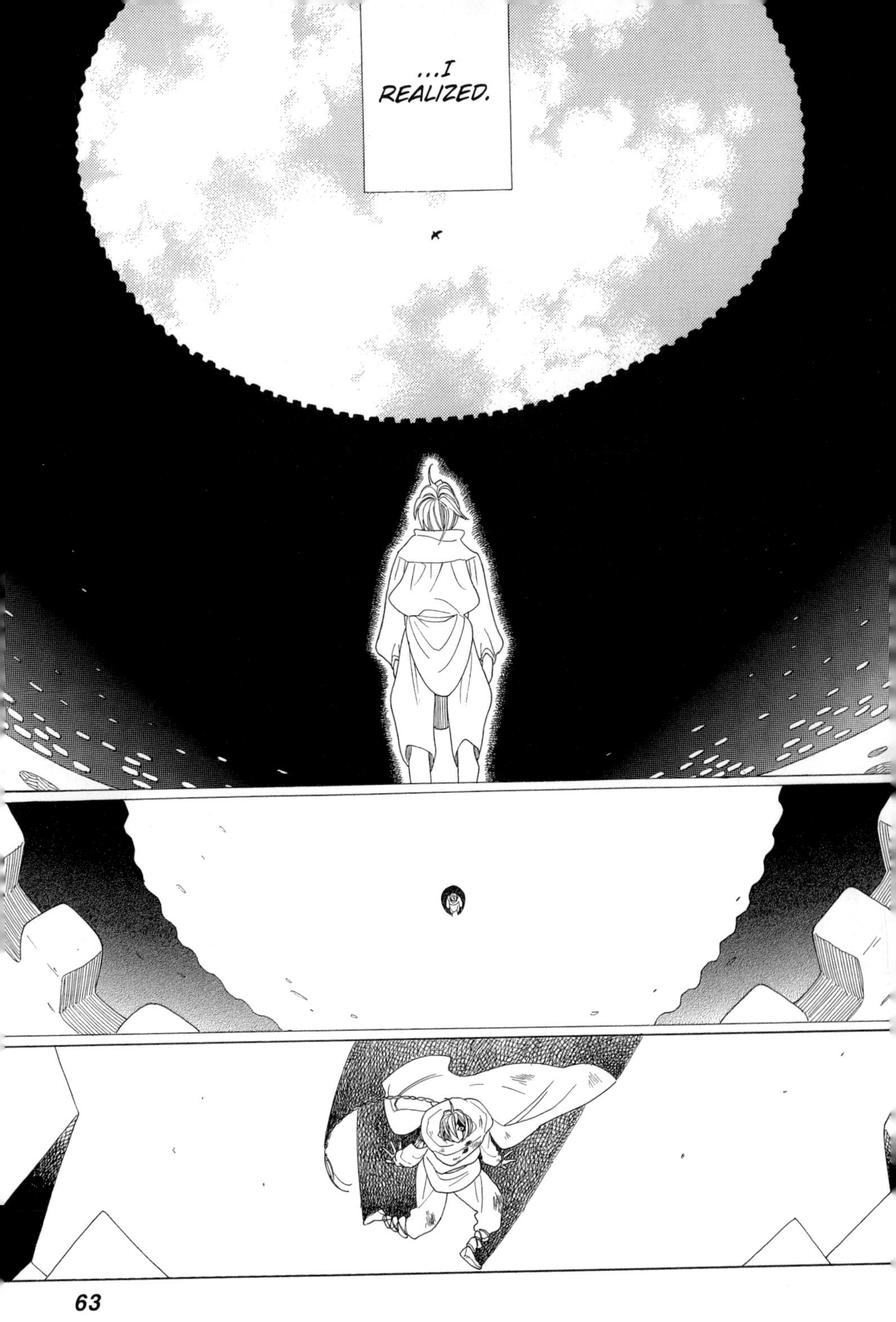
...I REALIZED.

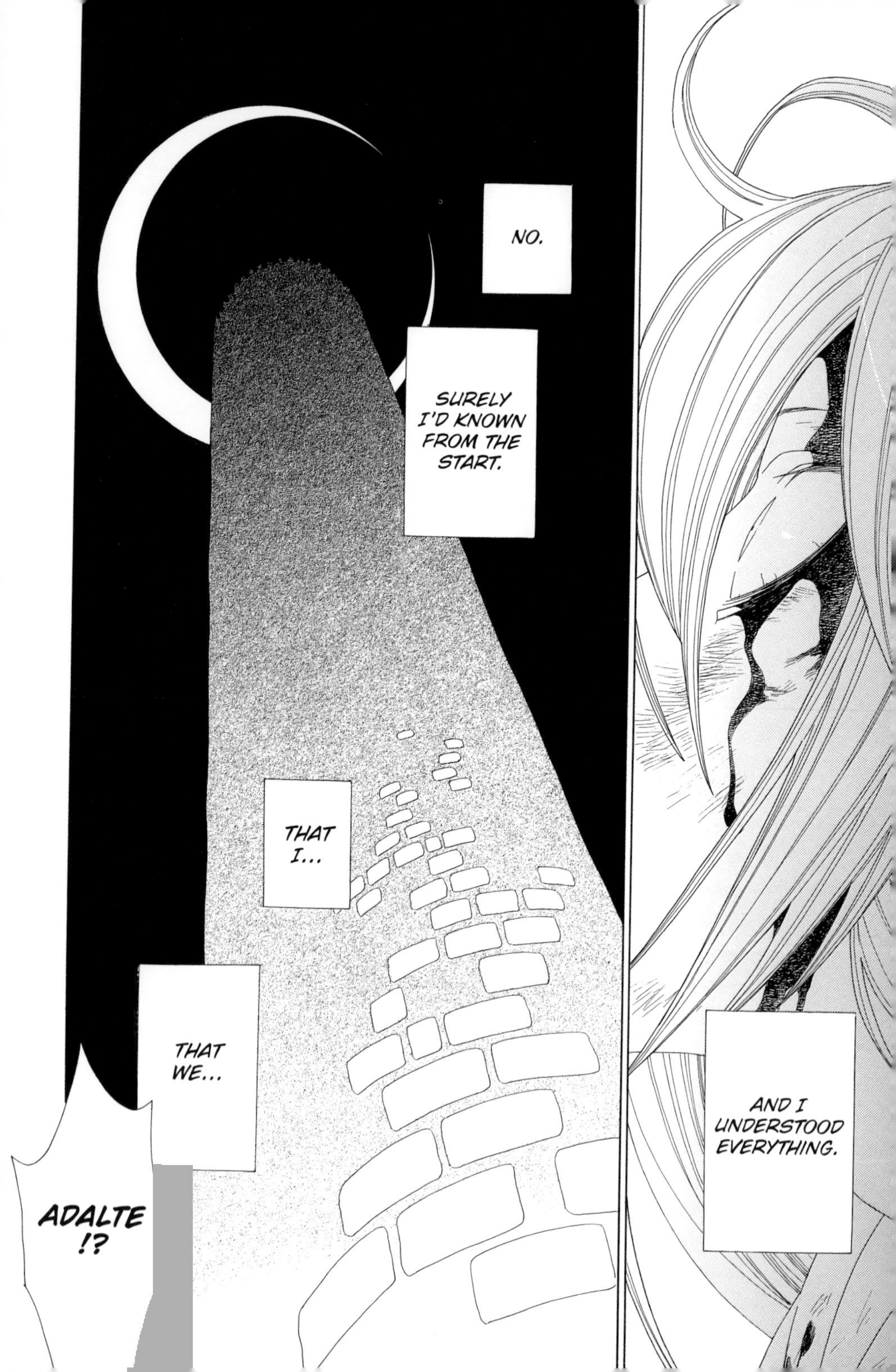
AND I UNDERSTOOD EVERYTHING.
NO.
SURELY I'D KNOWN FROM THE START.
THAT I...
THAT WE...
ADALTE !?

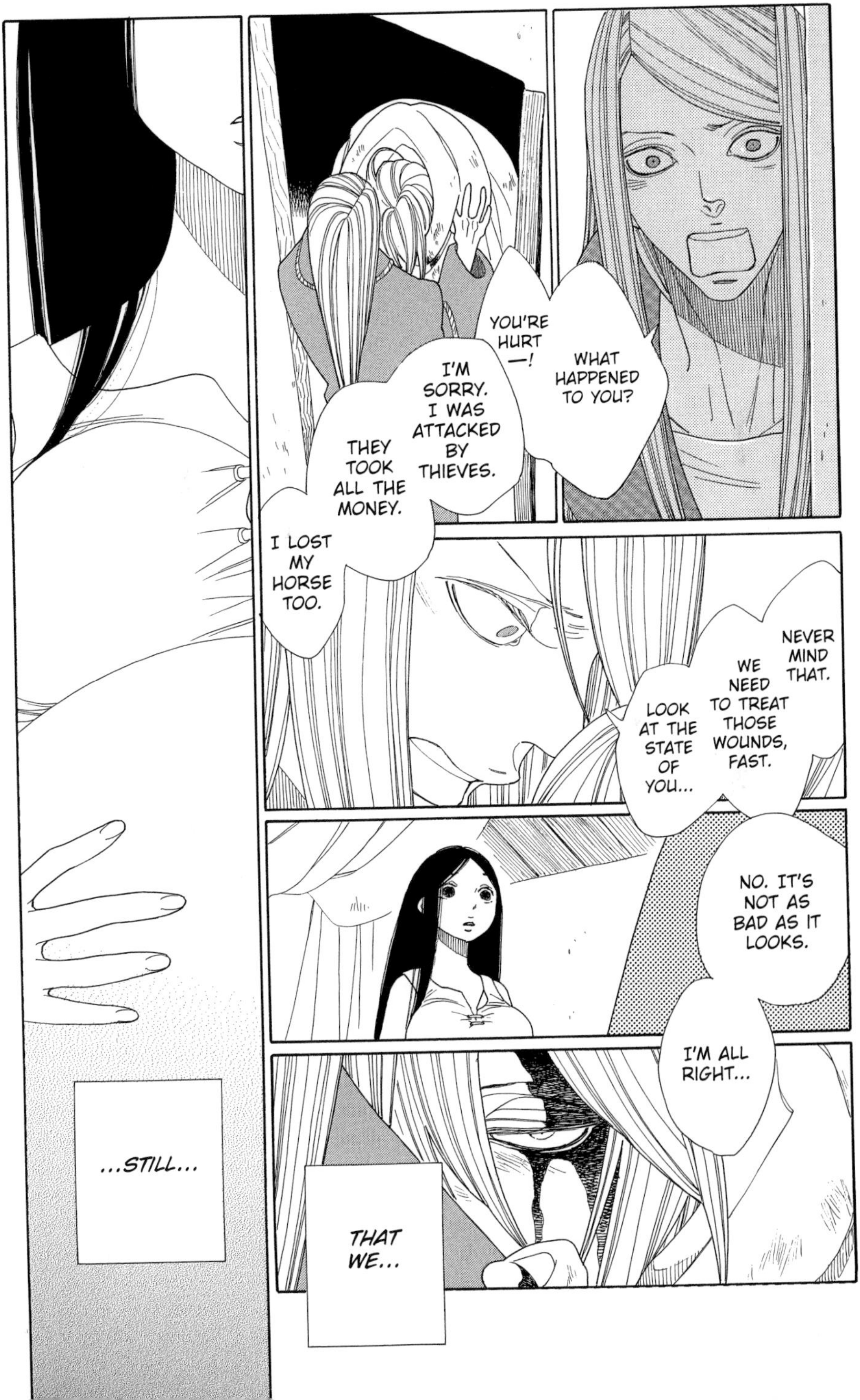

YOU'RE HURT—!
WHAT HAPPENED TO YOU?
I'M SORRY. I WAS ATTACKED BY THIEVES.
THEY TOOK ALL THE MONEY.
I LOST MY HORSE TOO.
NEVER MIND THAT.
WE NEED TO TREAT THOSE WOUNDS, FAST.
LOOK AT THE STATE OF YOU...
NO. IT'S NOT AS BAD AS IT LOOKS.
I'M ALL RIGHT...
THAT WE...
...STILL...

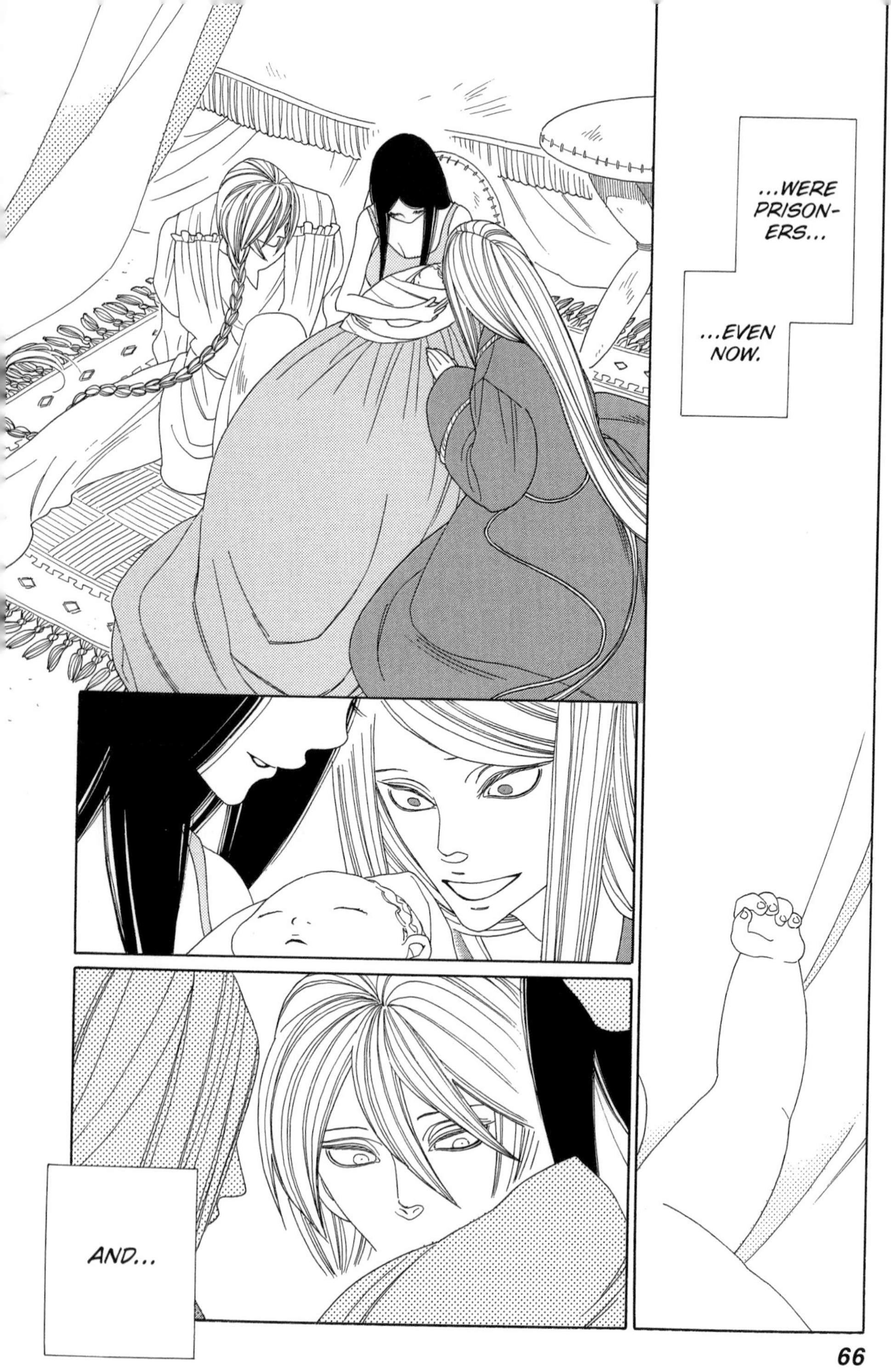
...WERE PRISON-ERS...
...EVEN NOW.
AND...

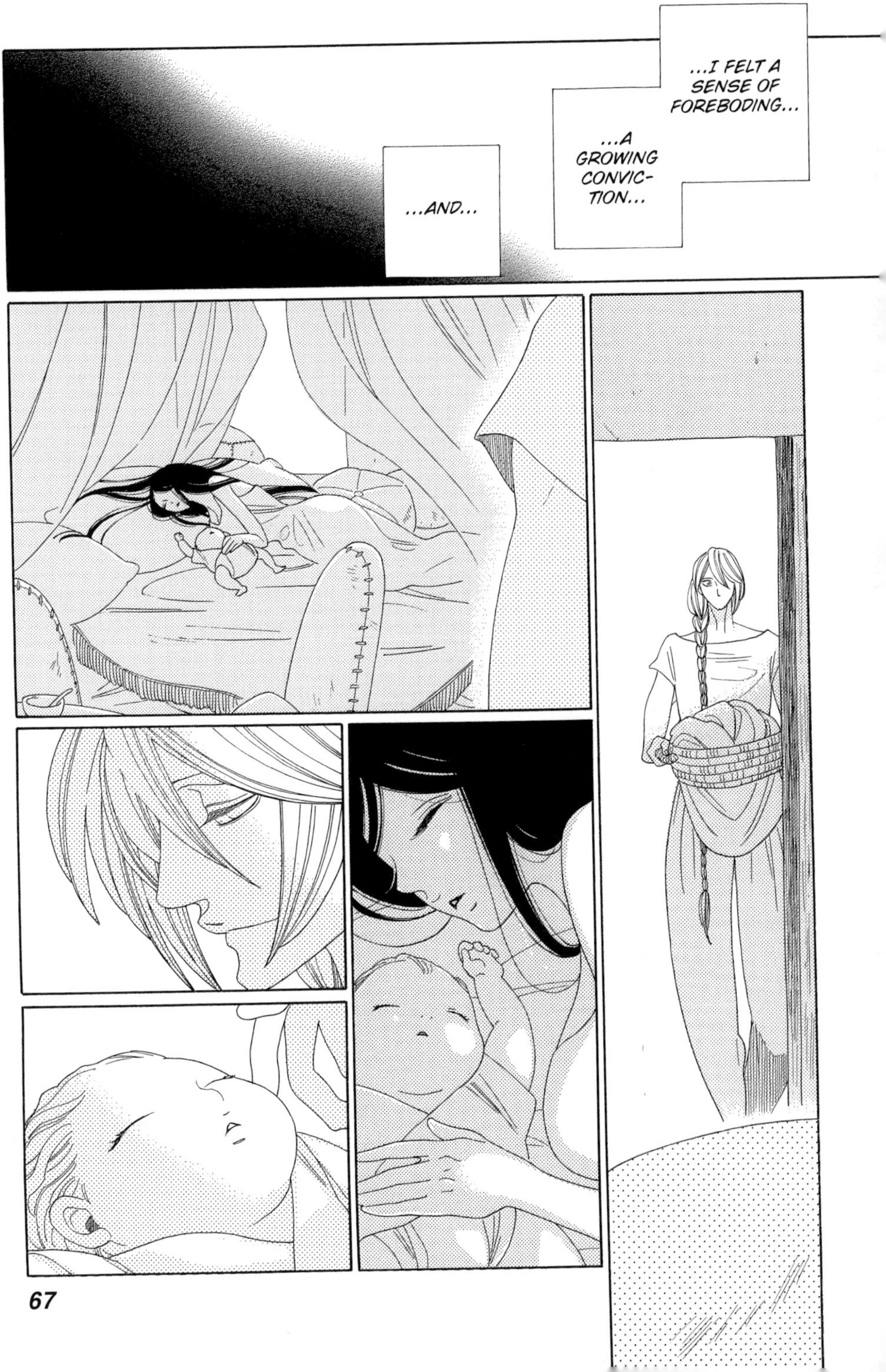
...I FELT A SENSE OF FOREBODING...
...A GROWING CONVIC-TION...
...AND...

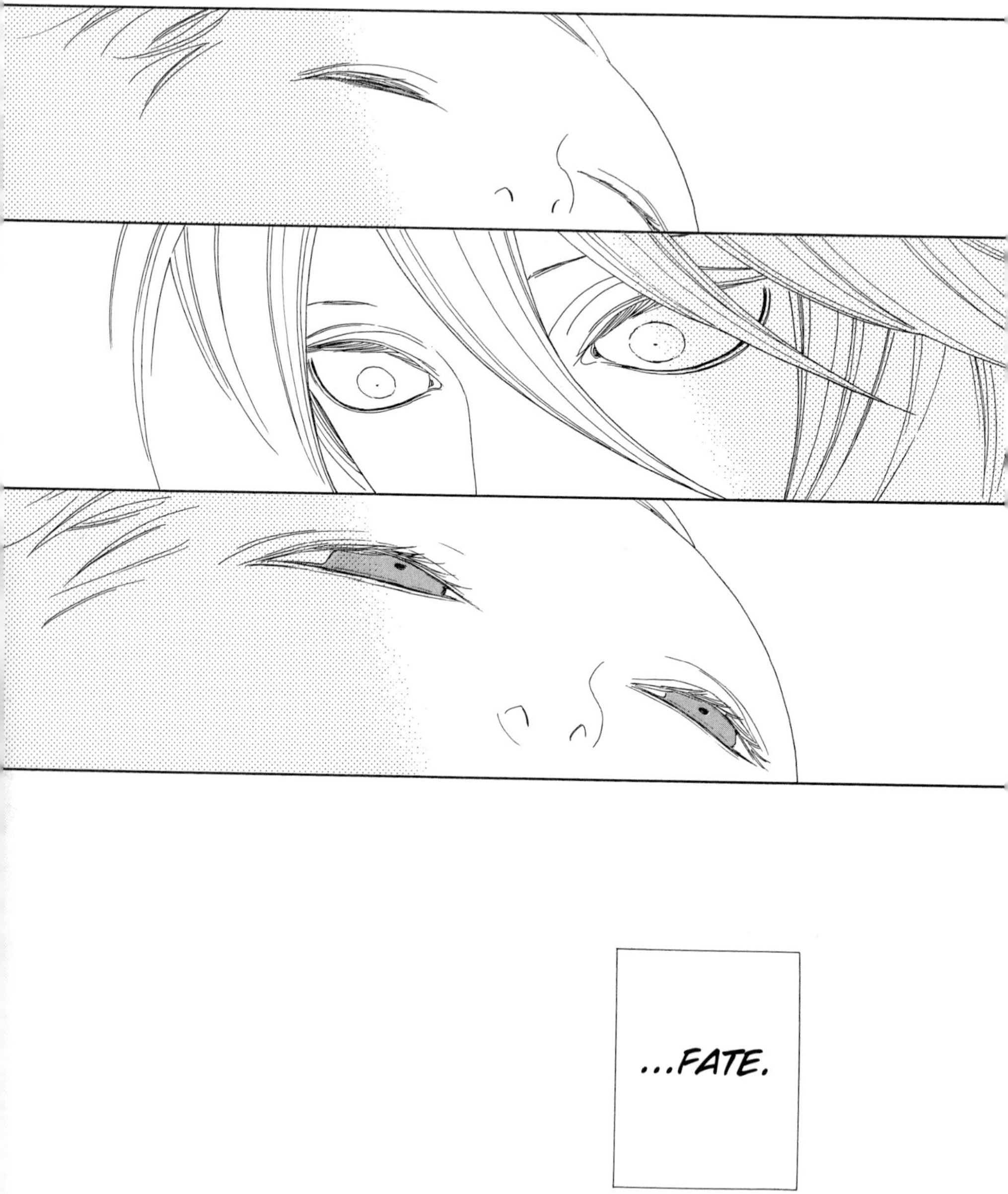
...FATE.

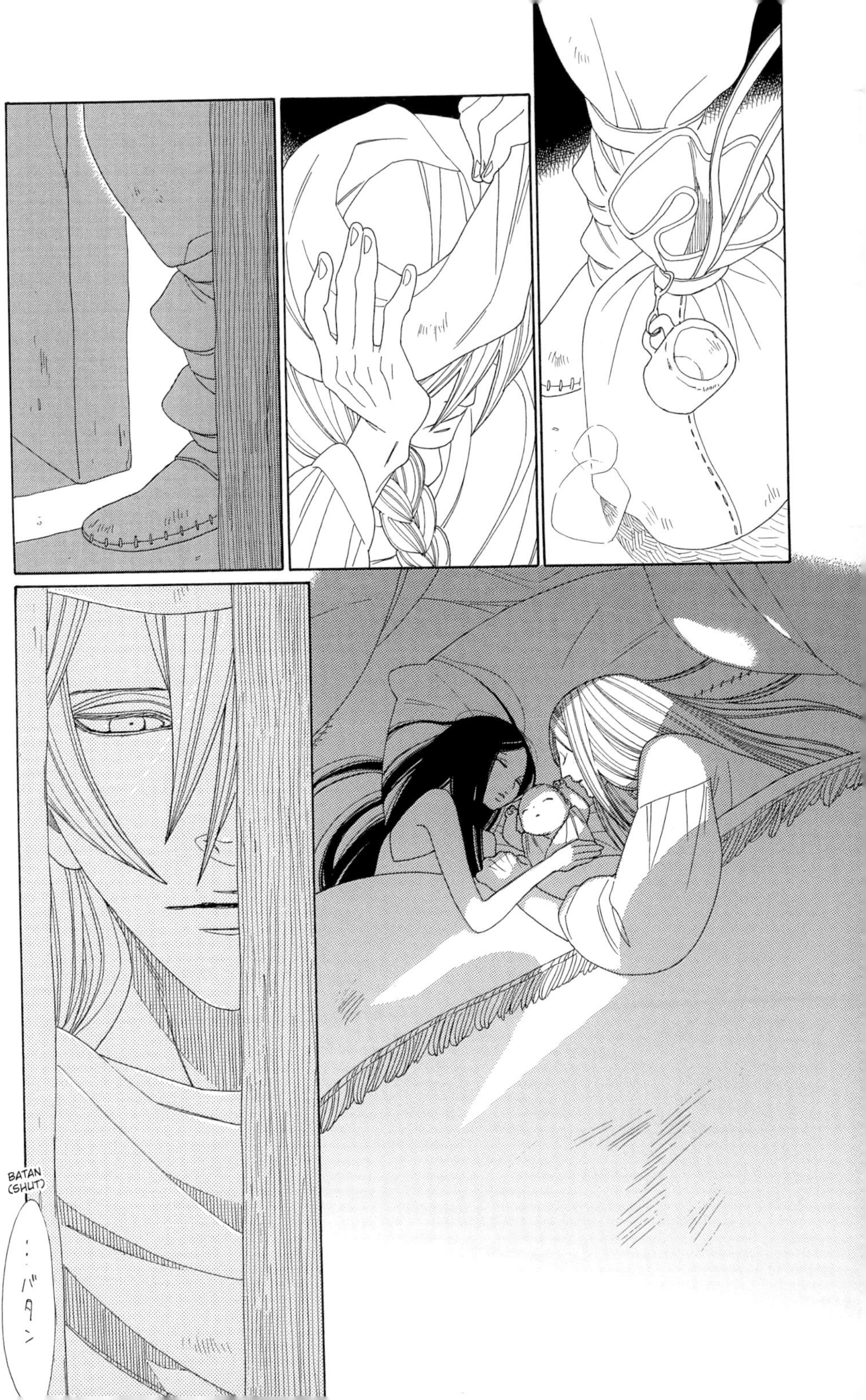
BATAN (SHUT)
…バタン

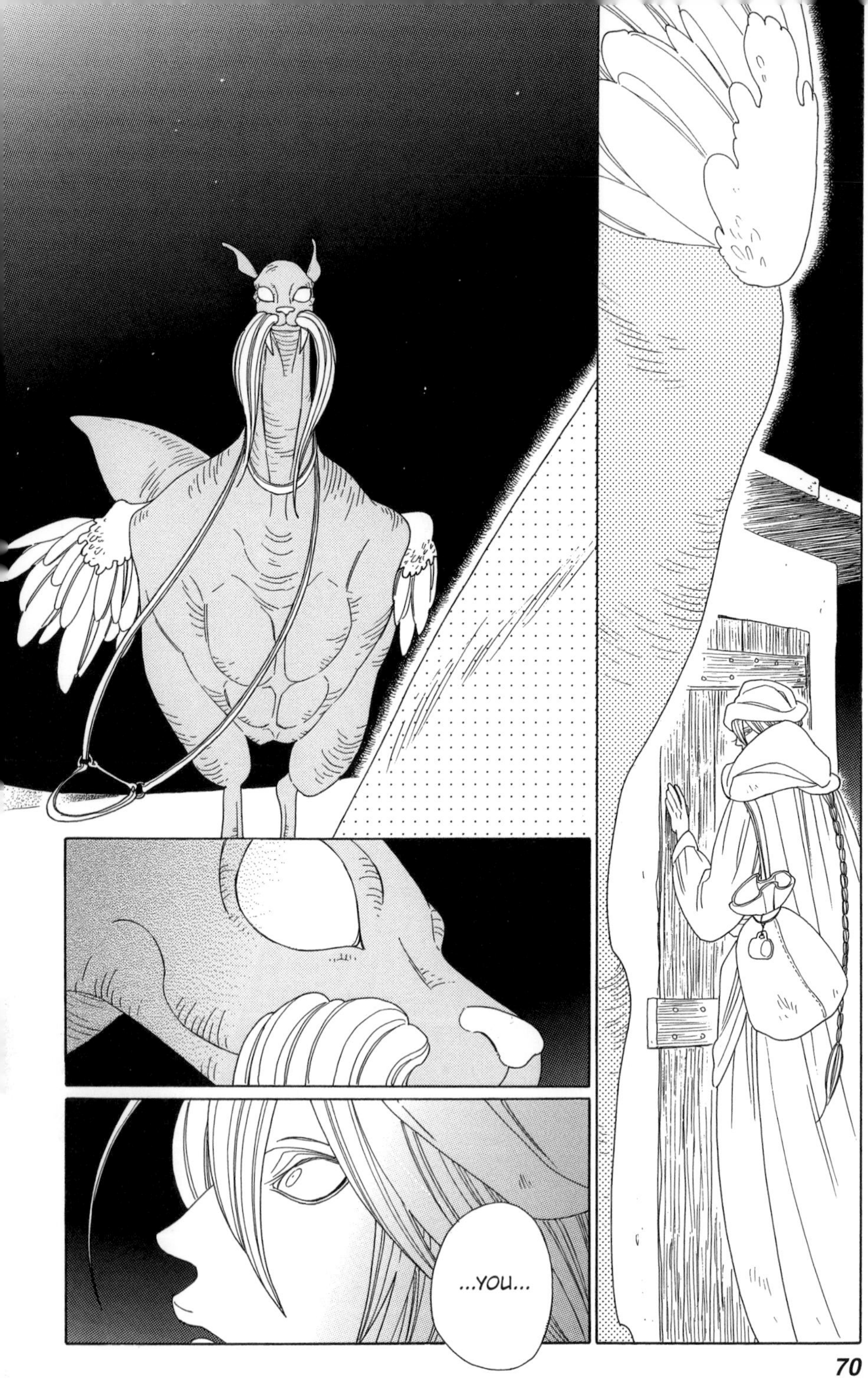
...YOU...

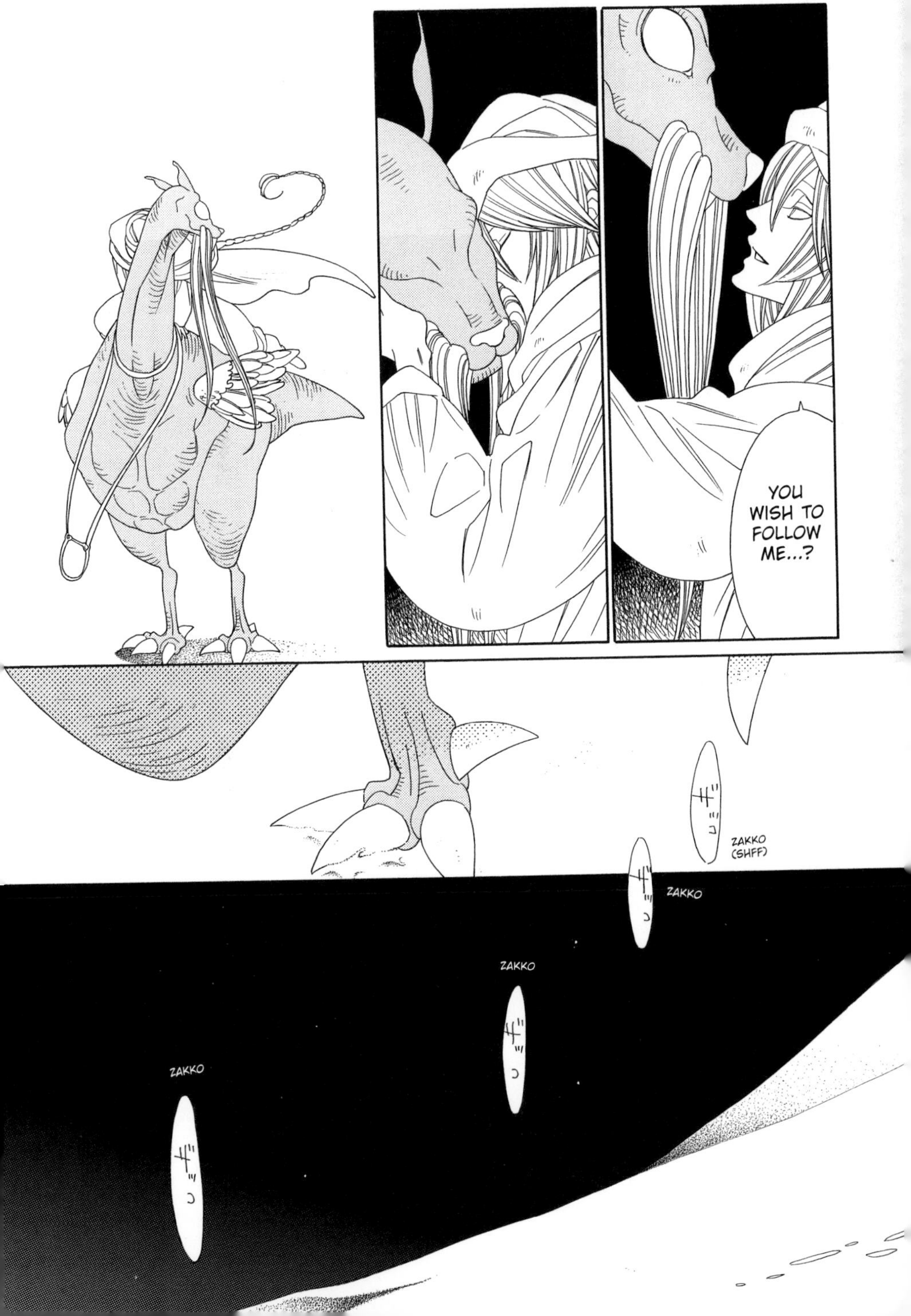
YOU WISH TO FOLLOW ME...?
ZAKKO (SHFF)
ZAKKO
ZAKKO
ZAKKO

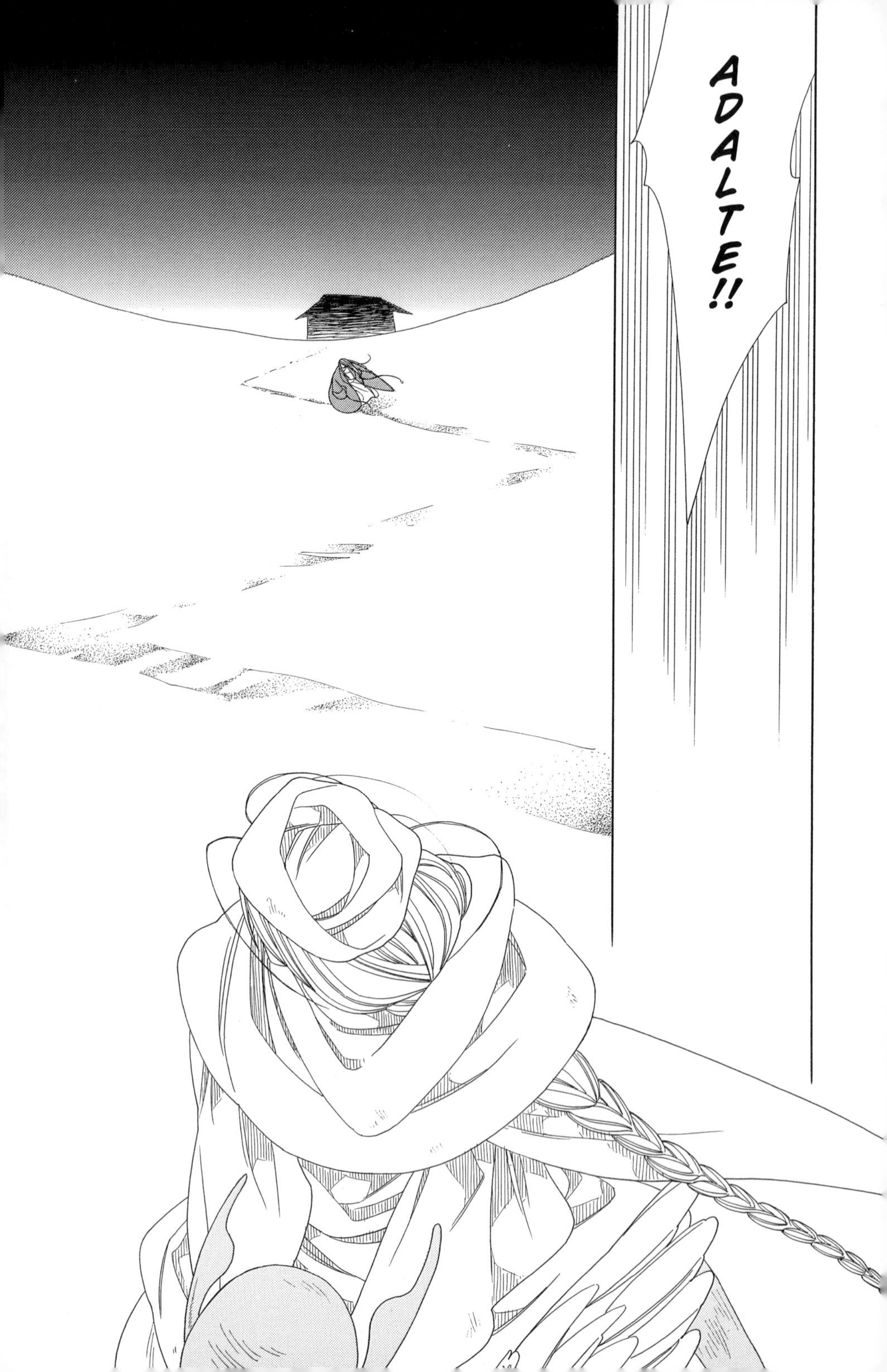
ADALTE!!

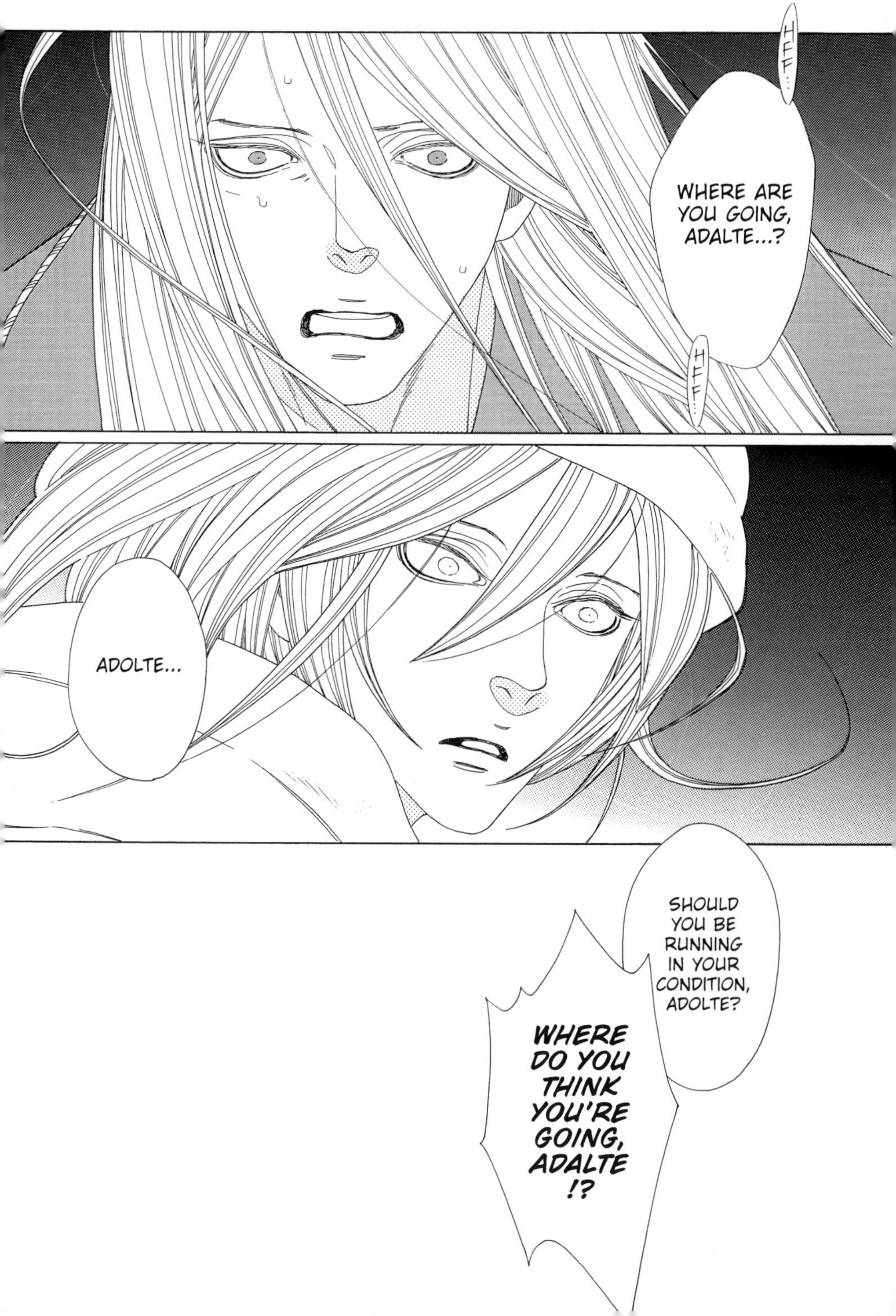
HFF...
WHERE ARE YOU GOING, ADALTE...?
HFF...
ADOLTE...
SHOULD YOU BE RUNNING IN YOUR CONDITION, ADOLTE?
WHERE DO YOU THINK YOU'RE GOING, ADALTE!?

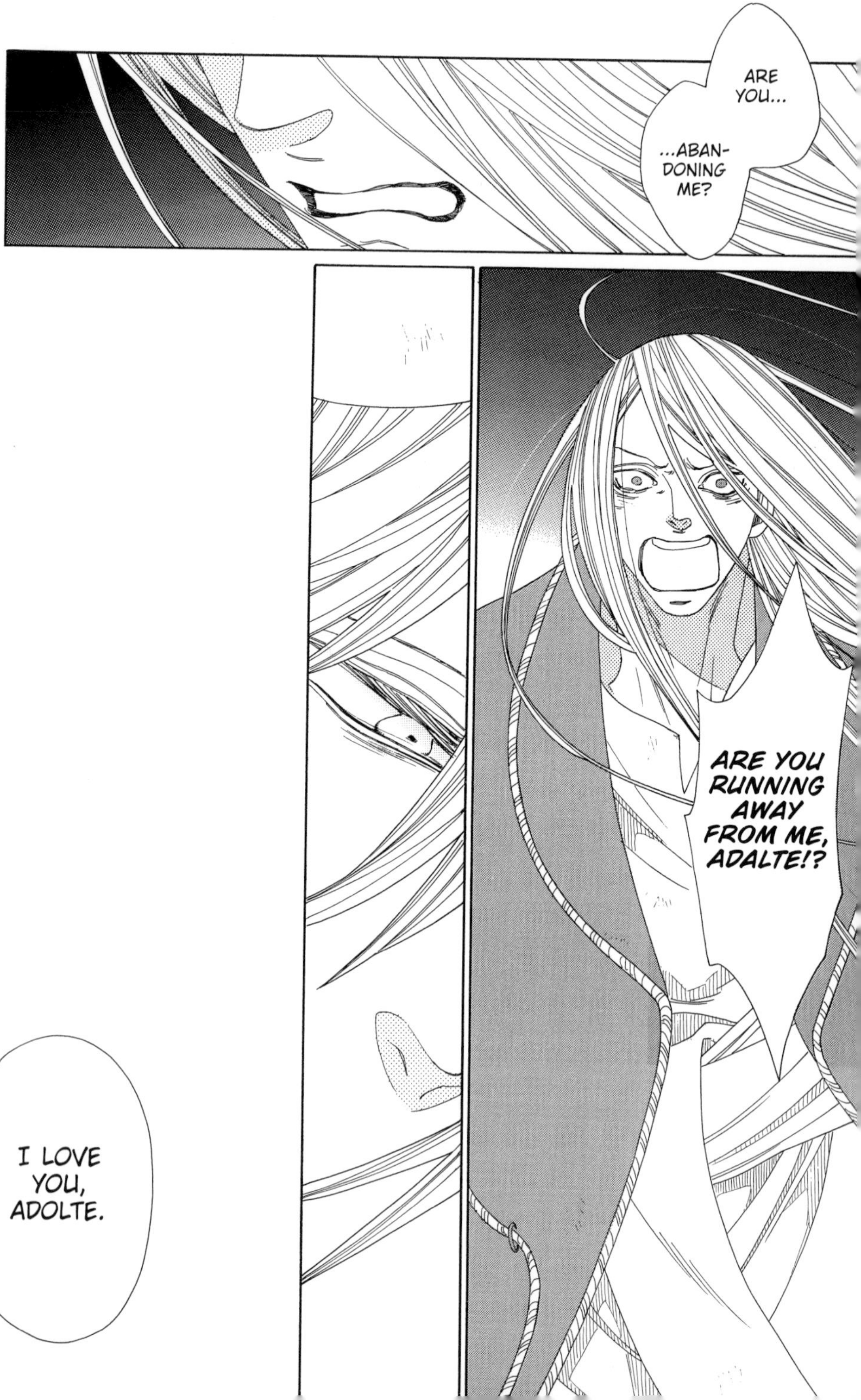
ARE YOU...
...ABAN-DONING ME?
ARE YOU RUNNING AWAY FROM ME, ADALTE!?
I LOVE YOU, ADOLTE.

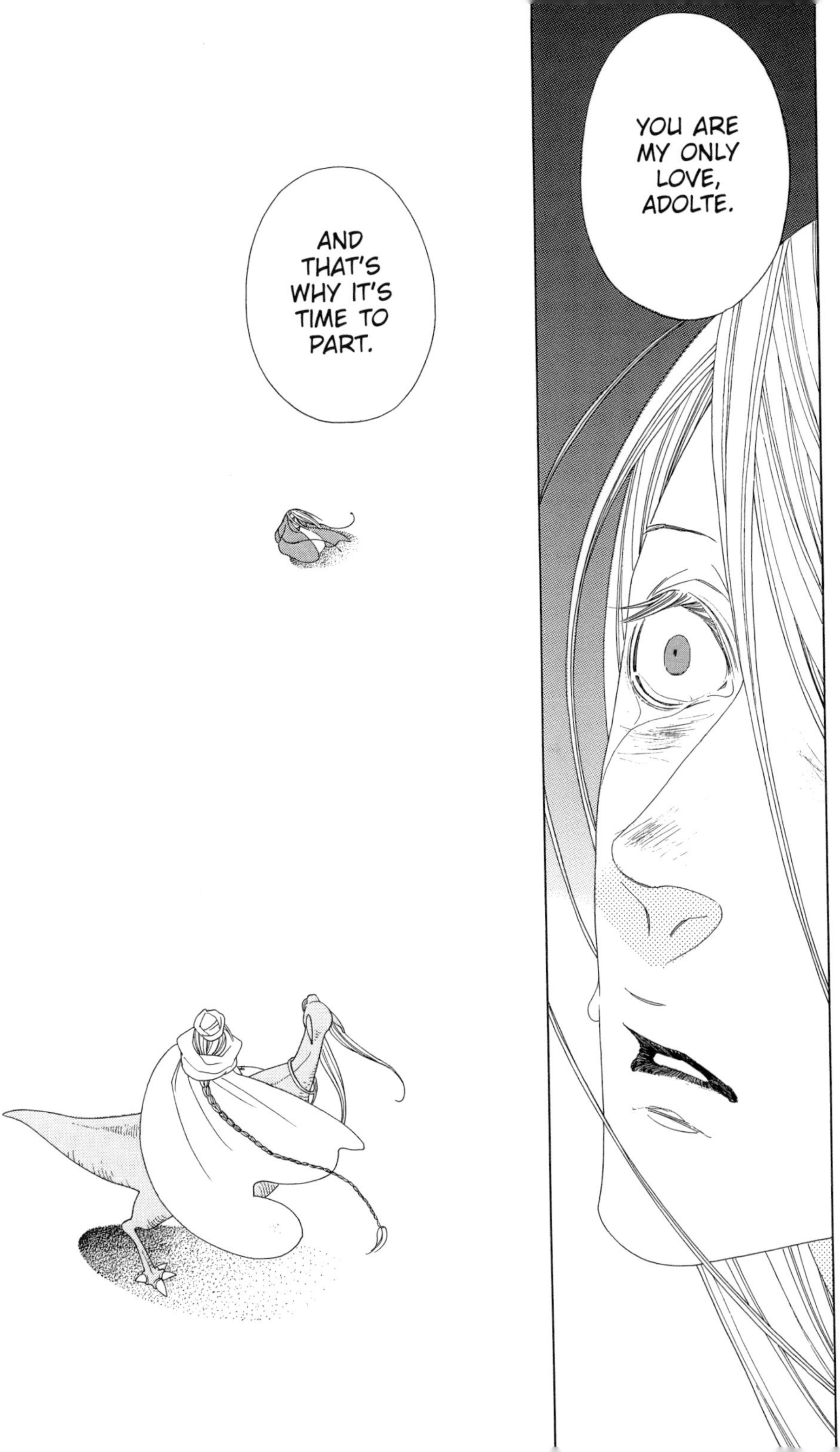
YOU ARE MY ONLY LOVE, ADOLTE.
AND THAT'S WHY IT'S TIME TO PART.

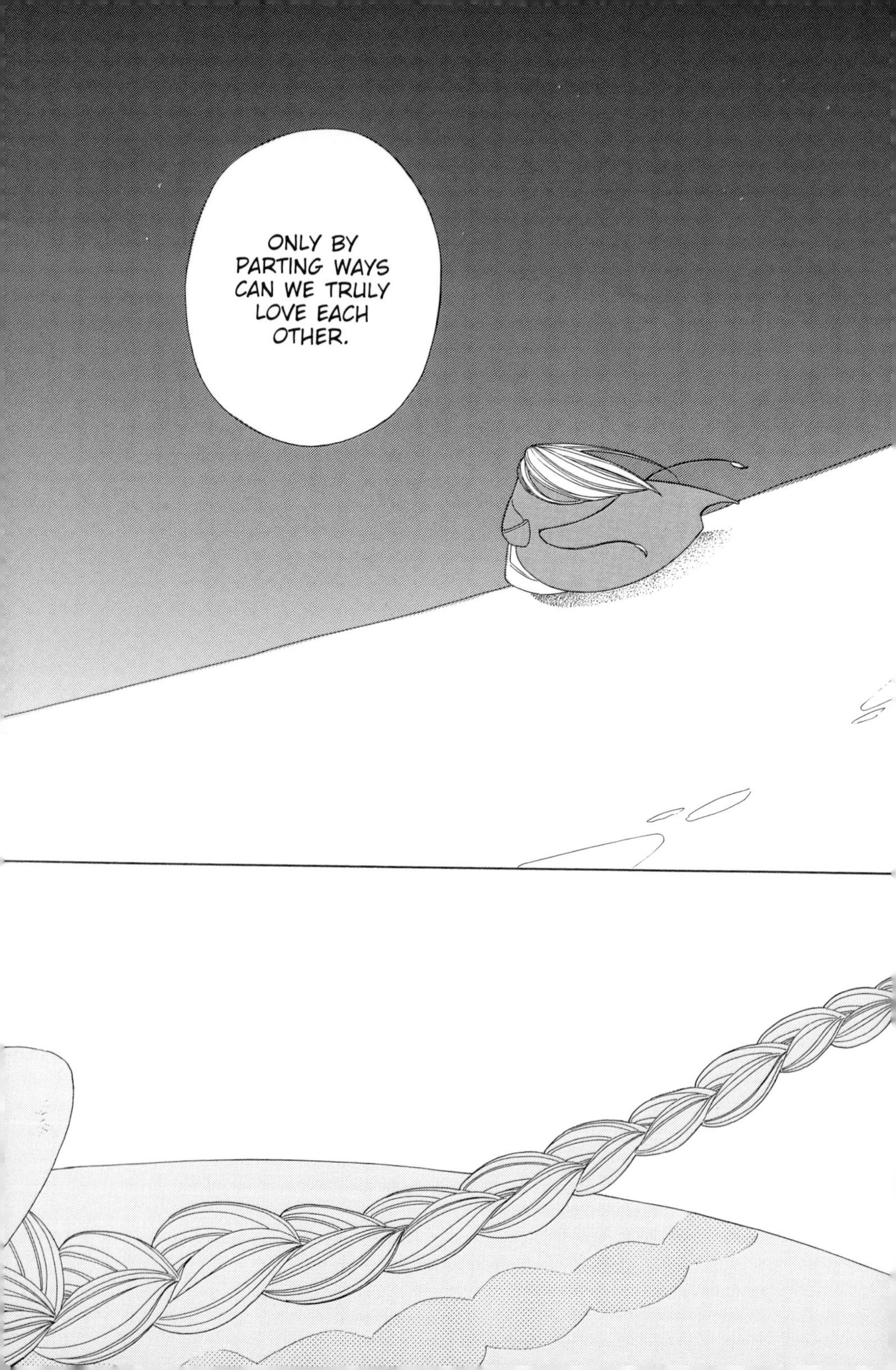
ONLY BY PARTING WAYS CAN WE TRULY LOVE EACH OTHER.

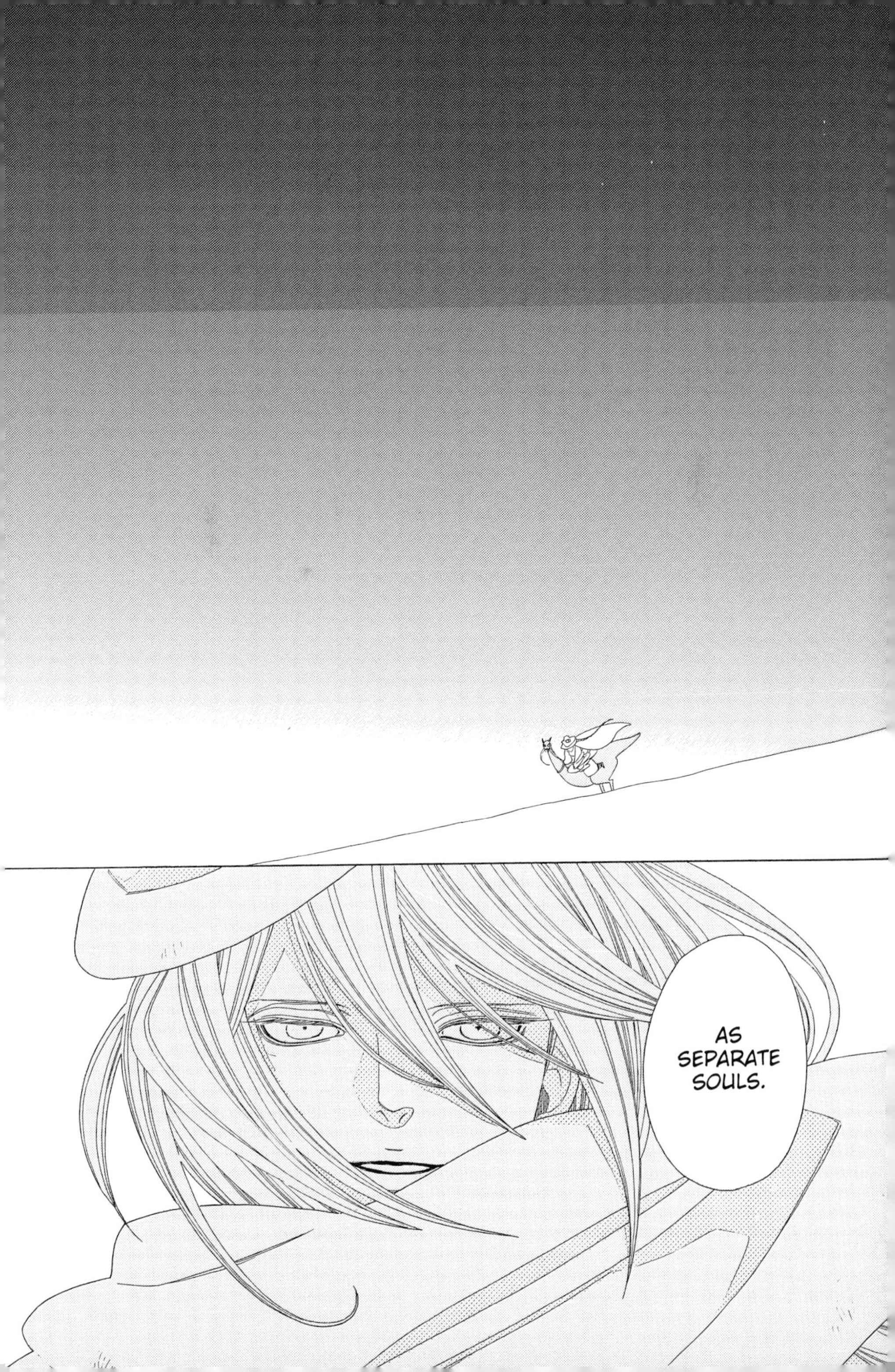
AS SEPARATE SOULS.

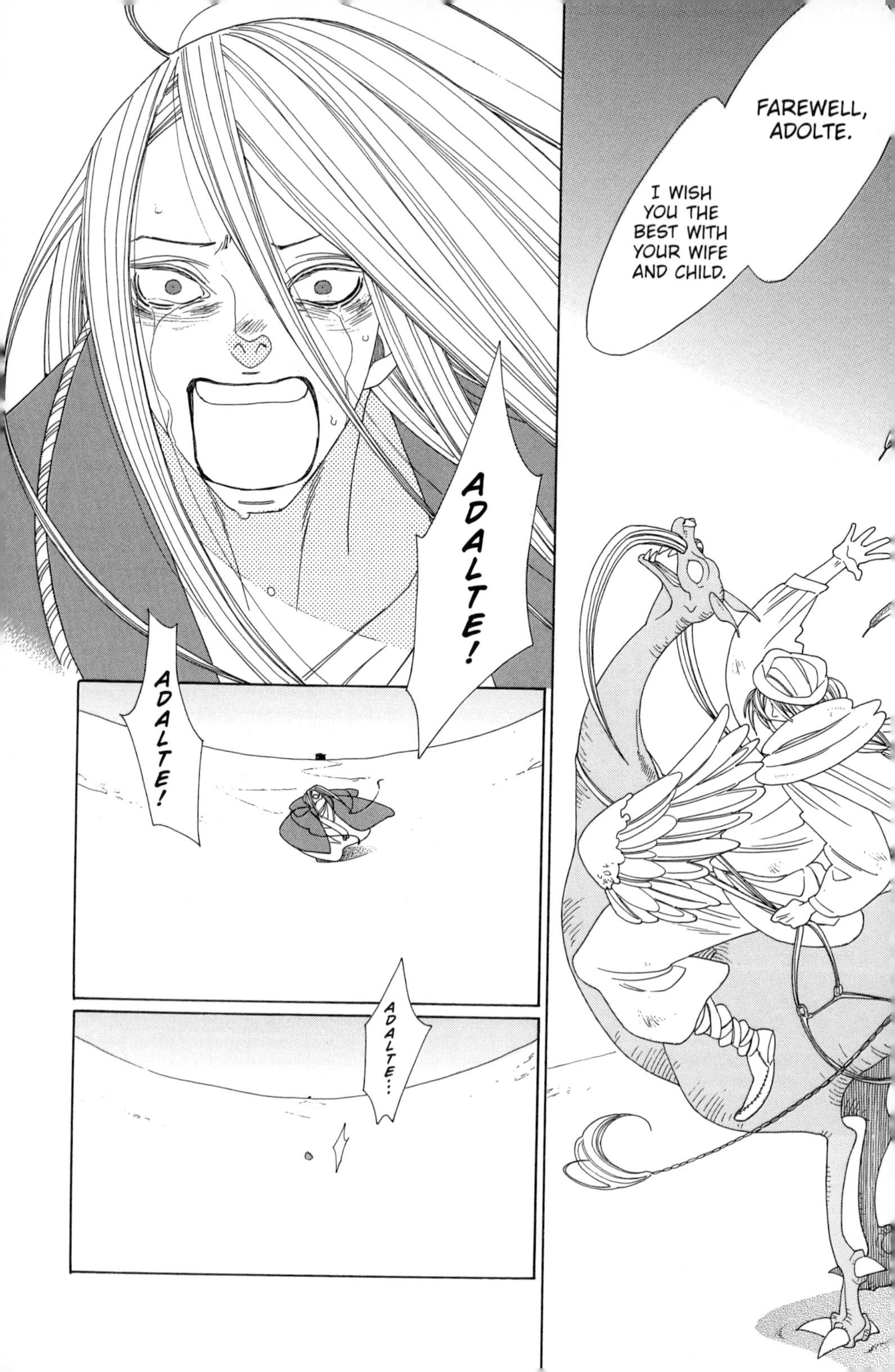

FAREWELL, ADOLTE.
I WISH YOU THE BEST WITH YOUR WIFE AND CHILD.
ADALTE!
ADALTE!
ADALTE...

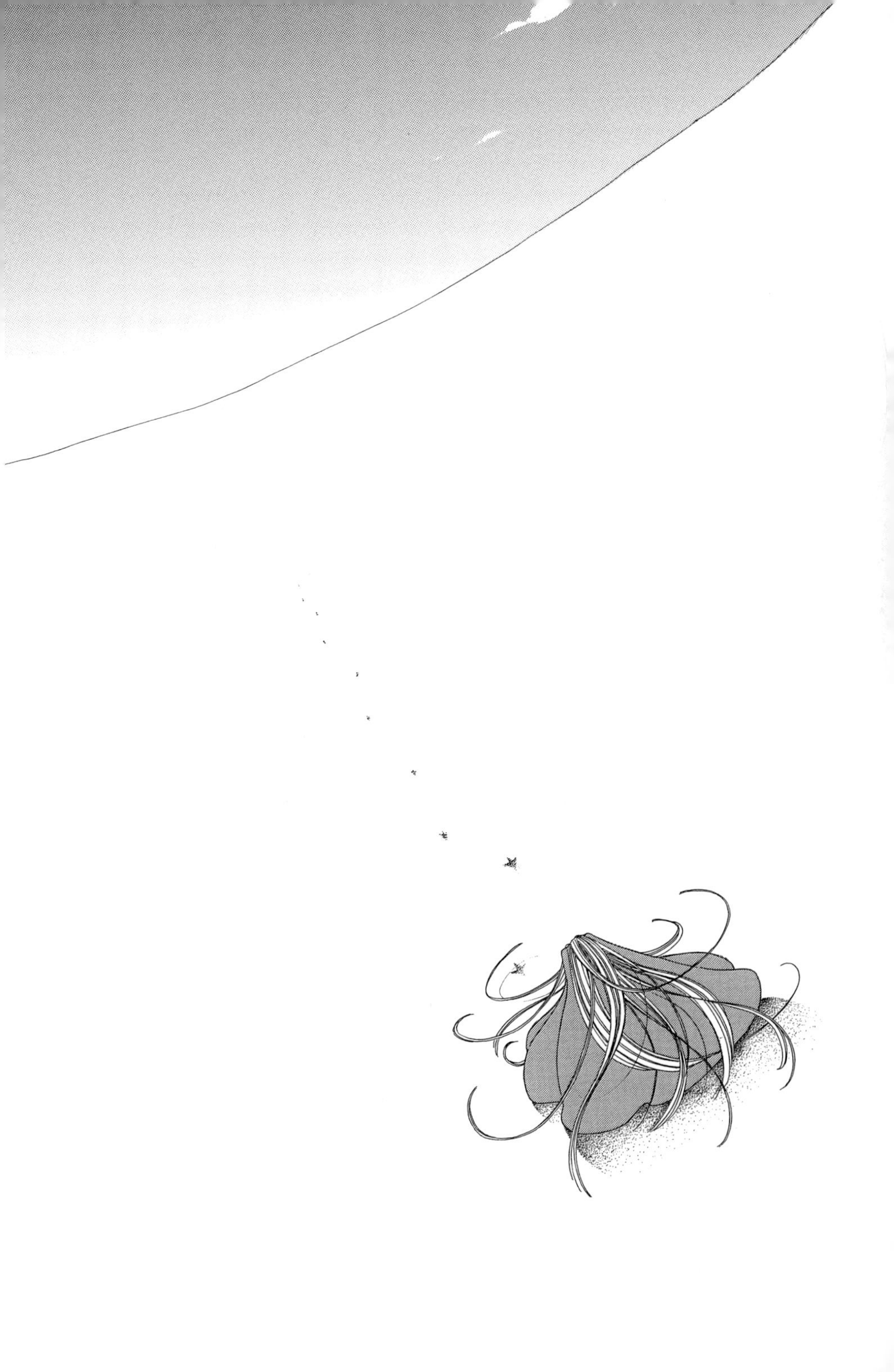

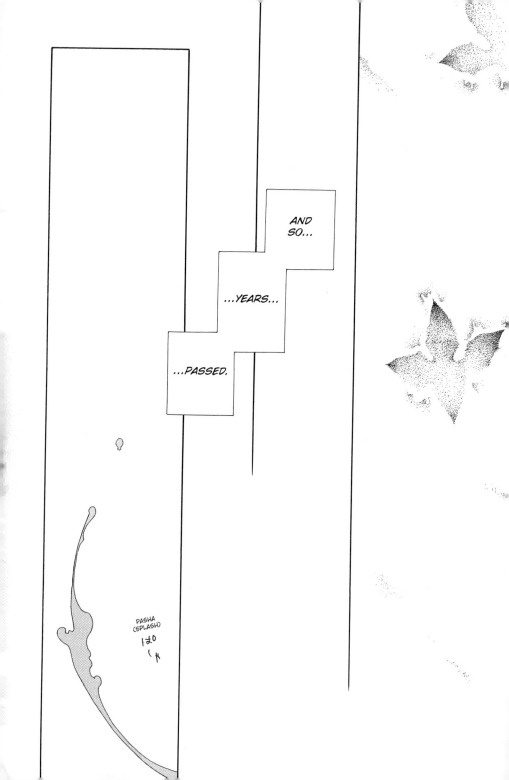

AND
SO...

...YEARS...

...PASSED.

PASHA
(SPLASH)

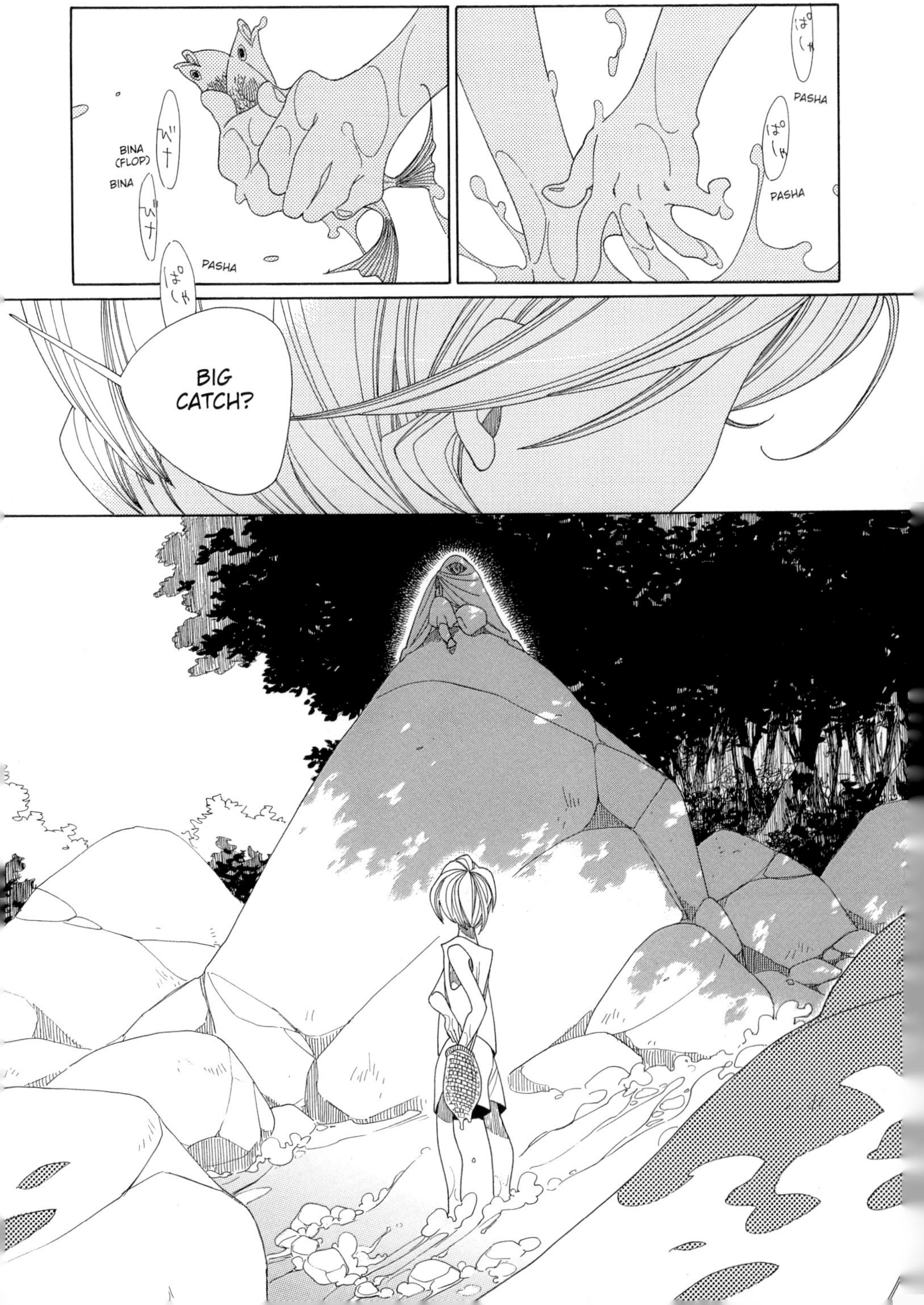
PASHA
PASHA
BINA (FLOP)
BINA
PASHA
BIG CATCH?

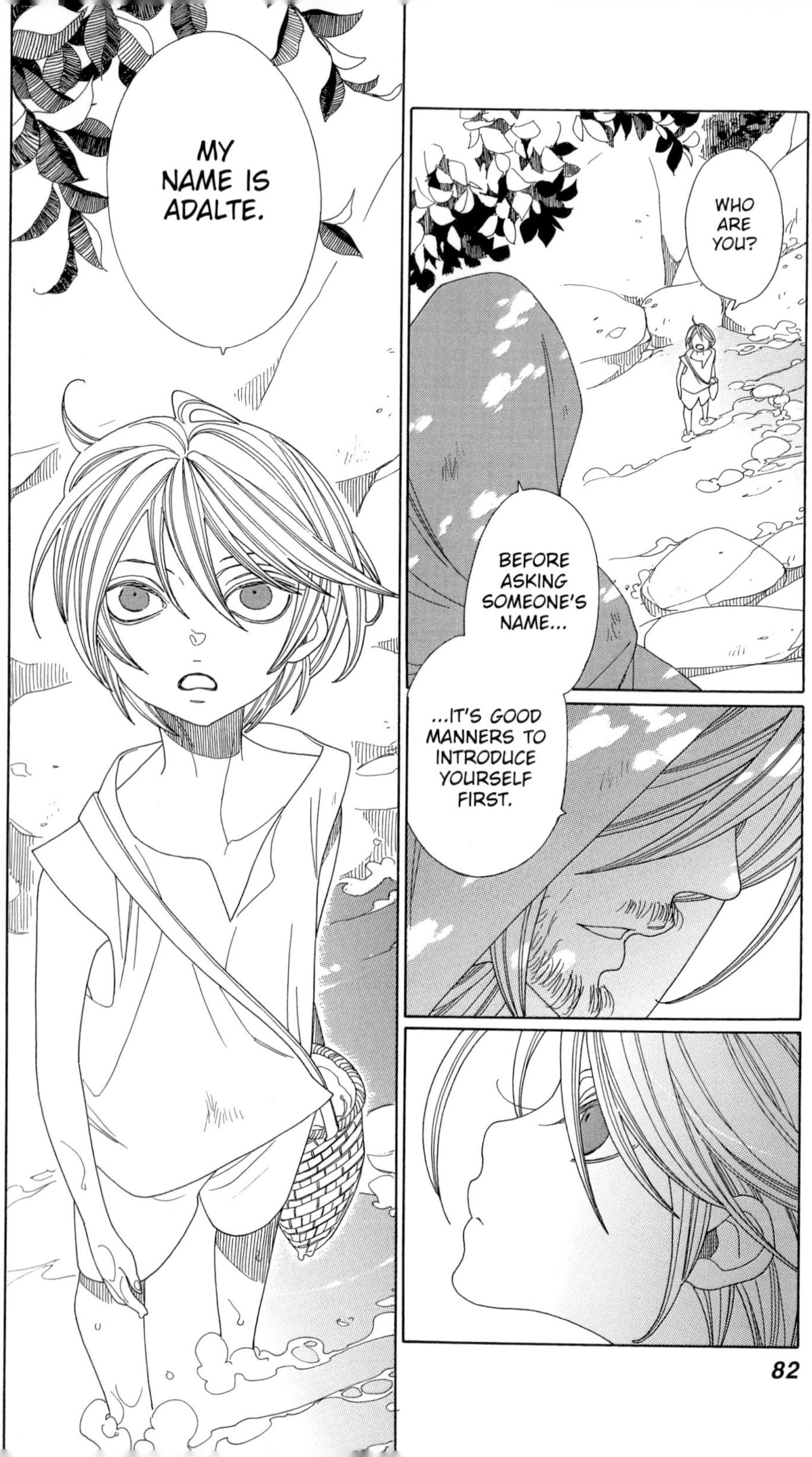
WHO ARE YOU?
BEFORE ASKING SOMEONE'S NAME...
...IT'S GOOD MANNERS TO INTRODUCE YOURSELF FIRST.
MY NAME IS ADALTE.

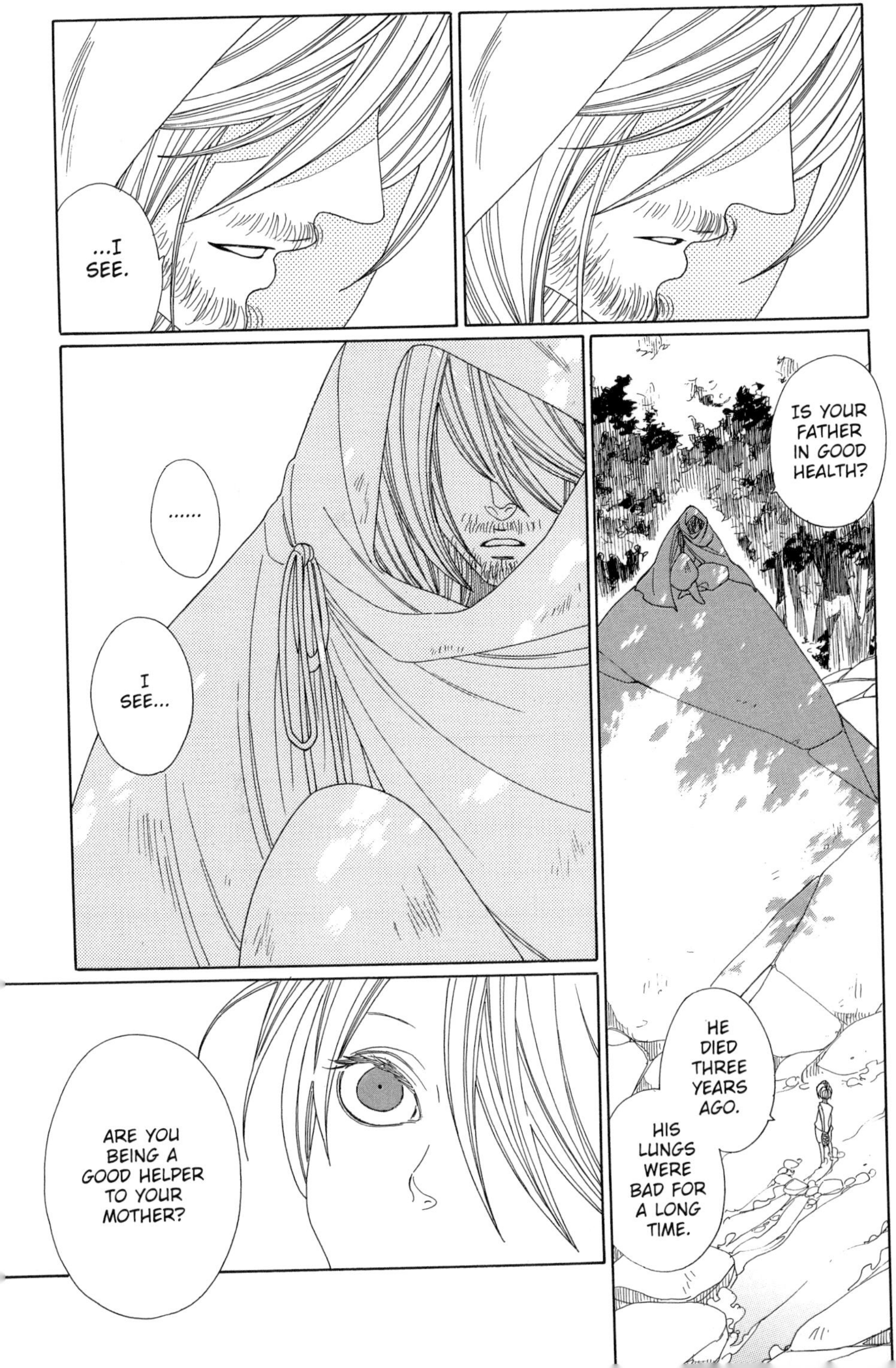
...I SEE.
IS YOUR FATHER IN GOOD HEALTH?
HE DIED THREE YEARS AGO.
HIS LUNGS WERE BAD FOR A LONG TIME.
......
I SEE...
ARE YOU BEING A GOOD HELPER TO YOUR MOTHER?

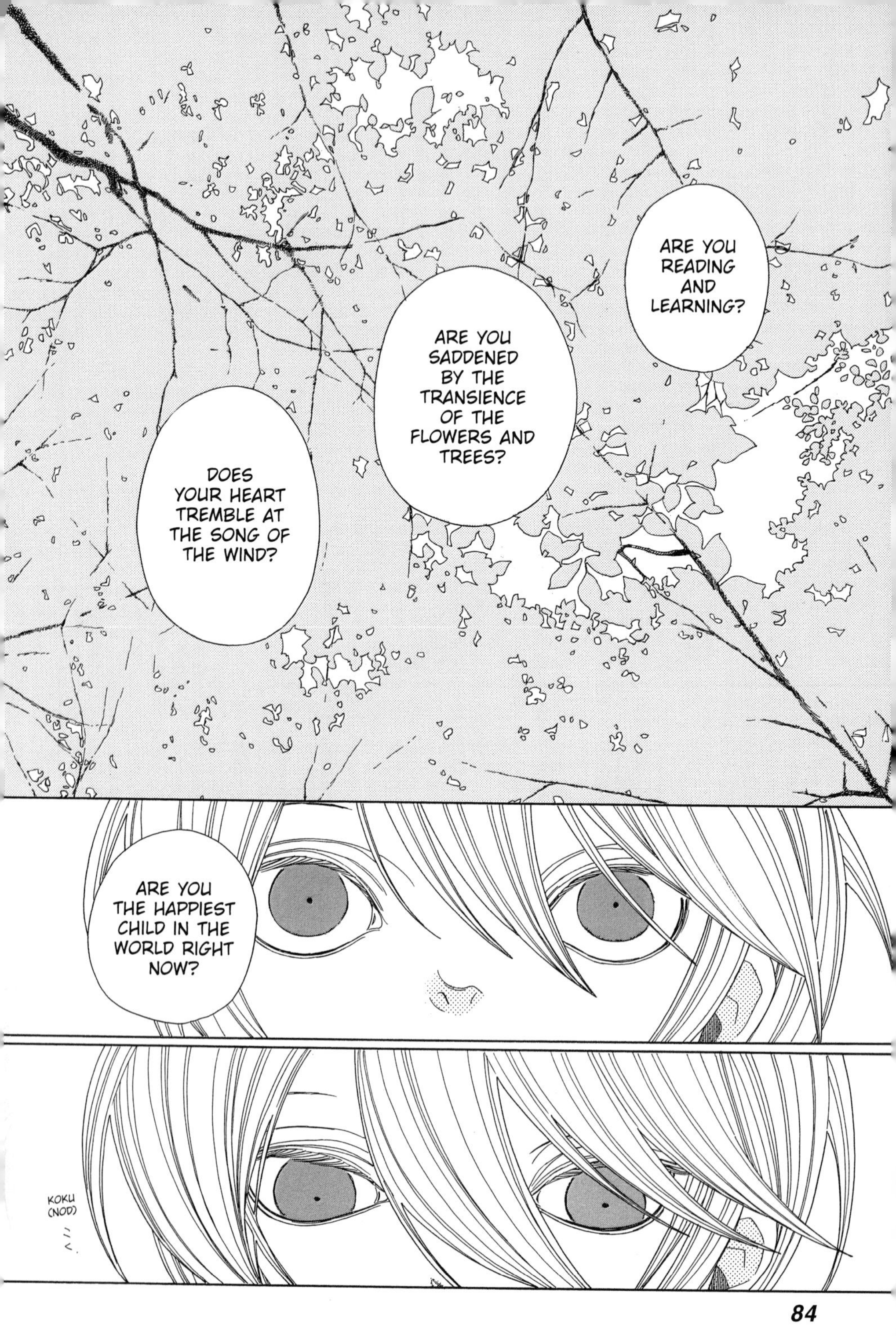
ARE YOU READING AND LEARNING?
ARE YOU SADDENED BY THE TRANSIENCE OF THE FLOWERS AND TREES?
DOES YOUR HEART TREMBLE AT THE SONG OF THE WIND?
ARE YOU THE HAPPIEST CHILD IN THE WORLD RIGHT NOW?
KOKU (NOD)

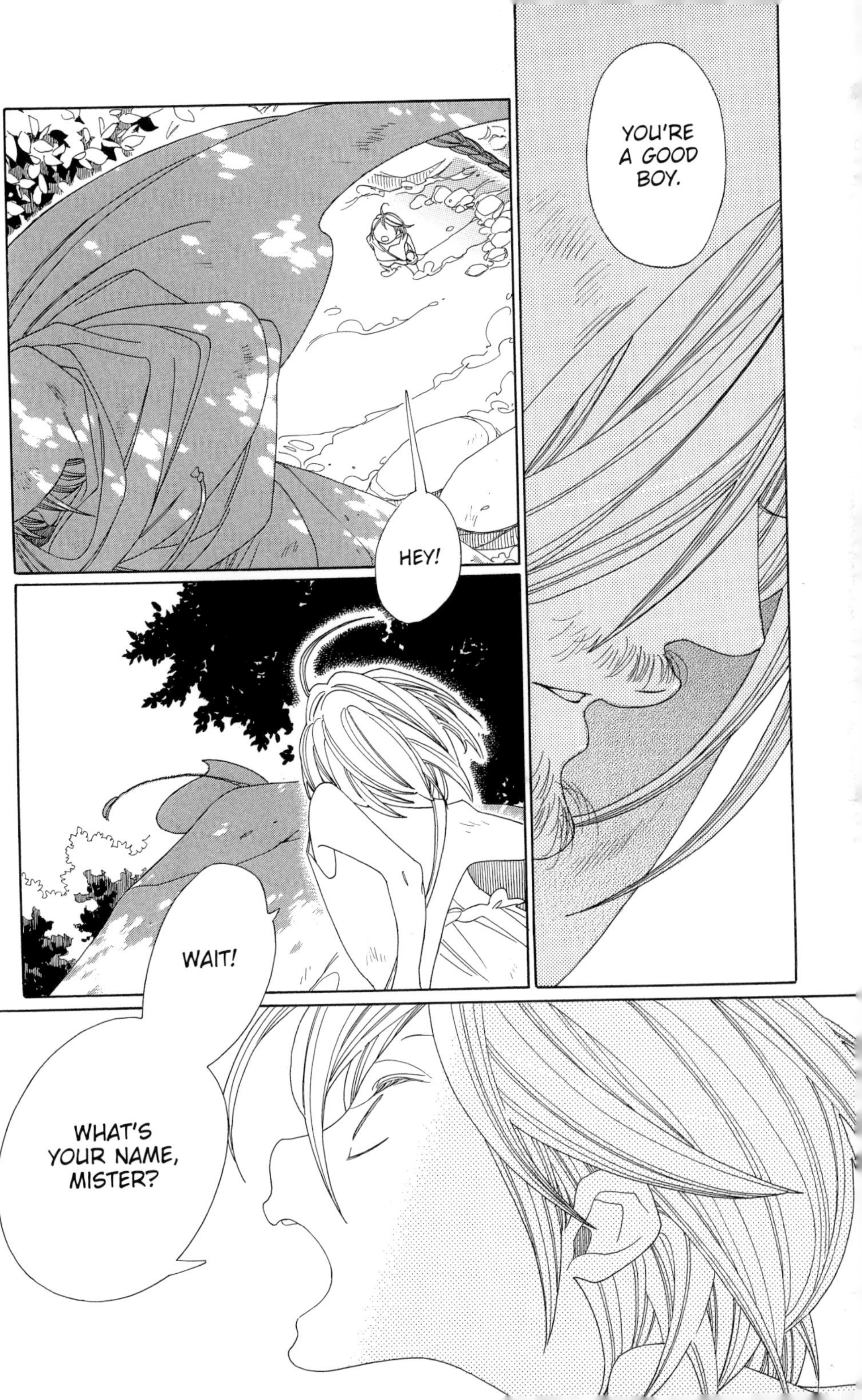
YOU'RE A GOOD BOY.
HEY!
WAIT!
WHAT'S YOUR NAME, MISTER?

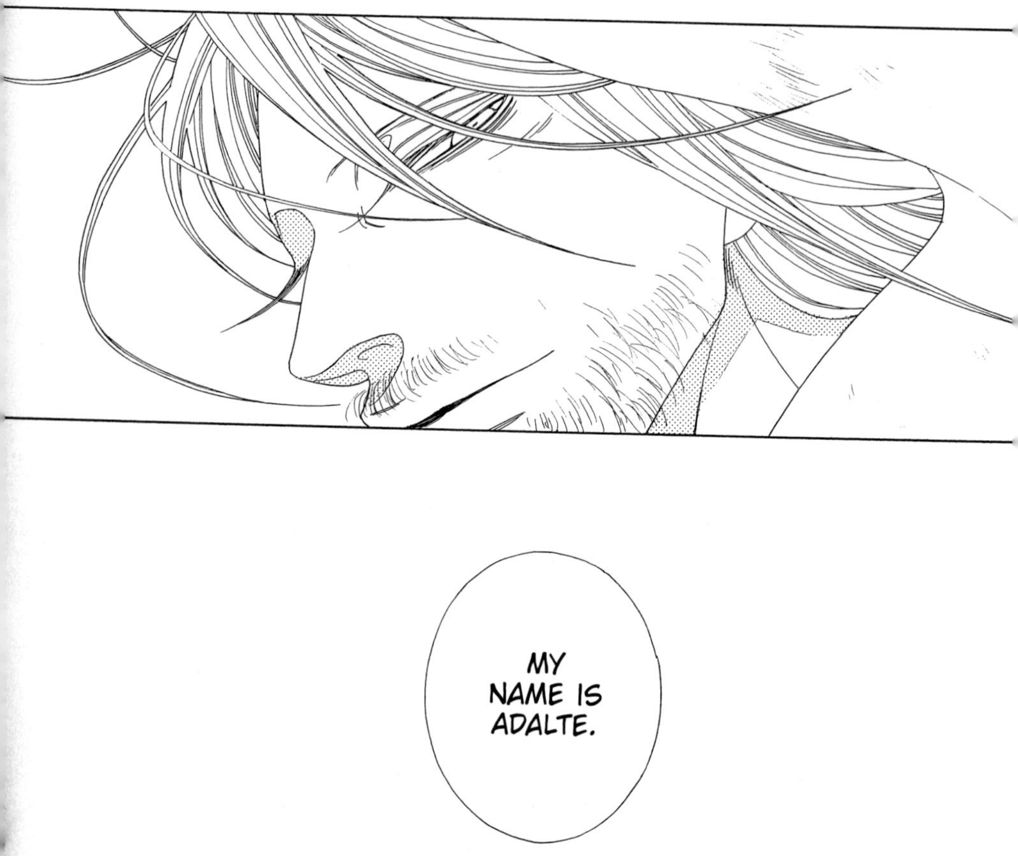
MY NAME IS ADALTE.

Tales
of the
Kingdom

I AM THE KING'S AIDE.

Chapter 3
**The King
and
His Aide**
episode 1

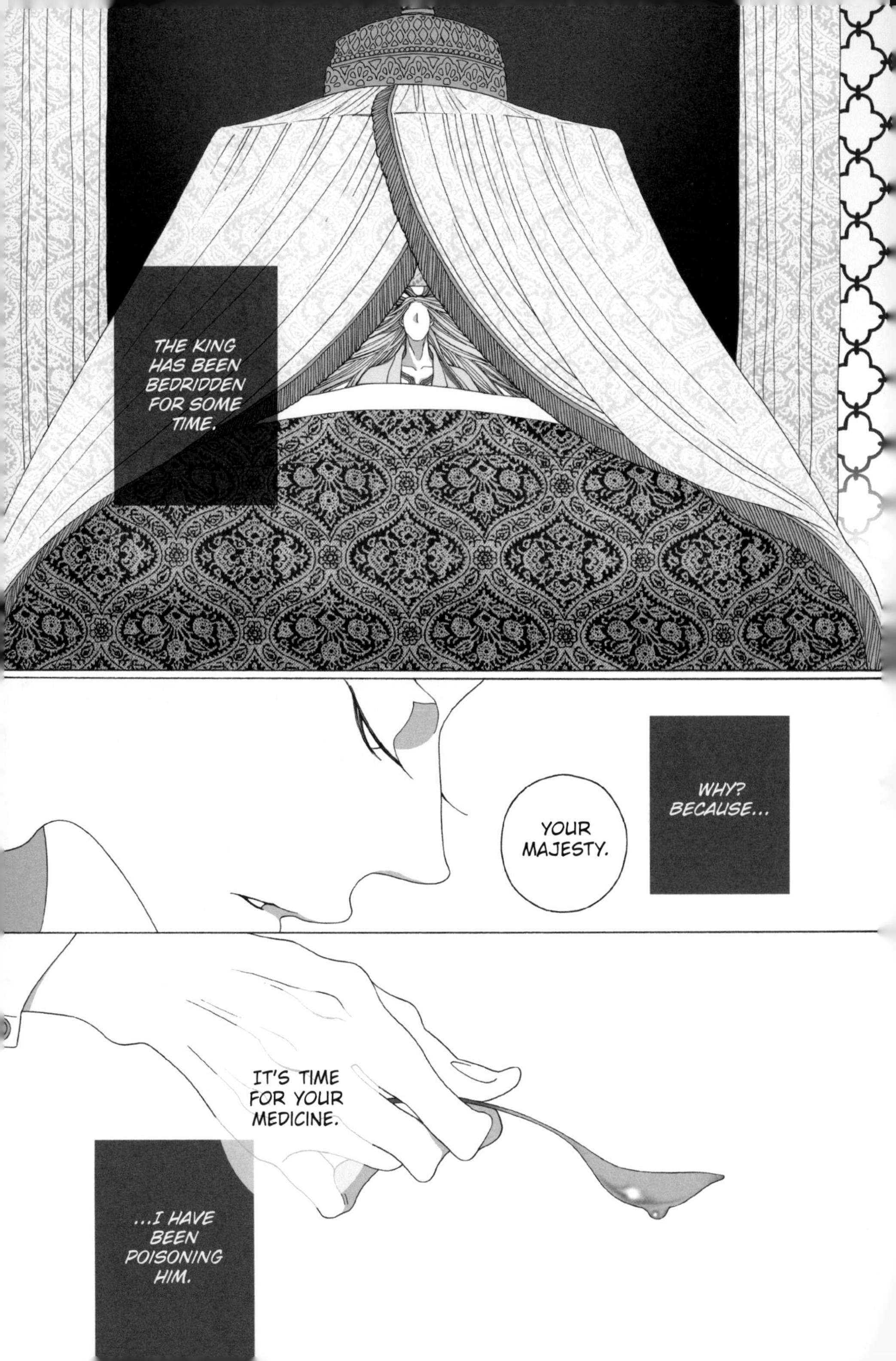
THE KING HAS BEEN BEDRIDDEN FOR SOME TIME.
WHY? BECAUSE...
YOUR MAJESTY.
IT'S TIME FOR YOUR MEDICINE.
...I HAVE BEEN POISONING HIM.

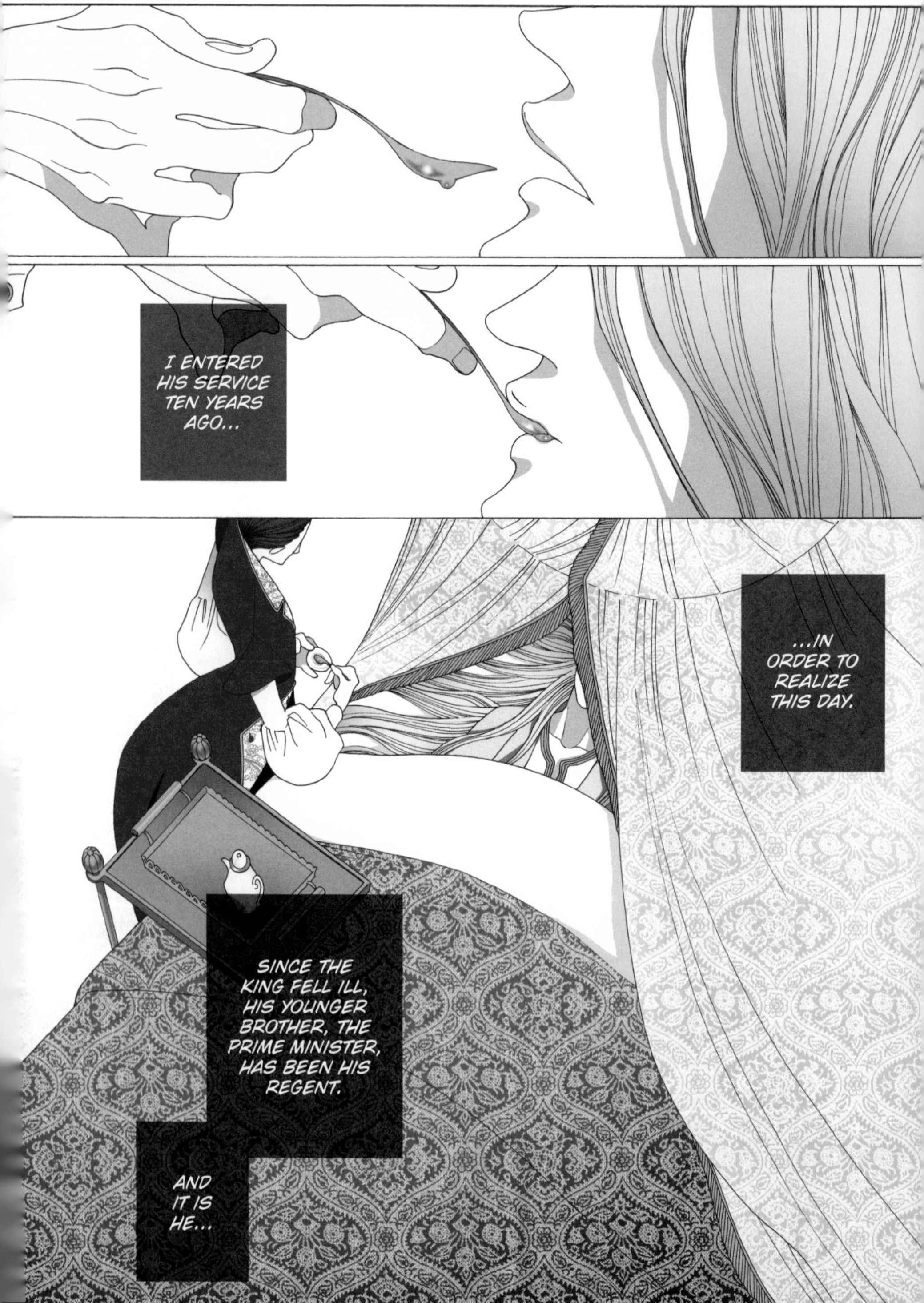
I ENTERED HIS SERVICE TEN YEARS AGO...
...IN ORDER TO REALIZE THIS DAY.
SINCE THE KING FELL ILL, HIS YOUNGER BROTHER, THE PRIME MINISTER, HAS BEEN HIS REGENT.
AND IT IS HE...

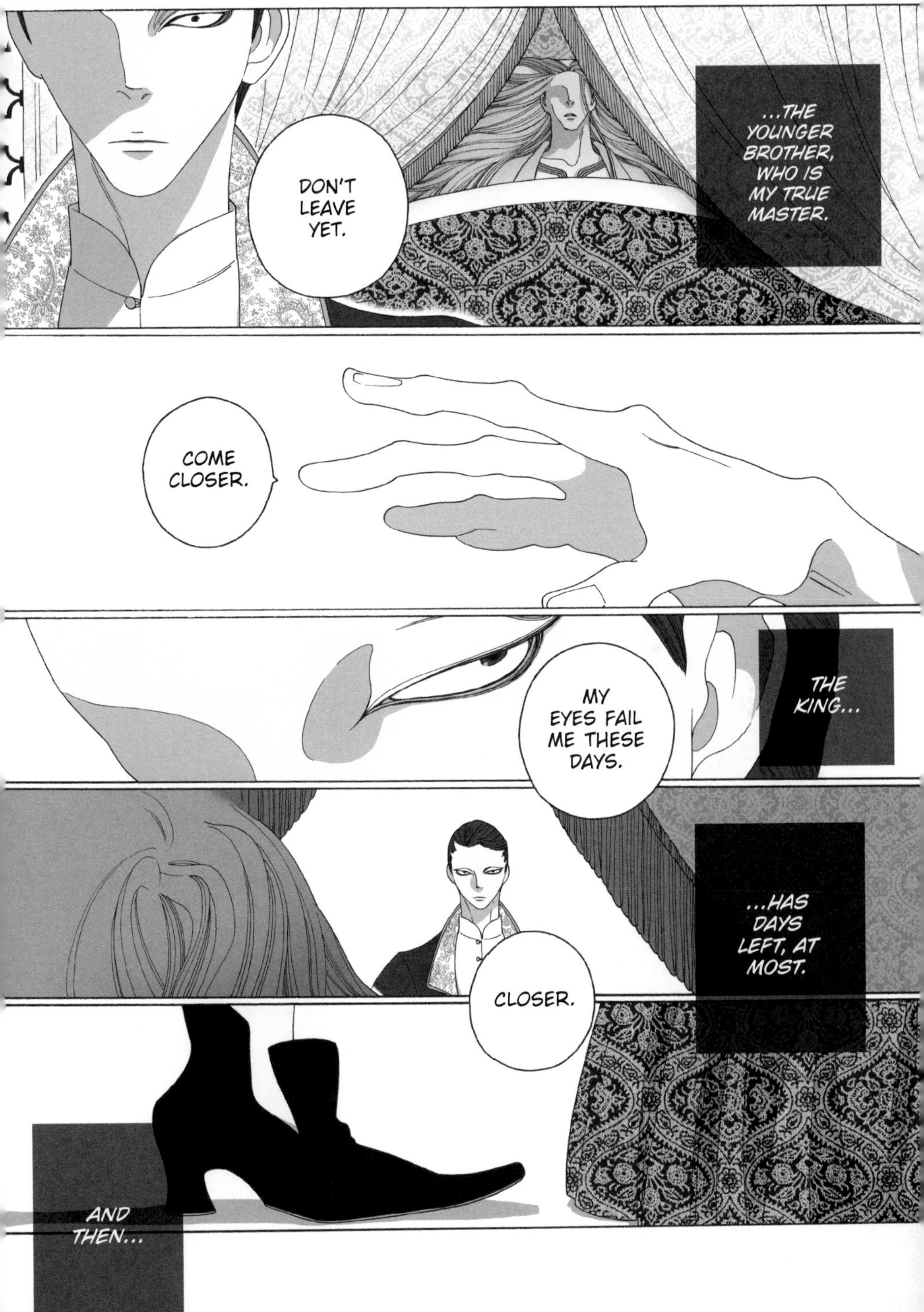
...THE YOUNGER BROTHER, WHO IS MY TRUE MASTER.
DON'T LEAVE YET.
COME CLOSER.
THE KING...
MY EYES FAIL ME THESE DAYS.
...HAS DAYS LEFT, AT MOST.
CLOSER.
AND THEN...

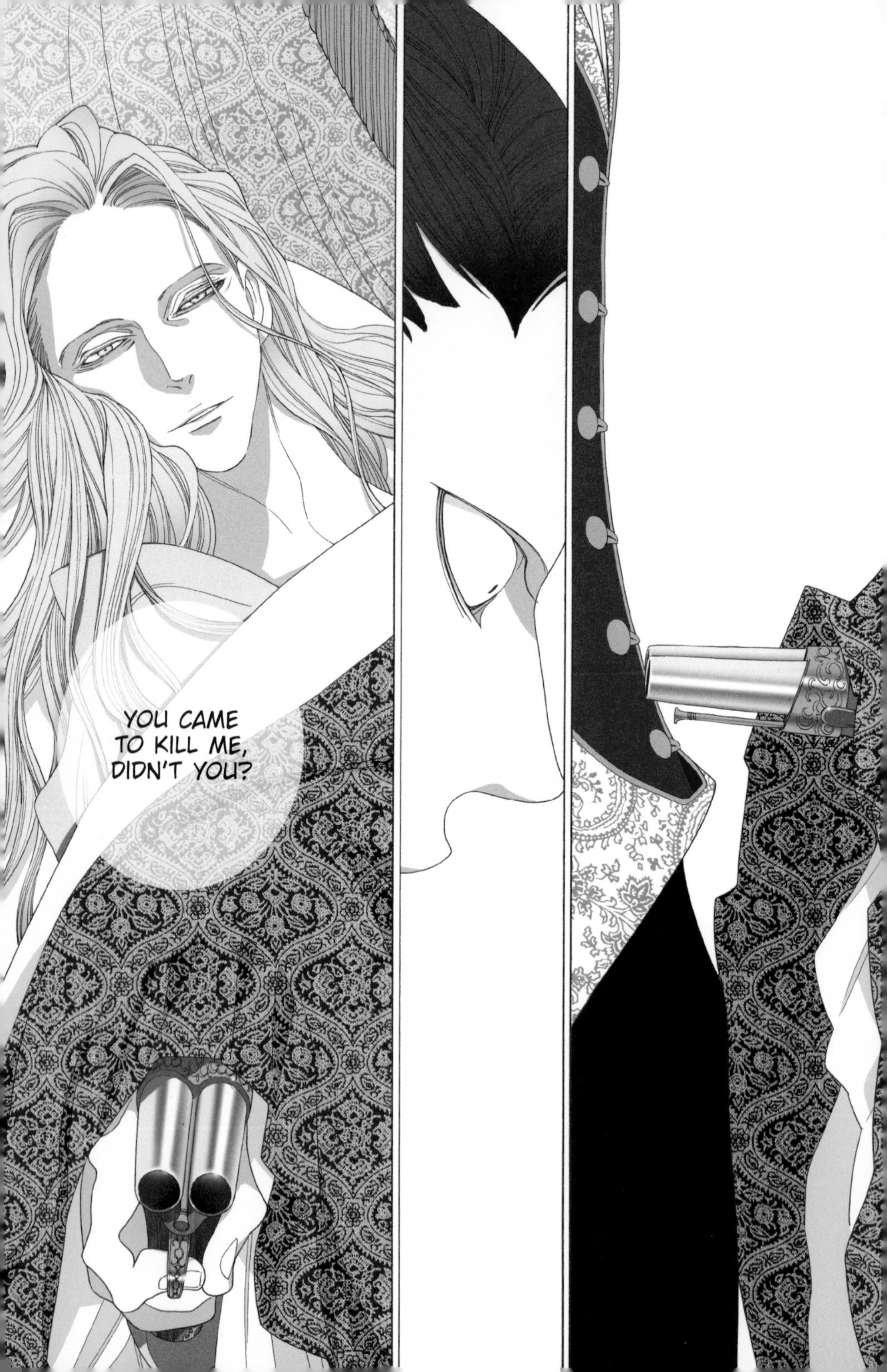
YOU CAME TO KILL ME, DIDN'T YOU?

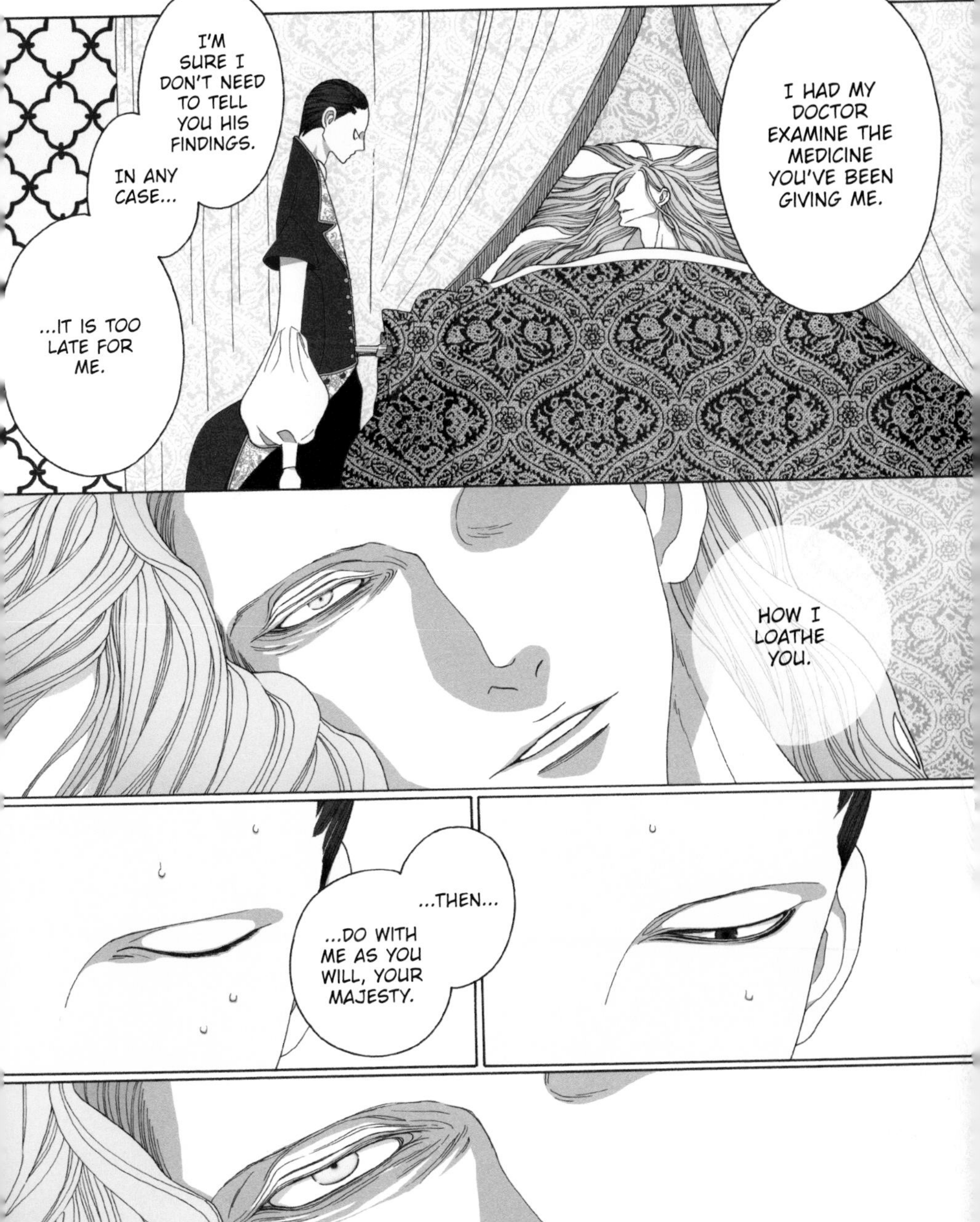
I HAD MY DOCTOR EXAMINE THE MEDICINE YOU'VE BEEN GIVING ME.
I'M SURE I DON'T NEED TO TELL YOU HIS FINDINGS.
IN ANY CASE...
...IT IS TOO LATE FOR ME.
HOW I LOATHE YOU.
...THEN...
...DO WITH ME AS YOU WILL, YOUR MAJESTY.

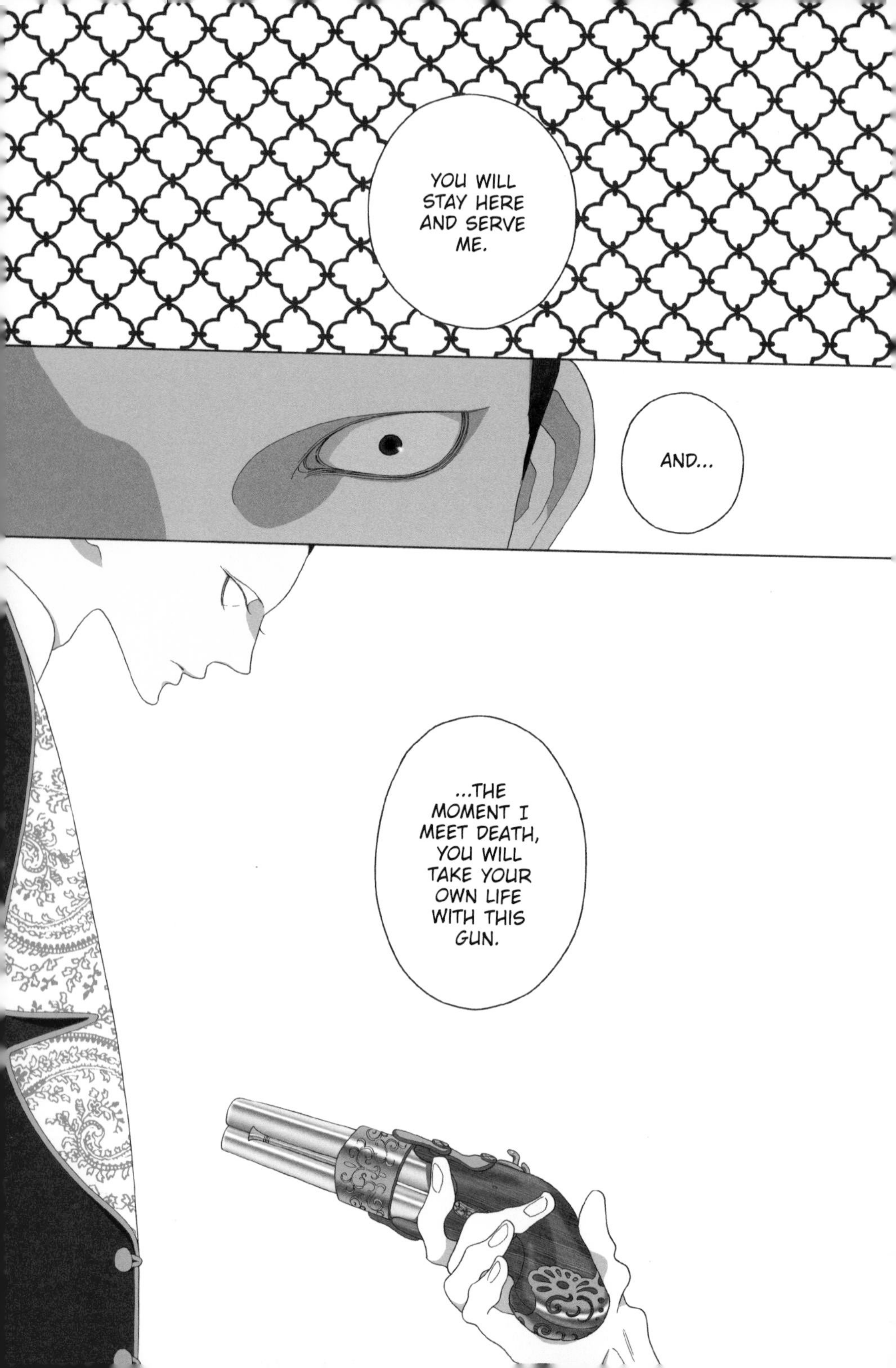
YOU WILL STAY HERE AND SERVE ME.
AND...
...THE MOMENT I MEET DEATH, YOU WILL TAKE YOUR OWN LIFE WITH THIS GUN.

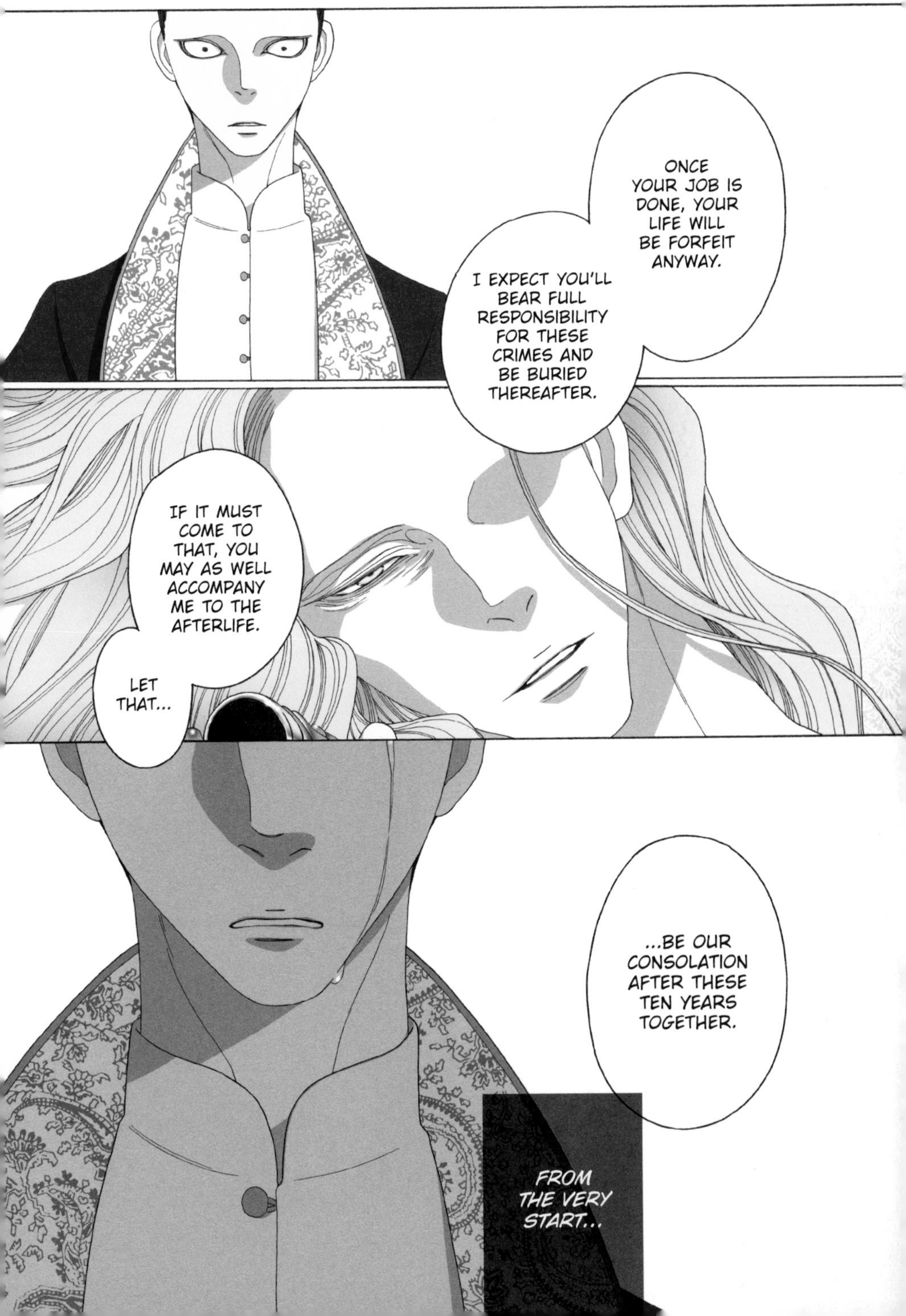
ONCE YOUR JOB IS DONE, YOUR LIFE WILL BE FORFEIT ANYWAY.
I EXPECT YOU'LL BEAR FULL RESPONSIBILITY FOR THESE CRIMES AND BE BURIED THEREAFTER.
IF IT MUST COME TO THAT, YOU MAY AS WELL ACCOMPANY ME TO THE AFTERLIFE.
LET THAT...
...BE OUR CONSOLATION AFTER THESE TEN YEARS TOGETHER.
FROM THE VERY START...

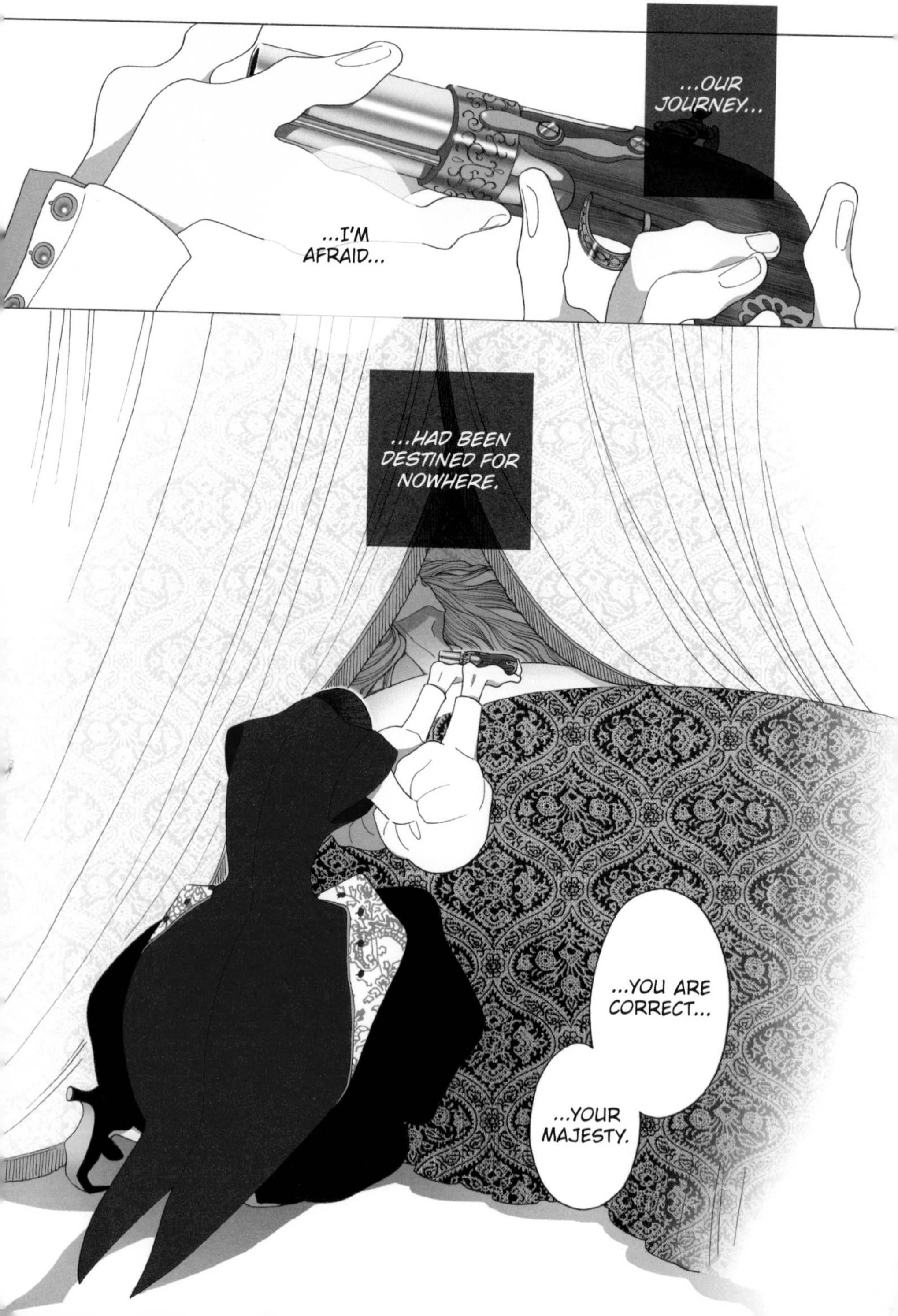
...OUR JOURNEY...
...I'M AFRAID...
...HAD BEEN DESTINED FOR NOWHERE.
...YOU ARE CORRECT...
...YOUR MAJESTY.

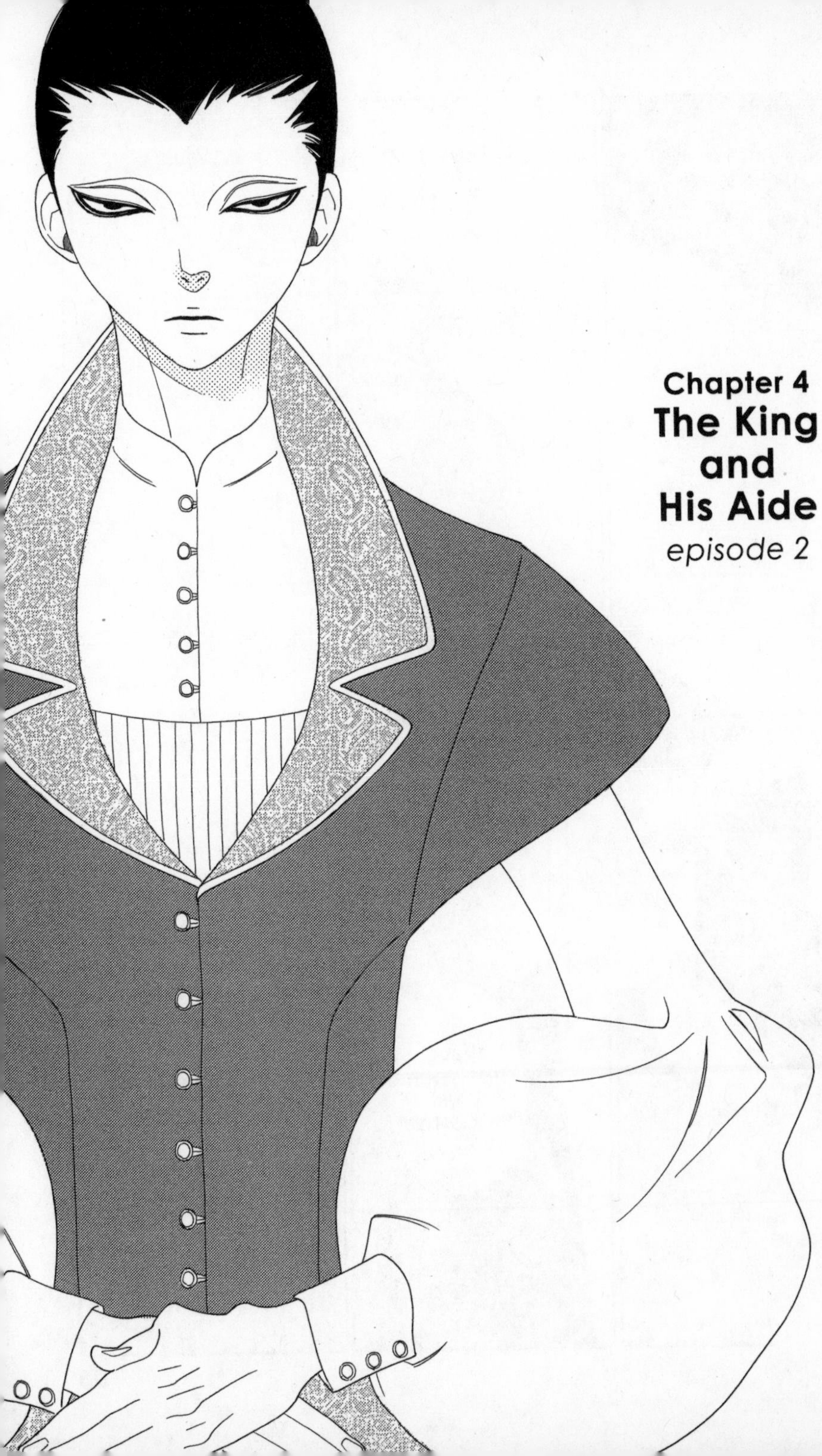

Chapter 4
The King and His Aide
episode 2

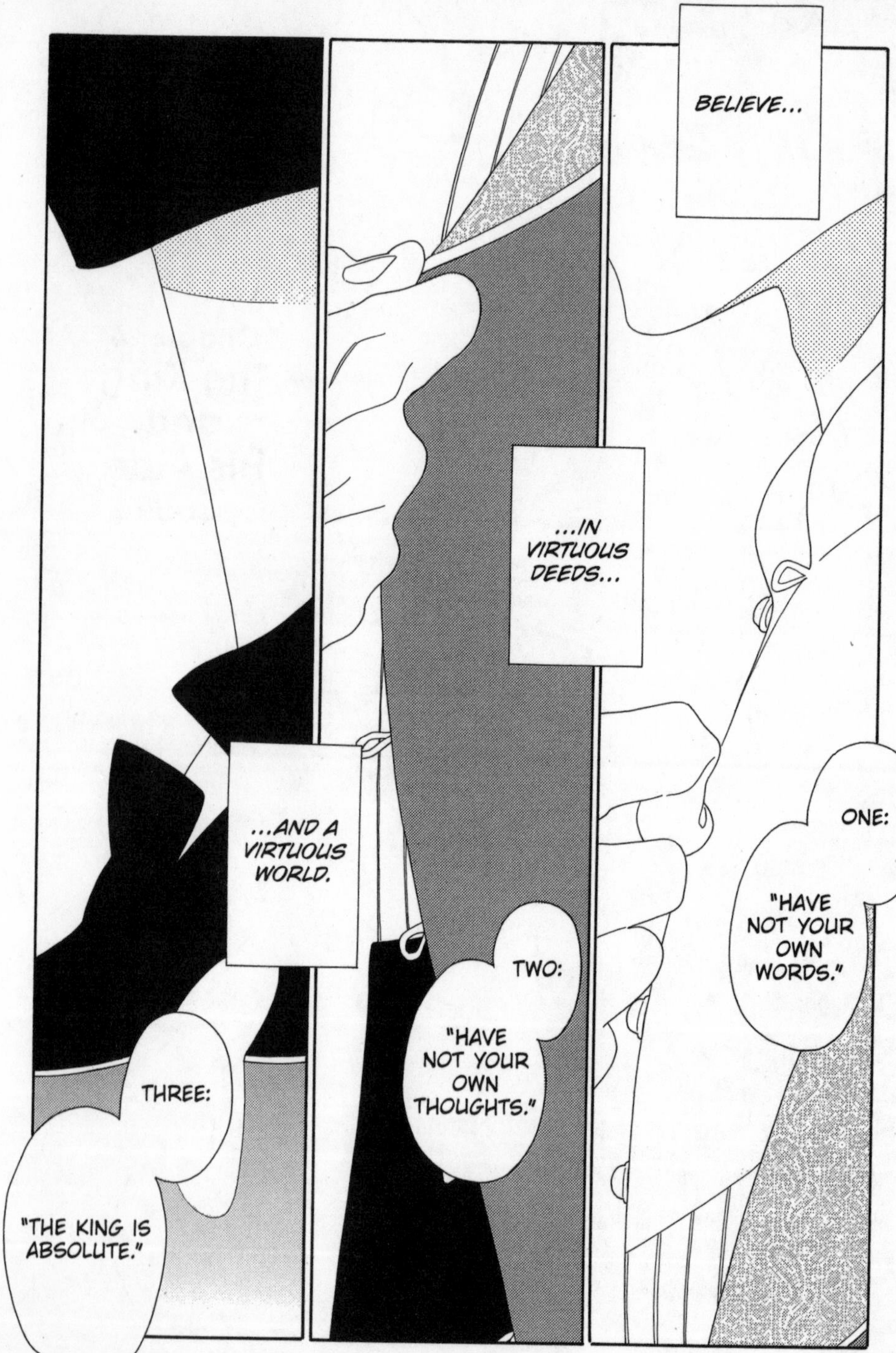
BELIEVE...
ONE:
"HAVE NOT YOUR OWN WORDS."
...IN VIRTUOUS DEEDS...
TWO:
"HAVE NOT YOUR OWN THOUGHTS."
...AND A VIRTUOUS WORLD.
THREE:
"THE KING IS ABSOLUTE."

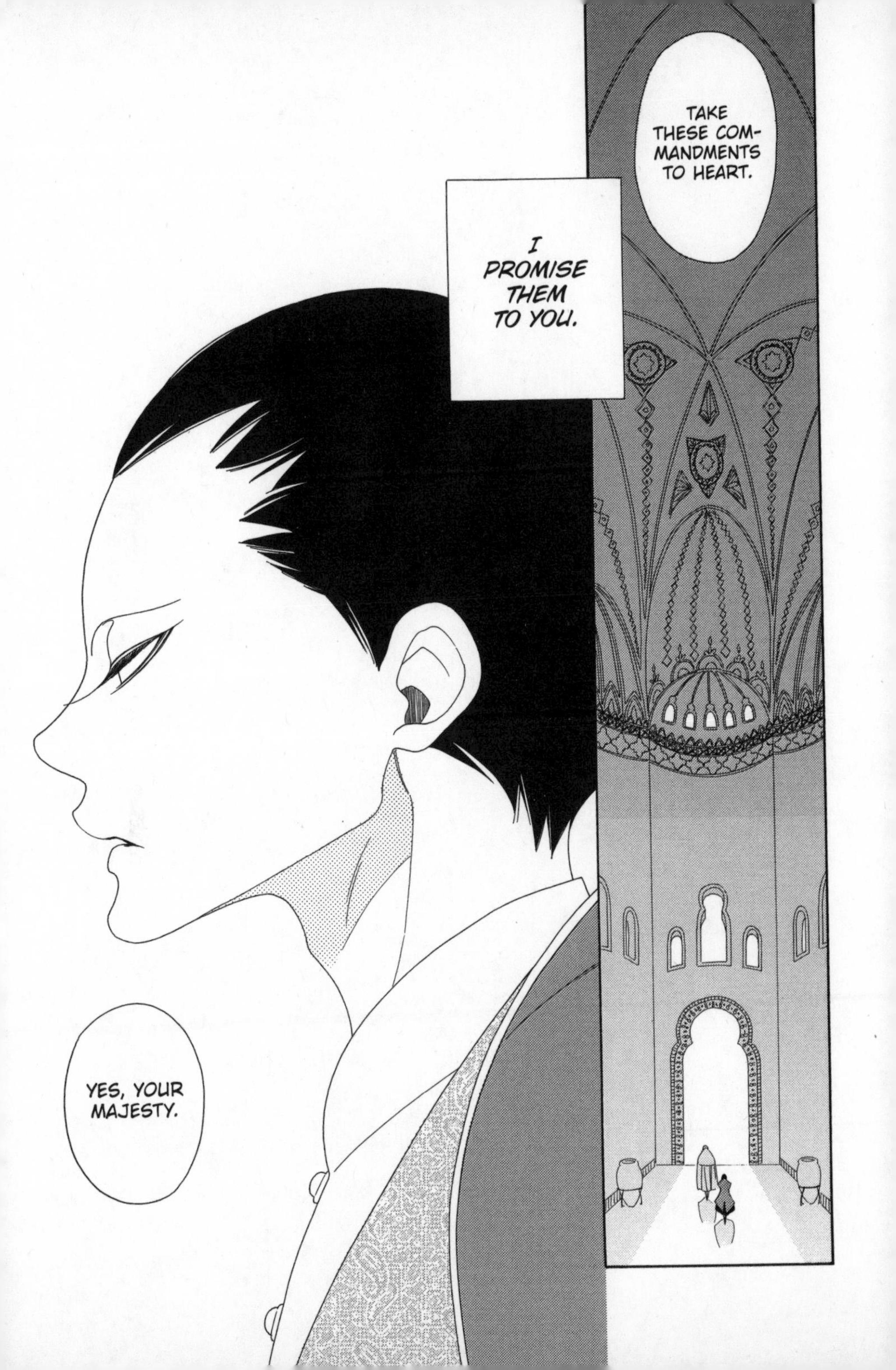
TAKE THESE COM-MANDMENTS TO HEART.
I PROMISE THEM TO YOU.
YES, YOUR MAJESTY.

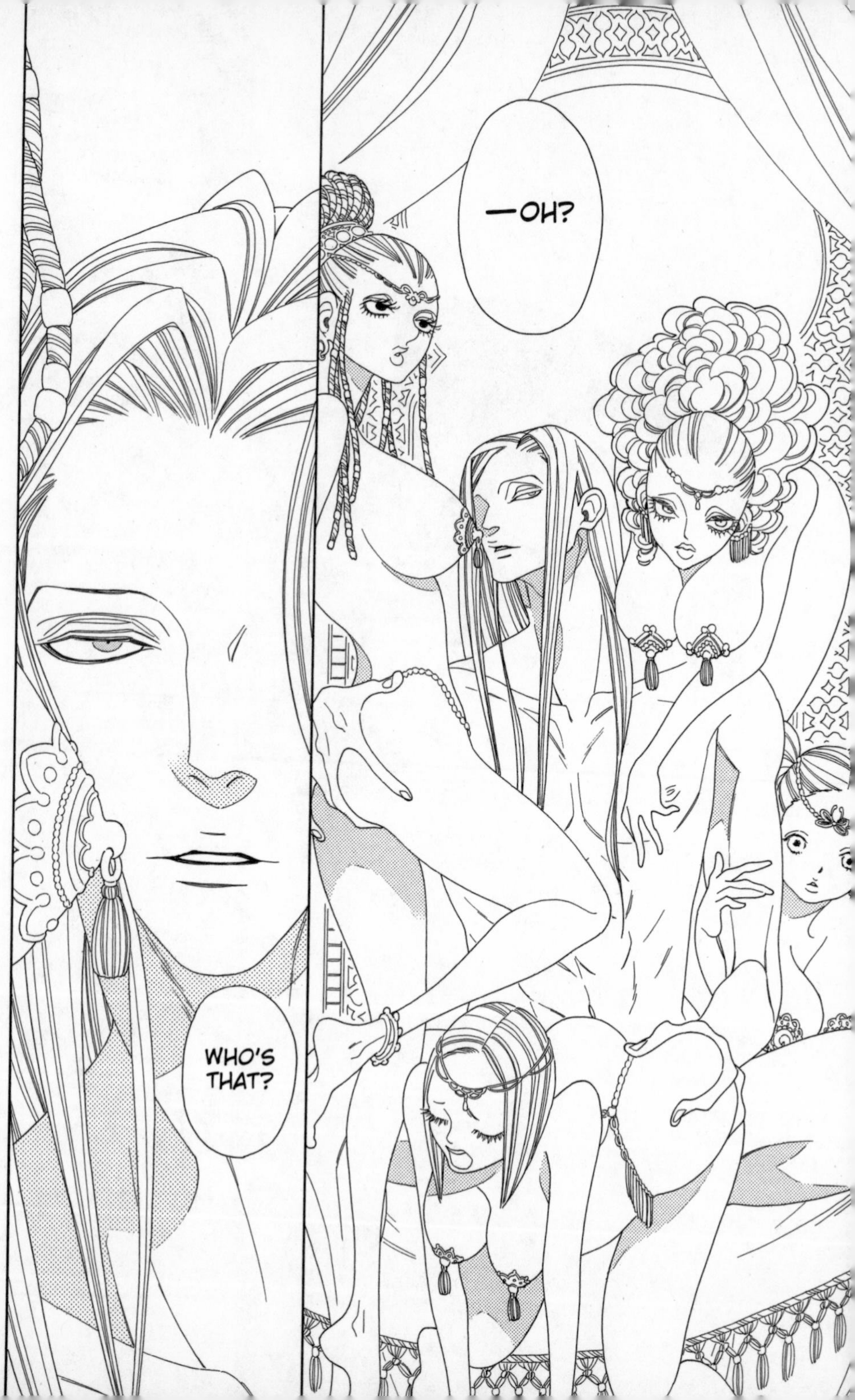
—OH?
WHO'S THAT?

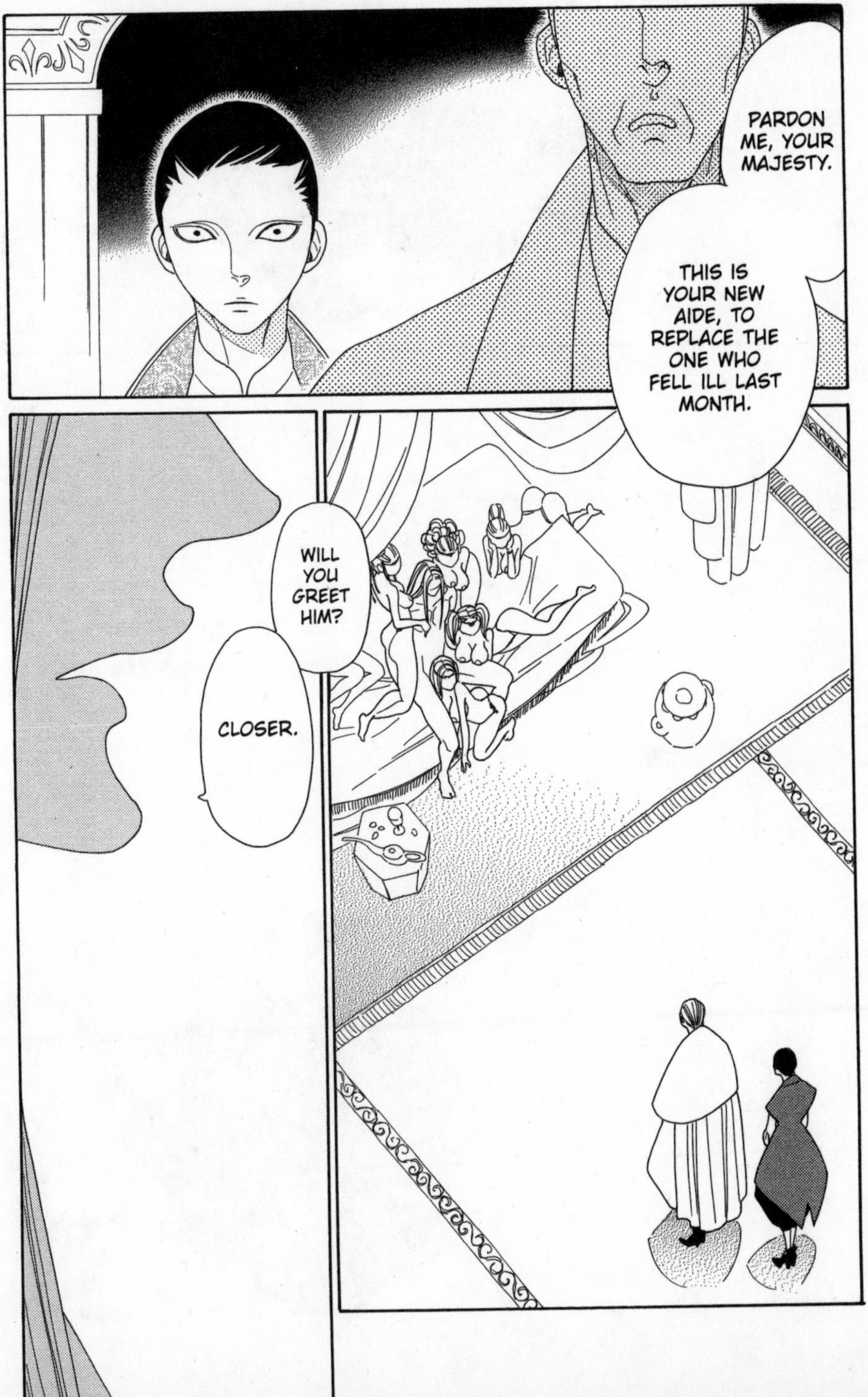
PARDON ME, YOUR MAJESTY.
THIS IS YOUR NEW AIDE, TO REPLACE THE ONE WHO FELL ILL LAST MONTH.
WILL YOU GREET HIM?
CLOSER.

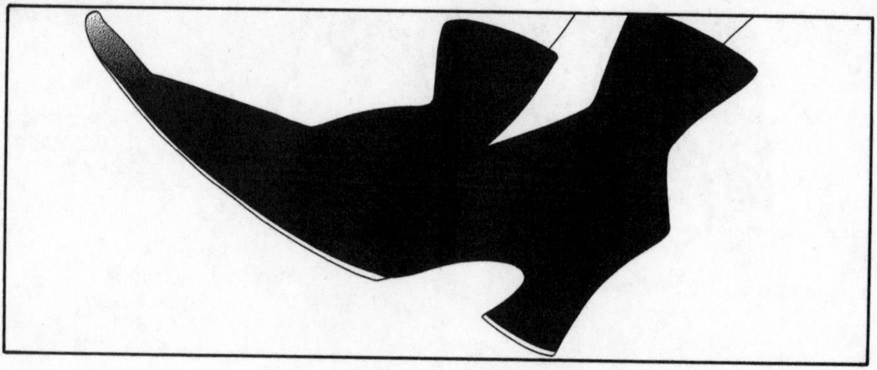

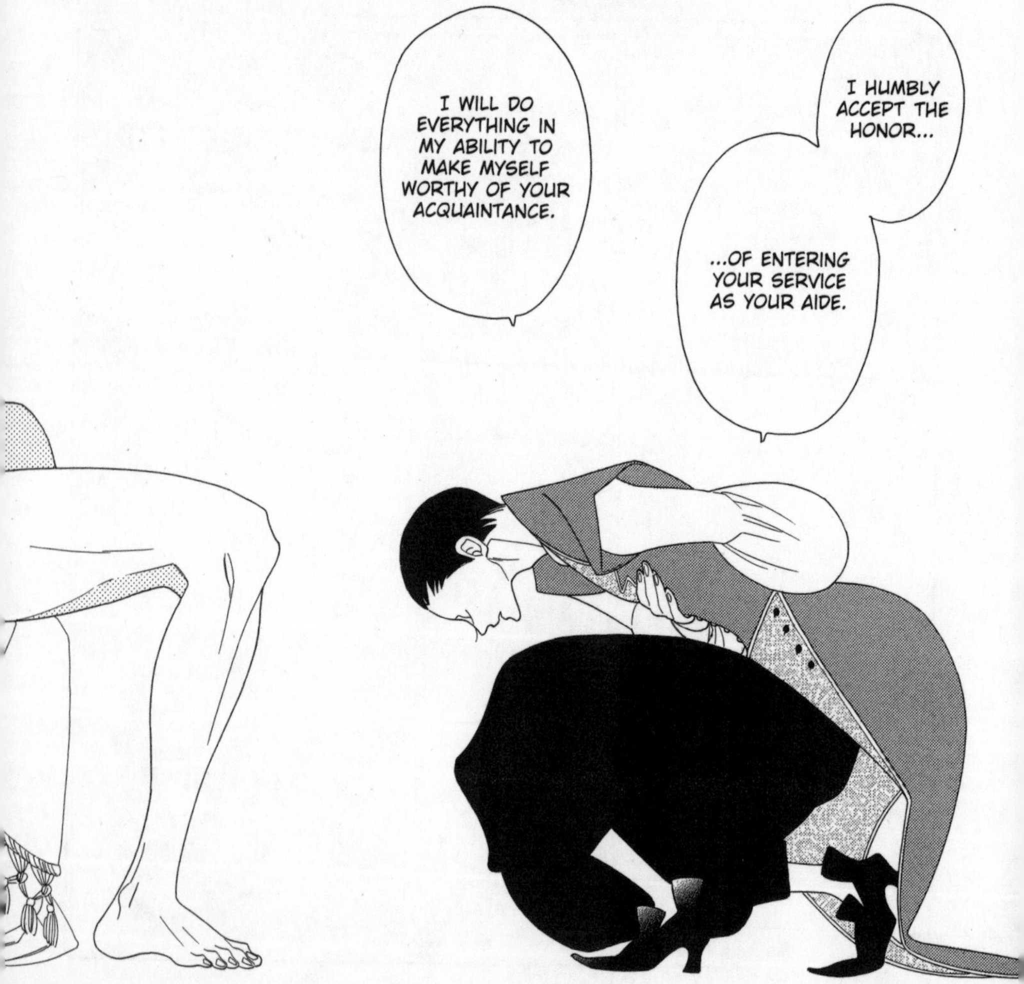
I HUMBLY ACCEPT THE HONOR...
...OF ENTERING YOUR SERVICE AS YOUR AIDE.
I WILL DO EVERYTHING IN MY ABILITY TO MAKE MYSELF WORTHY OF YOUR ACQUAINTANCE.

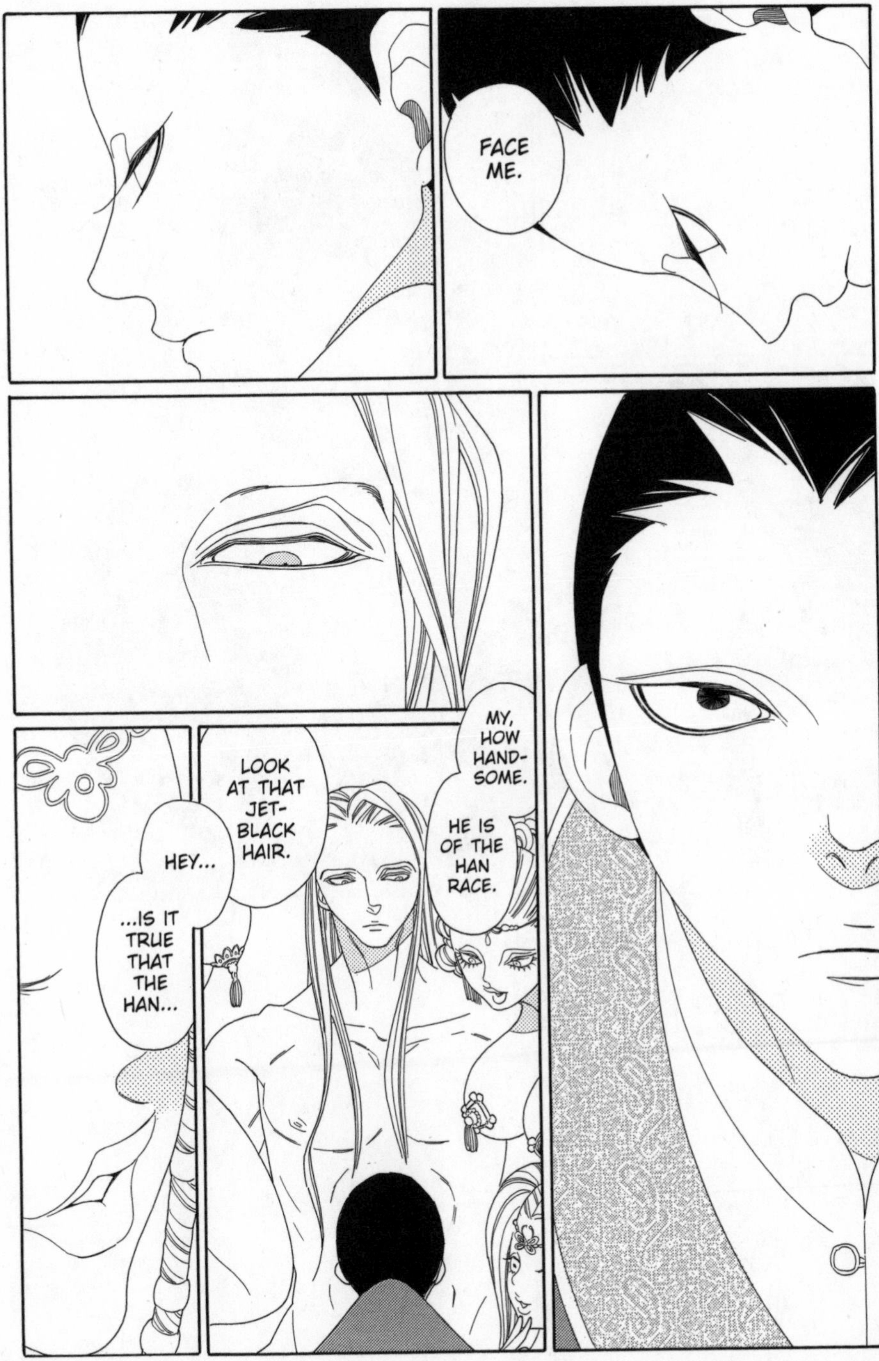
FACE ME.
MY, HOW HAND-SOME.
HE IS OF THE HAN RACE.
LOOK AT THAT JET-BLACK HAIR.
HEY...
...IS IT TRUE THAT THE HAN...

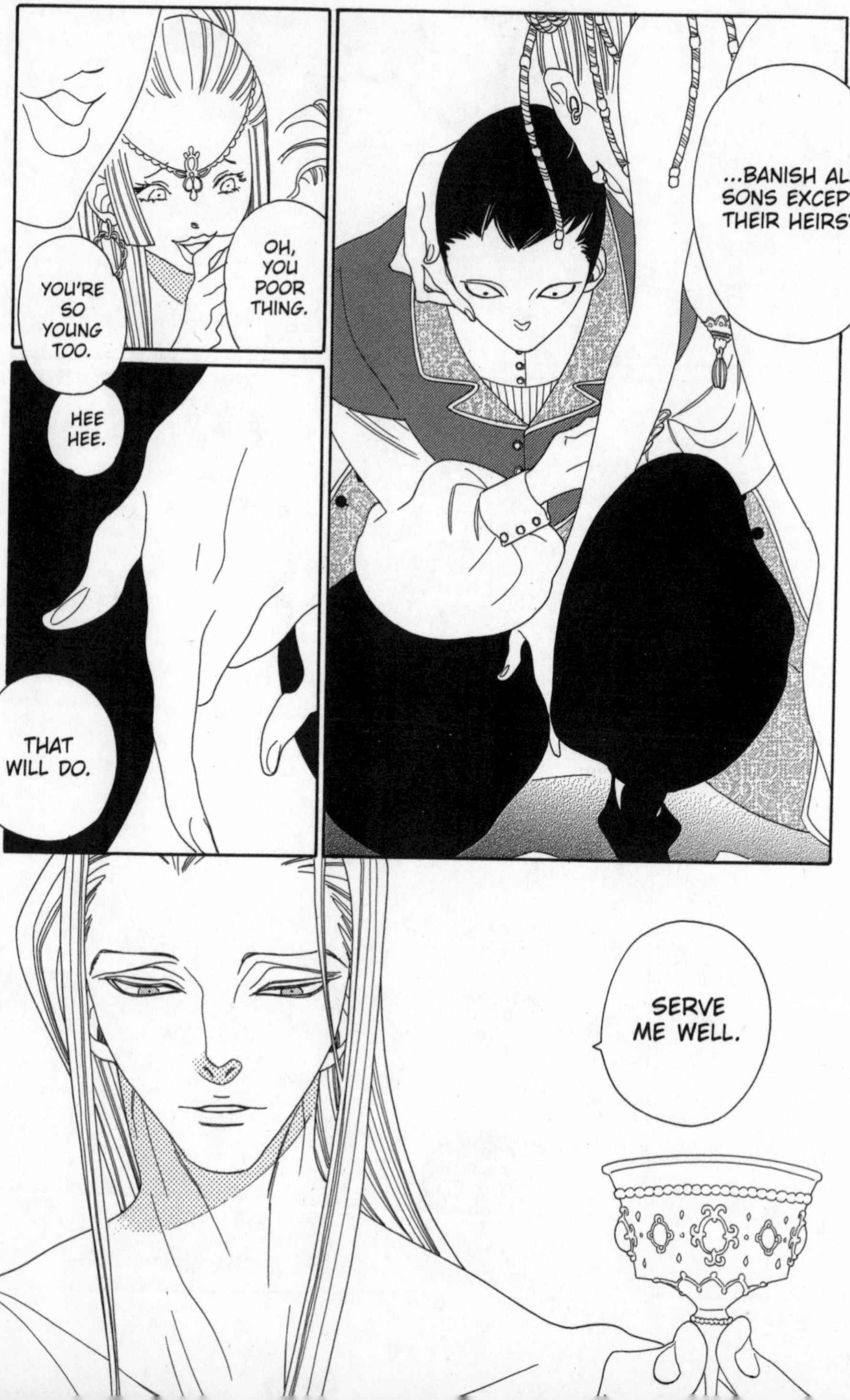
...BANISH ALL SONS EXCEPT THEIR HEIRS?
OH, YOU POOR THING.
YOU'RE SO YOUNG TOO.
HEE HEE.
THAT WILL DO.
SERVE ME WELL.

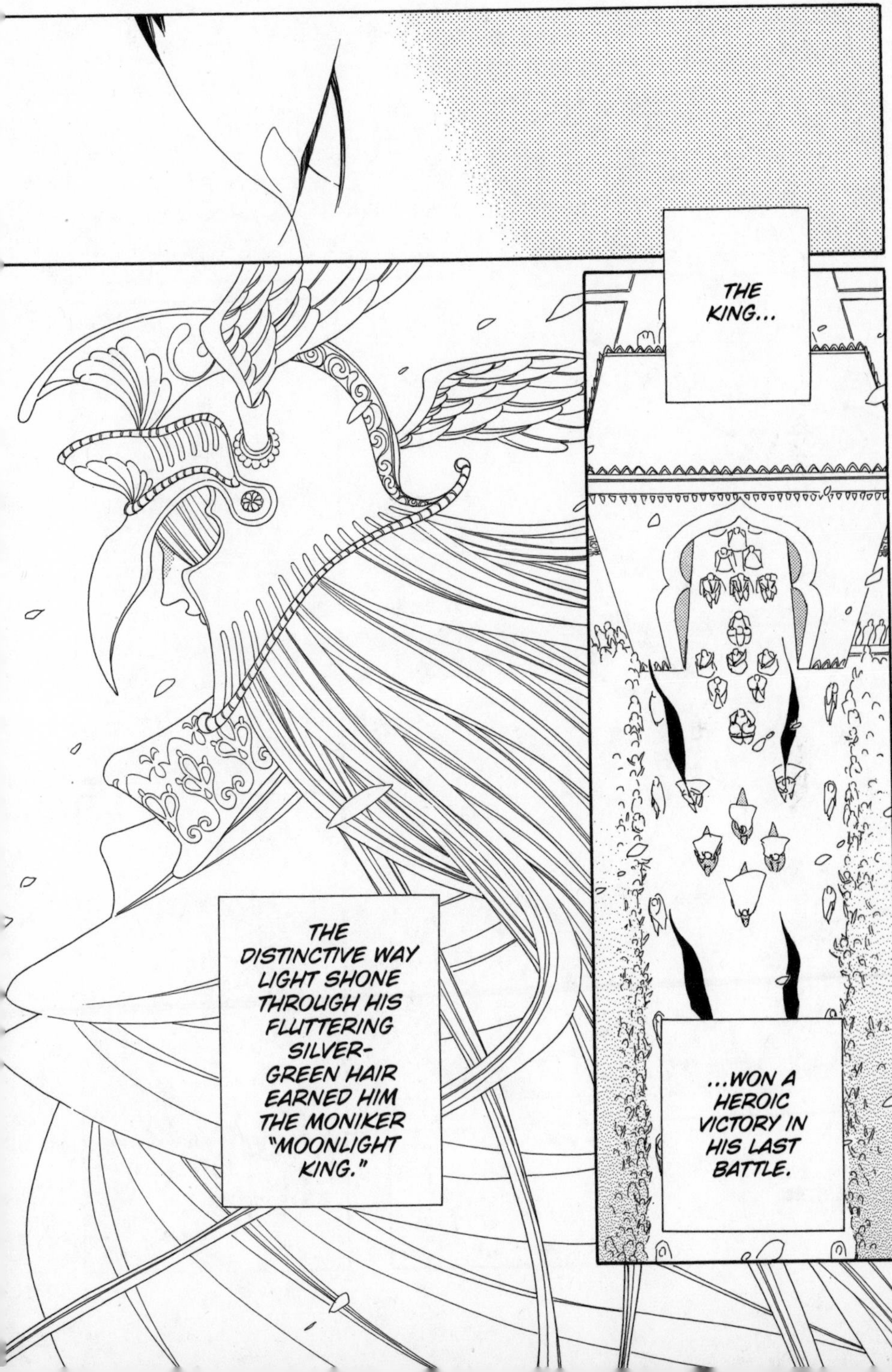
THE KING...
...WON A HEROIC VICTORY IN HIS LAST BATTLE.
THE DISTINCTIVE WAY LIGHT SHONE THROUGH HIS FLUTTERING SILVER-GREEN HAIR EARNED HIM THE MONIKER "MOONLIGHT KING."

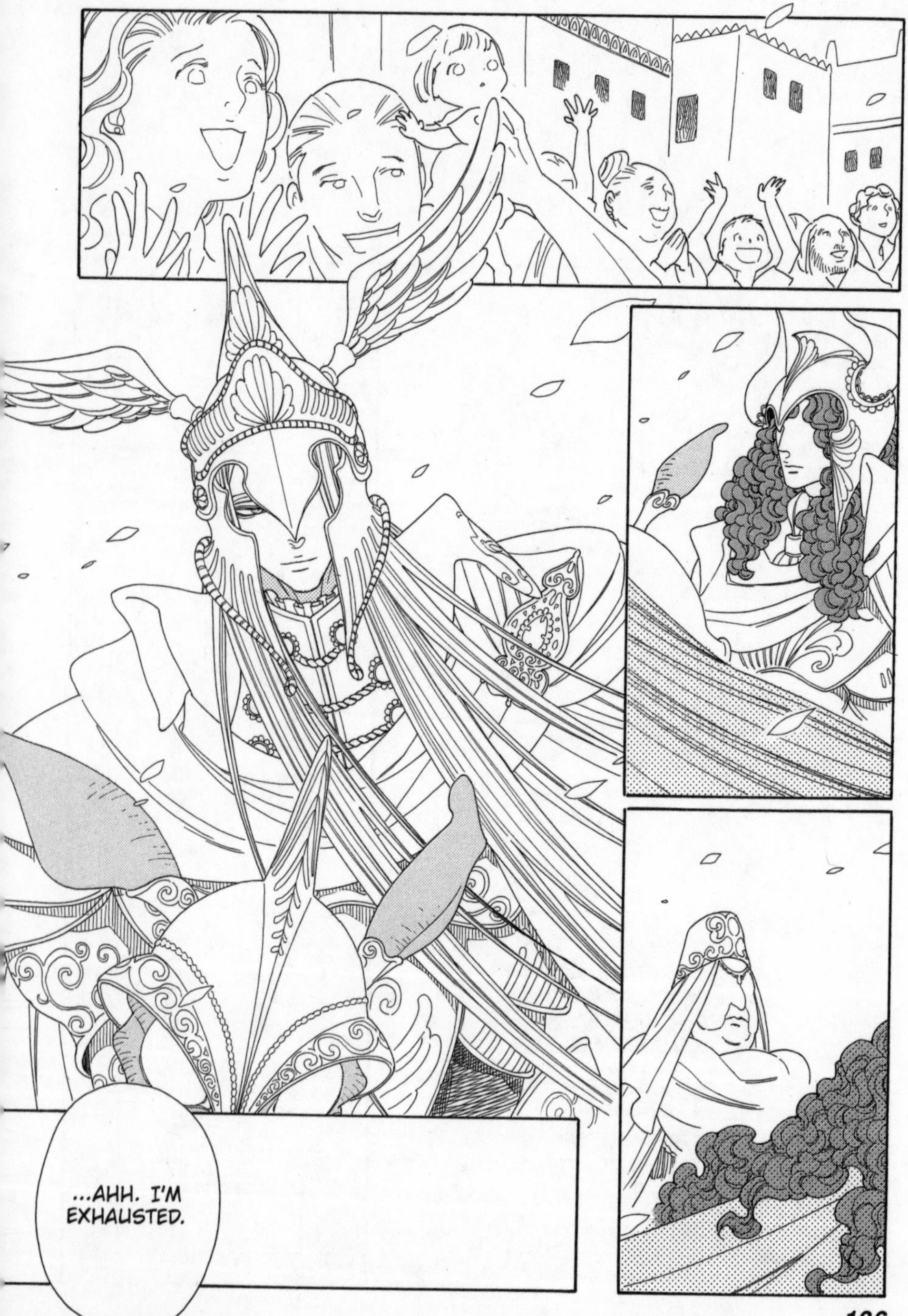
...AHH. I'M
EXHAUSTED.

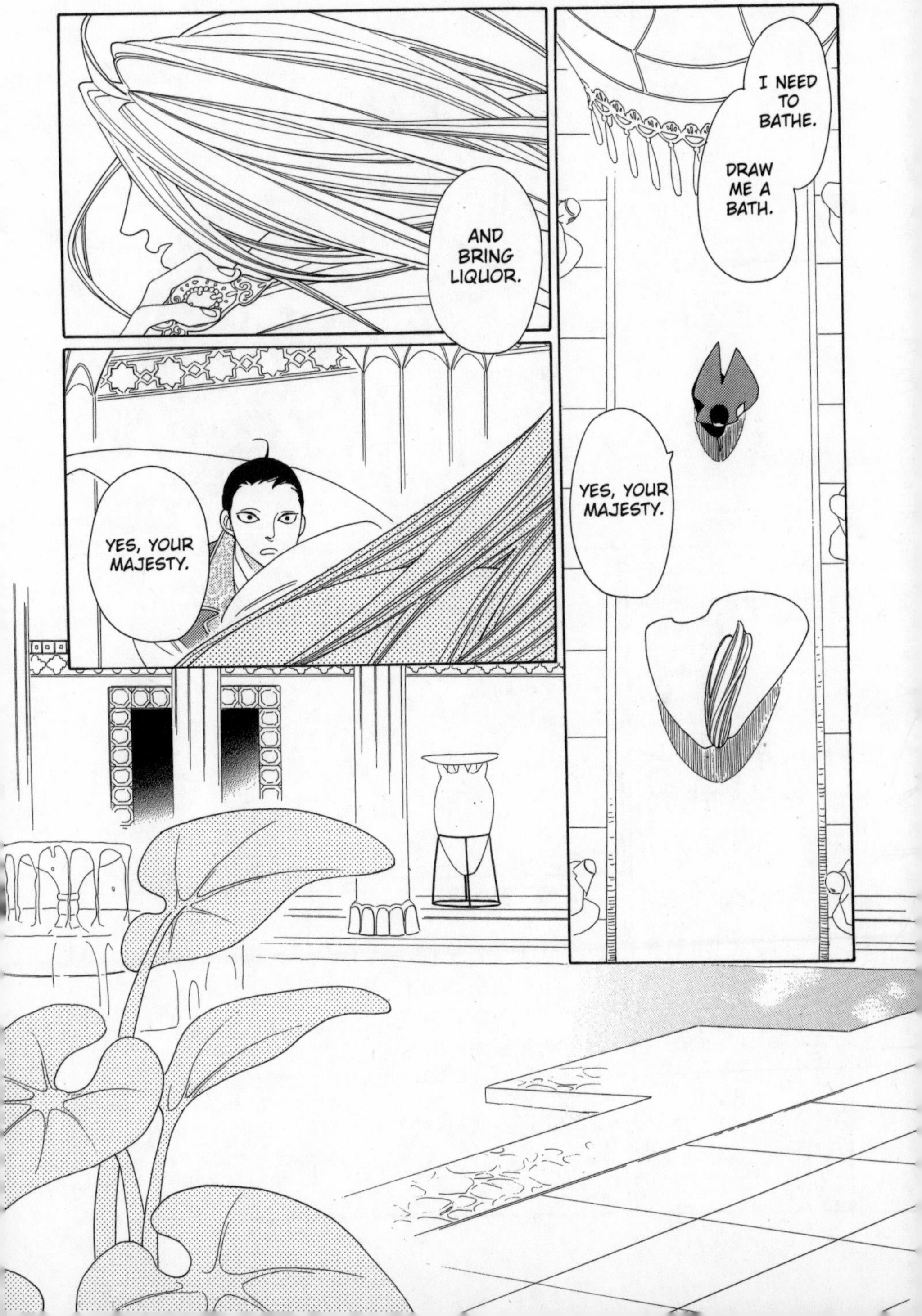
I NEED TO BATHE.
DRAW ME A BATH.
YES, YOUR MAJESTY.
AND BRING LIQUOR.
YES, YOUR MAJESTY.

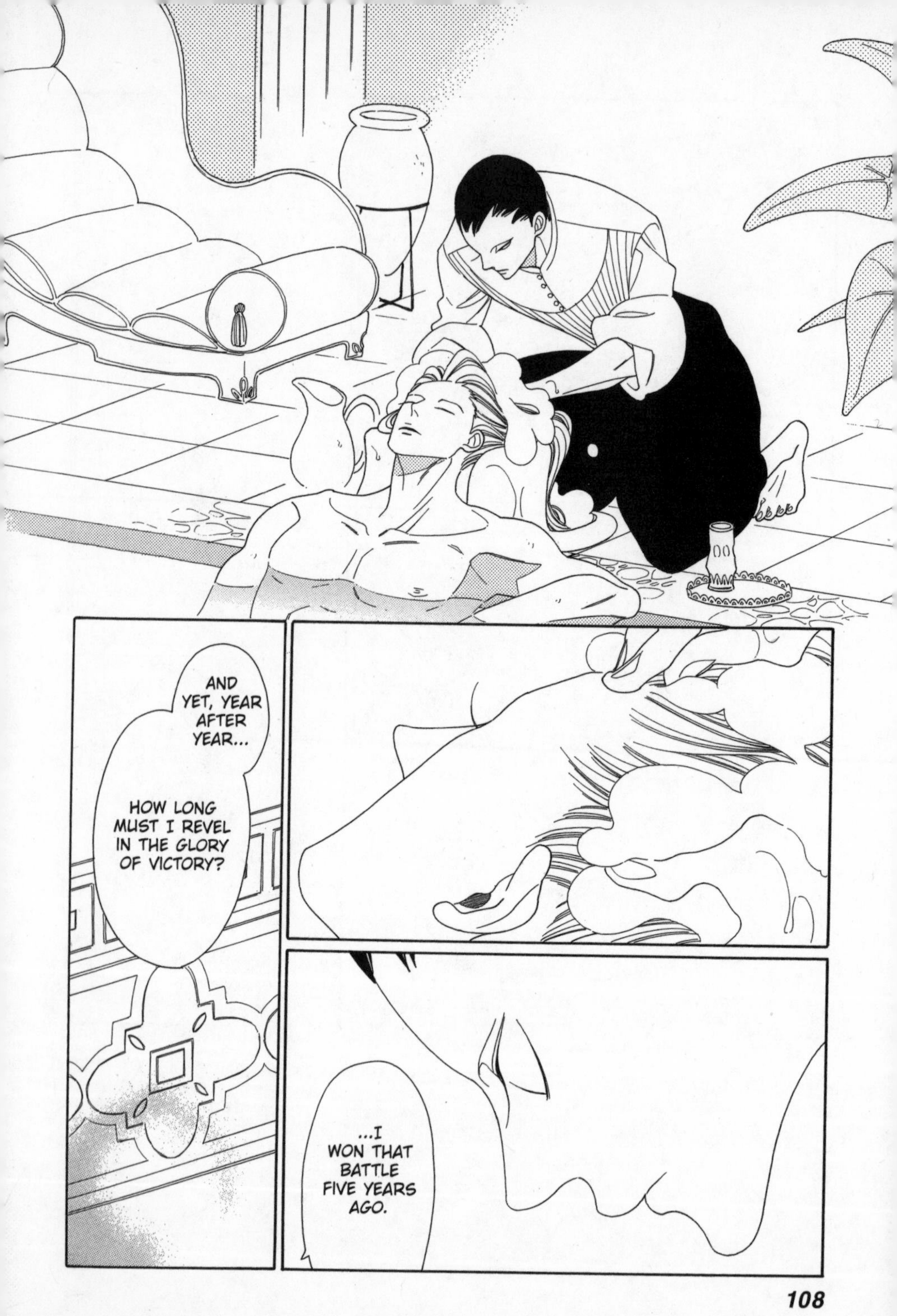
...I WON THAT BATTLE FIVE YEARS AGO.
AND YET, YEAR AFTER YEAR...
HOW LONG MUST I REVEL IN THE GLORY OF VICTORY?

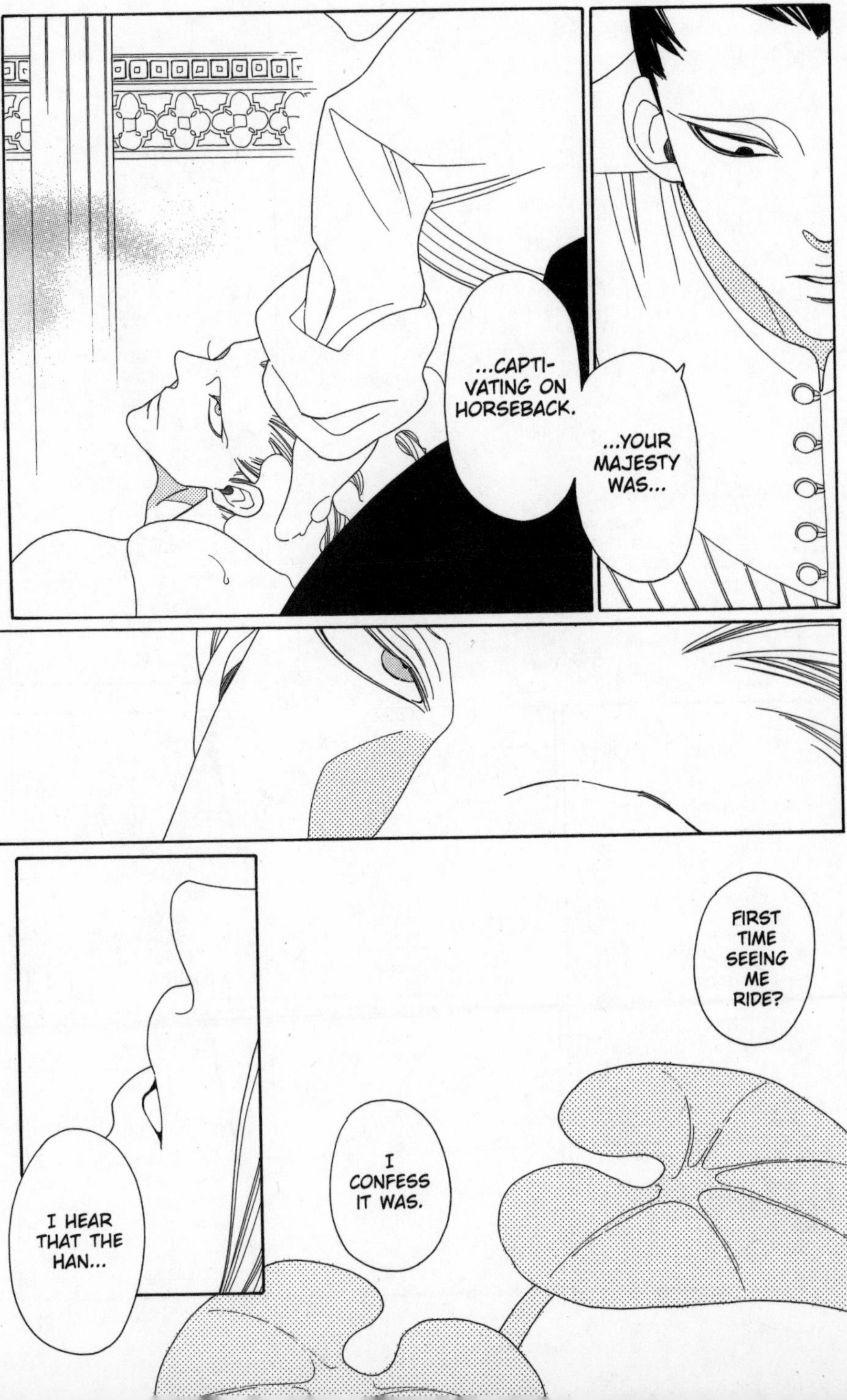
...YOUR MAJESTY WAS...
...CAPTIVATING ON HORSEBACK.
FIRST TIME SEEING ME RIDE?
I CONFESS IT WAS.
I HEAR THAT THE HAN...

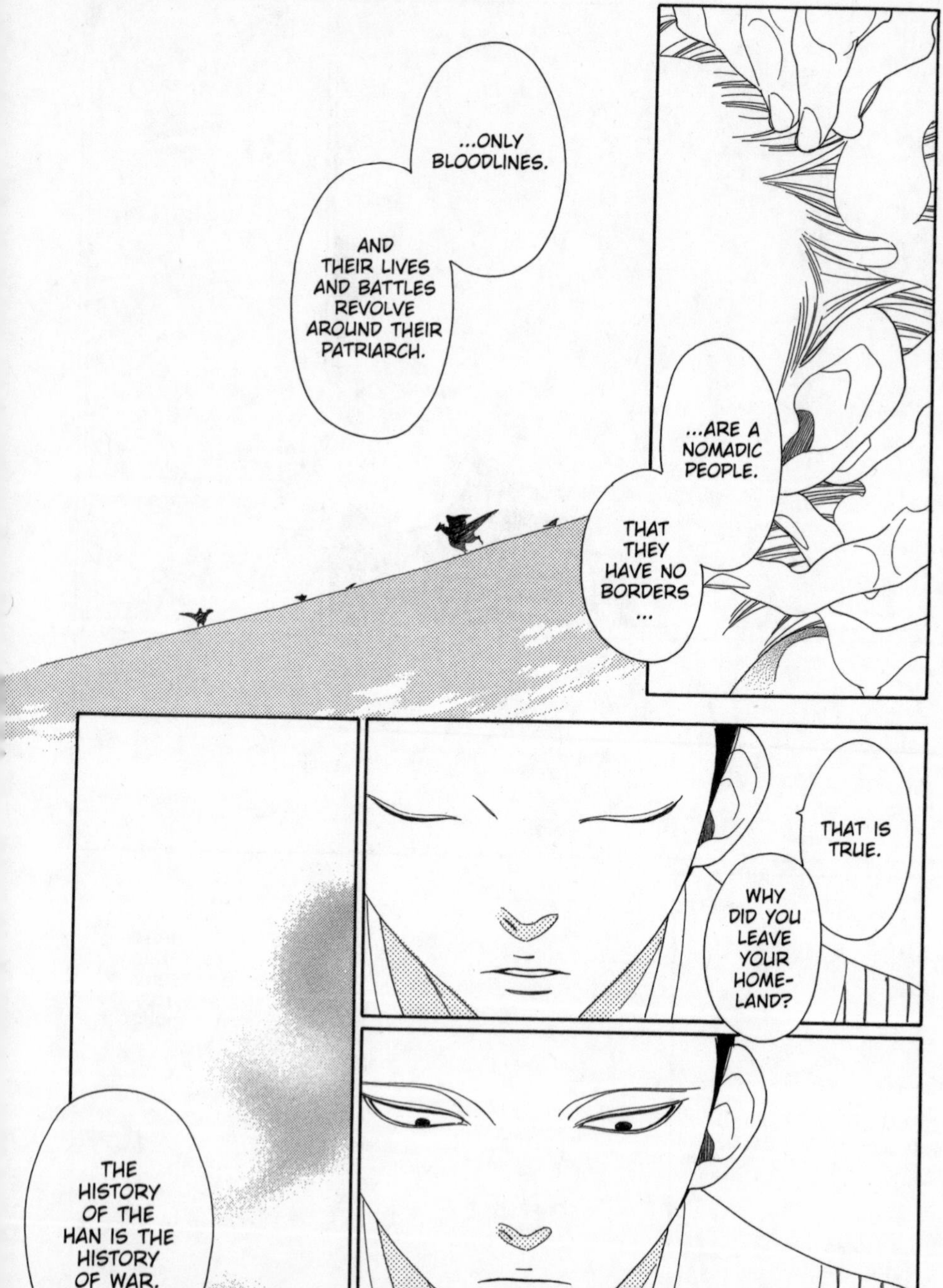
...ARE A NOMADIC PEOPLE.
THAT THEY HAVE NO BORDERS ...
...ONLY BLOODLINES.
AND THEIR LIVES AND BATTLES REVOLVE AROUND THEIR PATRIARCH.
THAT IS TRUE.
WHY DID YOU LEAVE YOUR HOME-LAND?
THE HISTORY OF THE HAN IS THE HISTORY OF WAR.

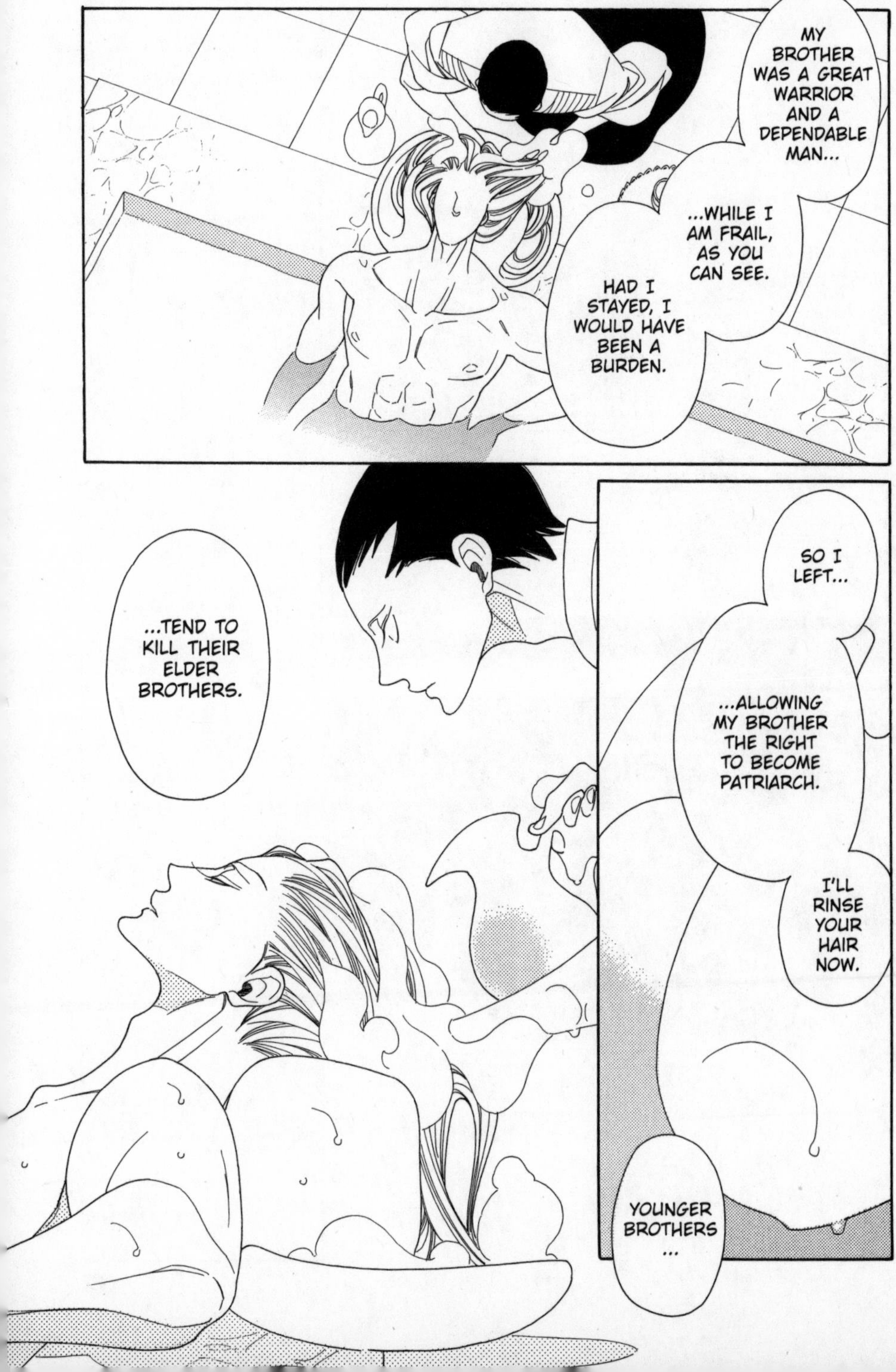
MY BROTHER WAS A GREAT WARRIOR AND A DEPENDABLE MAN...
...WHILE I AM FRAIL, AS YOU CAN SEE.
HAD I STAYED, I WOULD HAVE BEEN A BURDEN.
SO I LEFT...
...ALLOWING MY BROTHER THE RIGHT TO BECOME PATRIARCH.
I'LL RINSE YOUR HAIR NOW.
YOUNGER BROTHERS ...
...TEND TO KILL THEIR ELDER BROTHERS.

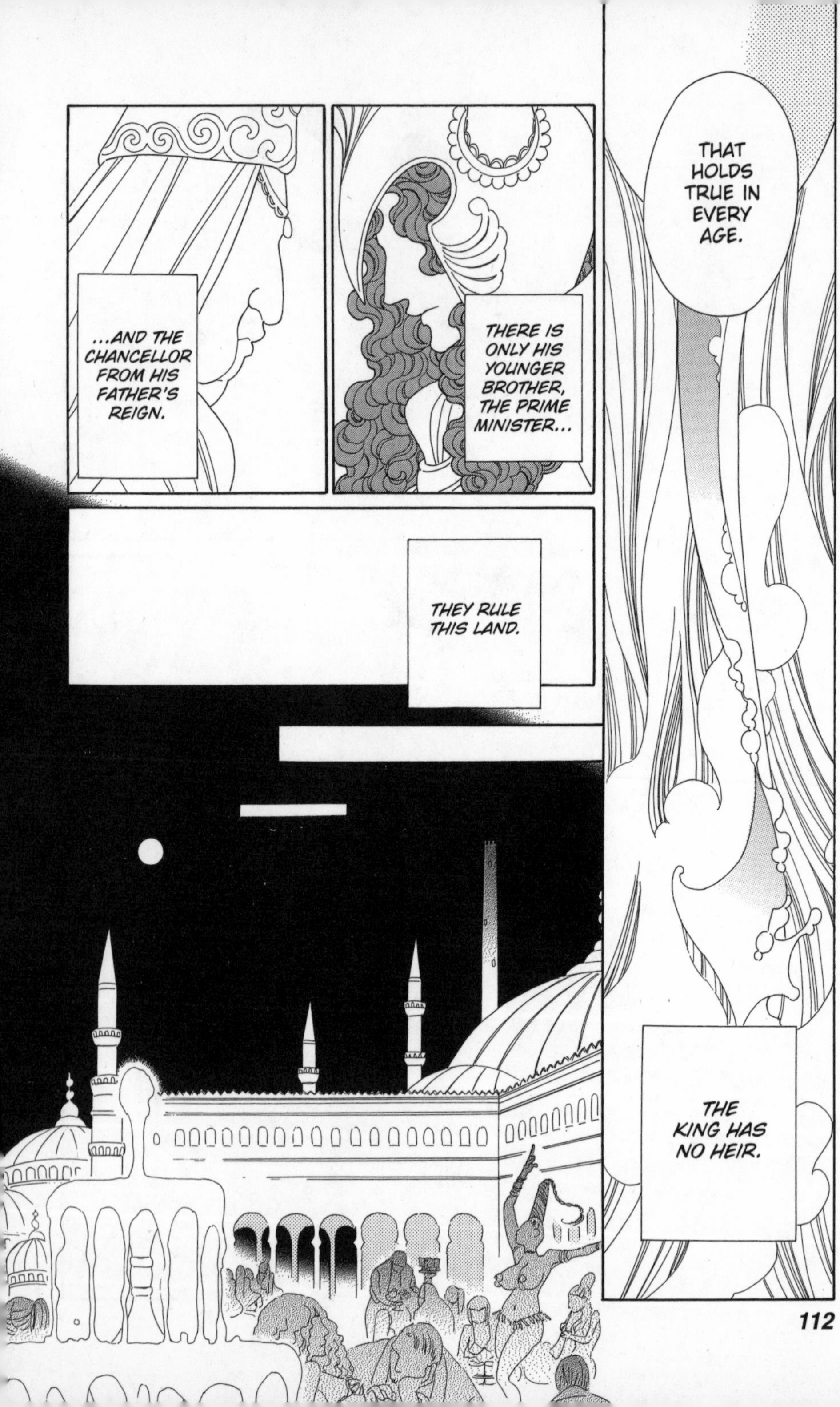
THAT HOLDS TRUE IN EVERY AGE.
THE KING HAS NO HEIR.
THERE IS ONLY HIS YOUNGER BROTHER, THE PRIME MINISTER...
...AND THE CHANCELLOR FROM HIS FATHER'S REIGN.
THEY RULE THIS LAND.

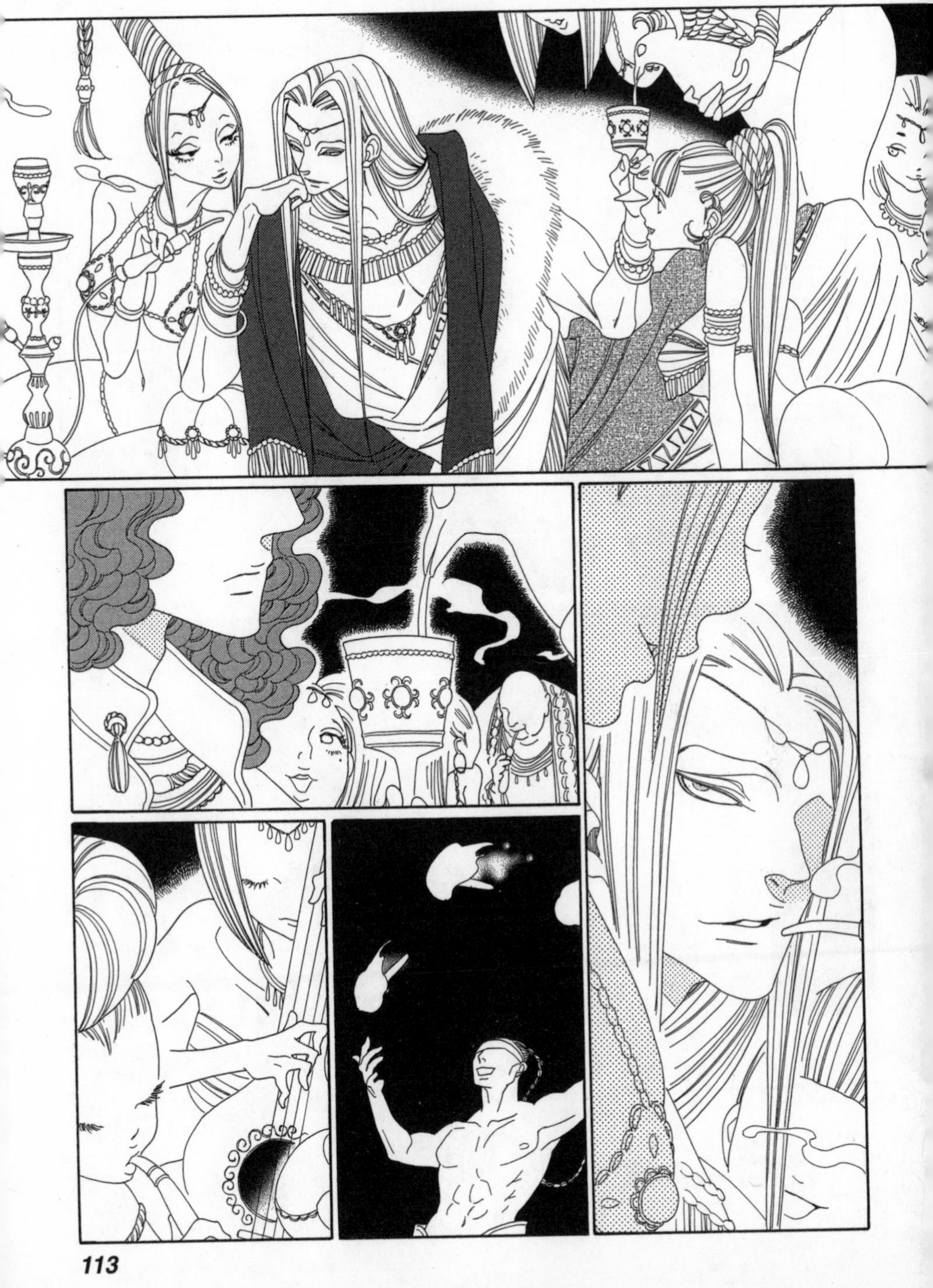

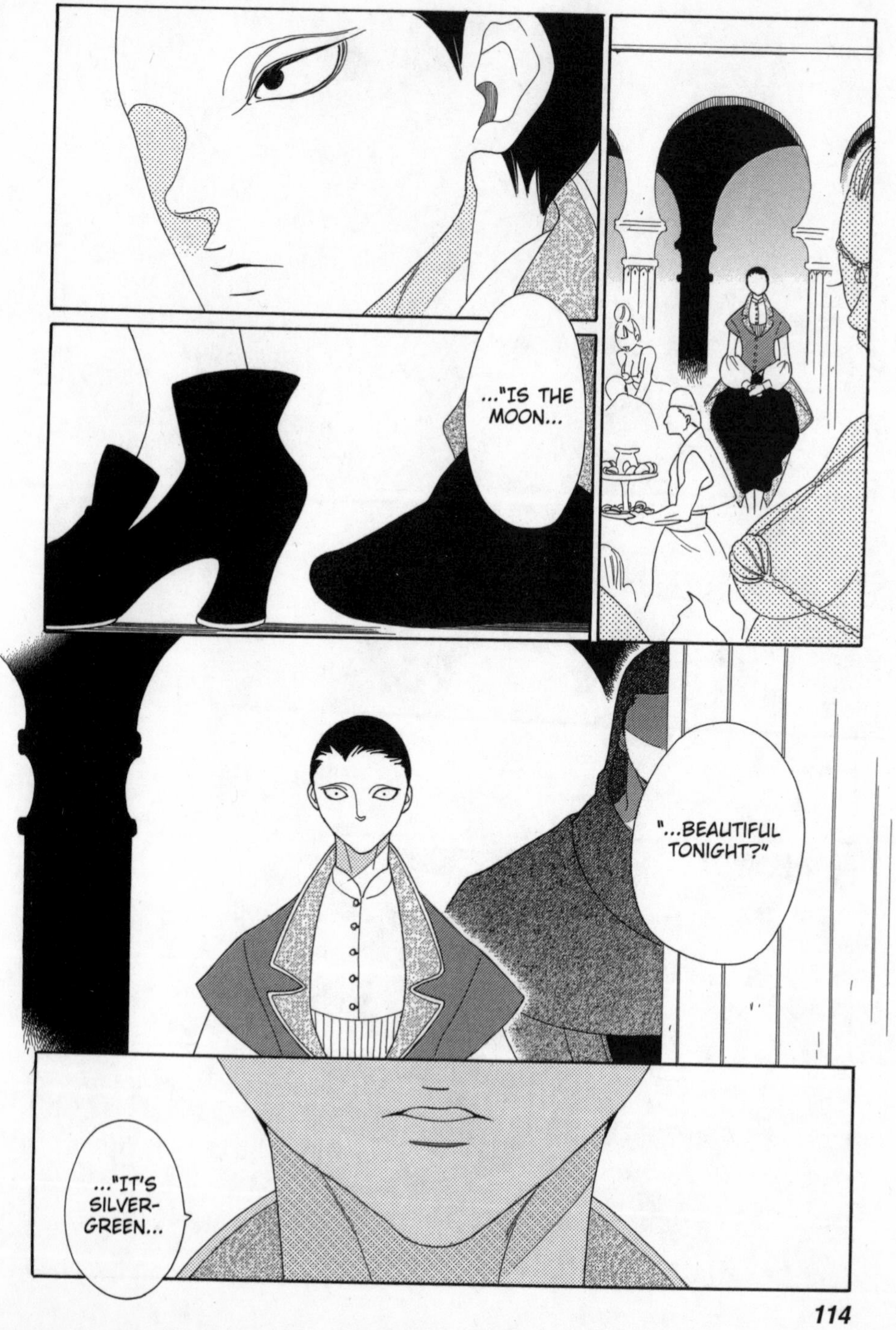
..."IS THE MOON...
"...BEAUTIFUL TONIGHT?"
..."IT'S SILVER-GREEN...

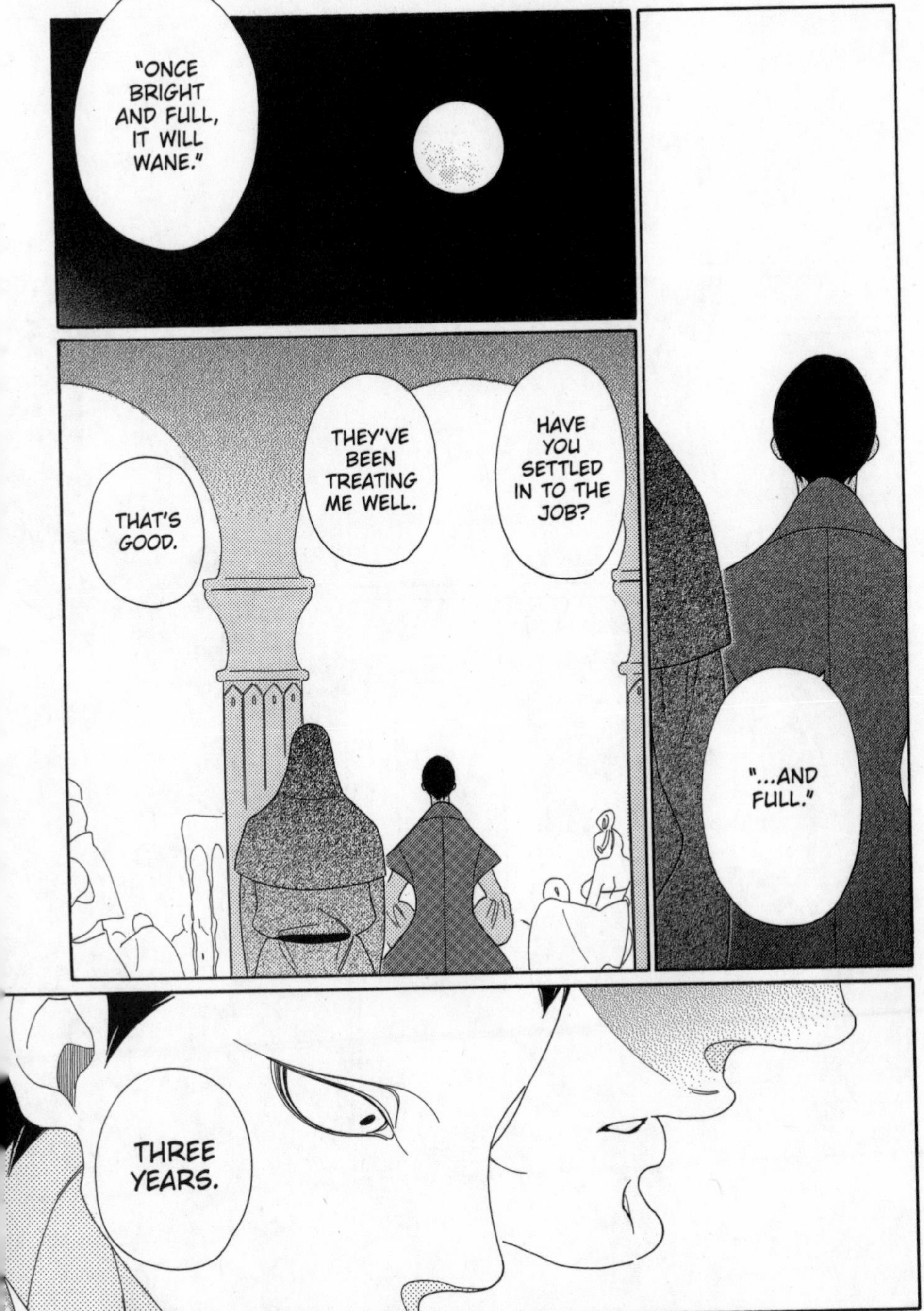
"ONCE BRIGHT AND FULL, IT WILL WANE."
HAVE YOU SETTLED IN TO THE JOB?
THEY'VE BEEN TREATING ME WELL.
THAT'S GOOD.
"...AND FULL."
THREE YEARS.

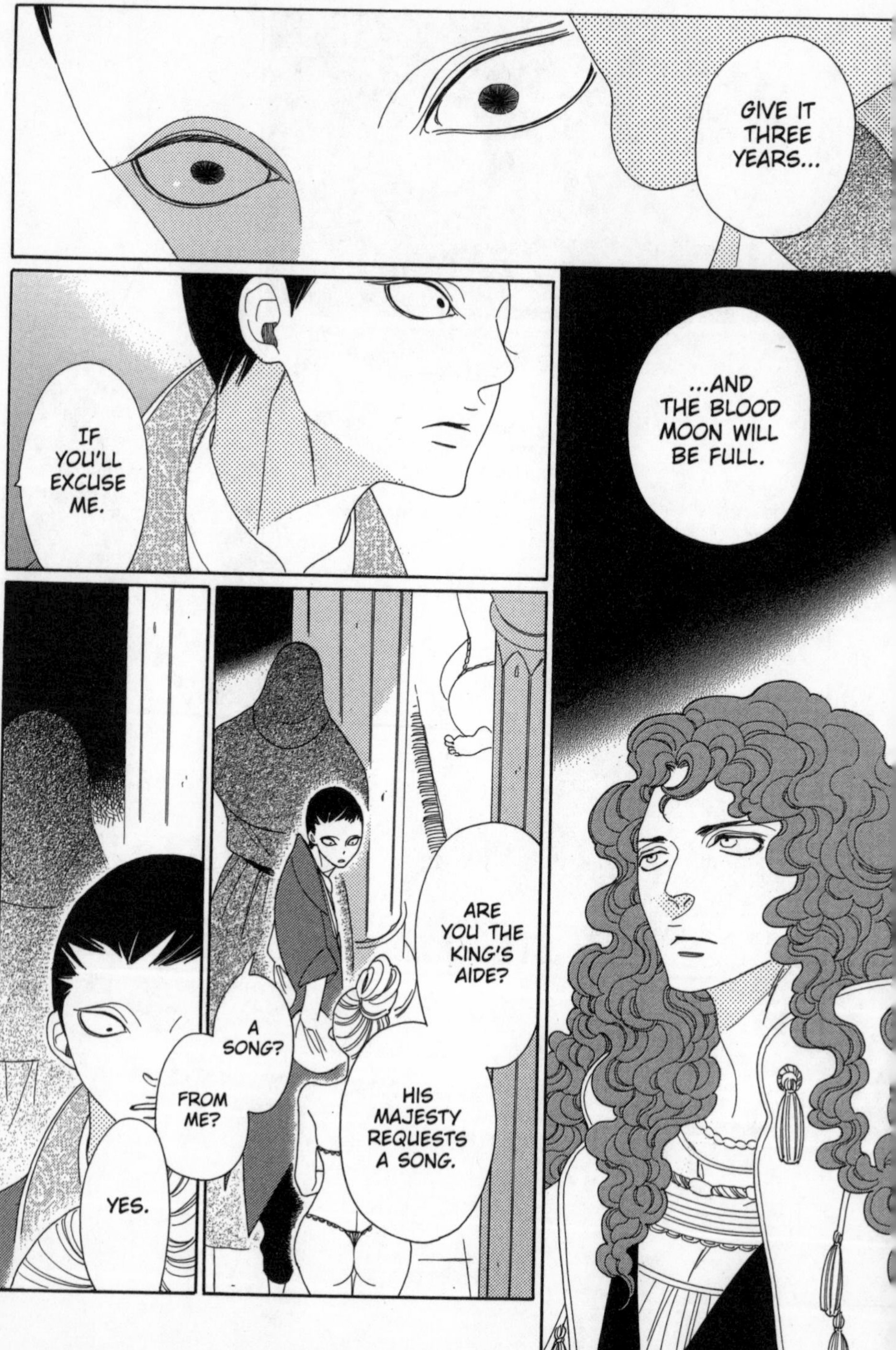
GIVE IT THREE YEARS...
...AND THE BLOOD MOON WILL BE FULL.
IF YOU'LL EXCUSE ME.
ARE YOU THE KING'S AIDE?
HIS MAJESTY REQUESTS A SONG.
A SONG?
FROM ME?
YES.

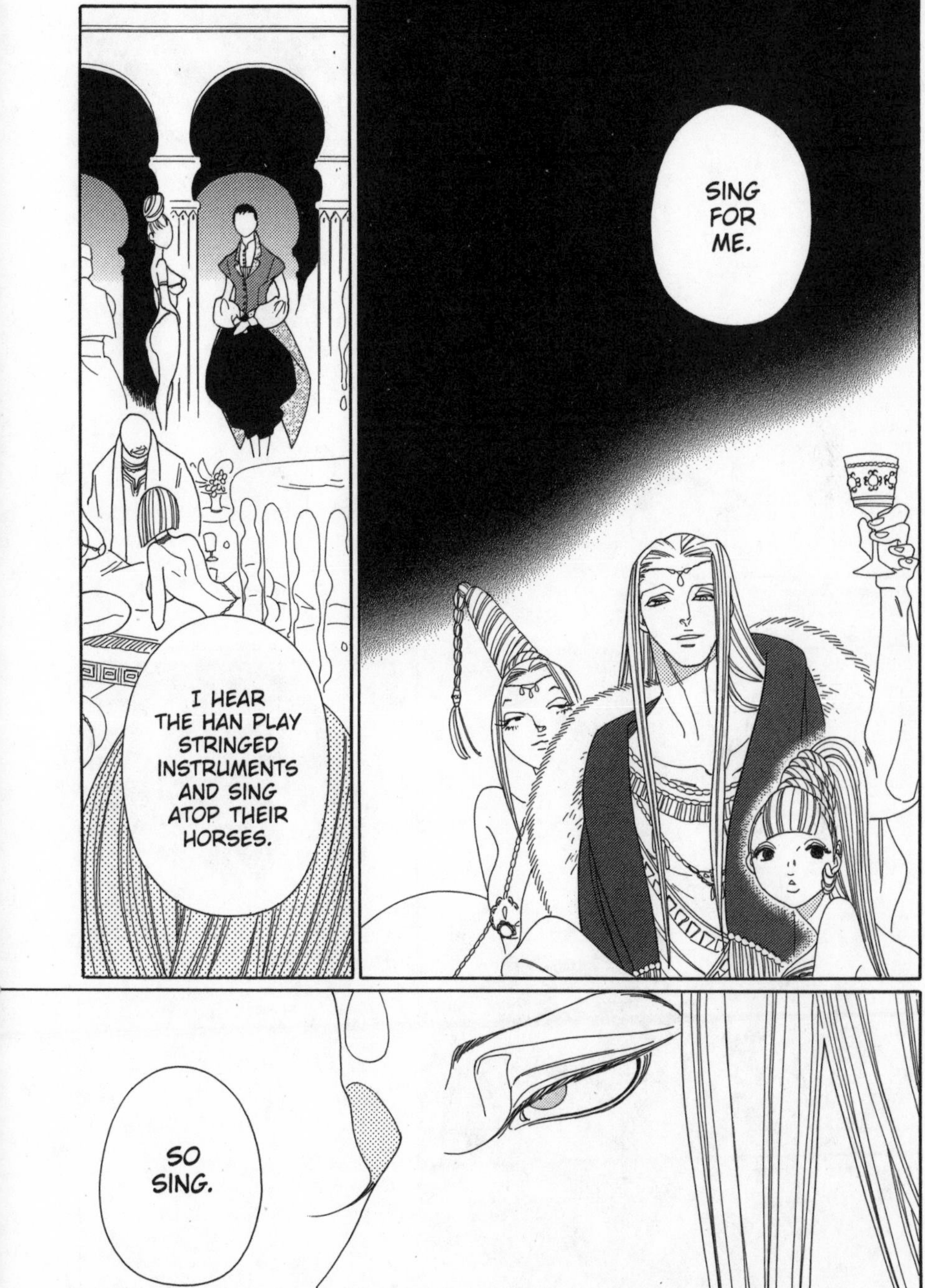
SING FOR ME.
I HEAR THE HAN PLAY STRINGED INSTRUMENTS AND SING ATOP THEIR HORSES.
SO SING.

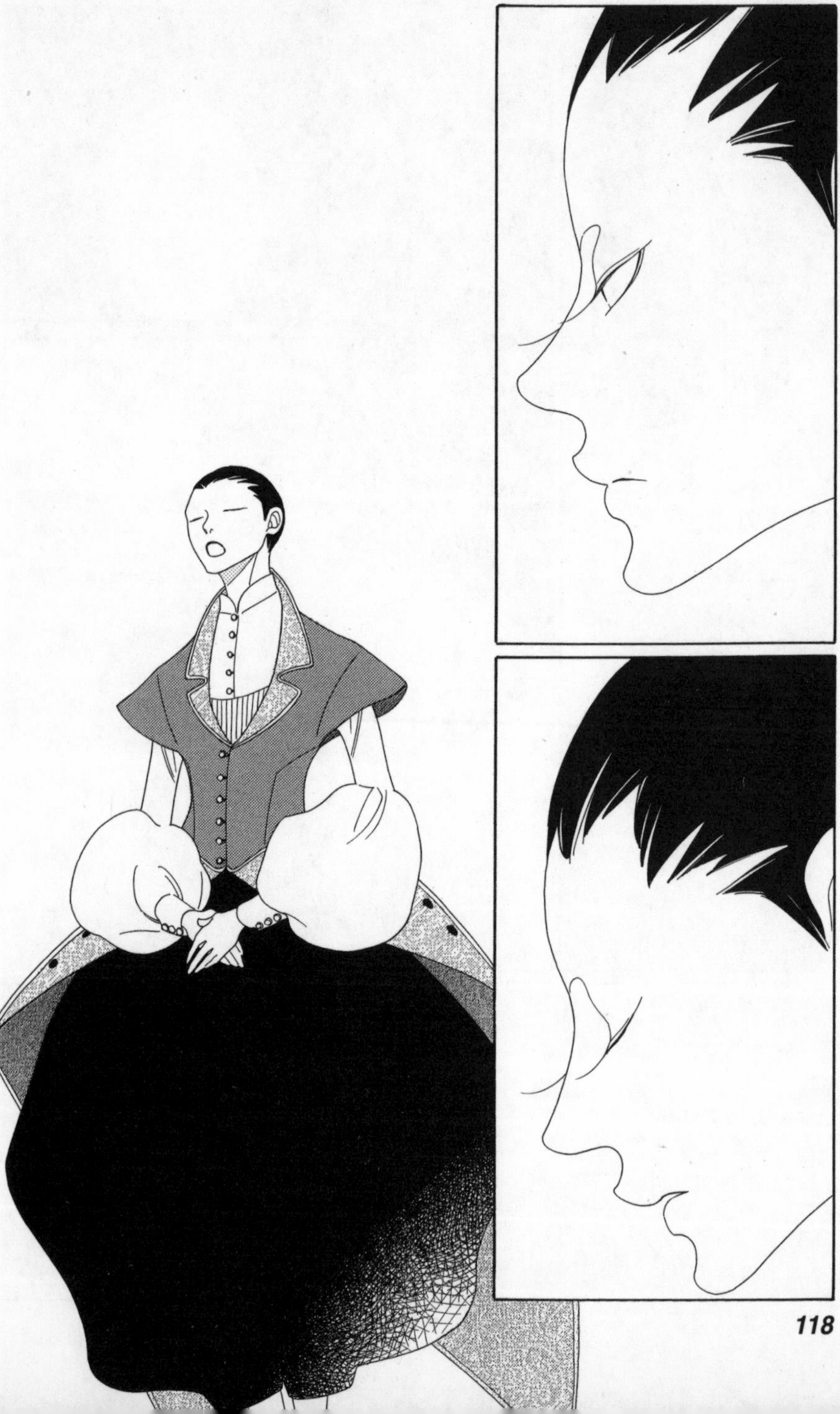

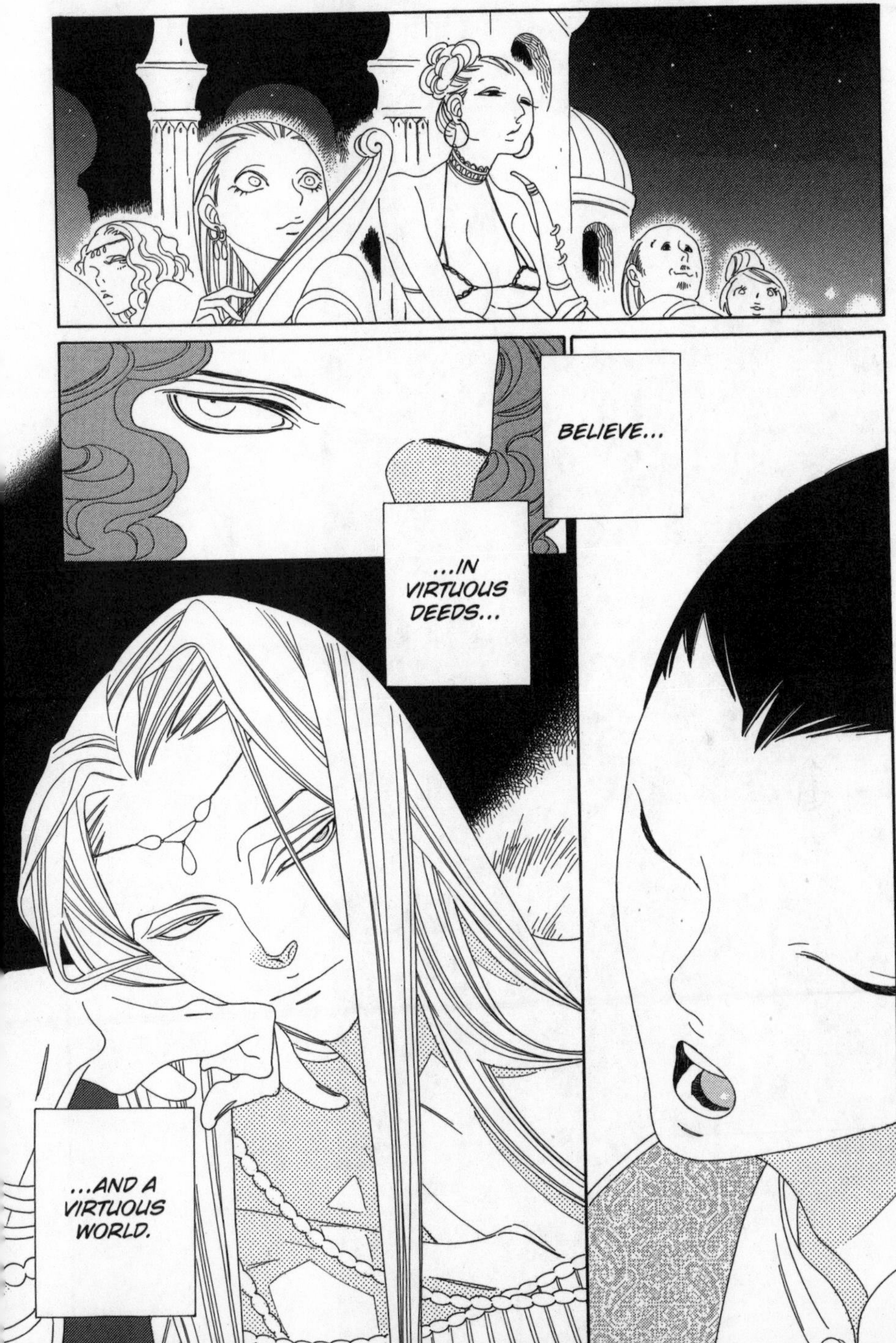
BELIEVE...
...IN VIRTUOUS DEEDS...
...AND A VIRTUOUS WORLD.

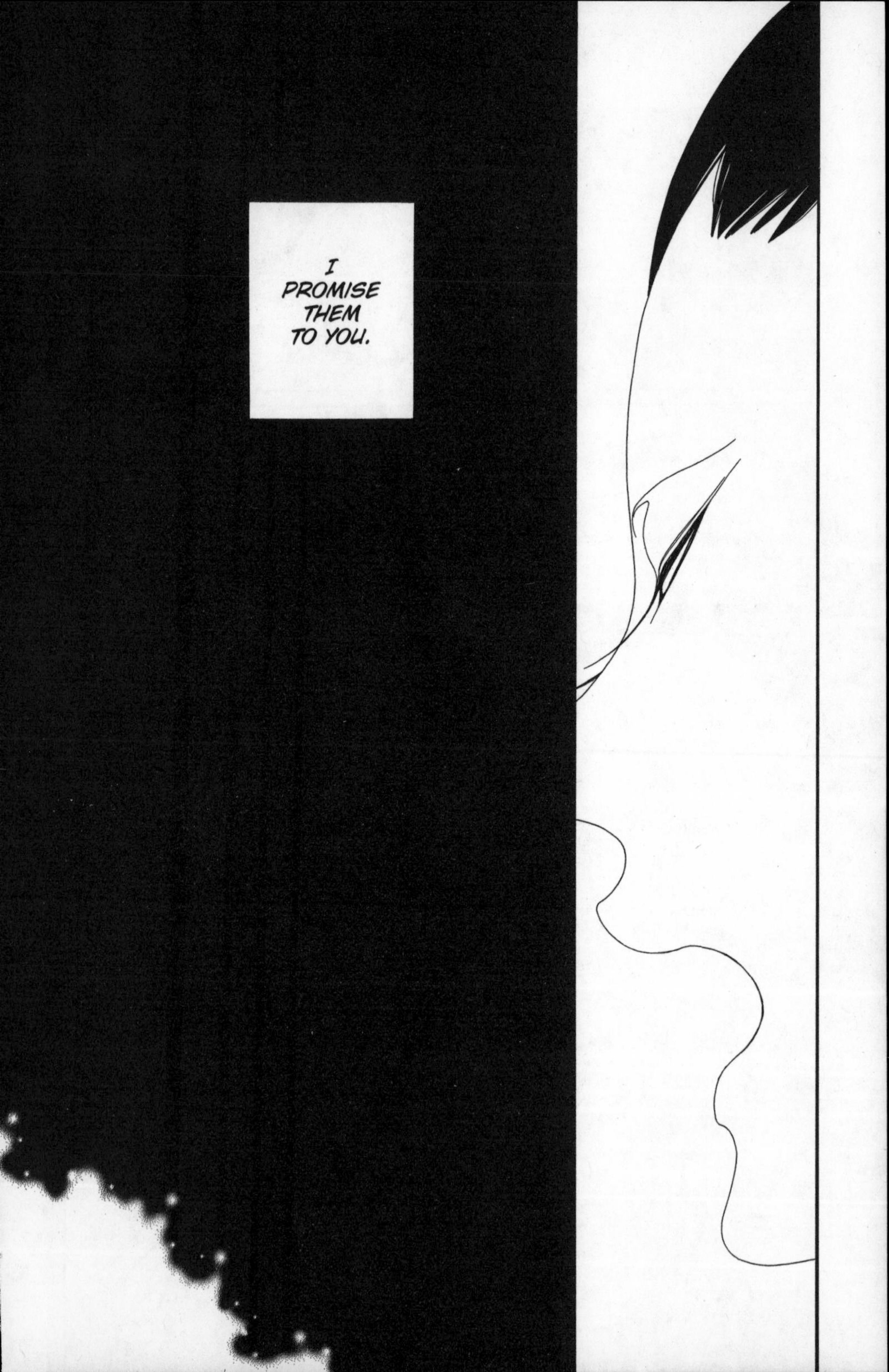
I PROMISE THEM TO YOU.

Chapter 5

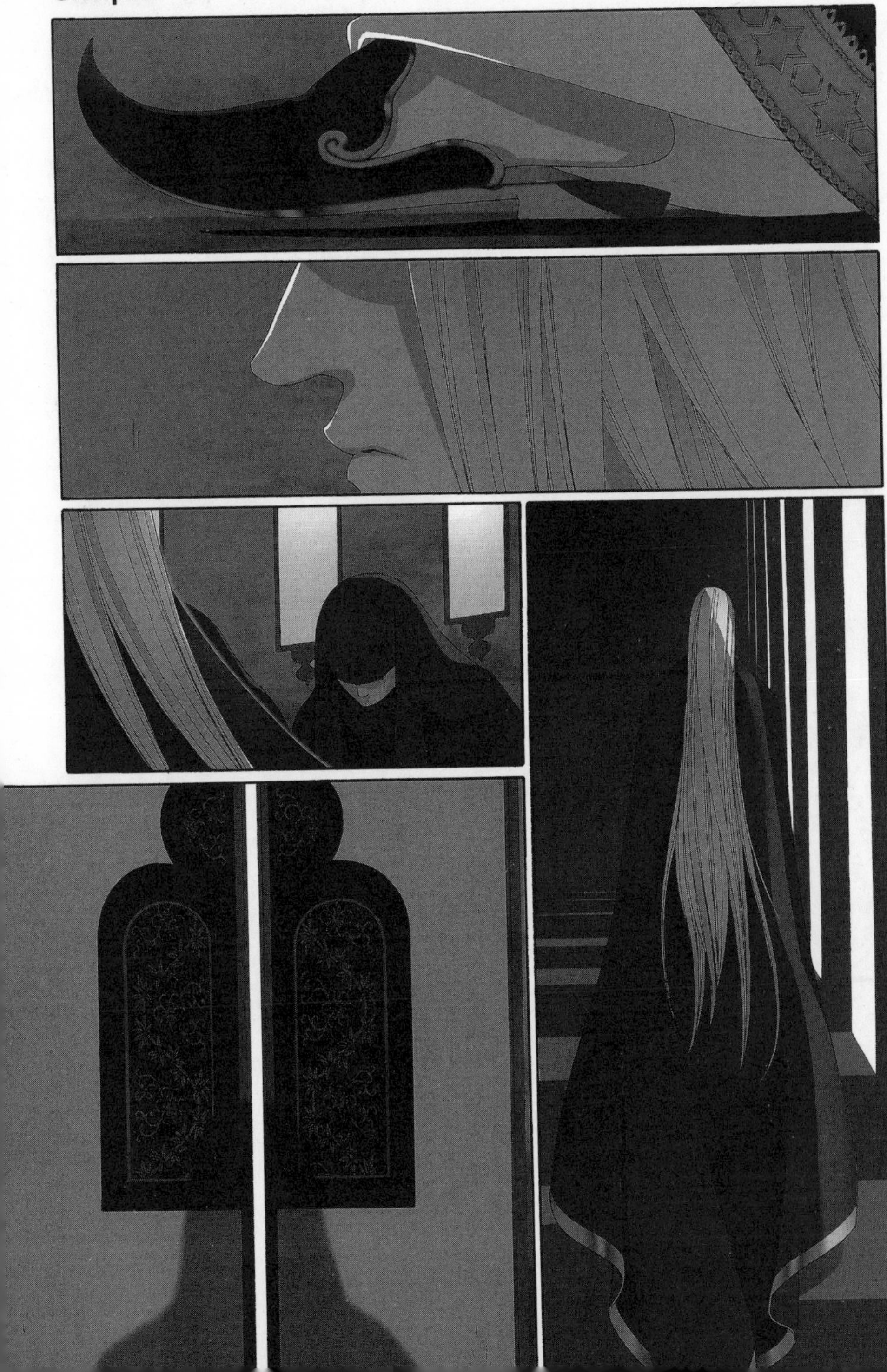

Chapter 5
The King and His Aide
episode 3

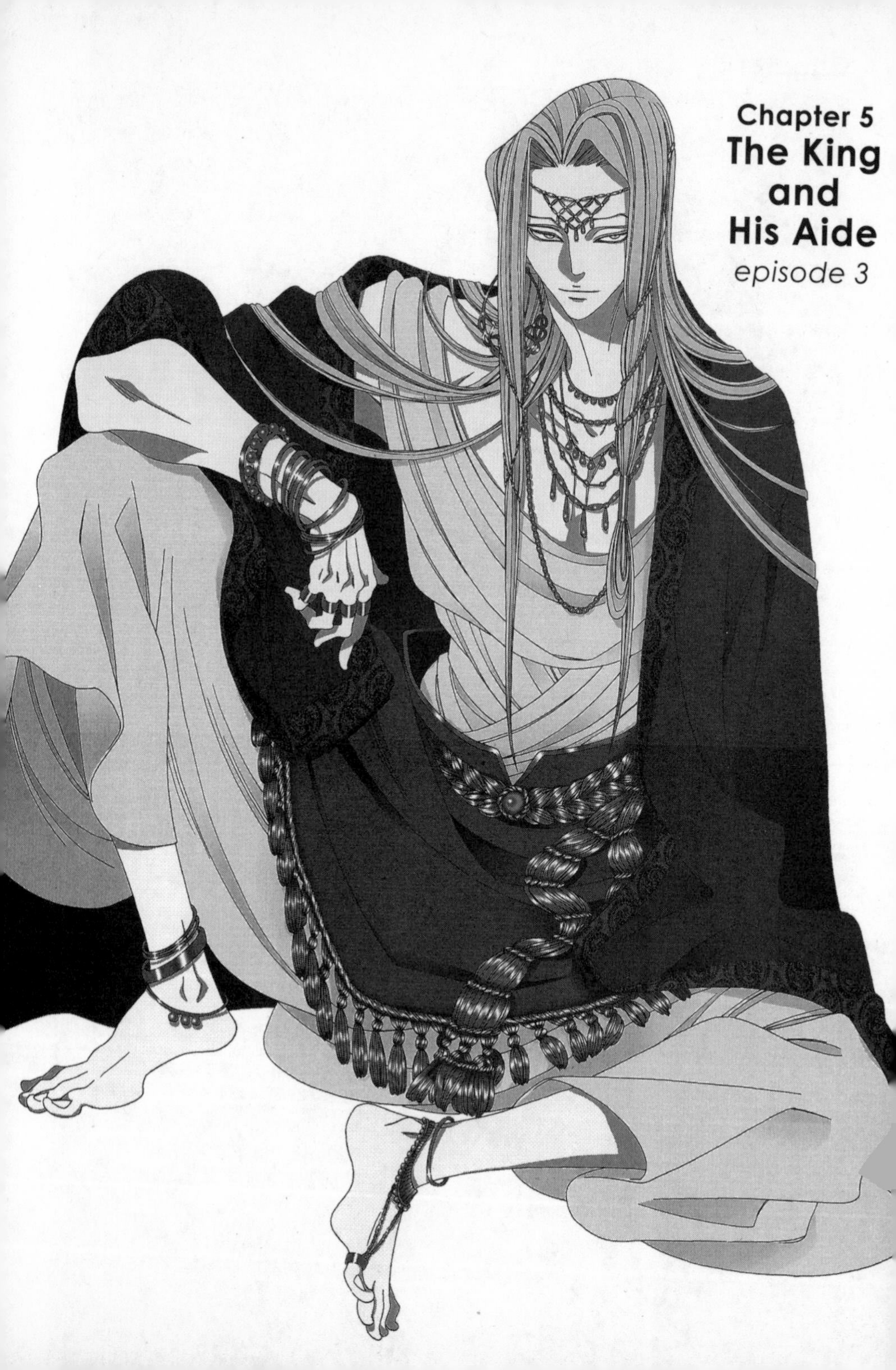

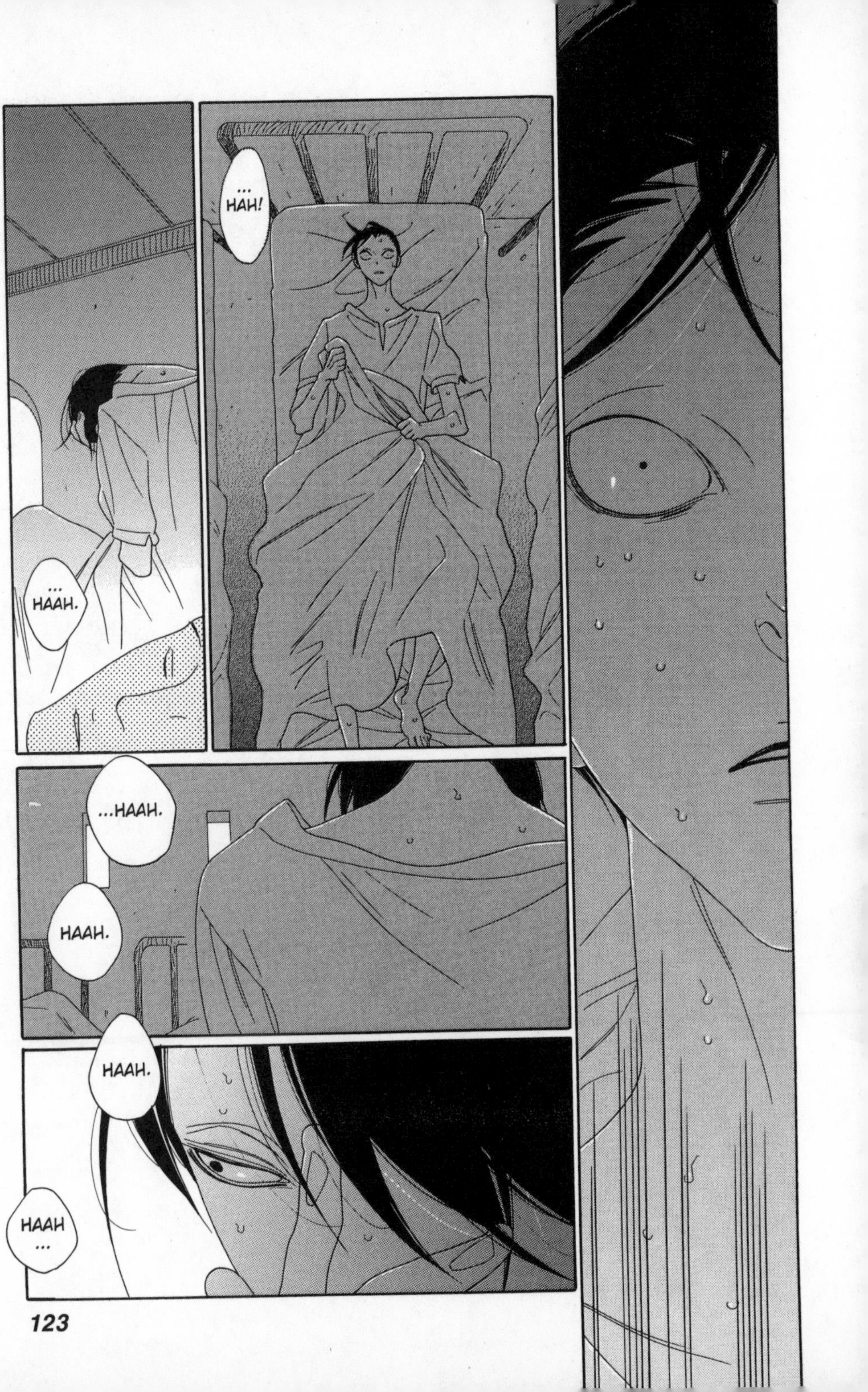
...HAH!
...HAAH.
...HAAH.
HAAH.
HAAH.
HAAH ...

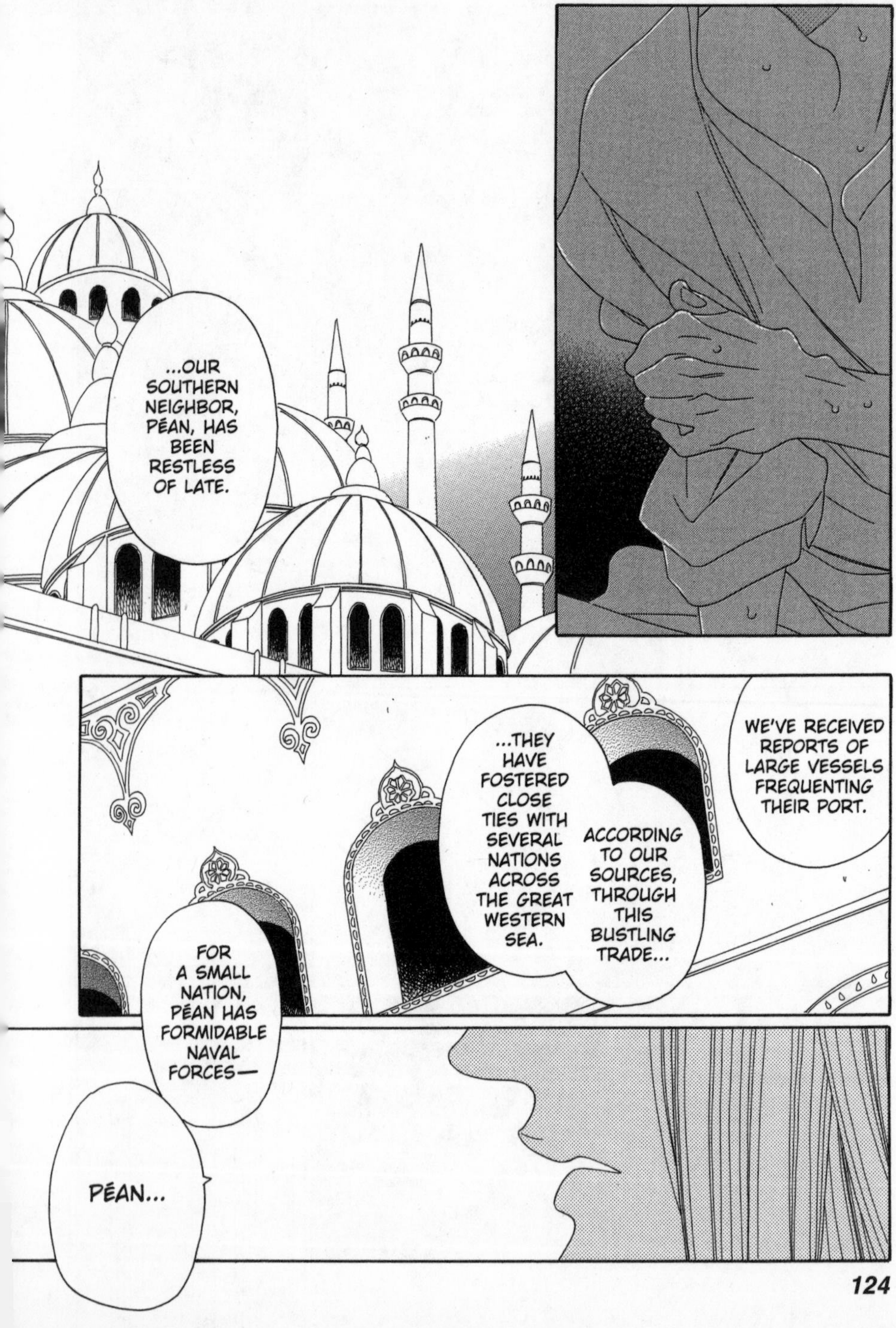
...OUR SOUTHERN NEIGHBOR, PÉAN, HAS BEEN RESTLESS OF LATE.
WE'VE RECEIVED REPORTS OF LARGE VESSELS FREQUENTING THEIR PORT.
ACCORDING TO OUR SOURCES, THROUGH THIS BUSTLING TRADE...
...THEY HAVE FOSTERED CLOSE TIES WITH SEVERAL NATIONS ACROSS THE GREAT WESTERN SEA.
FOR A SMALL NATION, PÉAN HAS FORMIDABLE NAVAL FORCES—
PÉAN...

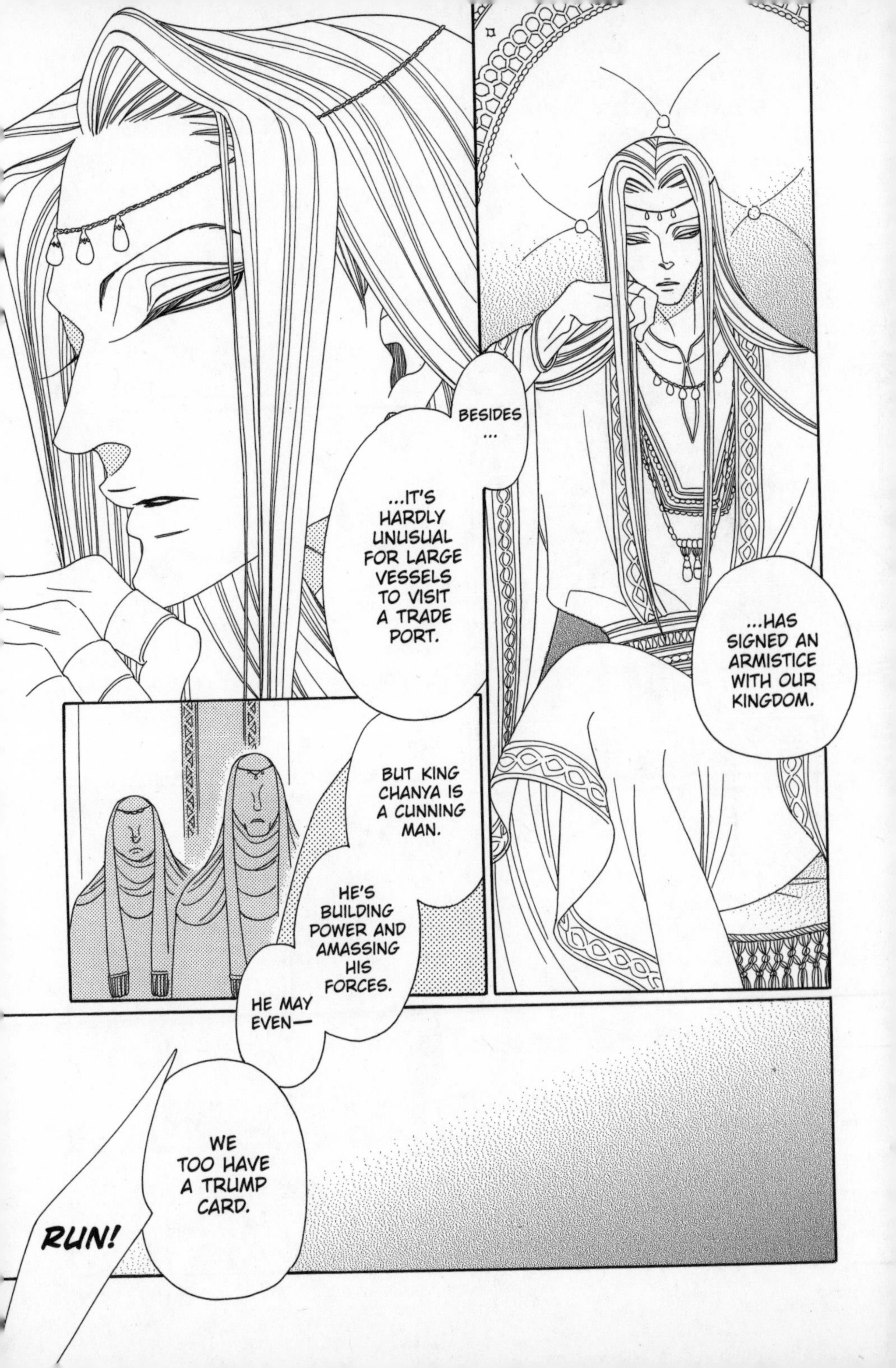
...HAS SIGNED AN ARMISTICE WITH OUR KINGDOM.
BESIDES...
...IT'S HARDLY UNUSUAL FOR LARGE VESSELS TO VISIT A TRADE PORT.
BUT KING CHANYA IS A CUNNING MAN.
HE'S BUILDING POWER AND AMASSING HIS FORCES.
HE MAY EVEN—
WE TOO HAVE A TRUMP CARD.
RUN!

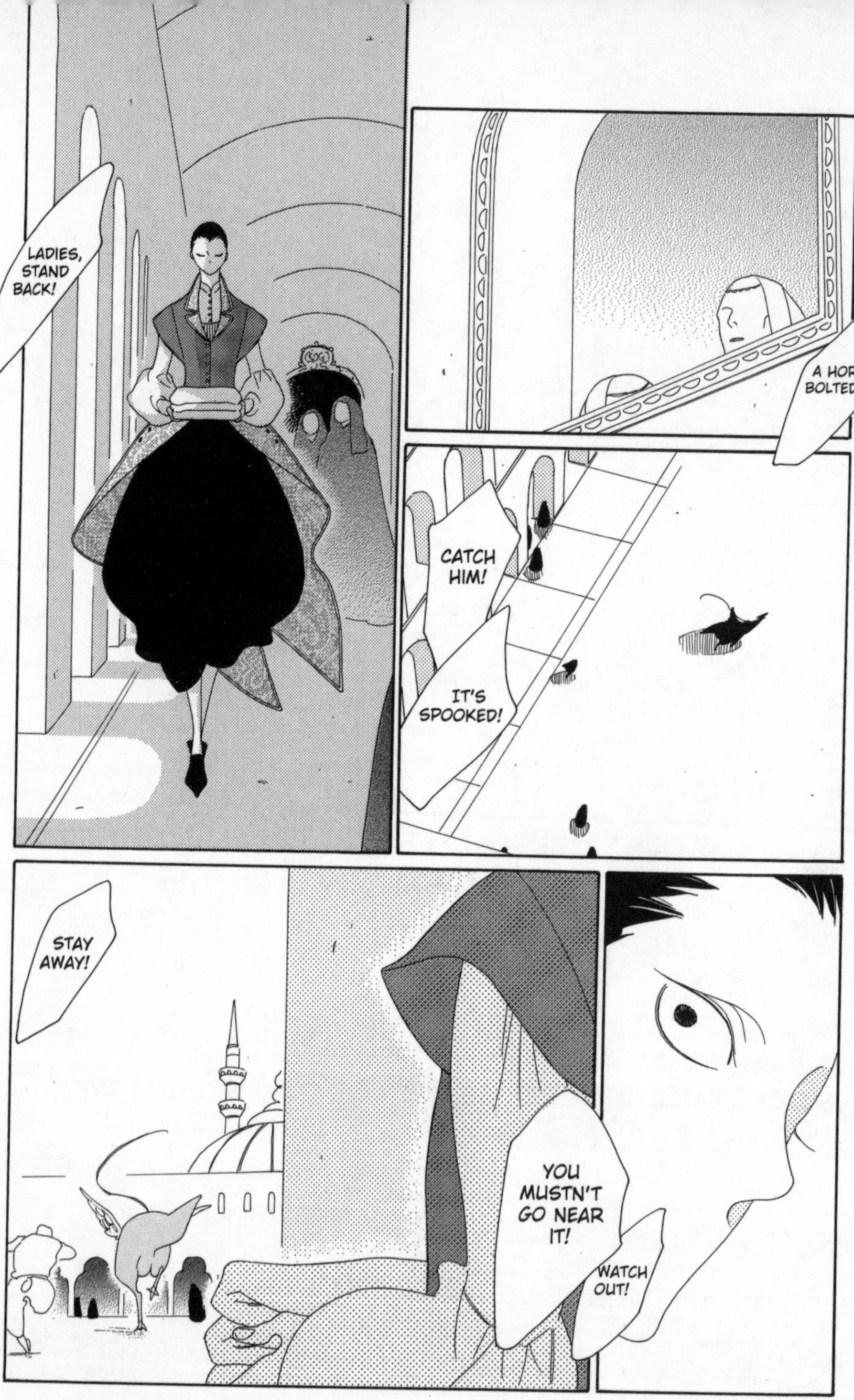
A HORSE BOLTED!
CATCH HIM!
IT'S SPOOKED!
LADIES, STAND BACK!
YOU MUSTN'T GO NEAR IT!
WATCH OUT!
STAY AWAY!

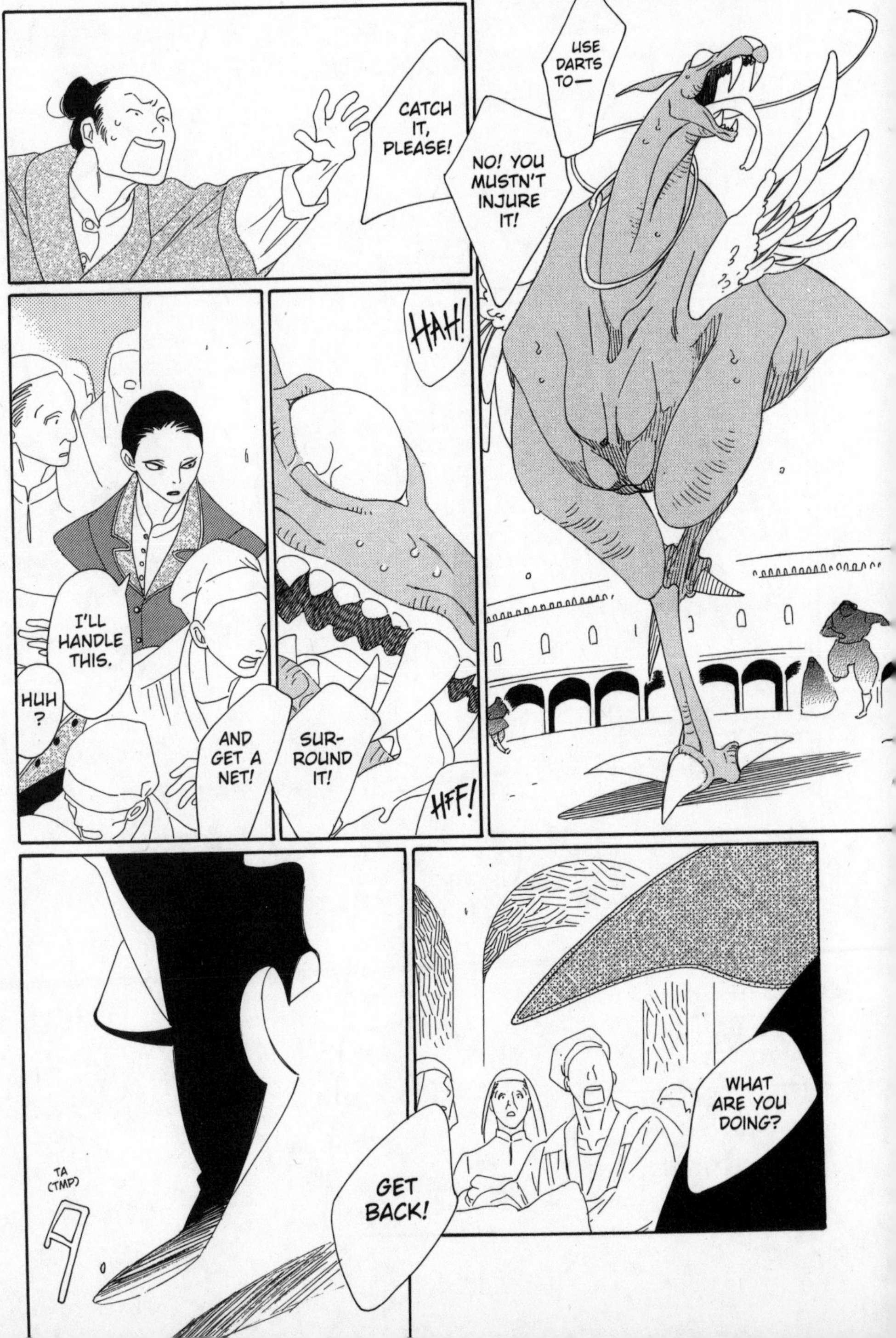
USE DARTS TO—
NO! YOU MUSTN'T INJURE IT!
CATCH IT, PLEASE!
HAH!
SUR-ROUND IT!
HFF!
AND GET A NET!
I'LL HANDLE THIS.
HUH?
WHAT ARE YOU DOING?
GET BACK!
TA (TMP)

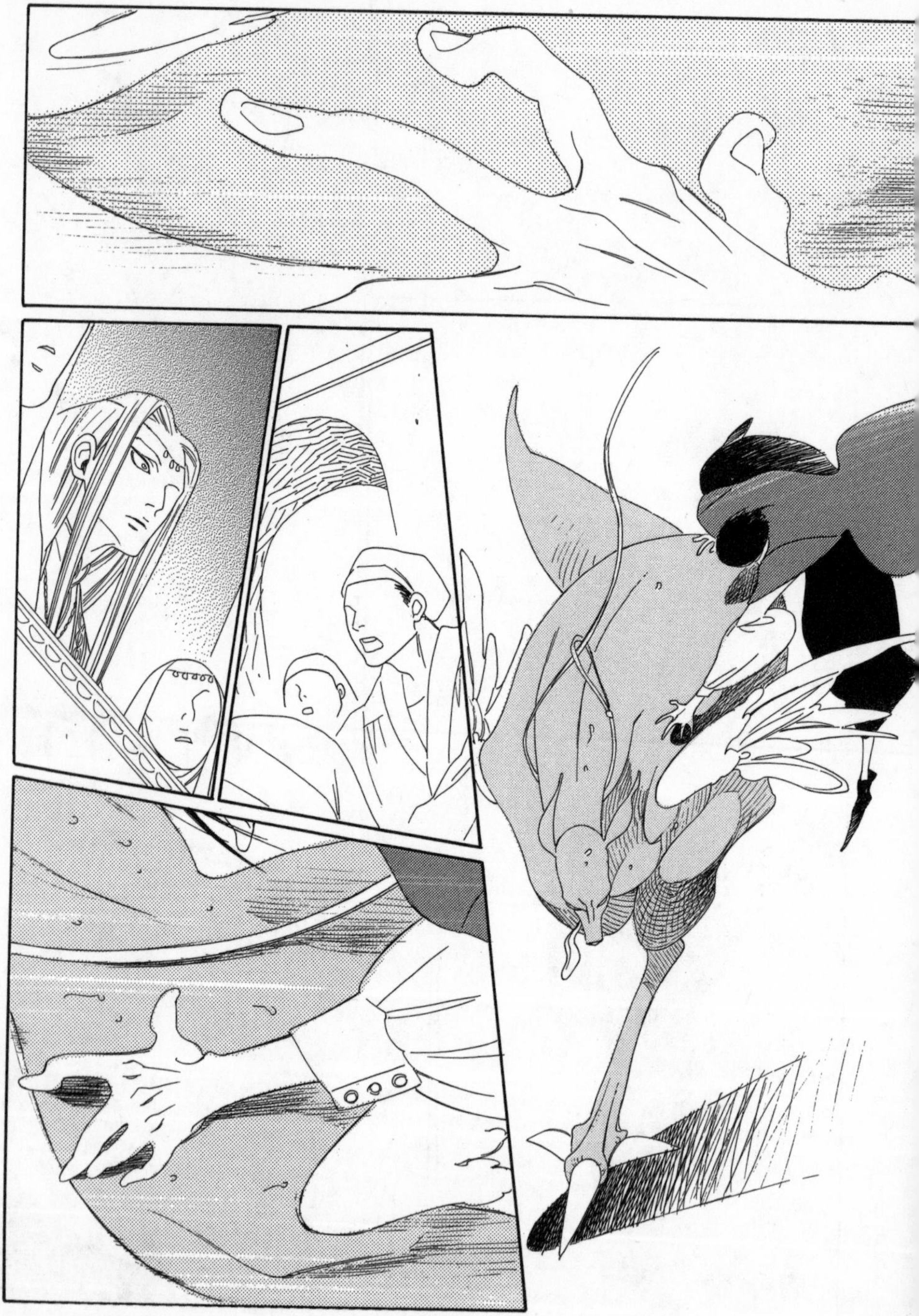

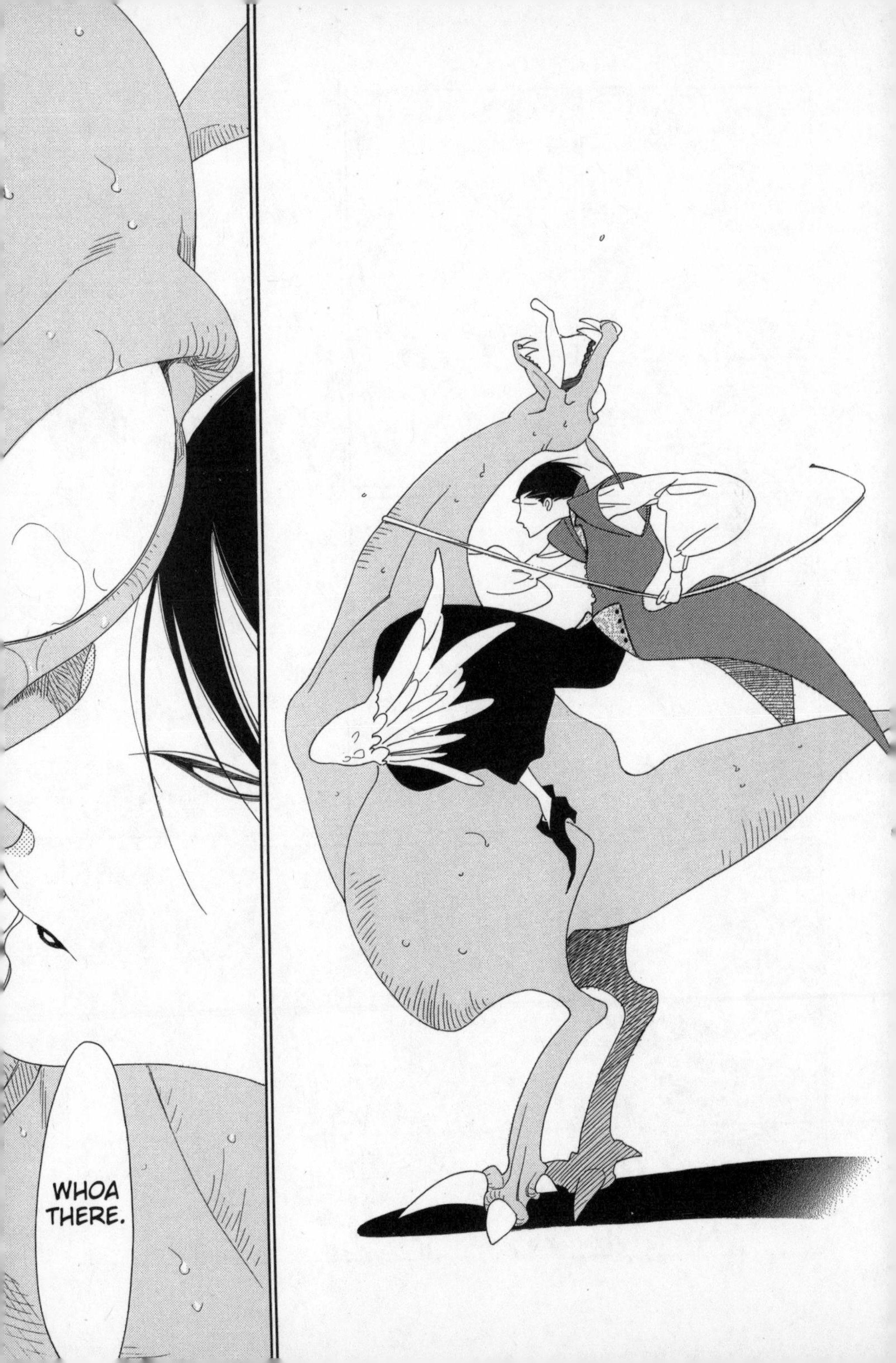
WHOA THERE.

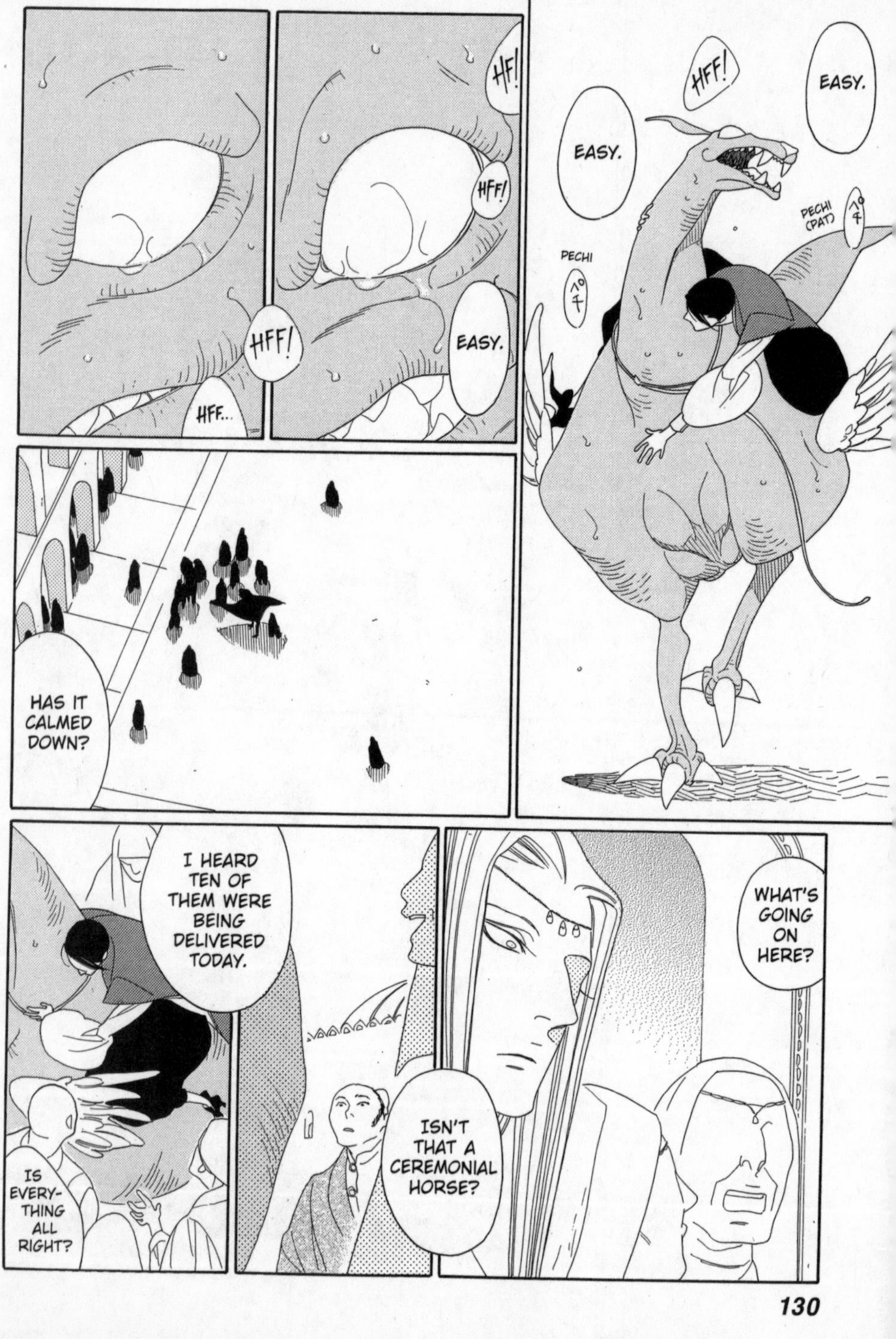
EASY.
HFF!
EASY.
PECHI (PAT)
ペチ
PECHI
ペチ
HF!
HFF!
EASY.
HFF!
HFF...
HAS IT CALMED DOWN?
WHAT'S GOING ON HERE?
ISN'T THAT A CEREMONIAL HORSE?
I HEARD TEN OF THEM WERE BEING DELIVERED TODAY.
IS EVERYTHING ALL RIGHT?

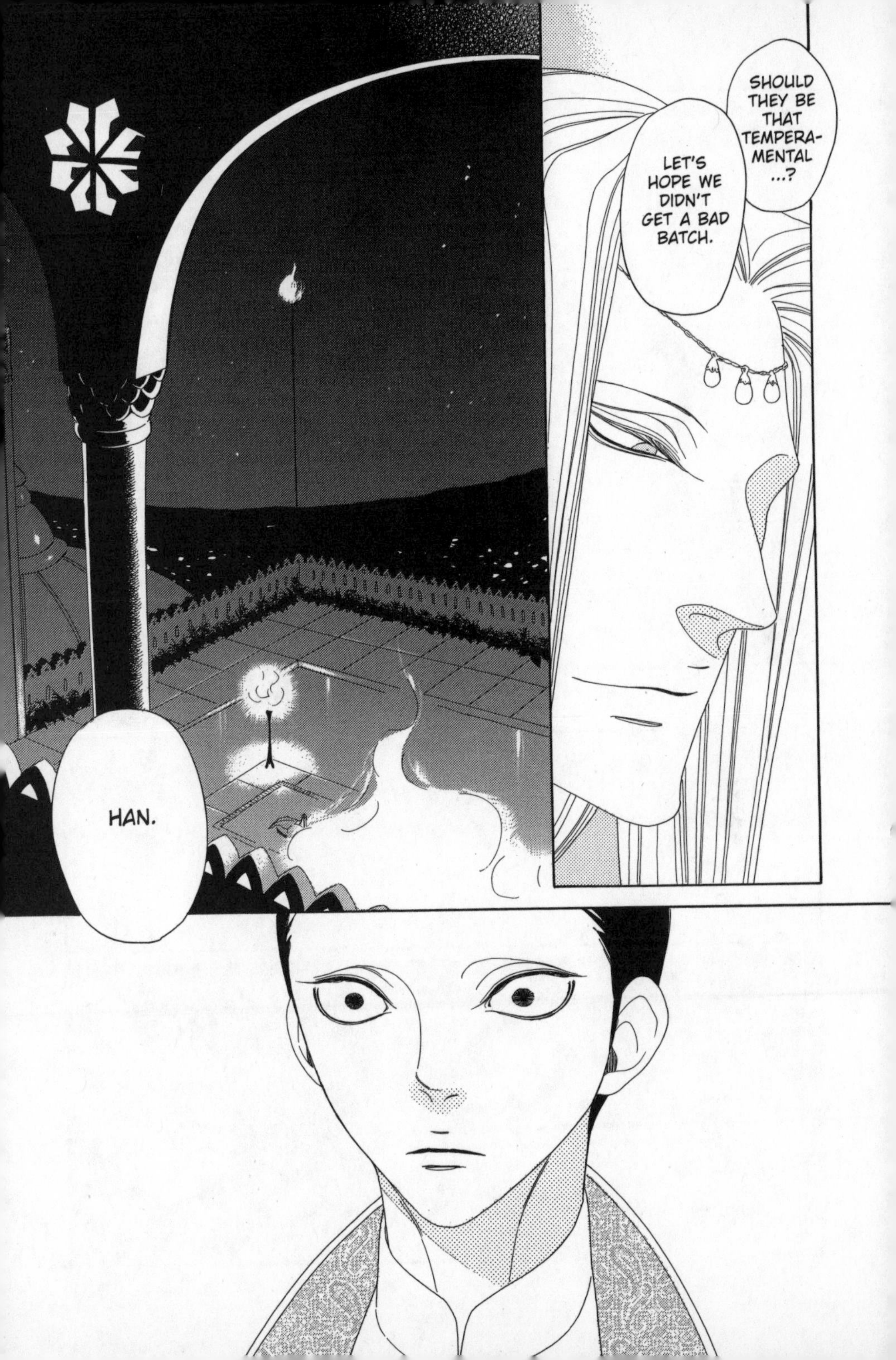
SHOULD THEY BE THAT TEMPERA-MENTAL ...?
LET'S HOPE WE DIDN'T GET A BAD BATCH.
HAN.

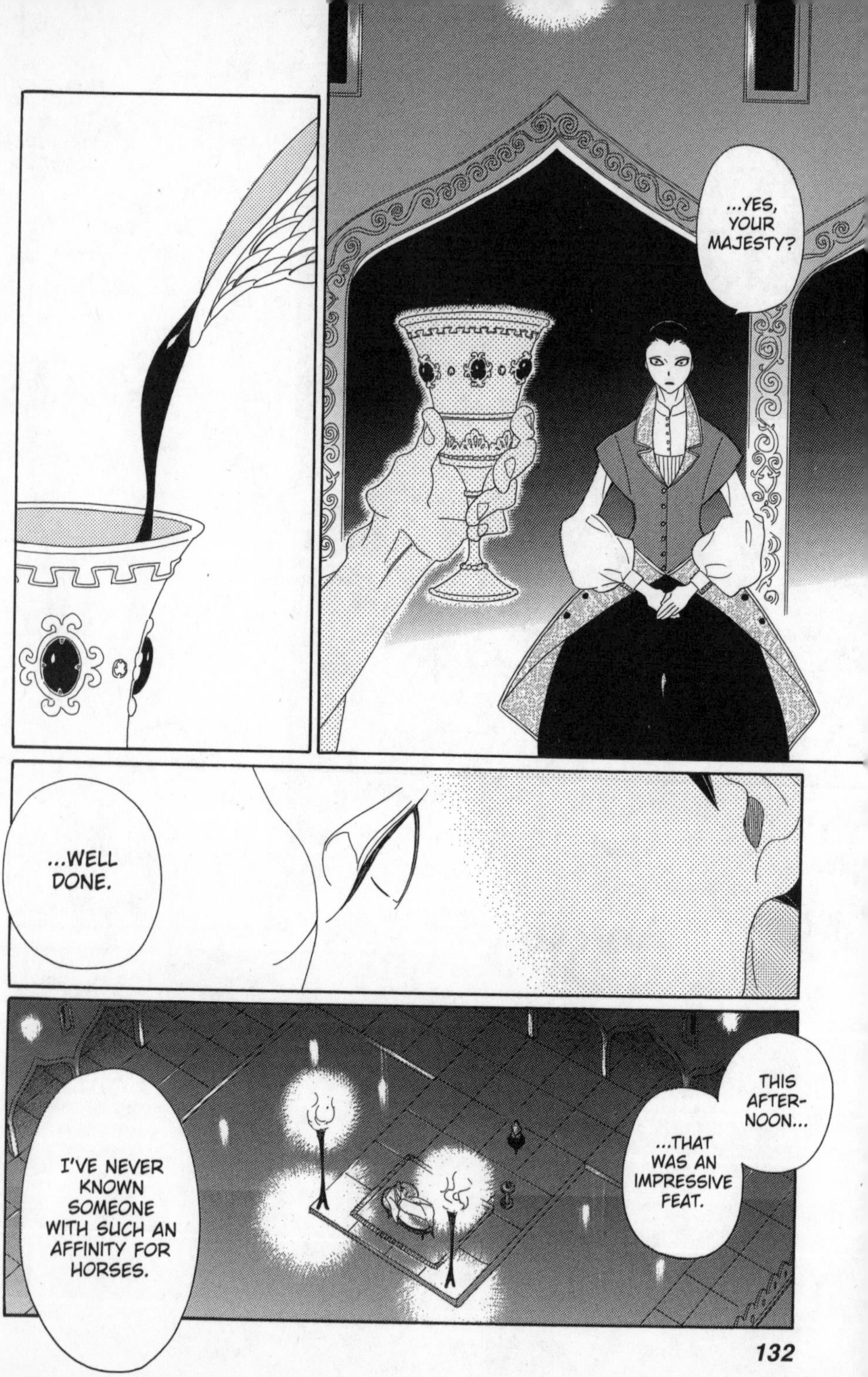
...YES, YOUR MAJESTY?
...WELL DONE.
THIS AFTER-NOON...
...THAT WAS AN IMPRESSIVE FEAT.
I'VE NEVER KNOWN SOMEONE WITH SUCH AN AFFINITY FOR HORSES.

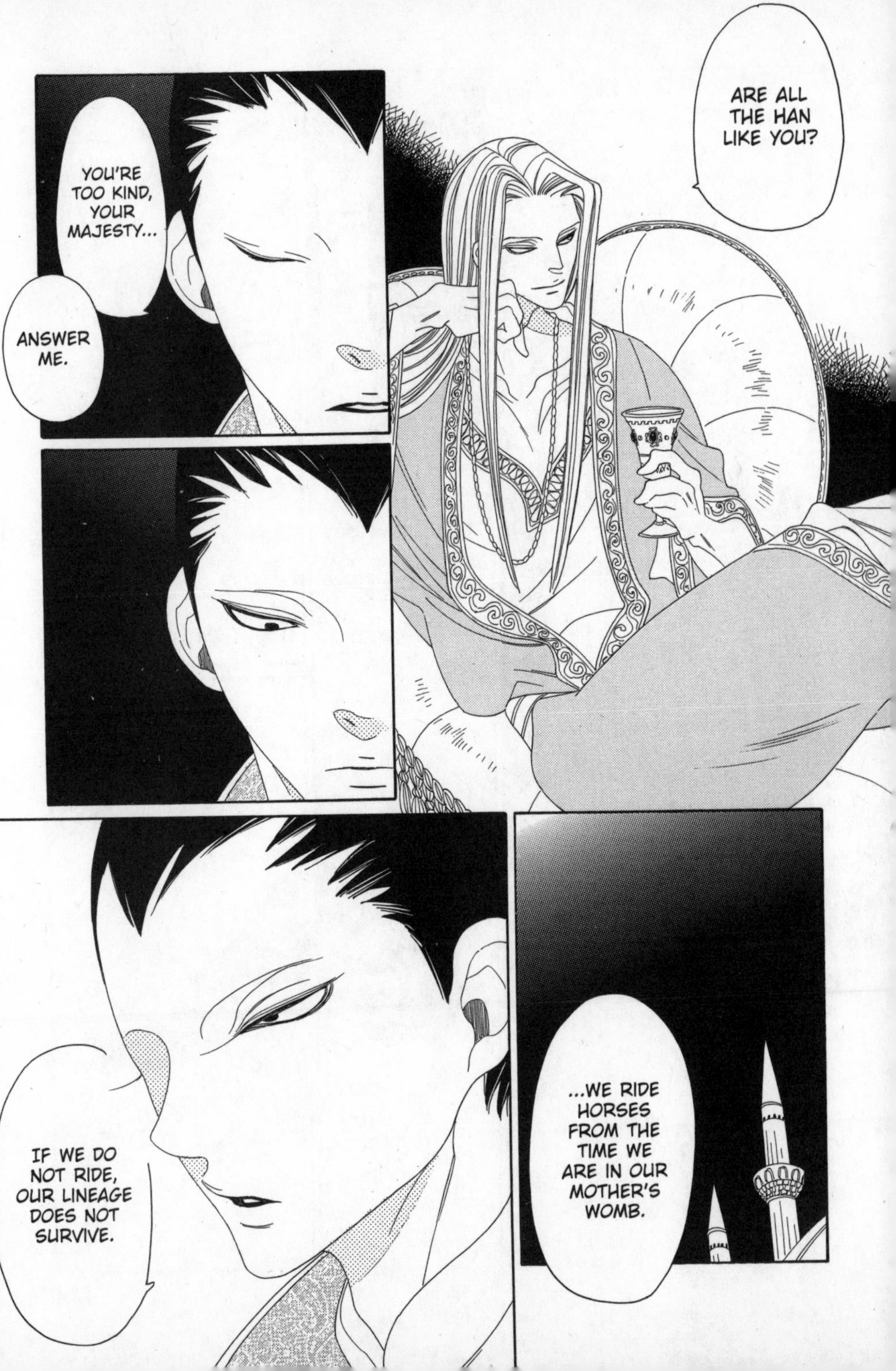
ARE ALL THE HAN LIKE YOU?
YOU'RE TOO KIND, YOUR MAJESTY...
ANSWER ME.
...WE RIDE HORSES FROM THE TIME WE ARE IN OUR MOTHER'S WOMB.
IF WE DO NOT RIDE, OUR LINEAGE DOES NOT SURVIVE.

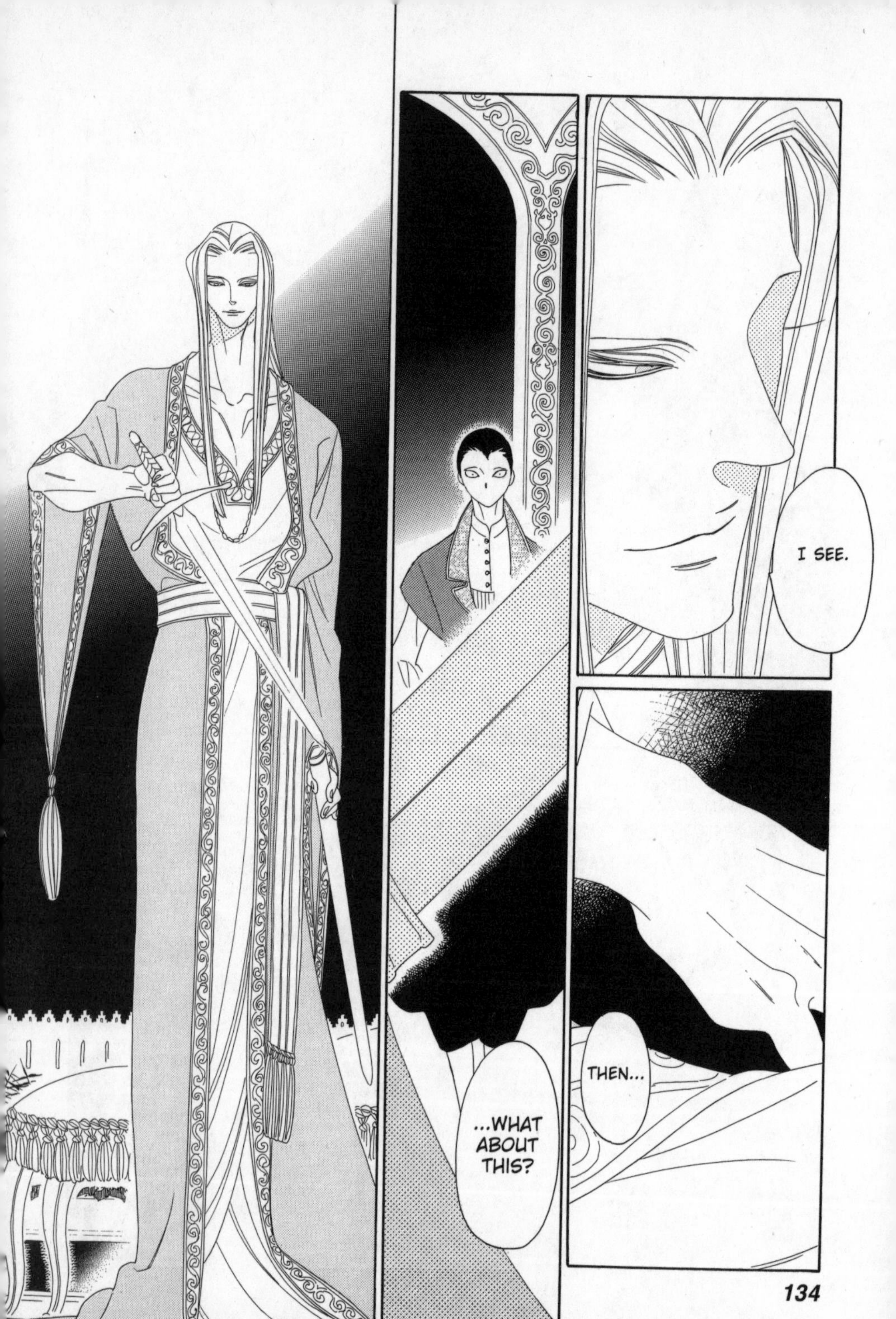
I SEE.
THEN...
...WHAT ABOUT THIS?

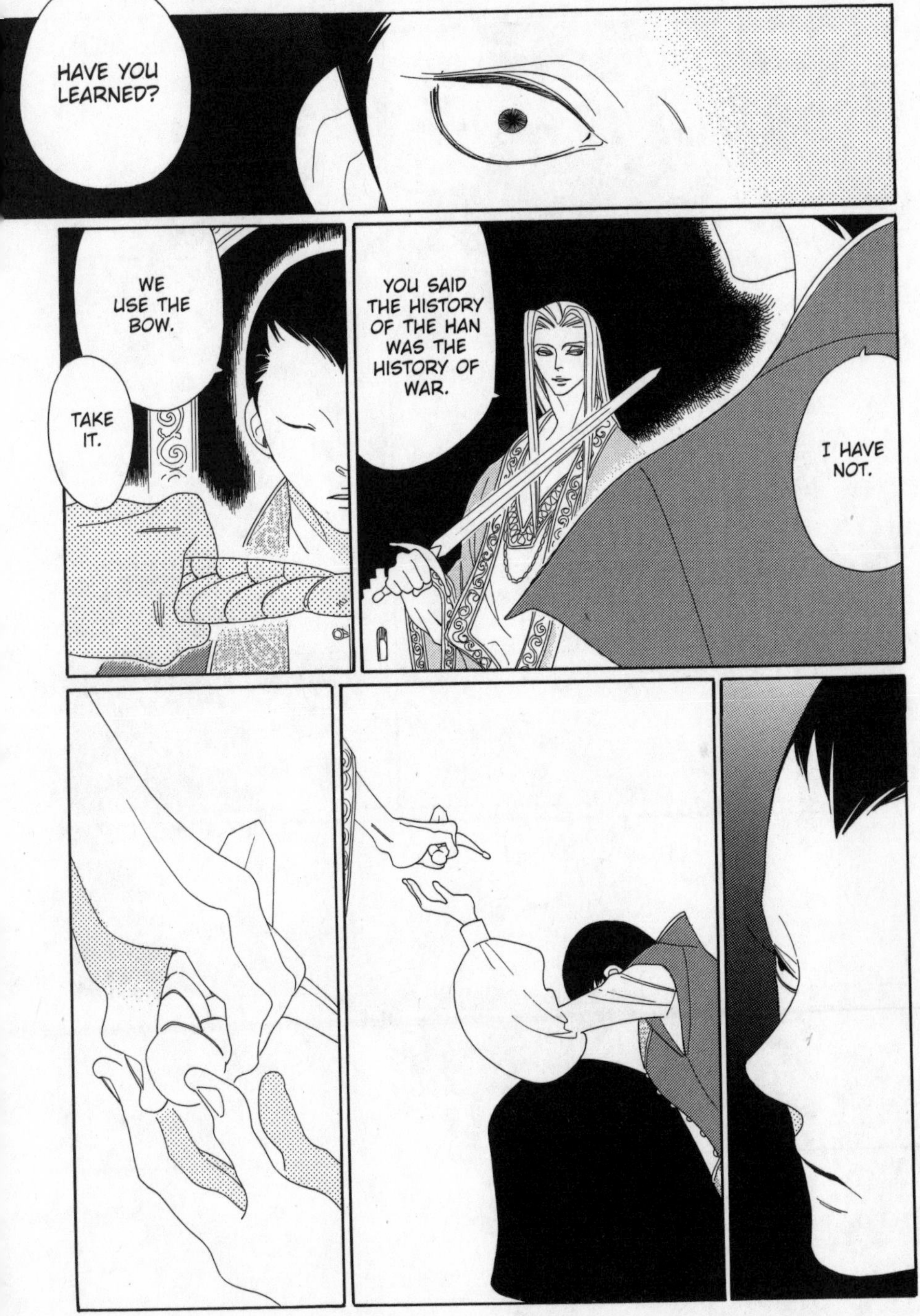
HAVE YOU LEARNED?
I HAVE NOT.
YOU SAID THE HISTORY OF THE HAN WAS THE HISTORY OF WAR.
WE USE THE BOW.
TAKE IT.

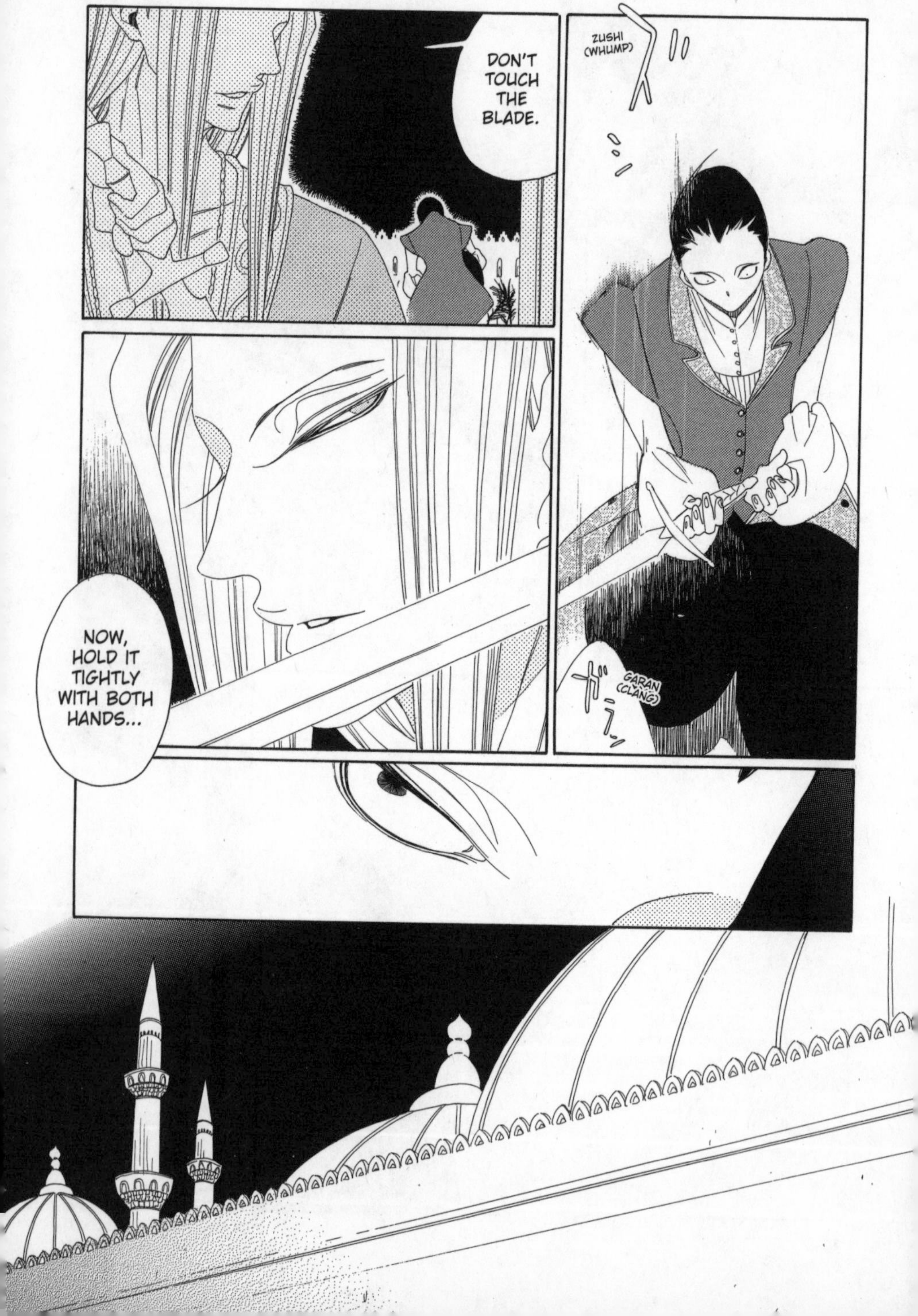
ZUSHI (WHUMP)
GARAN (CLANG)
DON'T TOUCH THE BLADE.
NOW, HOLD IT TIGHTLY WITH BOTH HANDS...

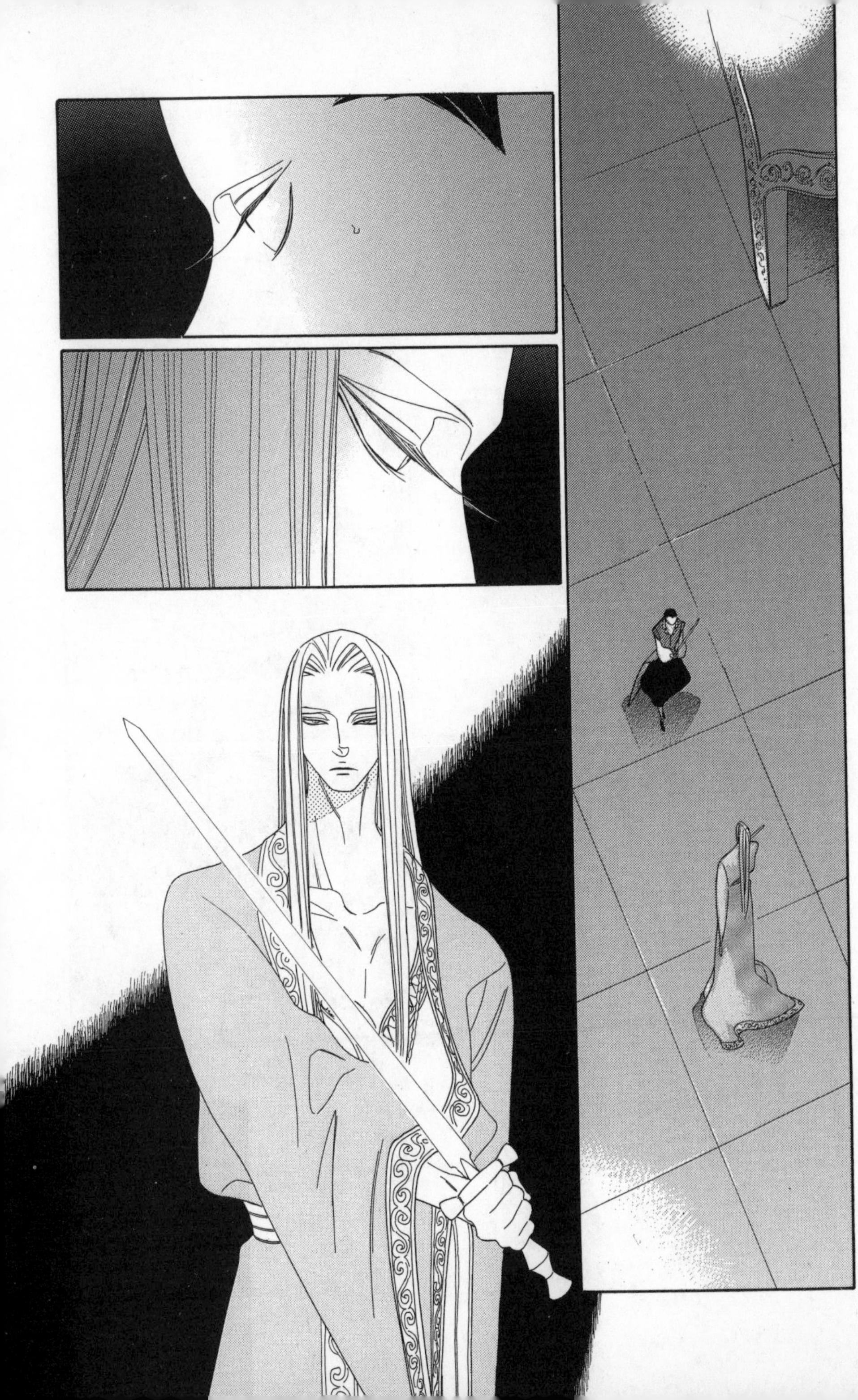

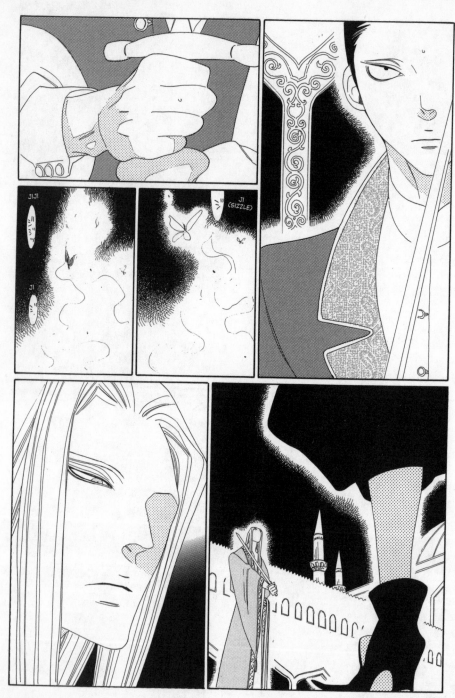

JIJI

JI
(SIZZLE)

JI

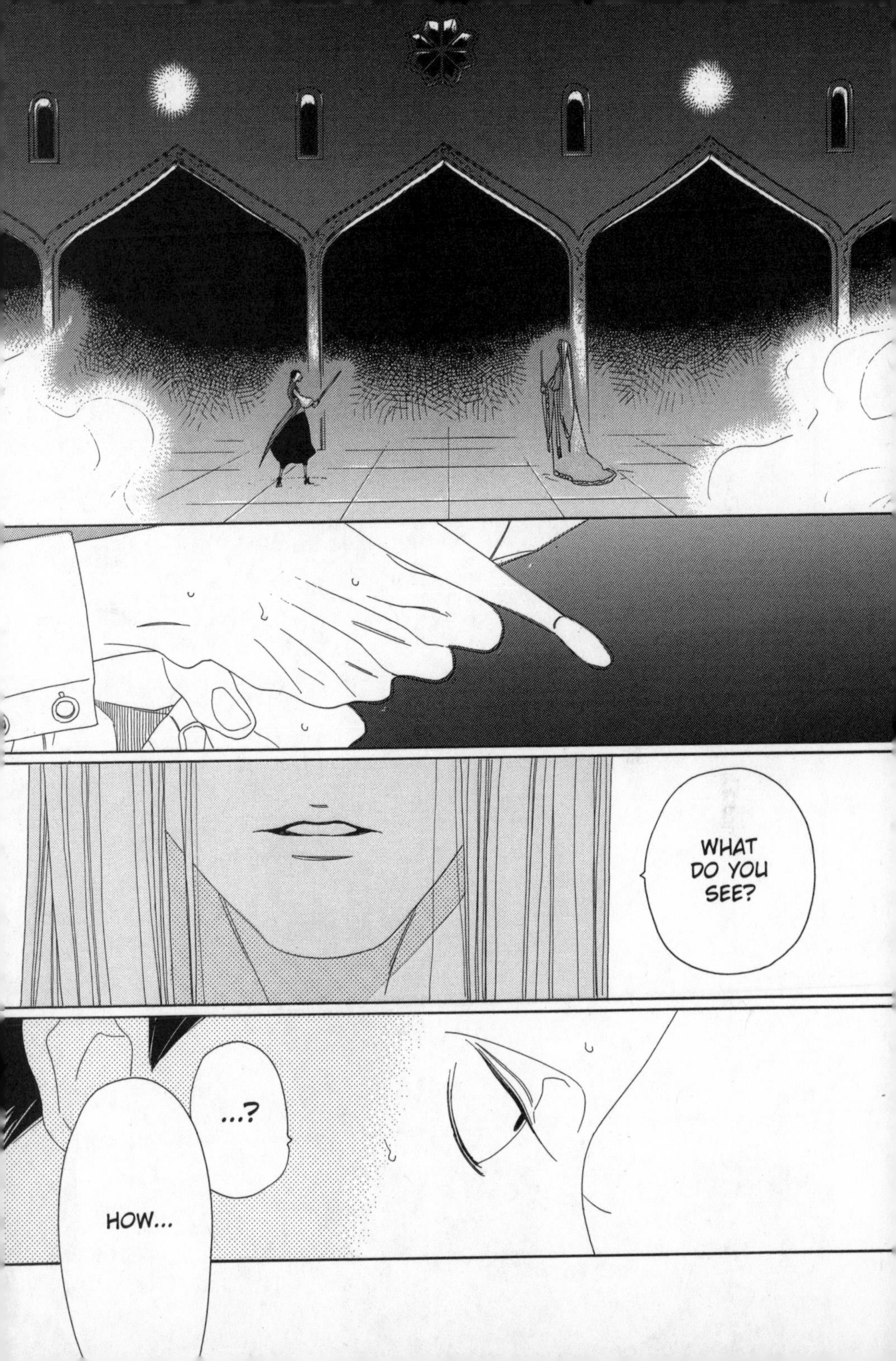
WHAT DO YOU SEE?
...?
HOW...

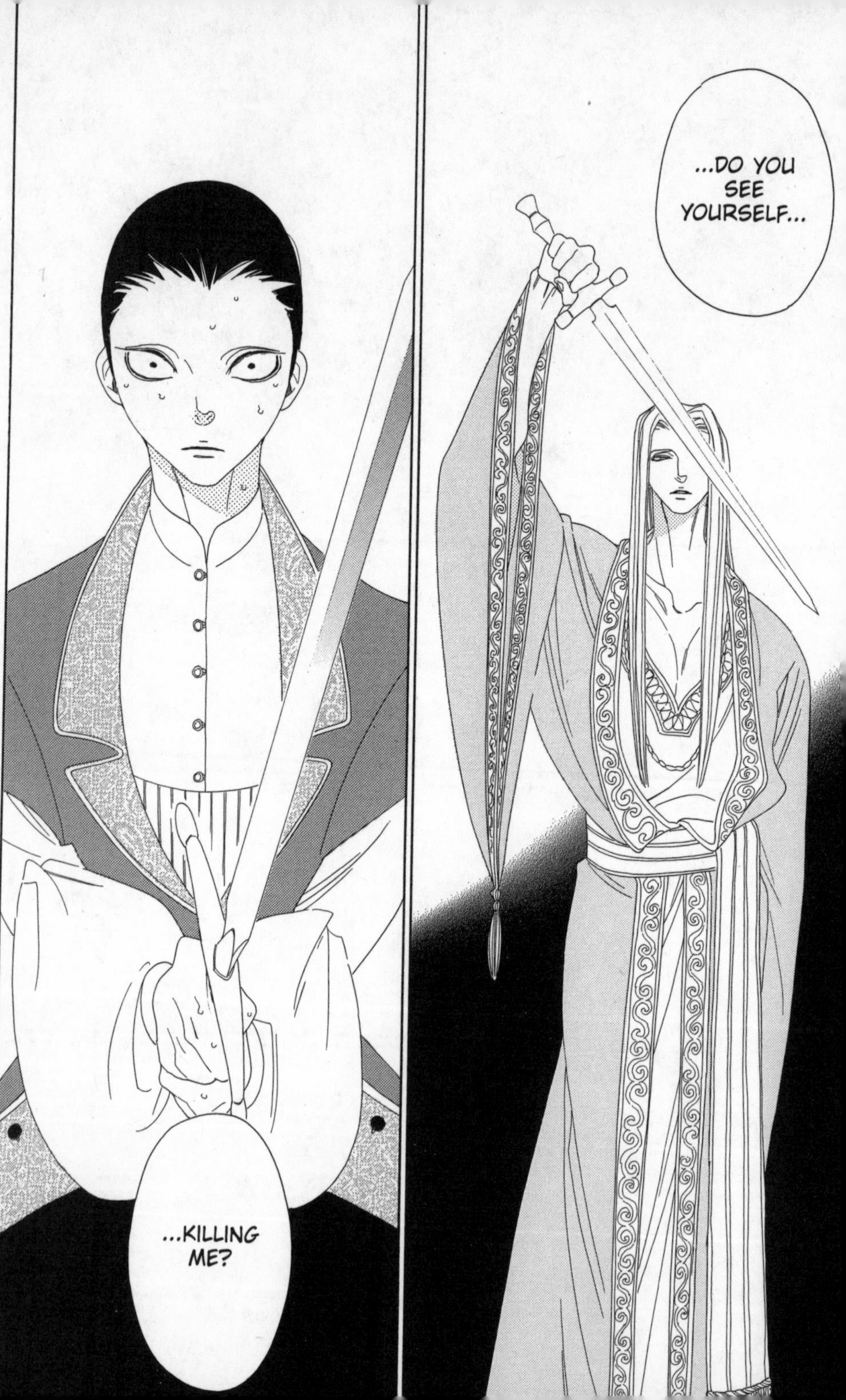
...DO YOU SEE YOURSELF...
...KILLING ME?

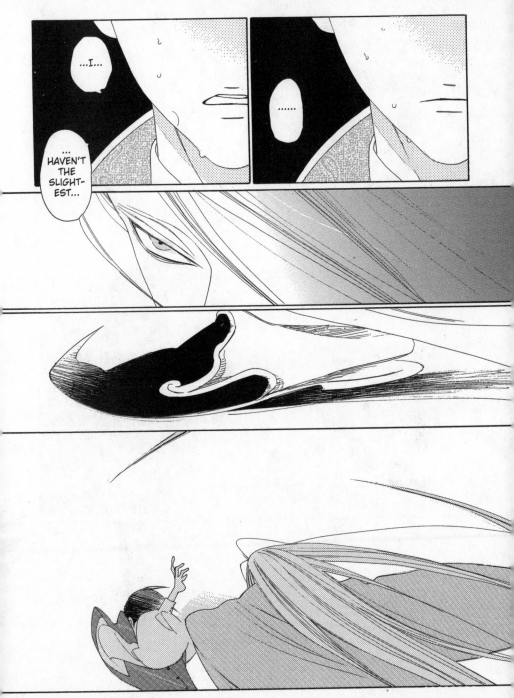

...I...

... HAVEN'T THE SLIGHT- EST...

......

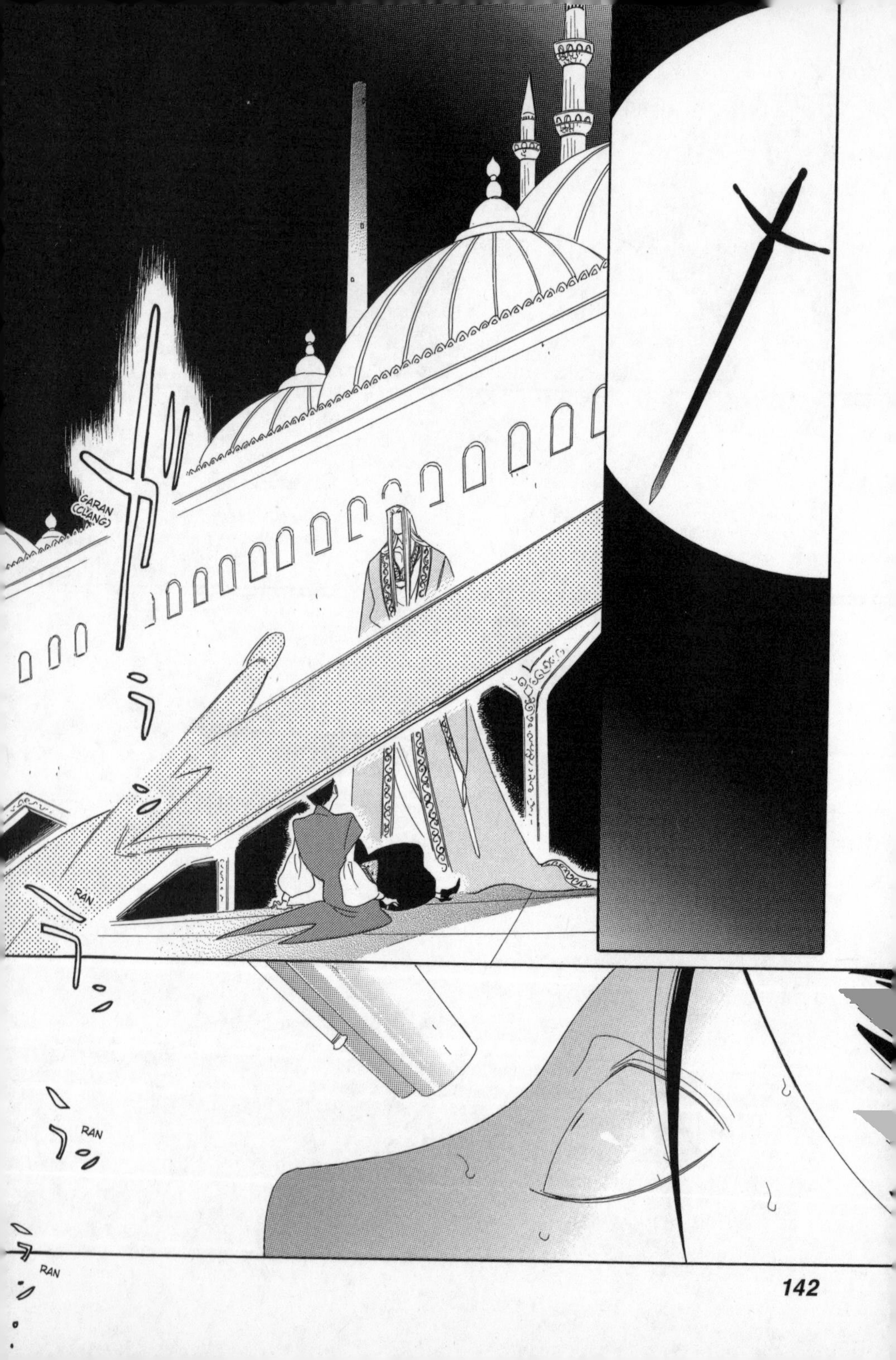
GARAN (CLANG)
RAN
RAN
RAN

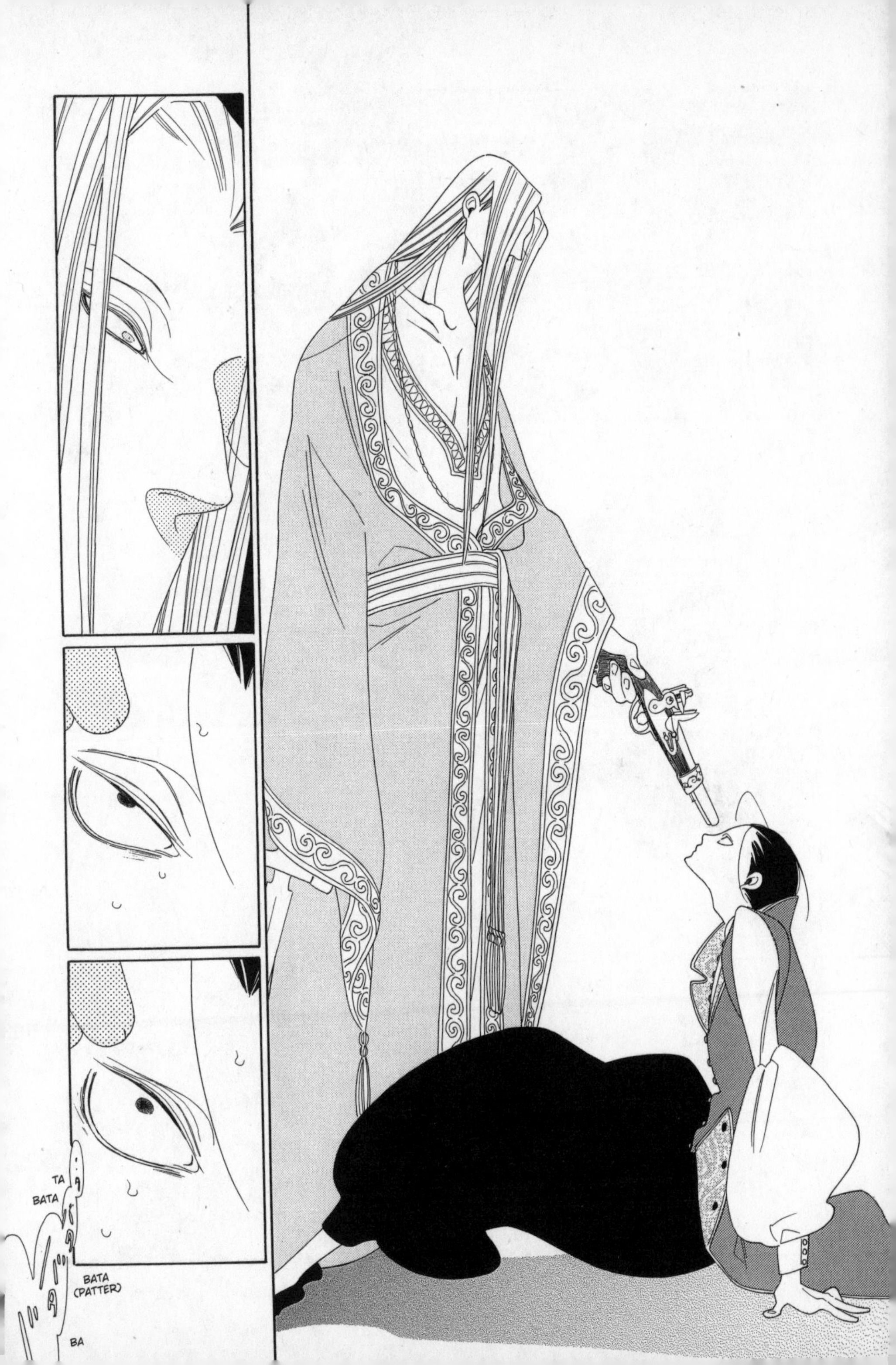
TA
BATA
BATA (PATTER)
BA

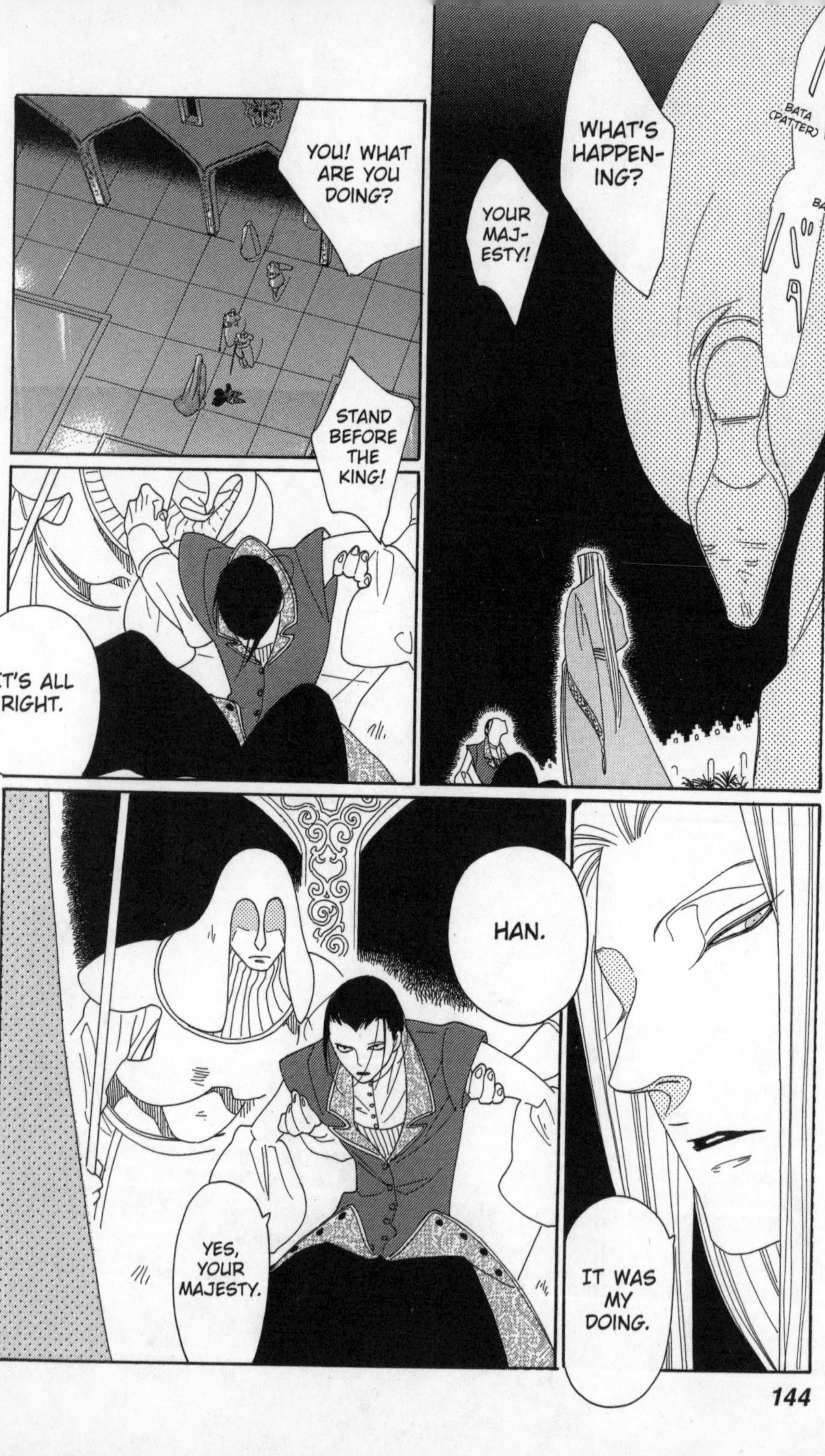
BATA (PATTER)
BATA
WHAT'S HAPPEN-ING?
YOUR MAJ-ESTY!
YOU! WHAT ARE YOU DOING?
STAND BEFORE THE KING!
IT'S ALL RIGHT.
IT WAS MY DOING.
HAN.
YES, YOUR MAJESTY.

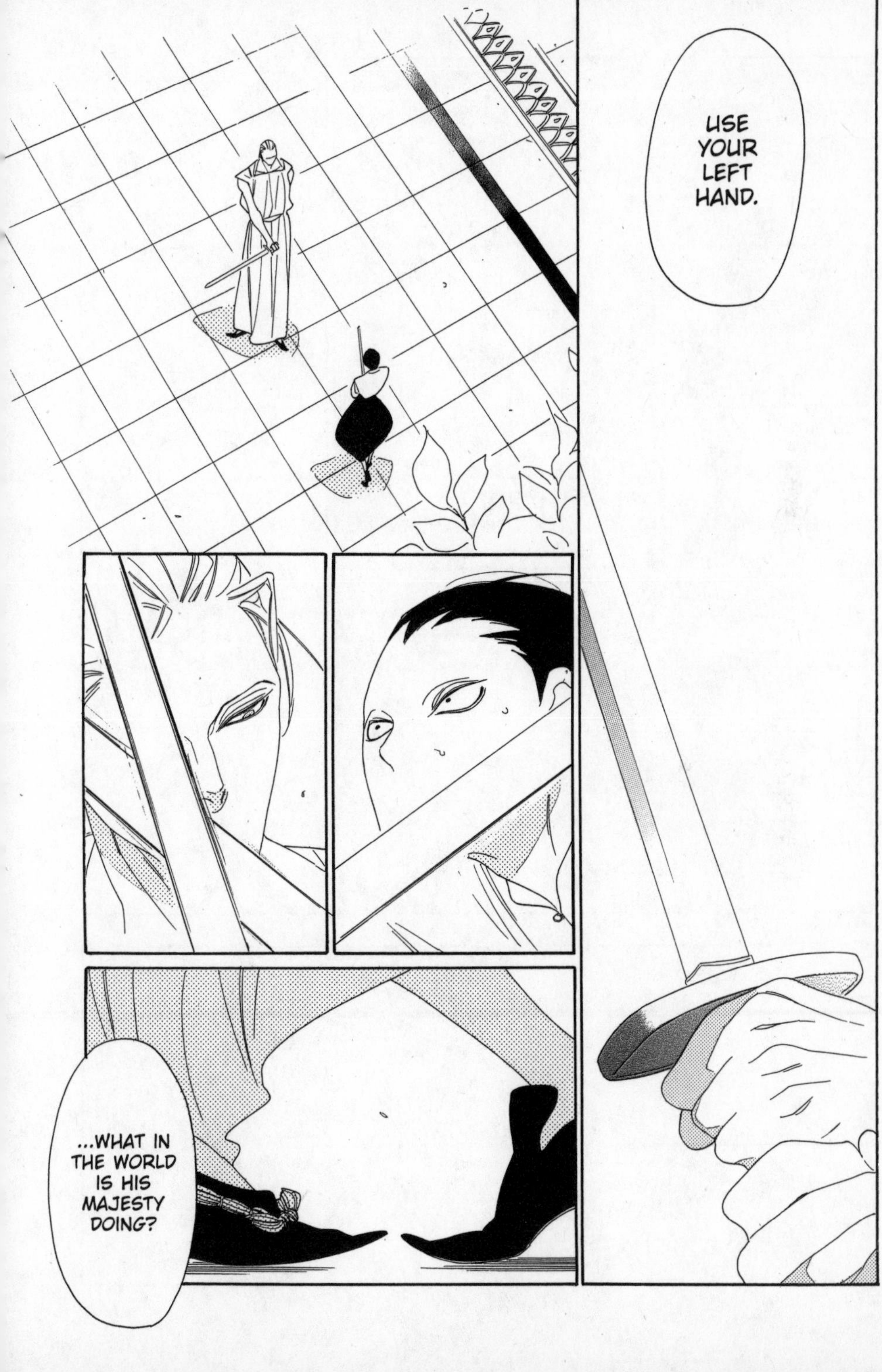
USE YOUR LEFT HAND.
...WHAT IN THE WORLD IS HIS MAJESTY DOING?

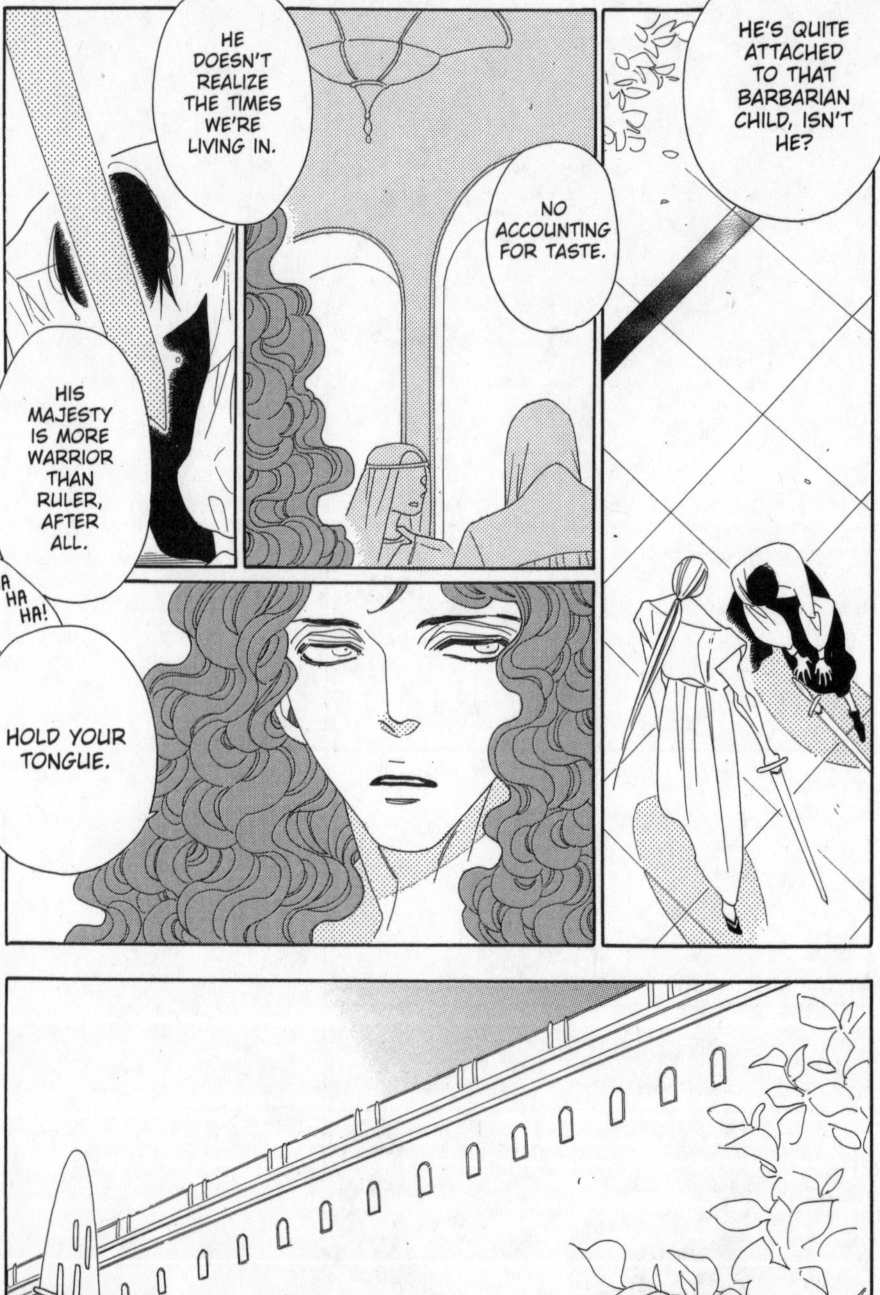
HE'S QUITE ATTACHED TO THAT BARBARIAN CHILD, ISN'T HE?
NO ACCOUNTING FOR TASTE.
HE DOESN'T REALIZE THE TIMES WE'RE LIVING IN.
HIS MAJESTY IS MORE WARRIOR THAN RULER, AFTER ALL.
HA HA HA!
HOLD YOUR TONGUE.
ZA (SPLSHHH)

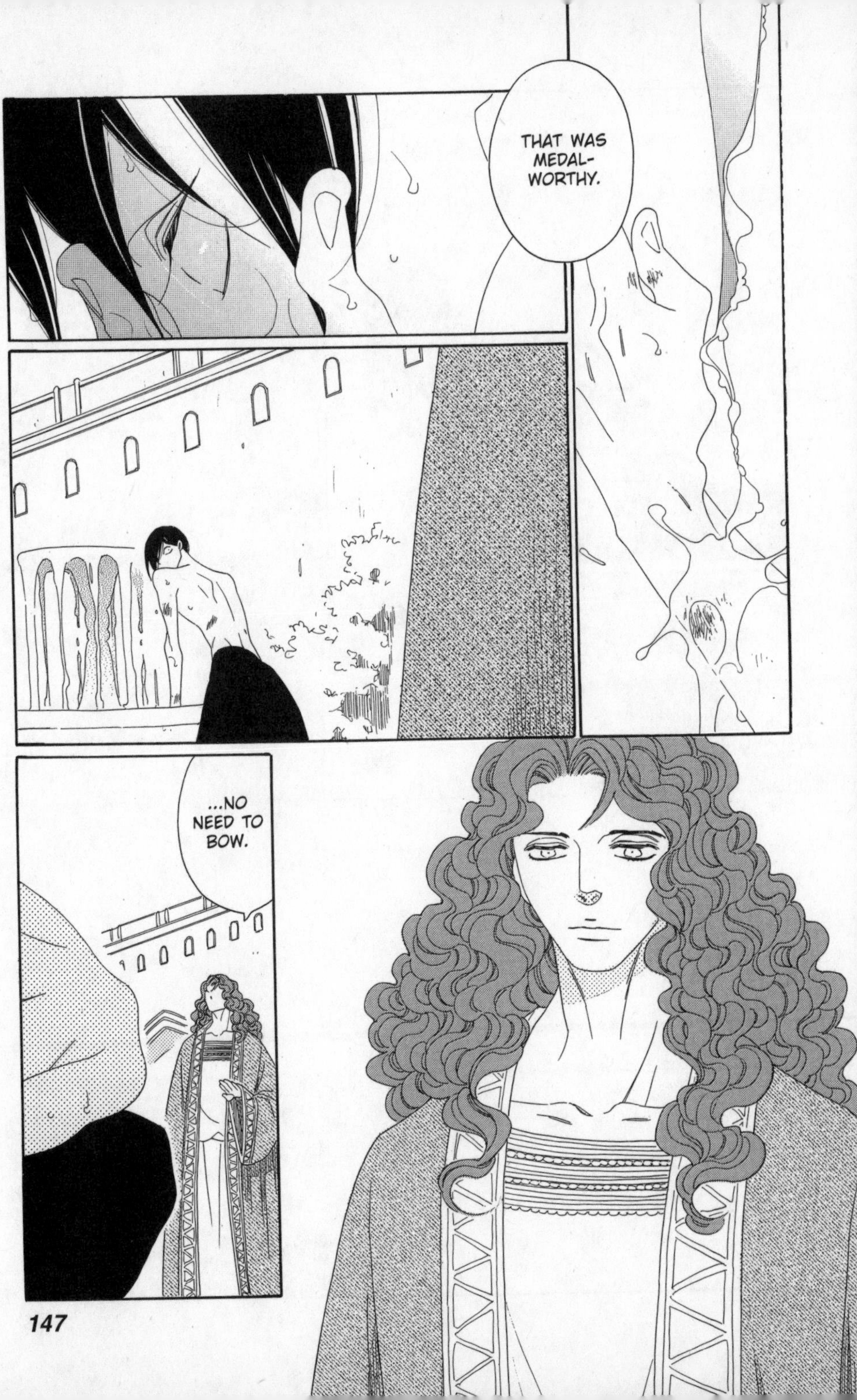
THAT WAS MEDAL-WORTHY.
...NO NEED TO BOW.

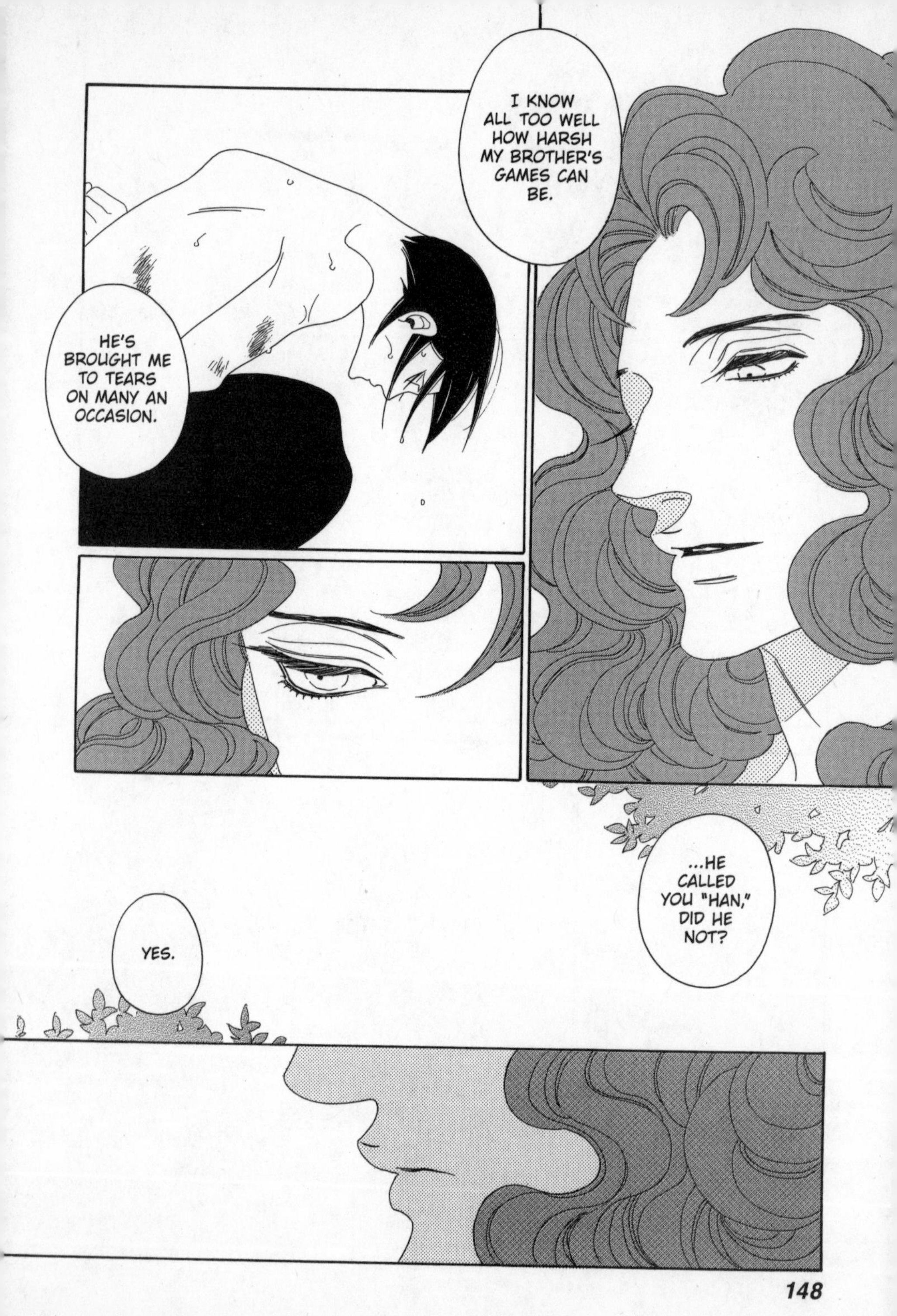
I KNOW ALL TOO WELL HOW HARSH MY BROTHER'S GAMES CAN BE.
HE'S BROUGHT ME TO TEARS ON MANY AN OCCASION.
...HE CALLED YOU "HAN," DID HE NOT?
YES.

TAKE CARE
OF MY
BROTHER
FOR ME.

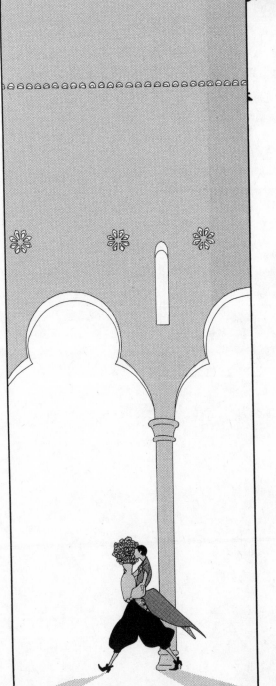

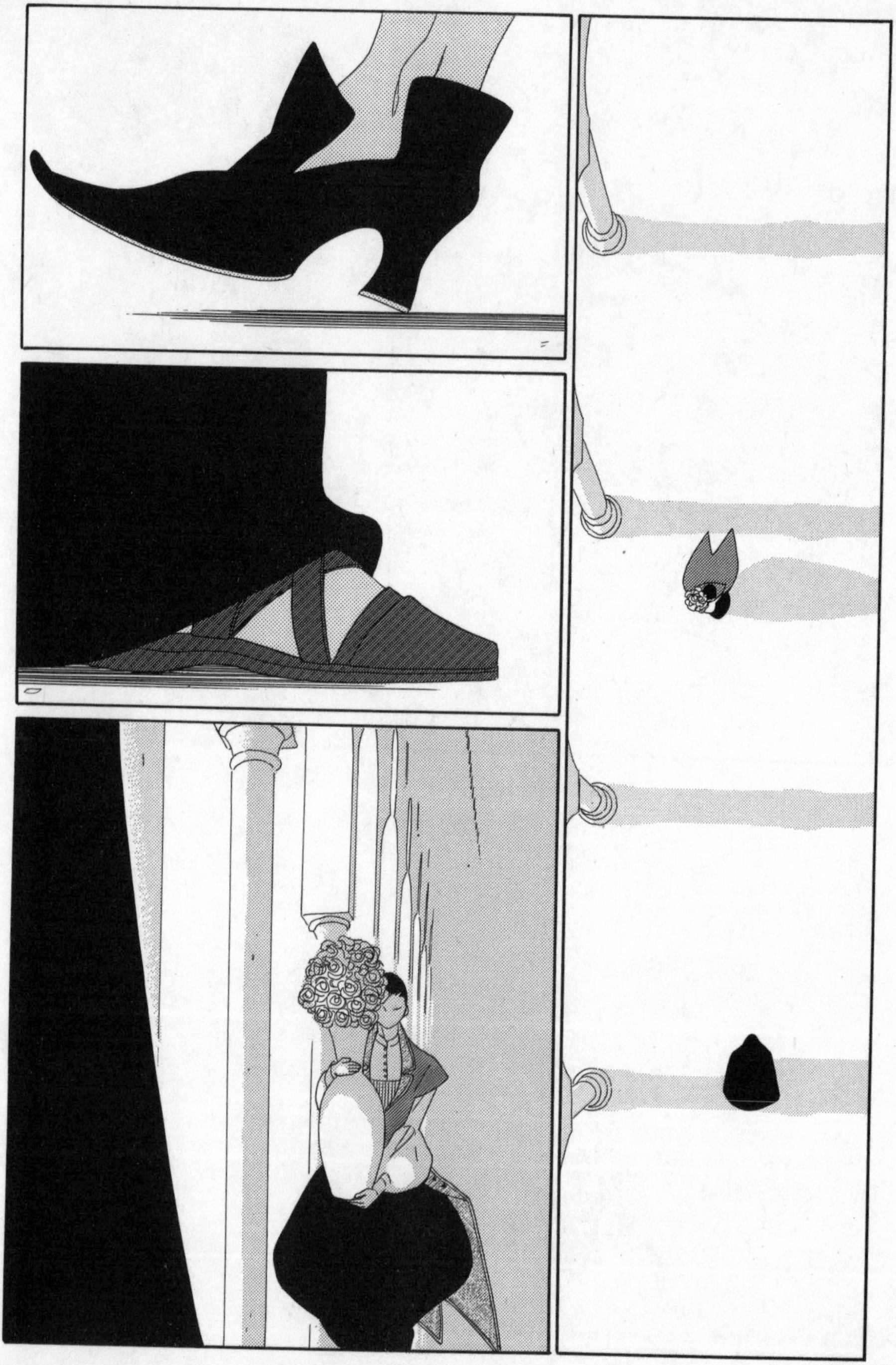

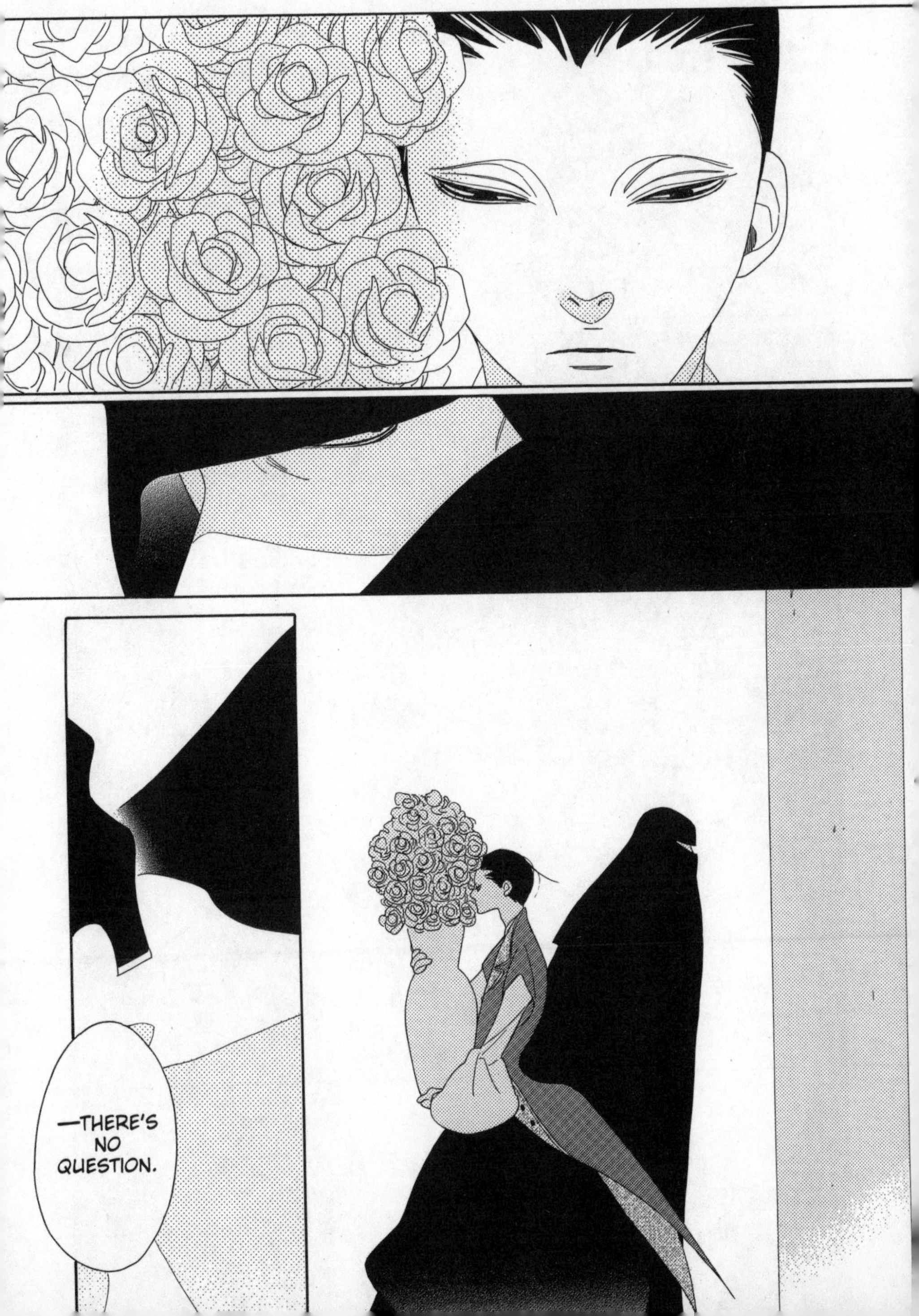
—THERE'S NO QUESTION.

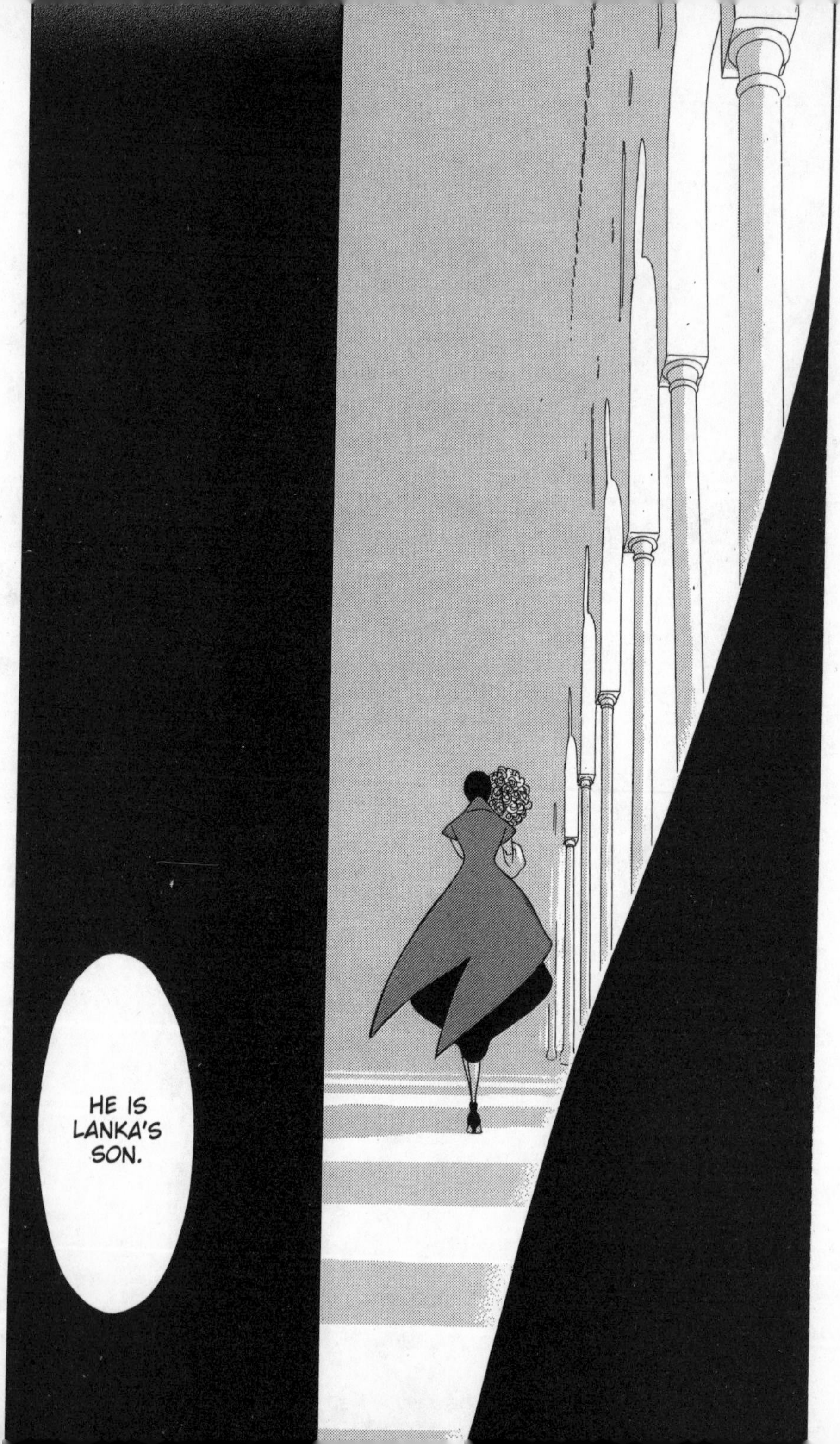
HE IS LANKA'S SON.

Chapter 6
Shao and Dao
episode 1

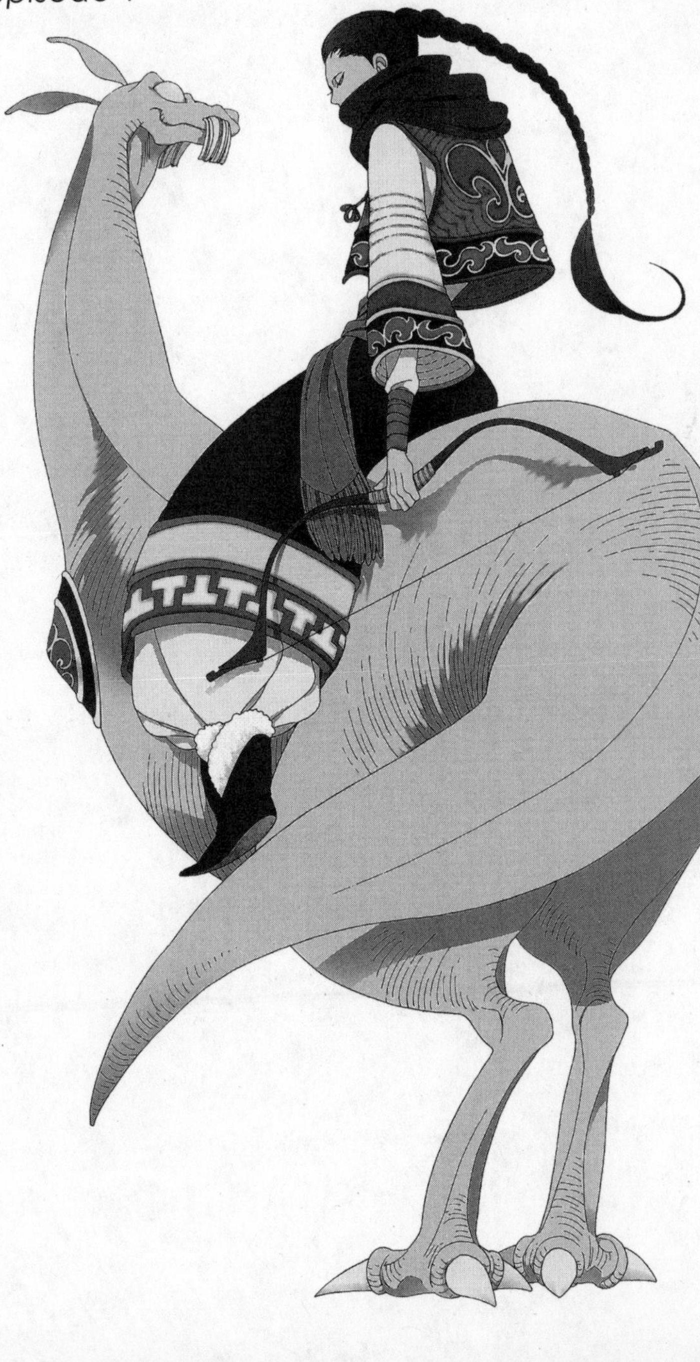

Tales
of the
Kingdom

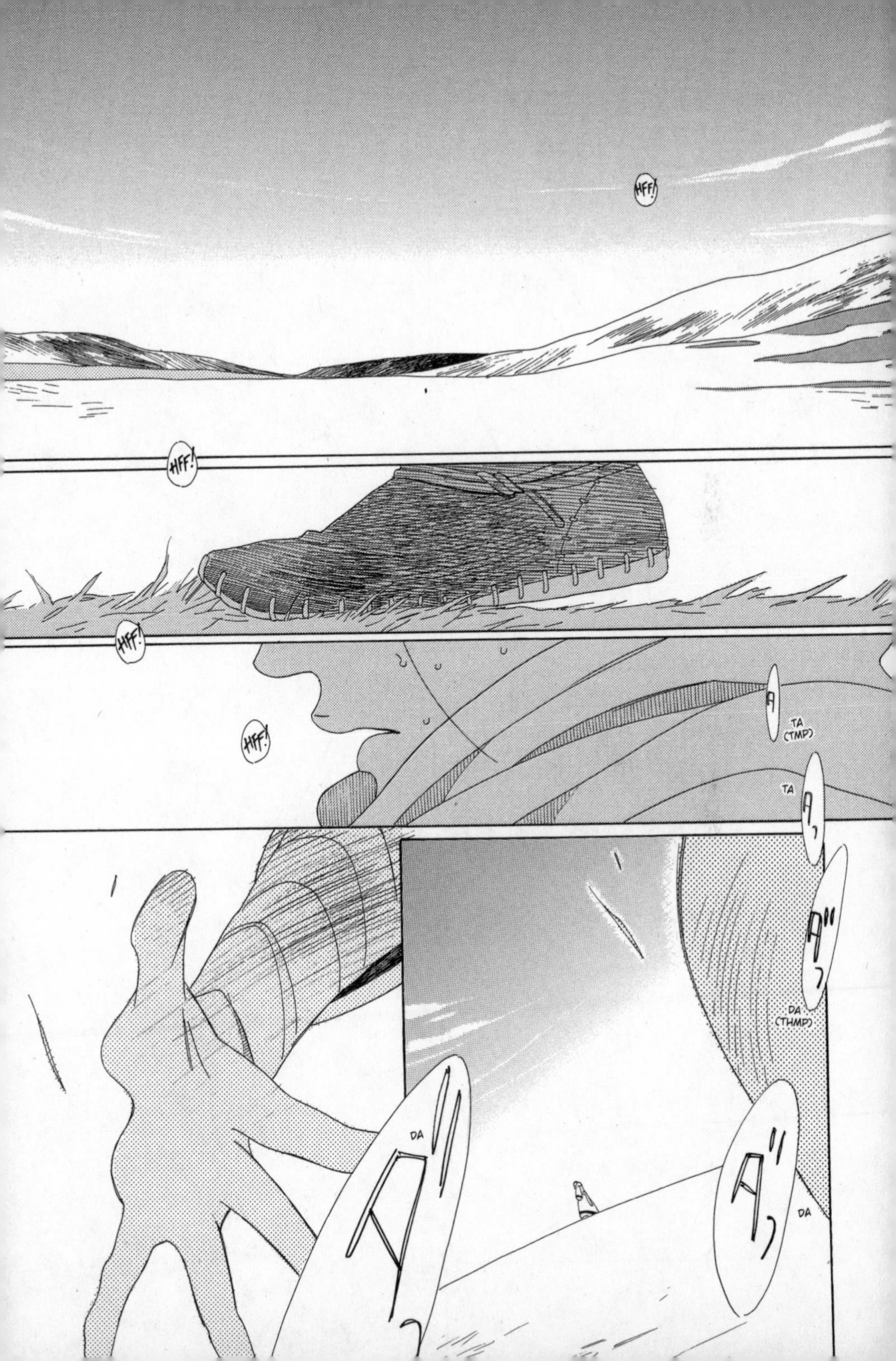
HFF!
HFF!
HFF!
HFF!
TA (TMP)
TA
DA (THMP)
DA
DA

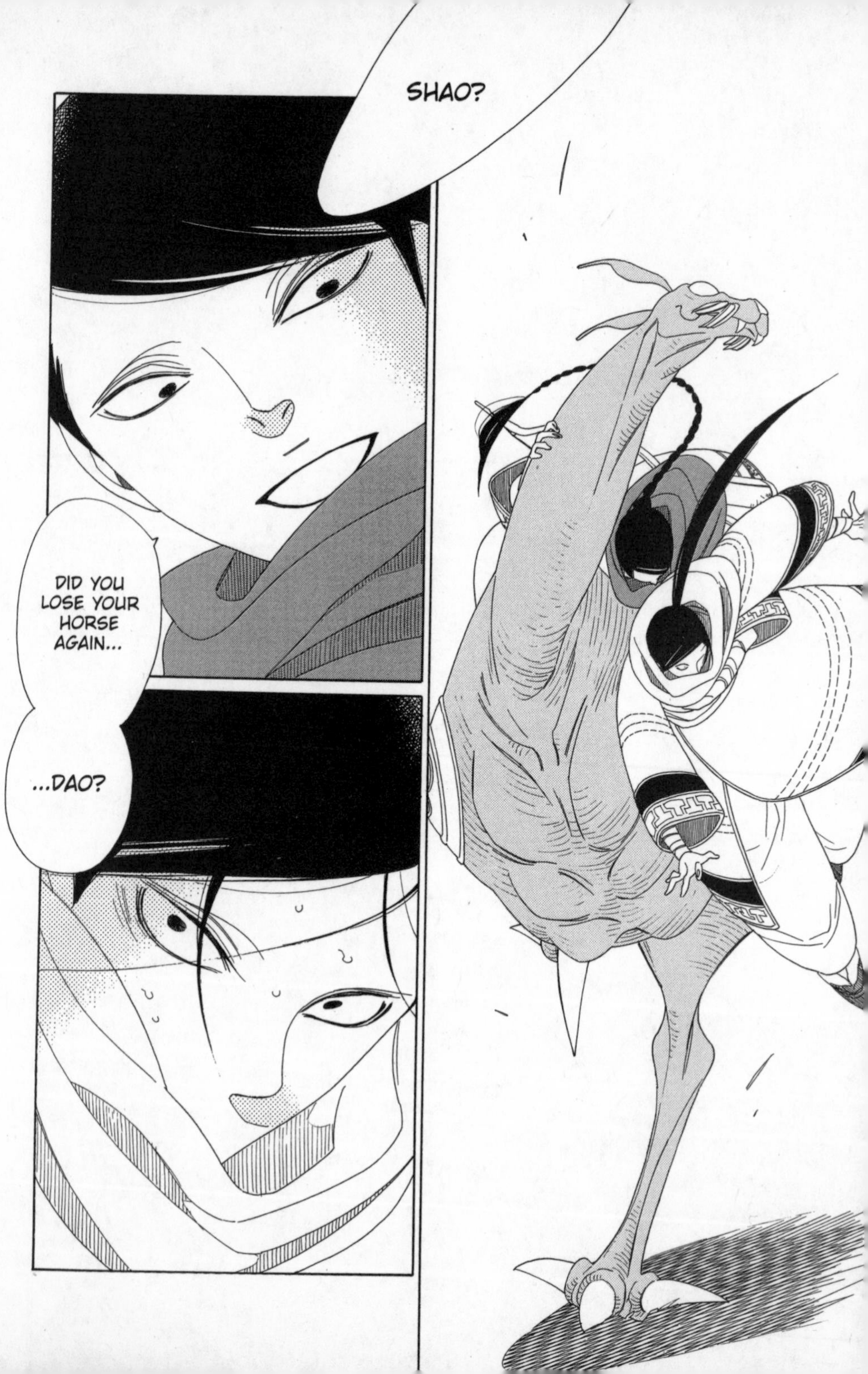
SHAO?
DID YOU LOSE YOUR HORSE AGAIN...
...DAO?

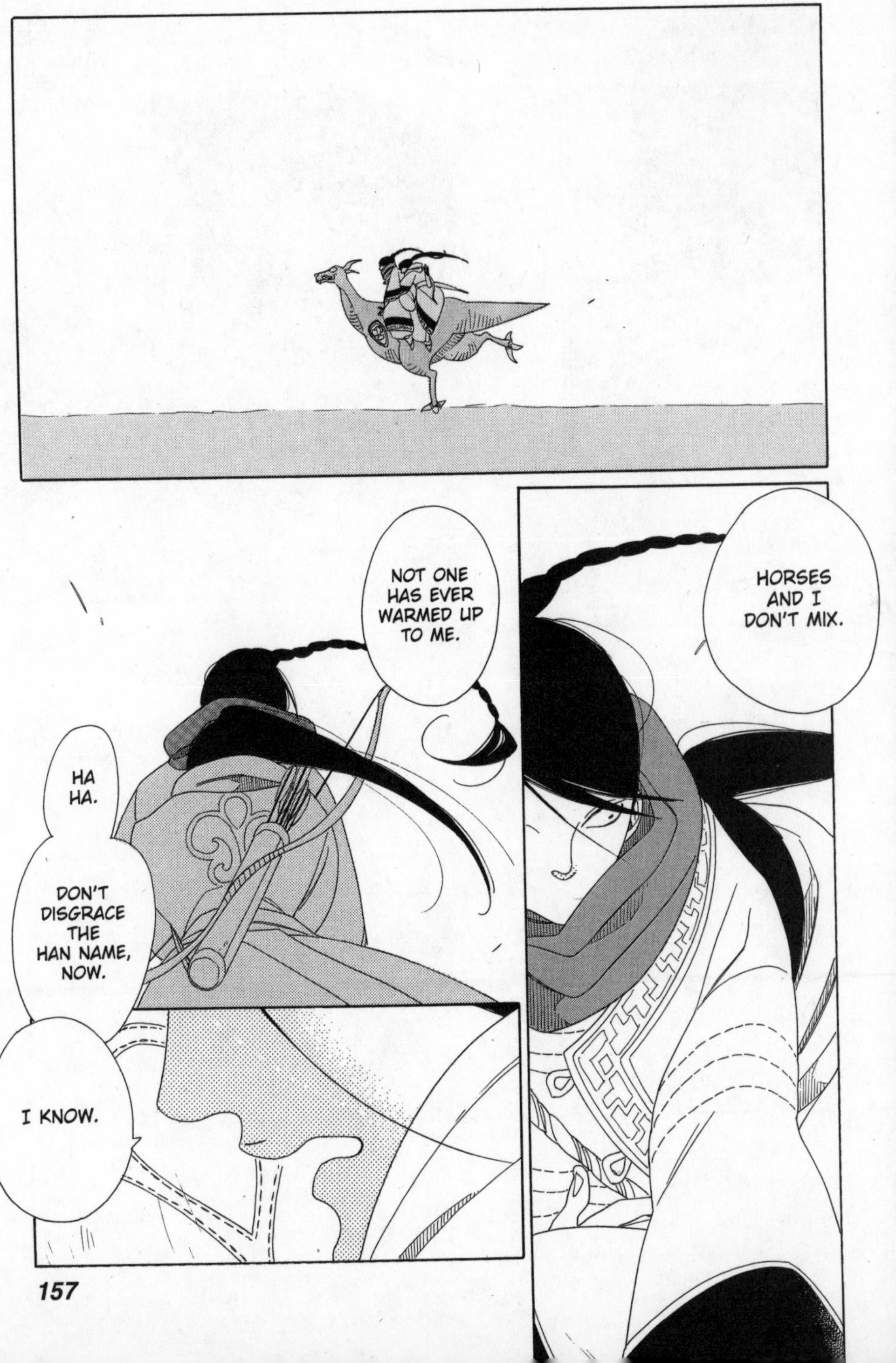
HORSES AND I DON'T MIX.
NOT ONE HAS EVER WARMED UP TO ME.
HA HA.
DON'T DISGRACE THE HAN NAME, NOW.
I KNOW.

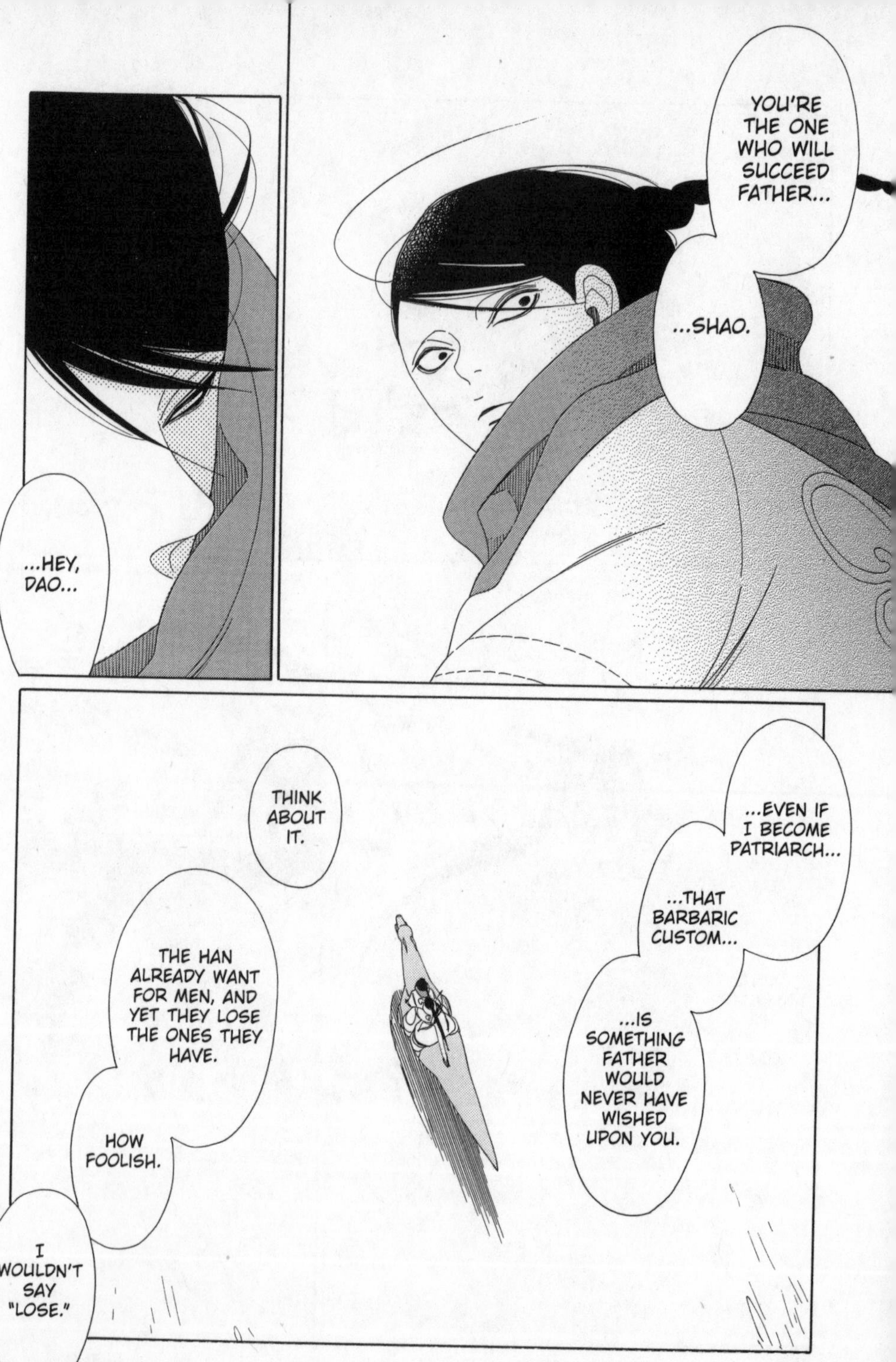
YOU'RE THE ONE WHO WILL SUCCEED FATHER...
...SHAO.
...HEY, DAO...
...EVEN IF I BECOME PATRIARCH...
...THAT BARBARIC CUSTOM...
...IS SOMETHING FATHER WOULD NEVER HAVE WISHED UPON YOU.
THINK ABOUT IT.
THE HAN ALREADY WANT FOR MEN, AND YET THEY LOSE THE ONES THEY HAVE.
HOW FOOLISH.
I WOULDN'T SAY "LOSE."

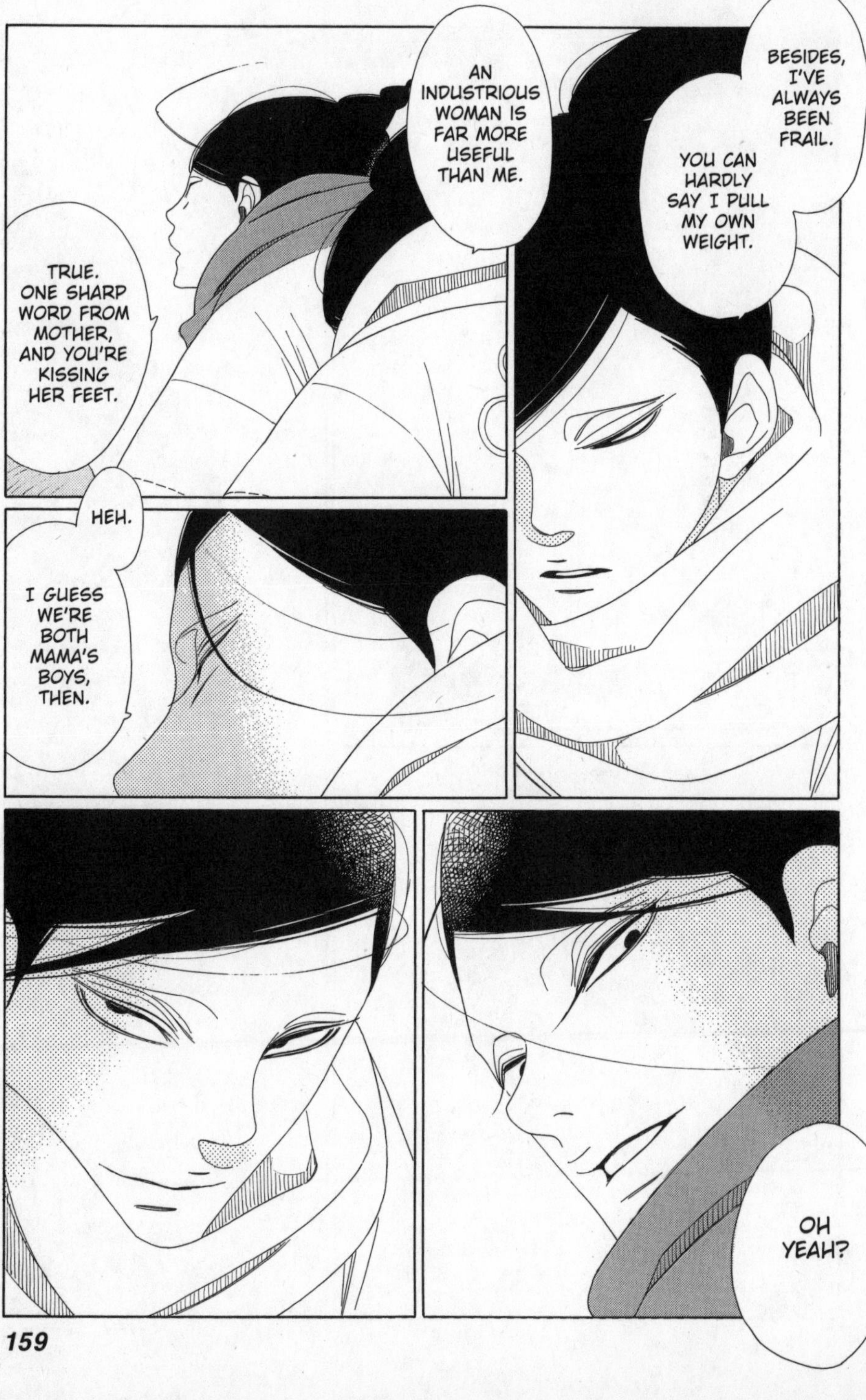
BESIDES, I'VE ALWAYS BEEN FRAIL.
YOU CAN HARDLY SAY I PULL MY OWN WEIGHT.
AN INDUSTRIOUS WOMAN IS FAR MORE USEFUL THAN ME.
TRUE. ONE SHARP WORD FROM MOTHER, AND YOU'RE KISSING HER FEET.
HEH.
I GUESS WE'RE BOTH MAMA'S BOYS, THEN.
OH YEAH?

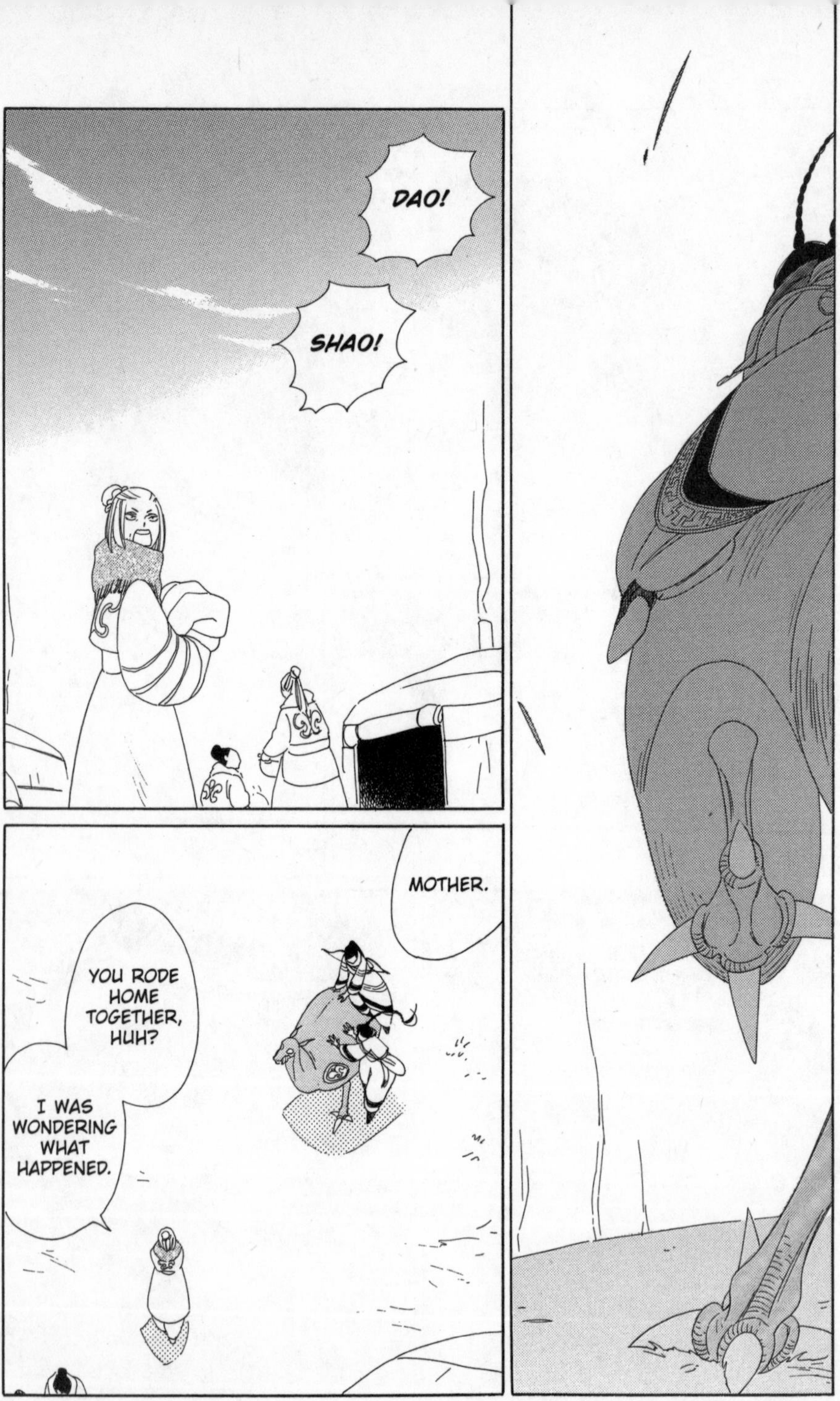
DAO!
SHAO!
MOTHER.
YOU RODE HOME TOGETHER, HUH?
I WAS WONDERING WHAT HAPPENED.

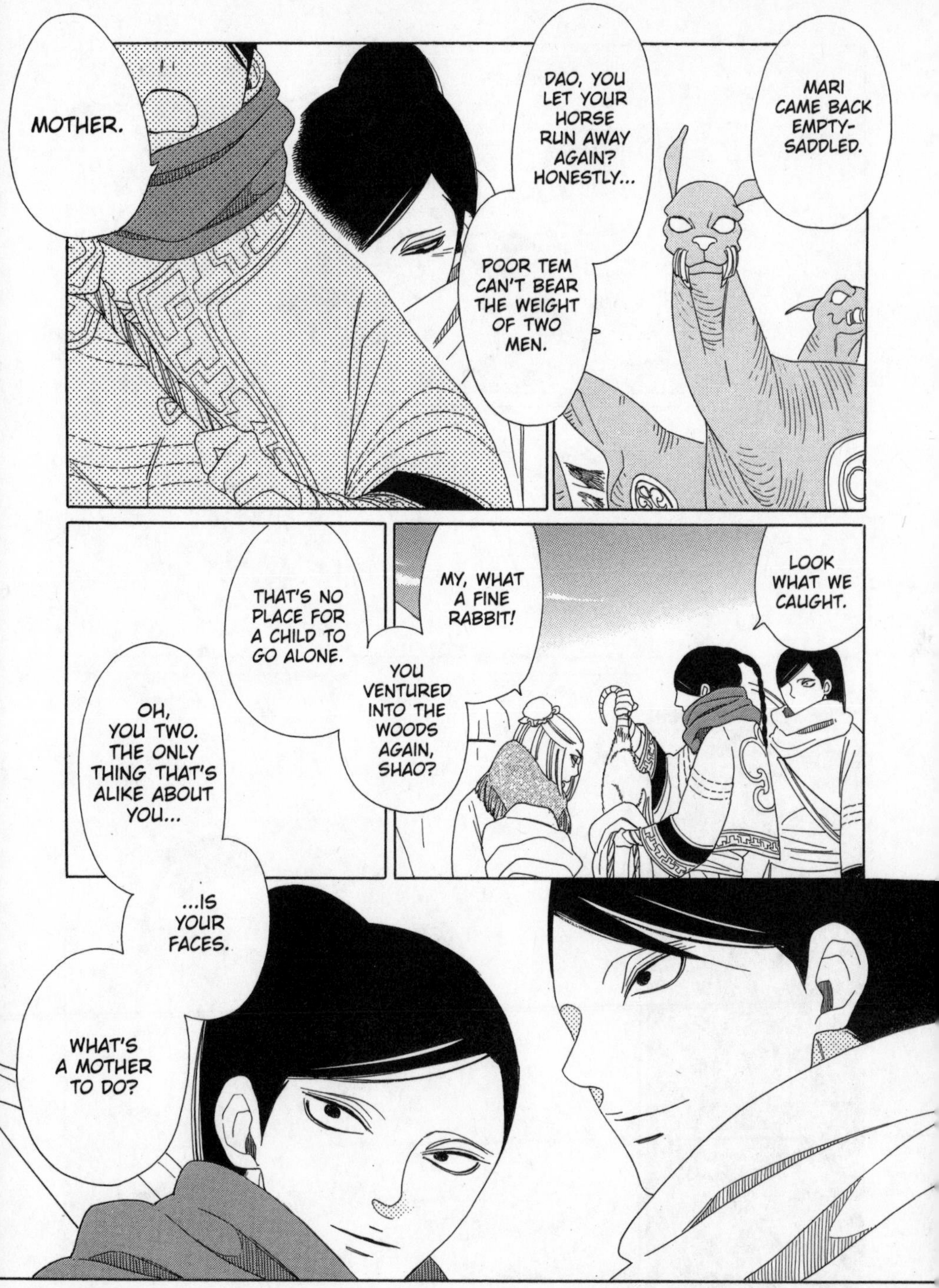
MARI CAME BACK EMPTY-SADDLED.
DAO, YOU LET YOUR HORSE RUN AWAY AGAIN? HONESTLY...
POOR TEM CAN'T BEAR THE WEIGHT OF TWO MEN.
MOTHER.
LOOK WHAT WE CAUGHT.
MY, WHAT A FINE RABBIT!
YOU VENTURED INTO THE WOODS AGAIN, SHAO?
THAT'S NO PLACE FOR A CHILD TO GO ALONE.
OH, YOU TWO. THE ONLY THING THAT'S ALIKE ABOUT YOU...
...IS YOUR FACES.
WHAT'S A MOTHER TO DO?

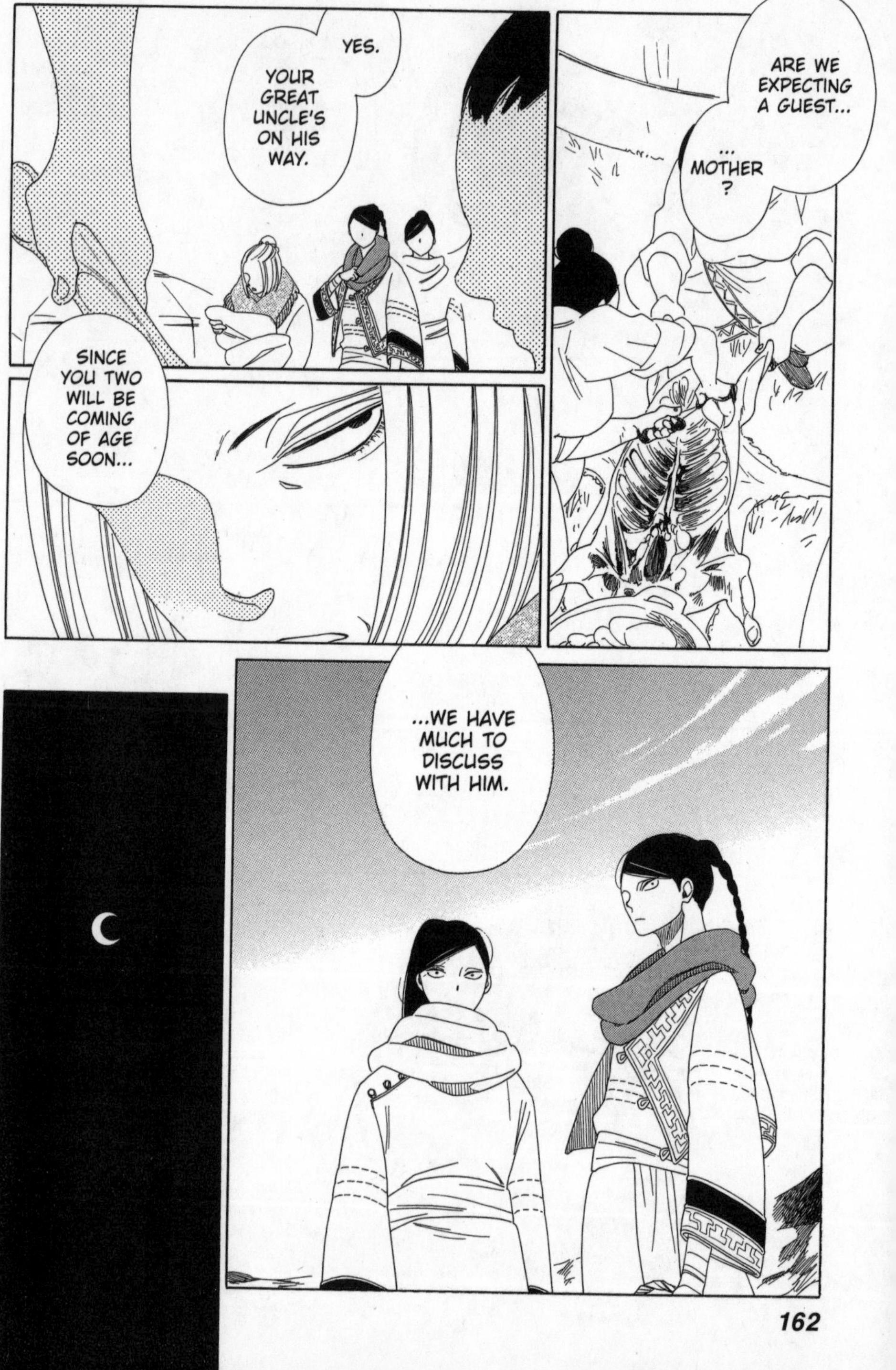
ARE WE EXPECTING A GUEST...
...MOTHER?
YES. YOUR GREAT UNCLE'S ON HIS WAY.
SINCE YOU TWO WILL BE COMING OF AGE SOON...
...WE HAVE MUCH TO DISCUSS WITH HIM.

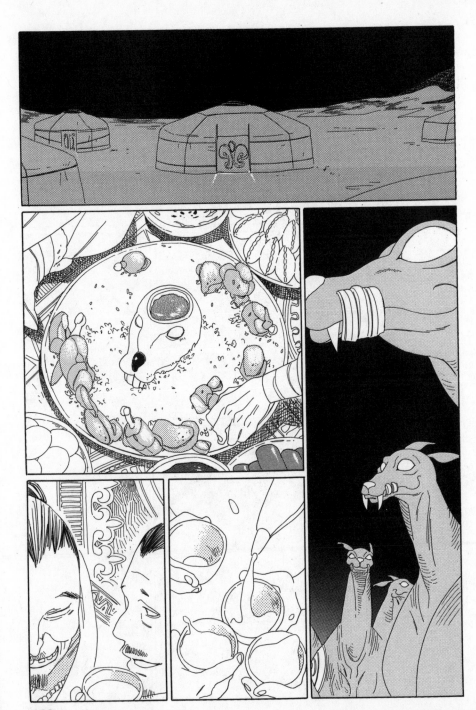

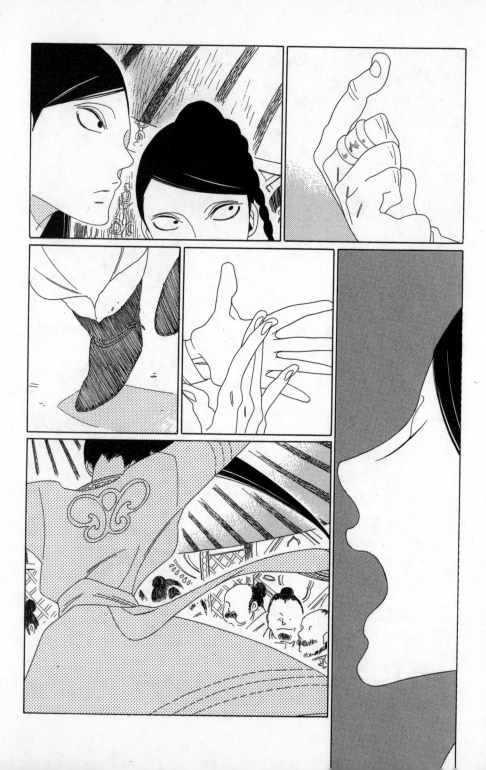

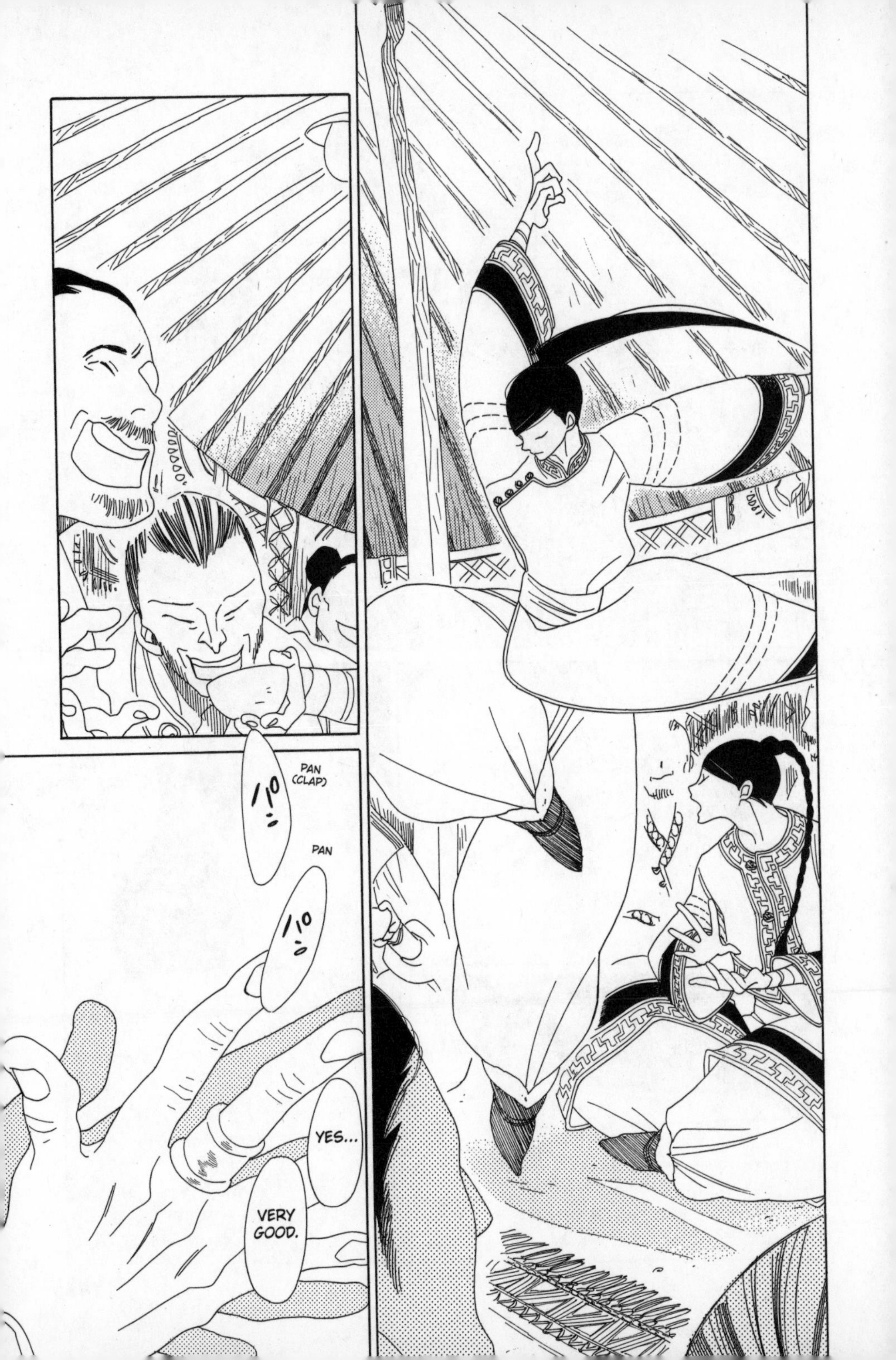
PAN (CLAP)
PAN
YES...
VERY GOOD.

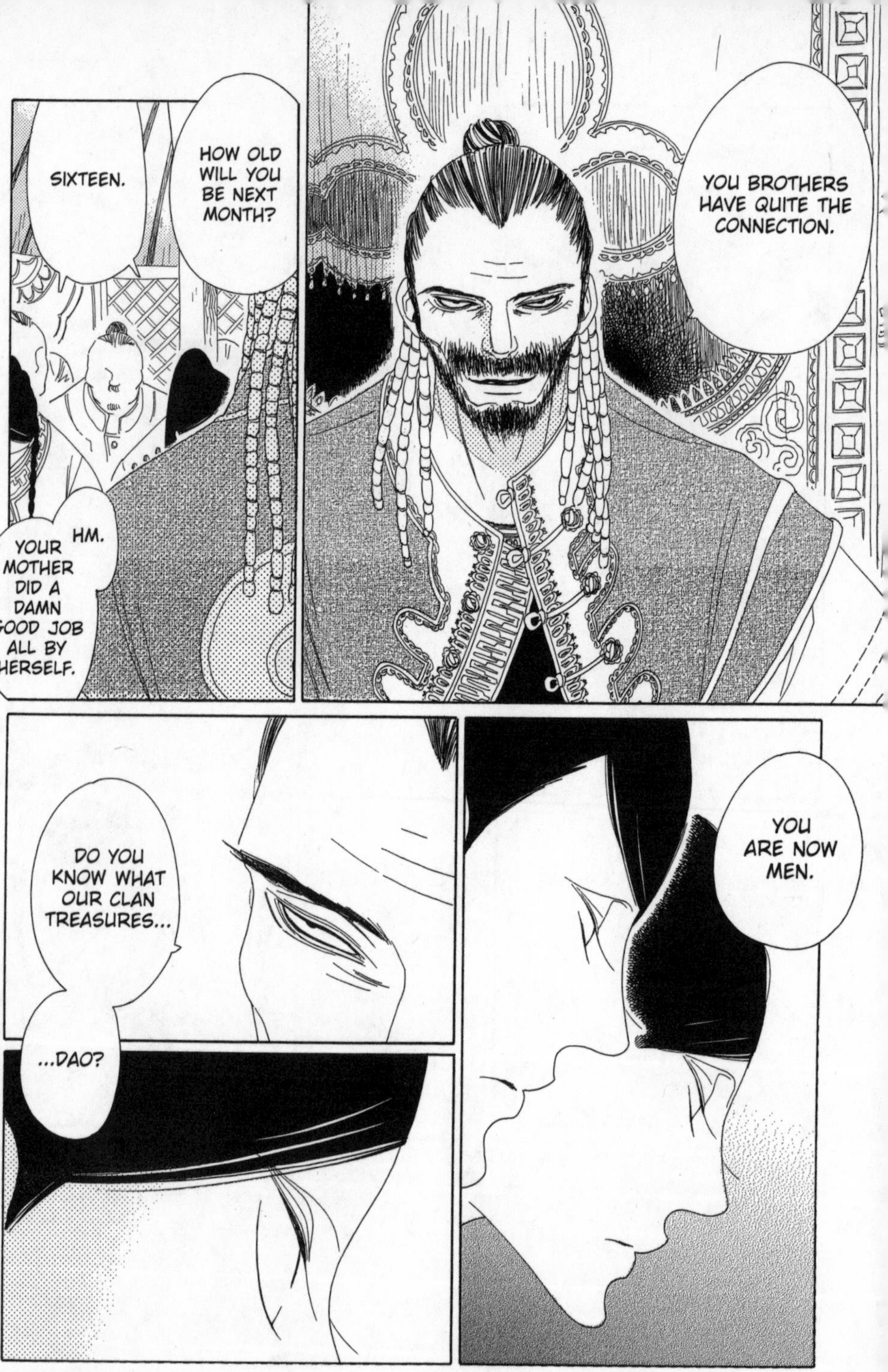
YOU BROTHERS HAVE QUITE THE CONNECTION.
HOW OLD WILL YOU BE NEXT MONTH?
SIXTEEN.
HM.
YOUR MOTHER DID A DAMN GOOD JOB ALL BY HERSELF.
YOU ARE NOW MEN.
DO YOU KNOW WHAT OUR CLAN TREASURES...
...DAO?

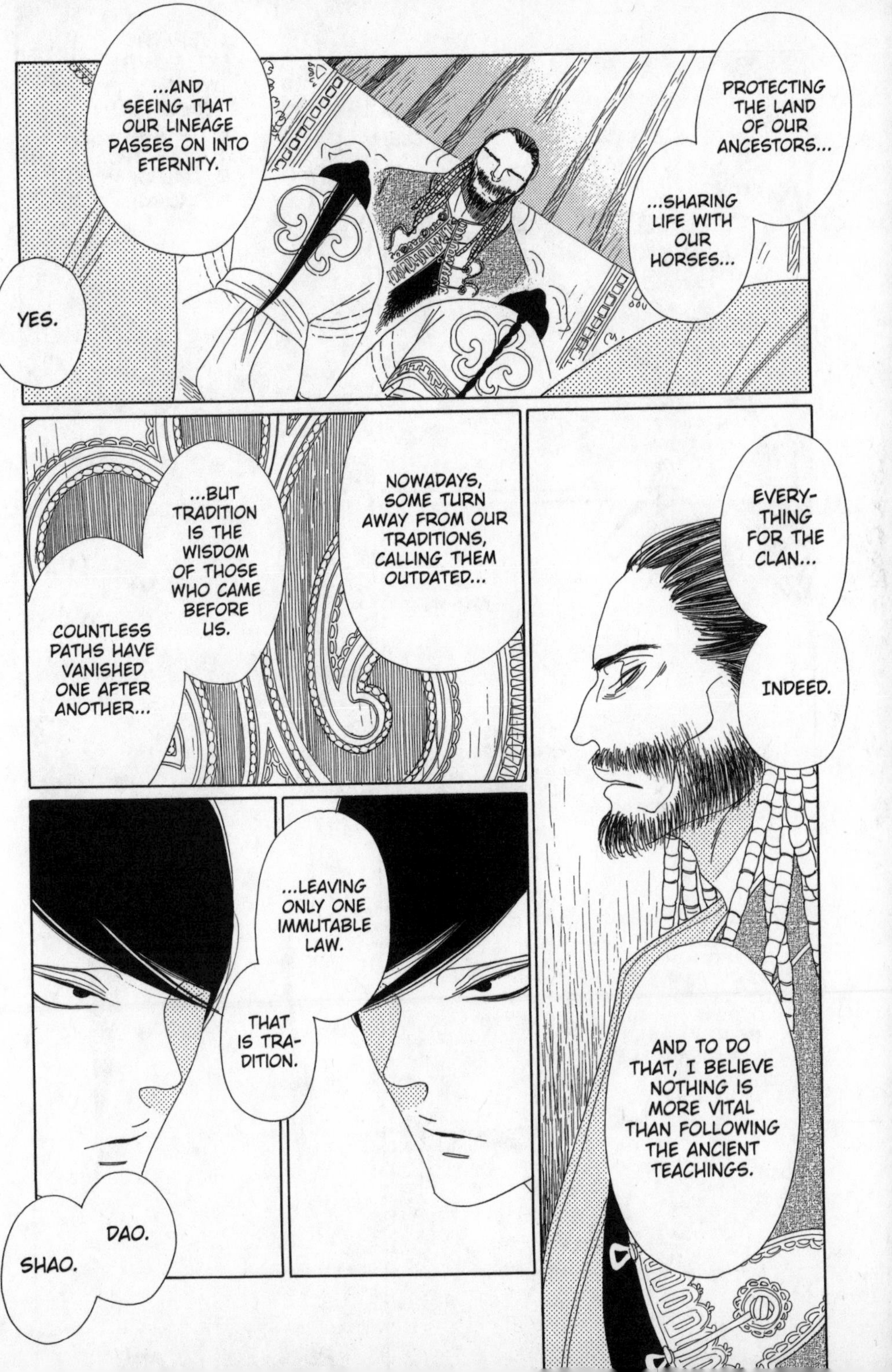
PROTECTING THE LAND OF OUR ANCESTORS...
...SHARING LIFE WITH OUR HORSES...
...AND SEEING THAT OUR LINEAGE PASSES ON INTO ETERNITY.
YES.
EVERY-THING FOR THE CLAN...
INDEED.
AND TO DO THAT, I BELIEVE NOTHING IS MORE VITAL THAN FOLLOWING THE ANCIENT TEACHINGS.
NOWADAYS, SOME TURN AWAY FROM OUR TRADITIONS, CALLING THEM OUTDATED...
...BUT TRADITION IS THE WISDOM OF THOSE WHO CAME BEFORE US.
COUNTLESS PATHS HAVE VANISHED ONE AFTER ANOTHER...
...LEAVING ONLY ONE IMMUTABLE LAW.
THAT IS TRA-DITION.
DAO.
SHAO.

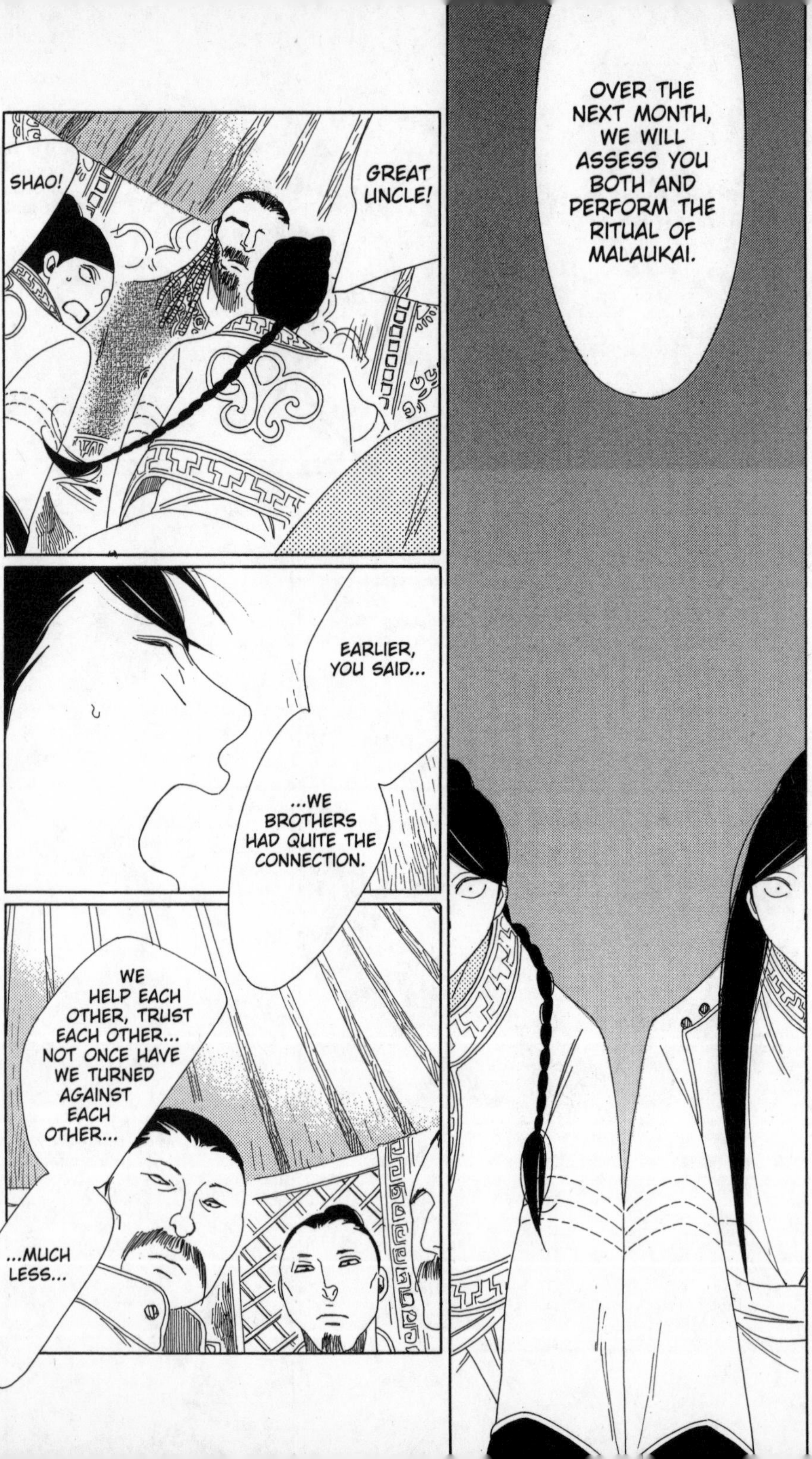
OVER THE NEXT MONTH, WE WILL ASSESS YOU BOTH AND PERFORM THE RITUAL OF MALAUKAI.
GREAT UNCLE!
SHAO!
EARLIER, YOU SAID...
...WE BROTHERS HAD QUITE THE CONNECTION.
WE HELP EACH OTHER, TRUST EACH OTHER... NOT ONCE HAVE WE TURNED AGAINST EACH OTHER...
...MUCH LESS...

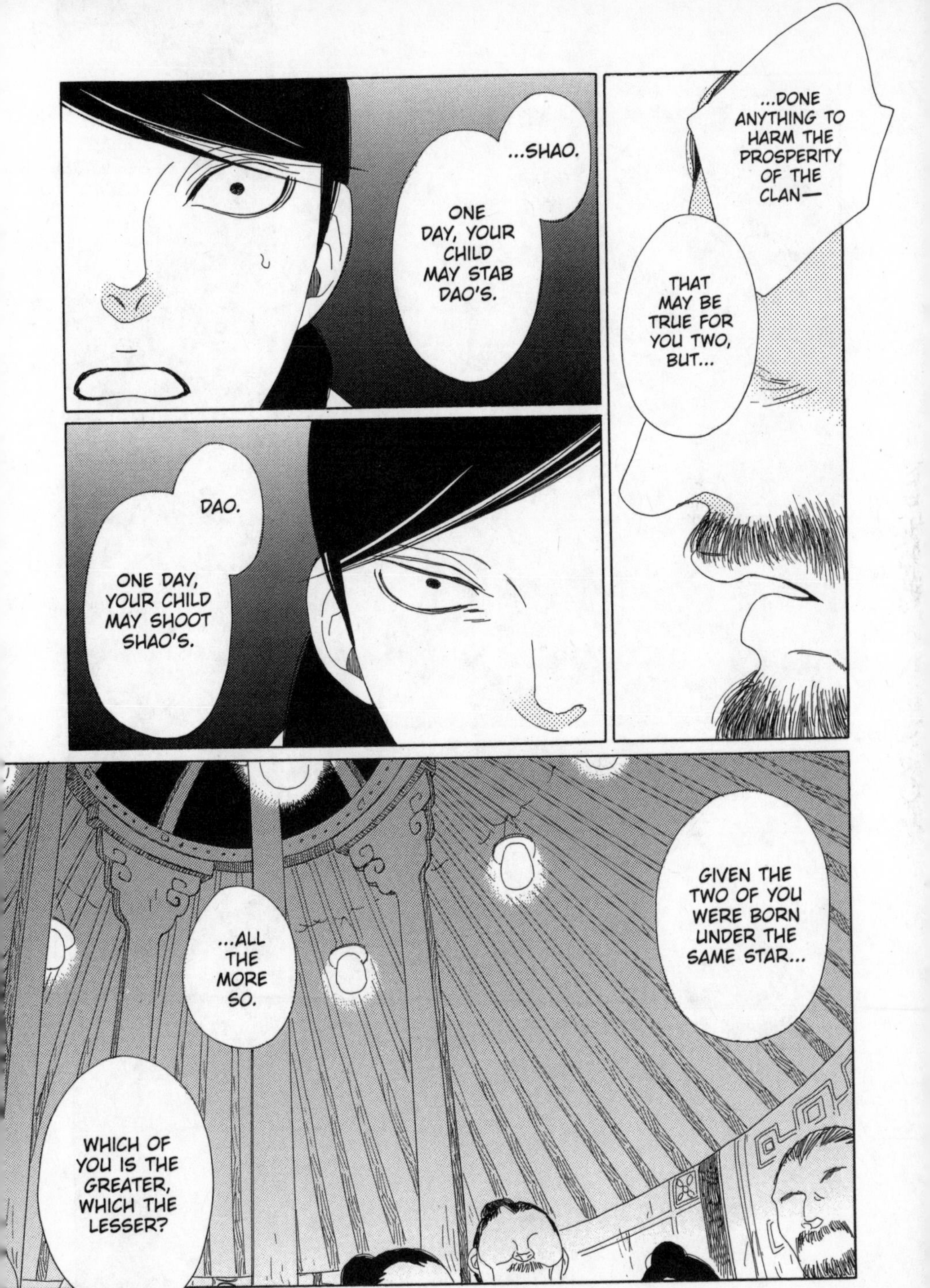
...DONE ANYTHING TO HARM THE PROSPERITY OF THE CLAN—
THAT MAY BE TRUE FOR YOU TWO, BUT...
...SHAO.
ONE DAY, YOUR CHILD MAY STAB DAO'S.
DAO.
ONE DAY, YOUR CHILD MAY SHOOT SHAO'S.
GIVEN THE TWO OF YOU WERE BORN UNDER THE SAME STAR...
...ALL THE MORE SO.
WHICH OF YOU IS THE GREATER, WHICH THE LESSER?

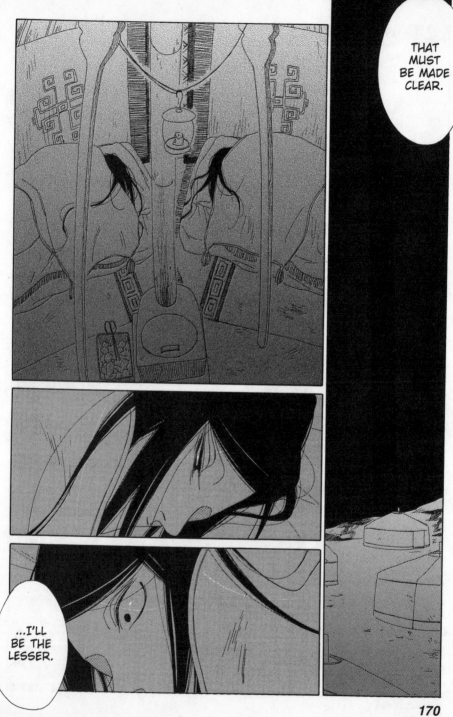

THAT
MUST
BE MADE
CLEAR.

...I'LL
BE THE
LESSER.

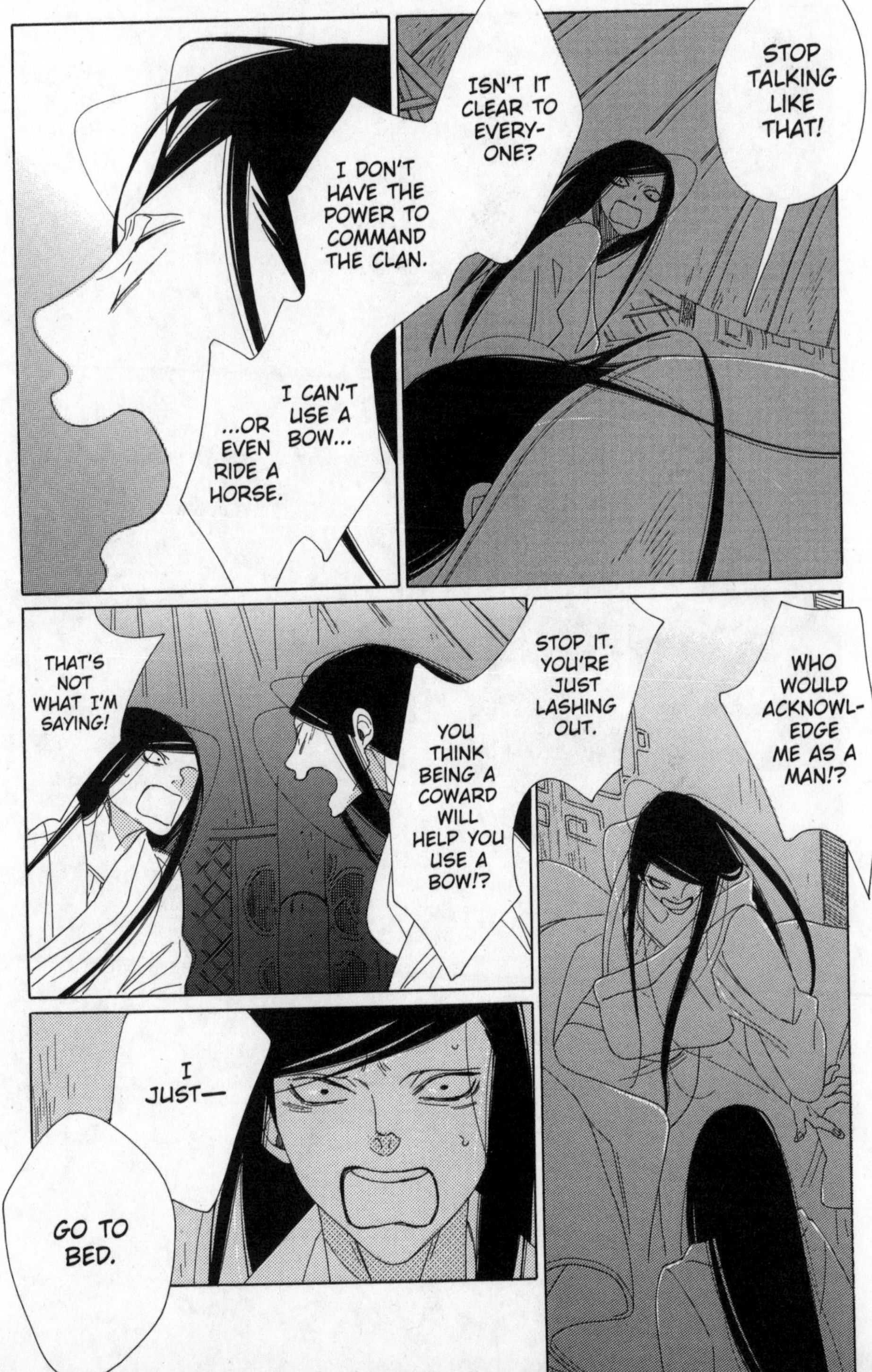
STOP TALKING LIKE THAT!
ISN'T IT CLEAR TO EVERY-ONE?
I DON'T HAVE THE POWER TO COMMAND THE CLAN.
I CAN'T USE A BOW...
...OR EVEN RIDE A HORSE.
WHO WOULD ACKNOWL-EDGE ME AS A MAN!?
STOP IT. YOU'RE JUST LASHING OUT.
YOU THINK BEING A COWARD WILL HELP YOU USE A BOW!?
THAT'S NOT WHAT I'M SAYING!
I JUST—
GO TO BED.

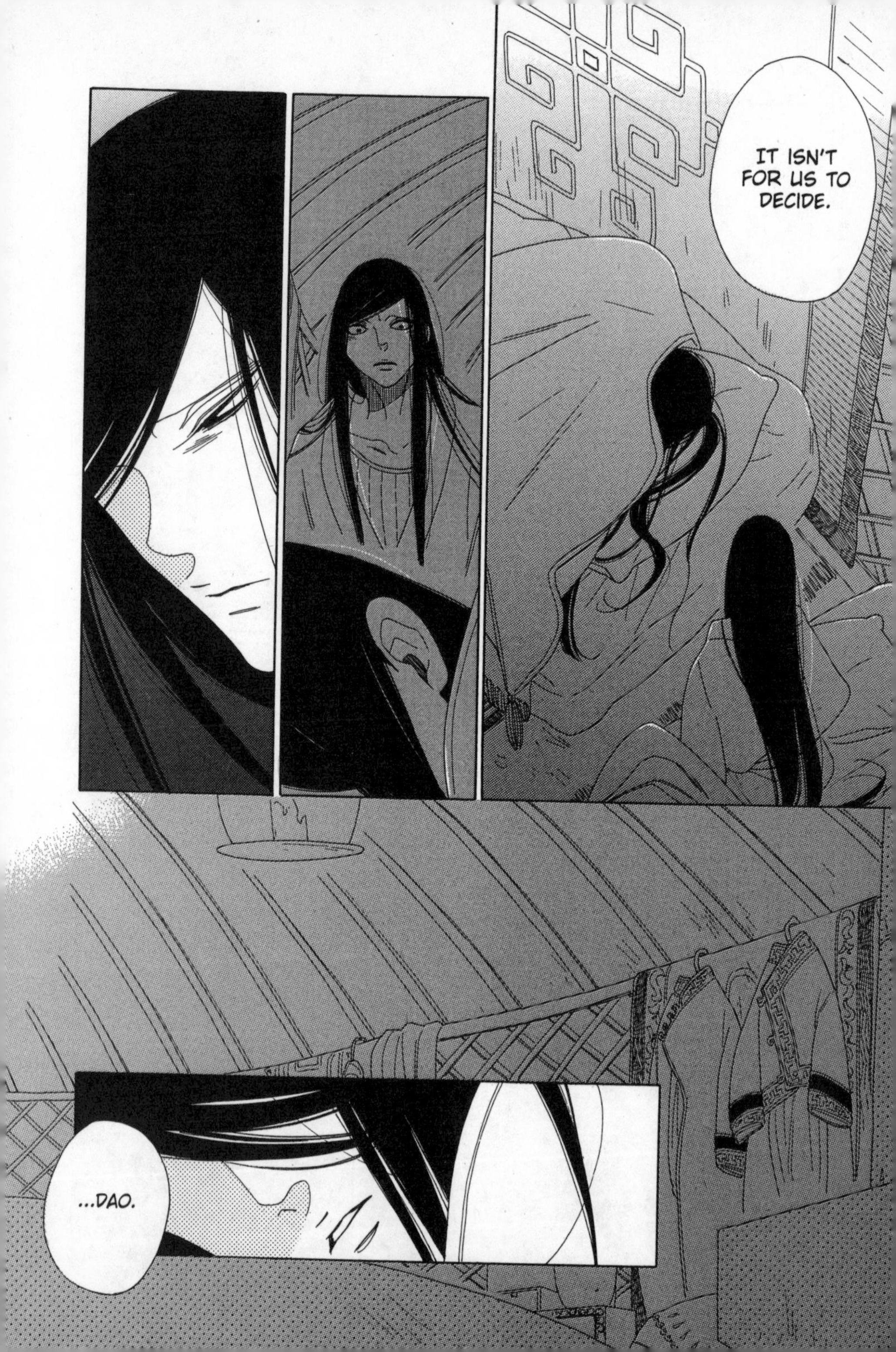
IT ISN'T FOR US TO DECIDE.
...DAO.

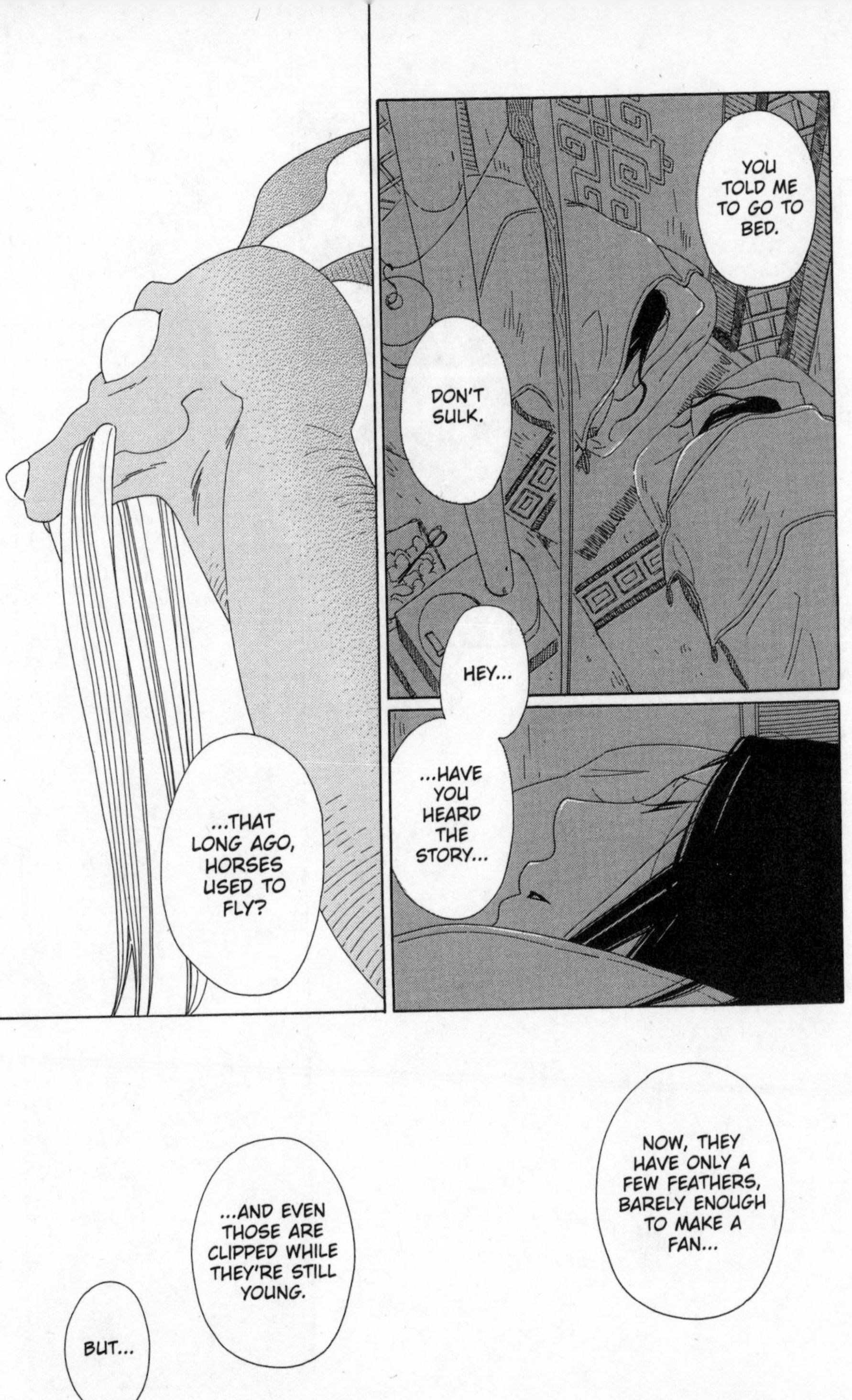
YOU TOLD ME TO GO TO BED.
DON'T SULK.
HEY...
...HAVE YOU HEARD THE STORY...
...THAT LONG AGO, HORSES USED TO FLY?
NOW, THEY HAVE ONLY A FEW FEATHERS, BARELY ENOUGH TO MAKE A FAN...
...AND EVEN THOSE ARE CLIPPED WHILE THEY'RE STILL YOUNG.
BUT...

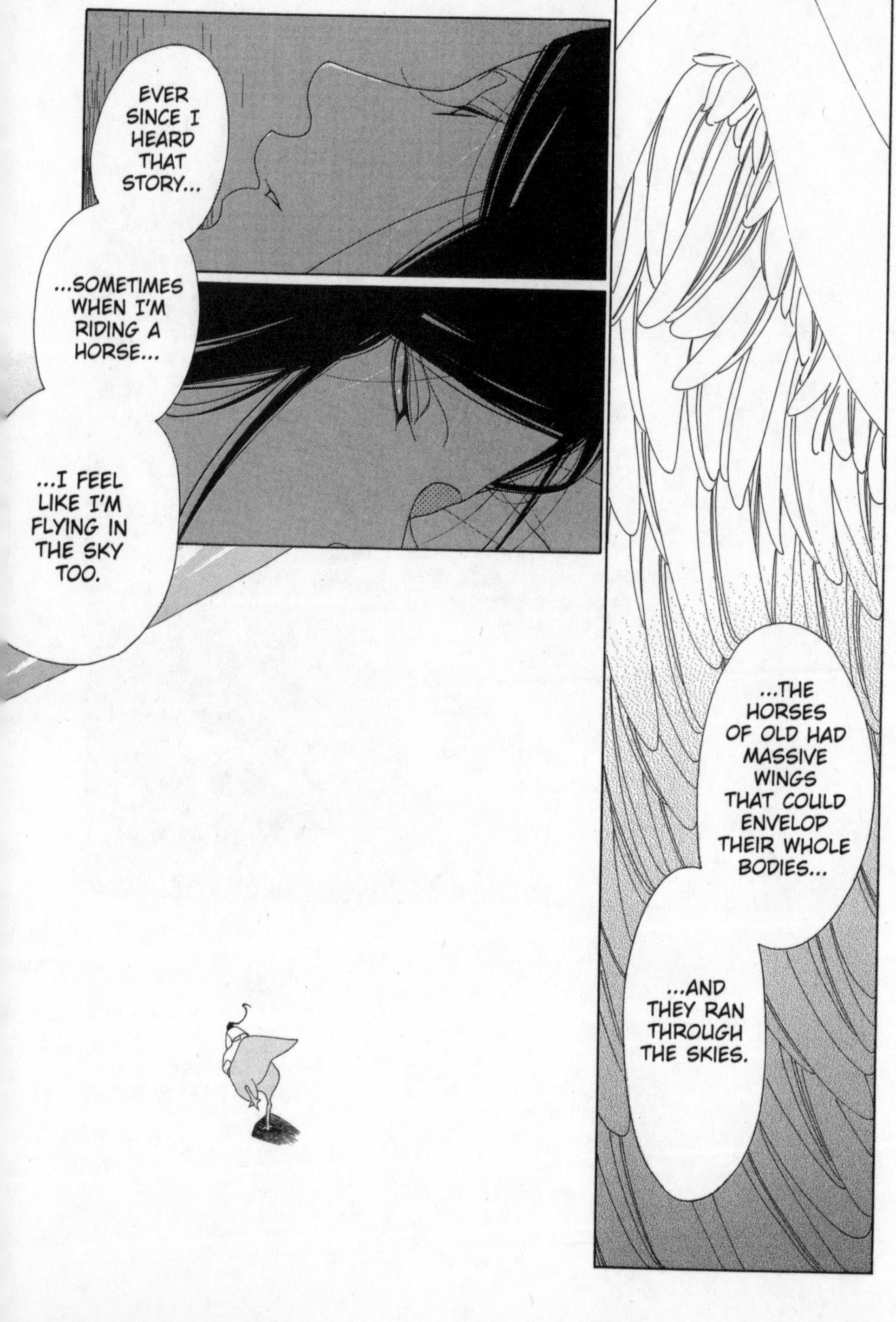
...THE HORSES OF OLD HAD MASSIVE WINGS THAT COULD ENVELOP THEIR WHOLE BODIES...
...AND THEY RAN THROUGH THE SKIES.
EVER SINCE I HEARD THAT STORY...
...SOMETIMES WHEN I'M RIDING A HORSE...
...I FEEL LIKE I'M FLYING IN THE SKY TOO.

HEY...
DAO...

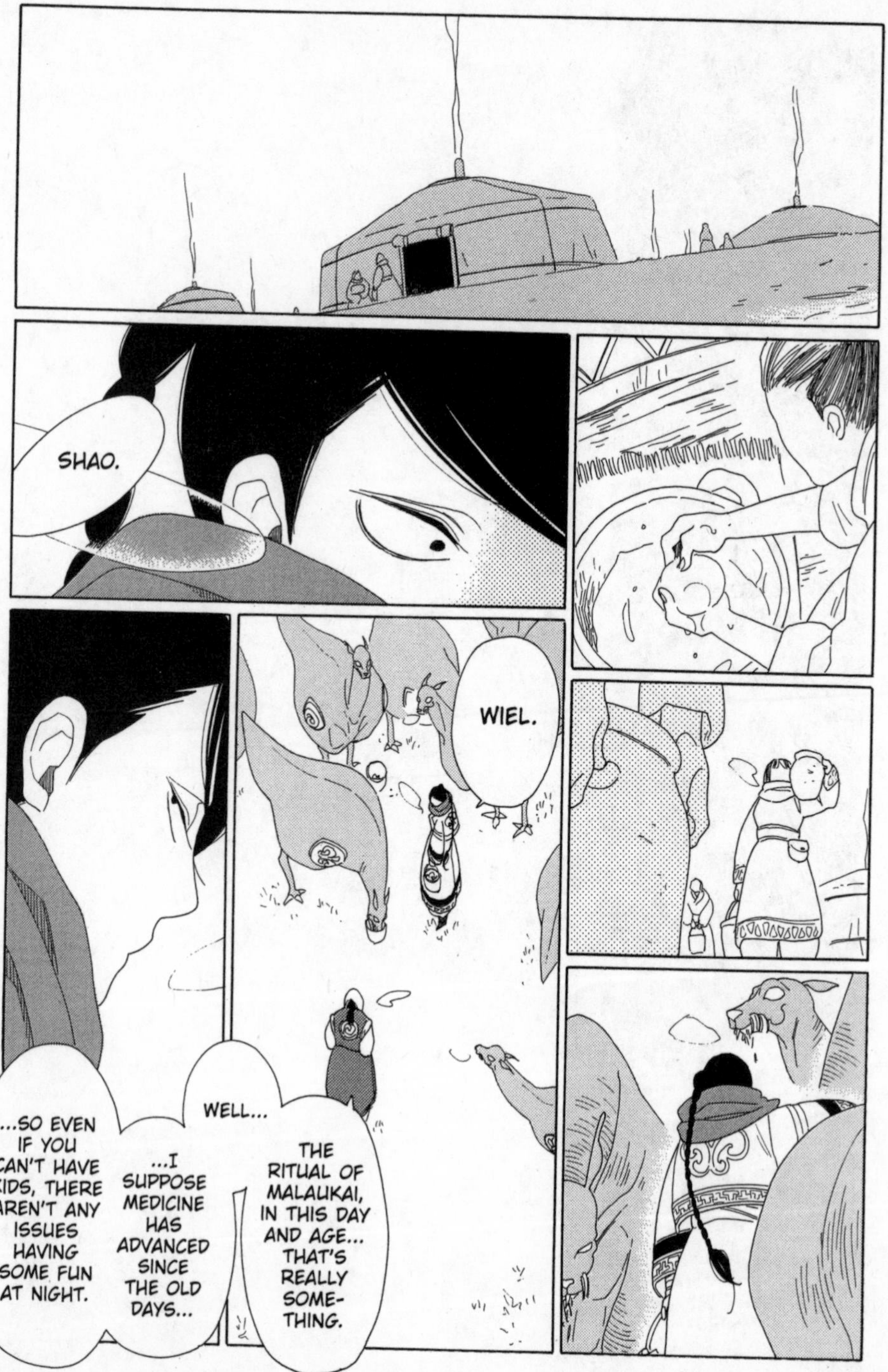
SHAO.
WIEL.
THE RITUAL OF MALAUKAI, IN THIS DAY AND AGE... THAT'S REALLY SOME-THING.
WELL...
...I SUPPOSE MEDICINE HAS ADVANCED SINCE THE OLD DAYS...
...SO EVEN IF YOU CAN'T HAVE KIDS, THERE AREN'T ANY ISSUES HAVING SOME FUN AT NIGHT.

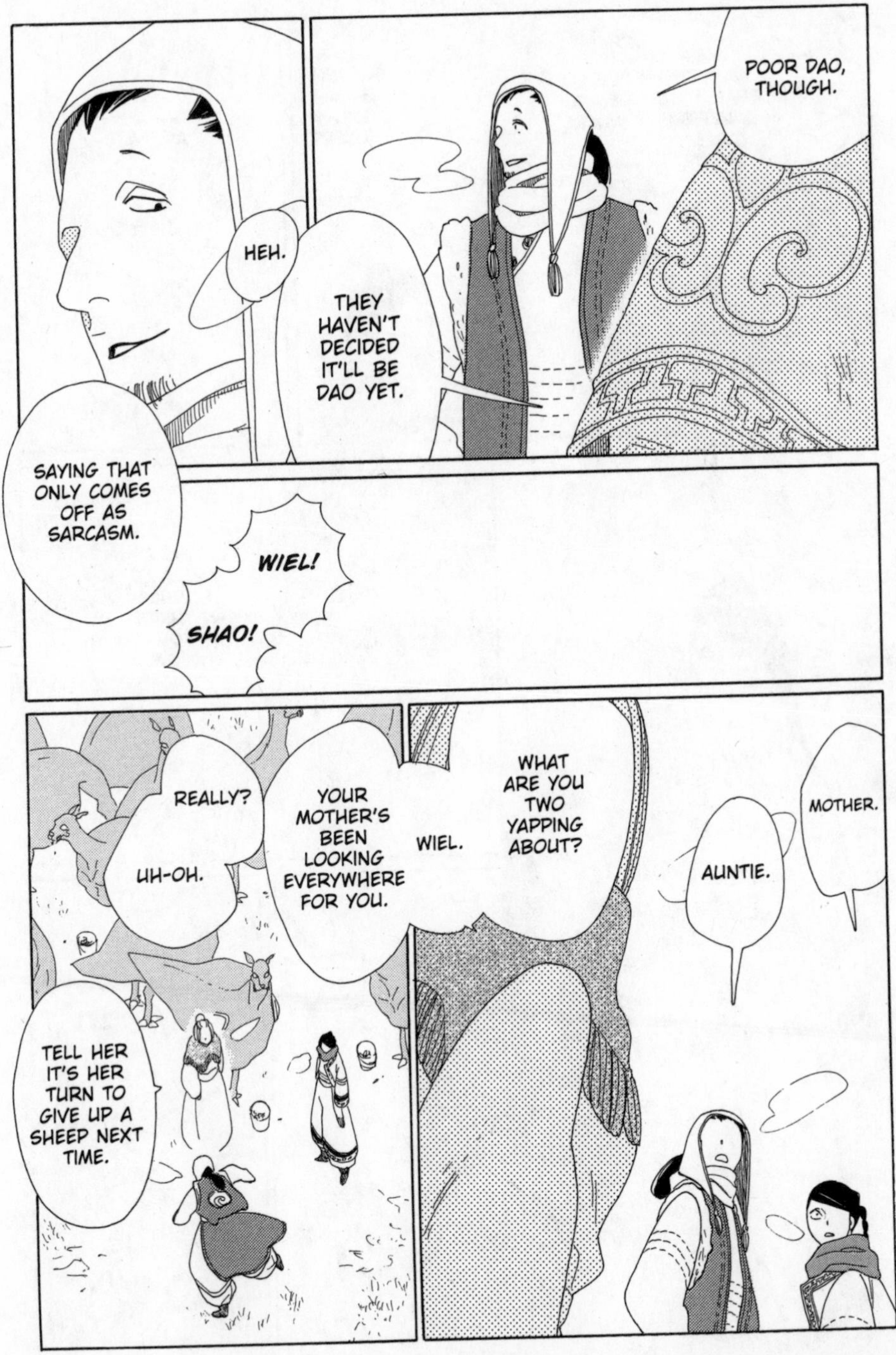
POOR DAO, THOUGH.
THEY HAVEN'T DECIDED IT'LL BE DAO YET.
HEH.
SAYING THAT ONLY COMES OFF AS SARCASM.
WIEL!
SHAO!
MOTHER.
AUNTIE.
WHAT ARE YOU TWO YAPPING ABOUT?
WIEL.
YOUR MOTHER'S BEEN LOOKING EVERYWHERE FOR YOU.
REALLY?
UH-OH.
TELL HER IT'S HER TURN TO GIVE UP A SHEEP NEXT TIME.

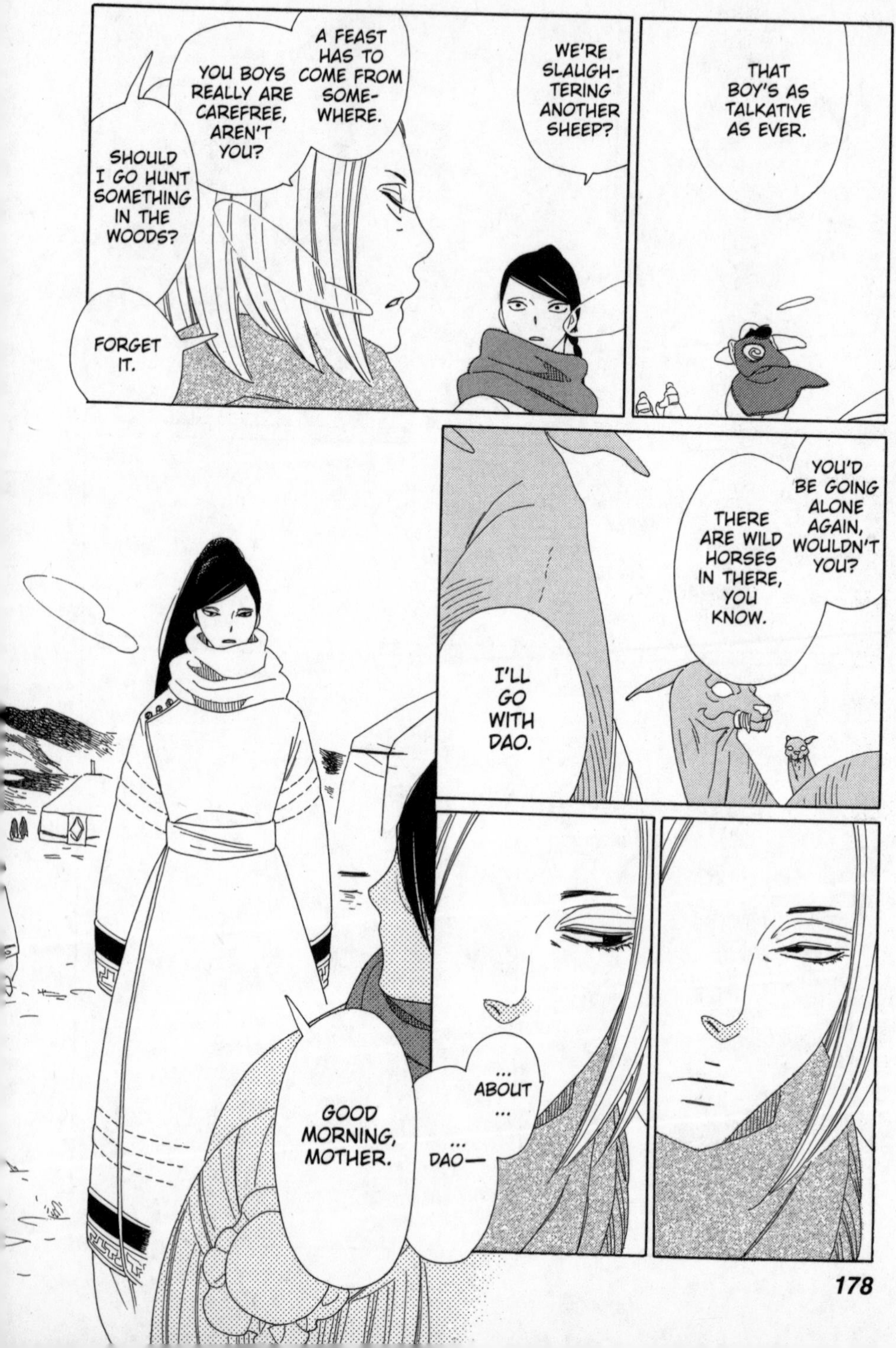
THAT BOY'S AS TALKATIVE AS EVER.
WE'RE SLAUGHTERING ANOTHER SHEEP?
A FEAST HAS TO COME FROM SOMEWHERE.
YOU BOYS REALLY ARE CAREFREE, AREN'T YOU?
SHOULD I GO HUNT SOMETHING IN THE WOODS?
FORGET IT.
YOU'D BE GOING ALONE AGAIN, WOULDN'T YOU?
THERE ARE WILD HORSES IN THERE, YOU KNOW.
I'LL GO WITH DAO.
... ABOUT ...
... DAO—
GOOD MORNING, MOTHER.

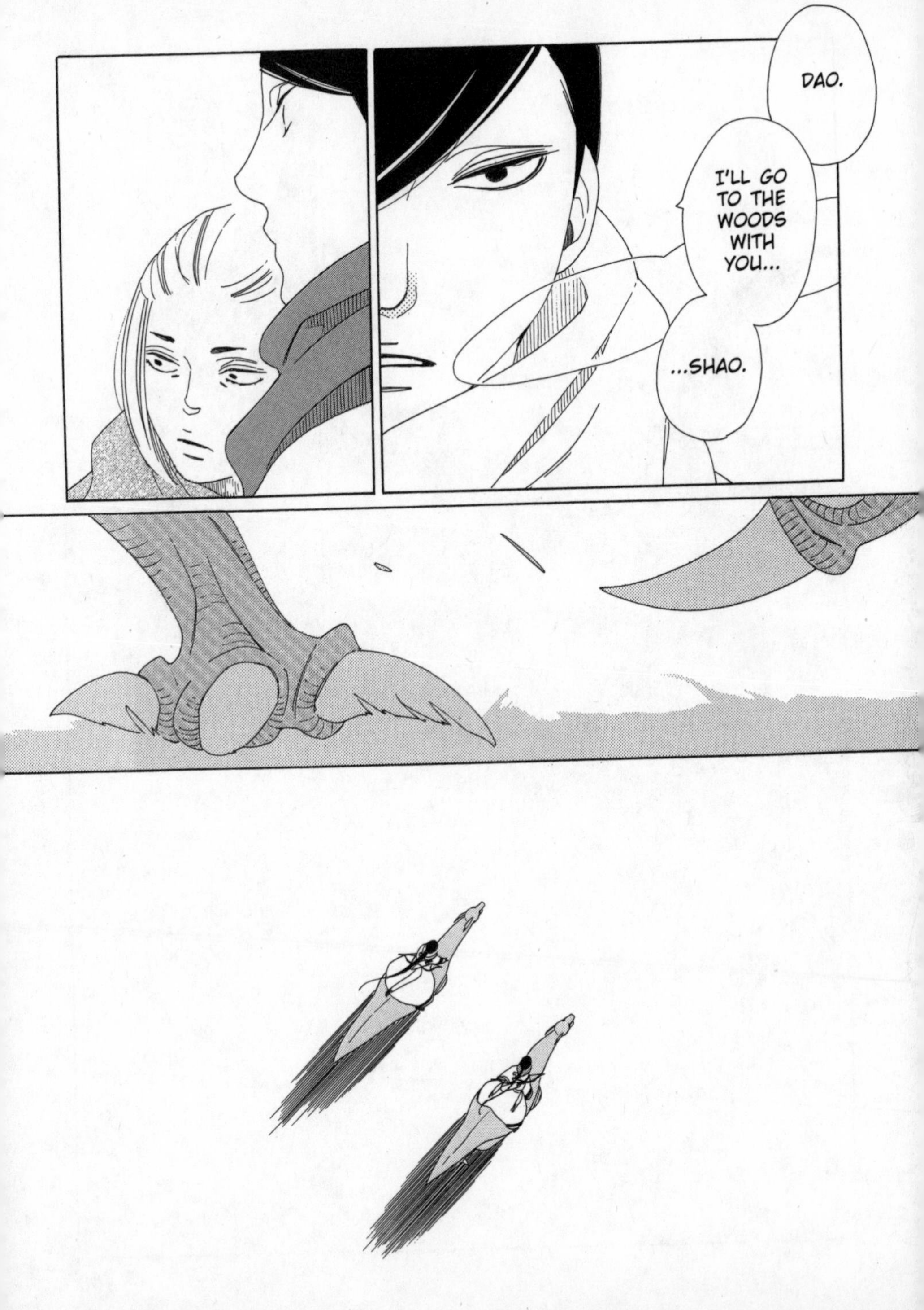
DAO.
I'LL GO TO THE WOODS WITH YOU...
...SHAO.

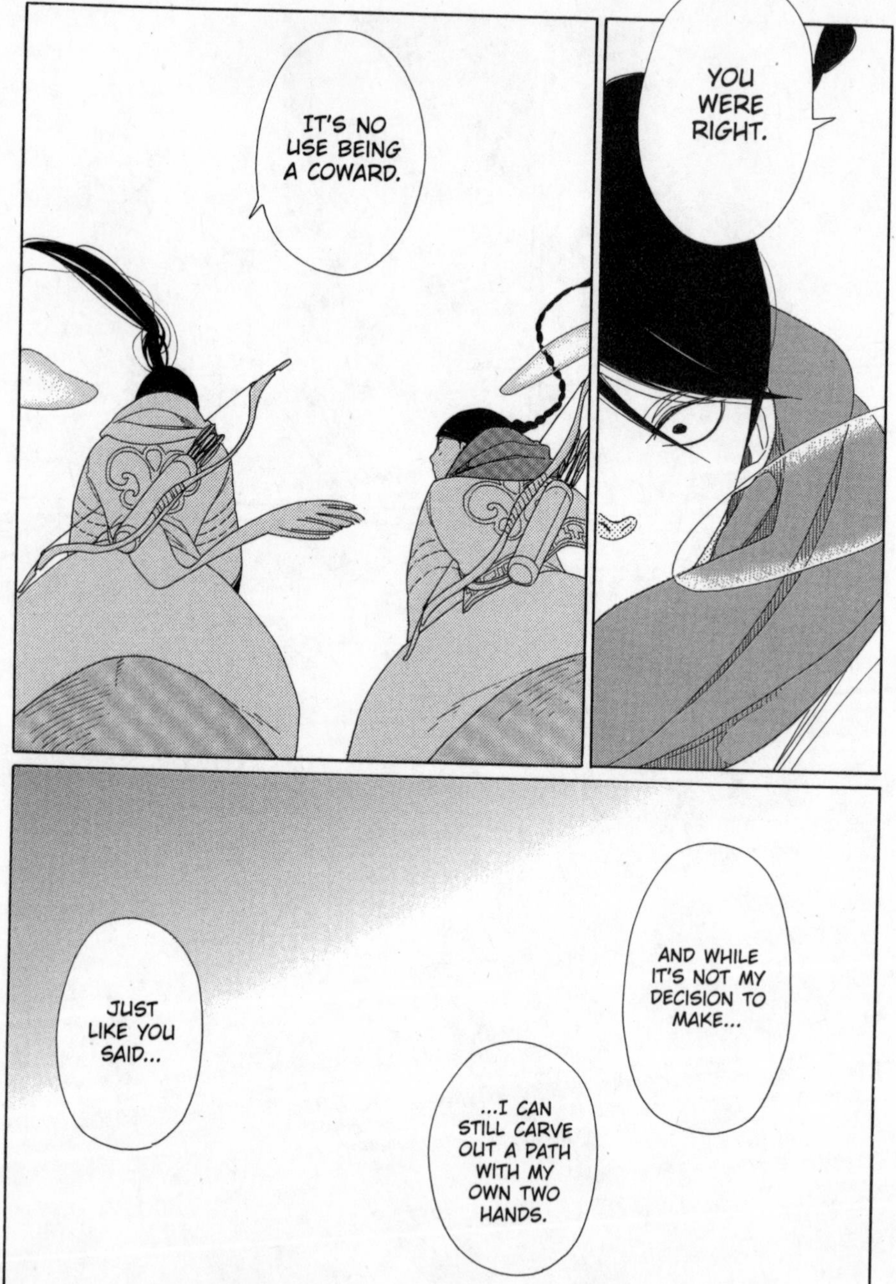
YOU WERE RIGHT.
IT'S NO USE BEING A COWARD.
AND WHILE IT'S NOT MY DECISION TO MAKE...
...I CAN STILL CARVE OUT A PATH WITH MY OWN TWO HANDS.
JUST LIKE YOU SAID...

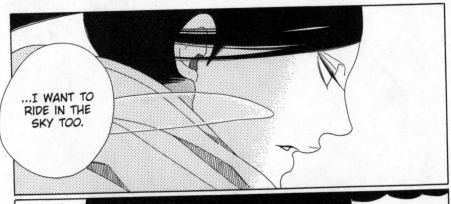

...I WANT TO RIDE IN THE SKY TOO.

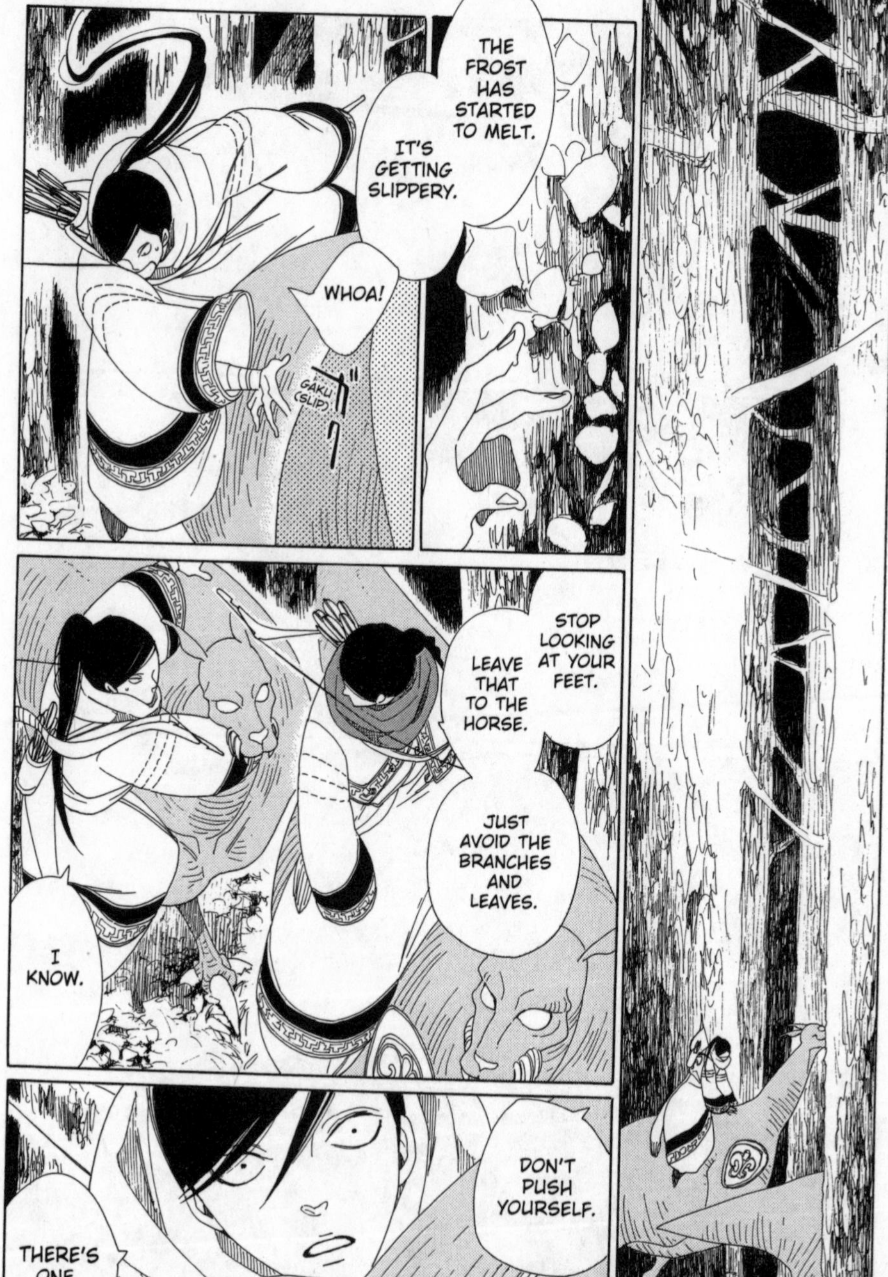
THE FROST HAS STARTED TO MELT.
IT'S GETTING SLIPPERY.
WHOA!
GAKU (SLIP)
STOP LOOKING AT YOUR FEET.
LEAVE THAT TO THE HORSE.
JUST AVOID THE BRANCHES AND LEAVES.
I KNOW.
DON'T PUSH YOURSELF.
THERE'S ONE.

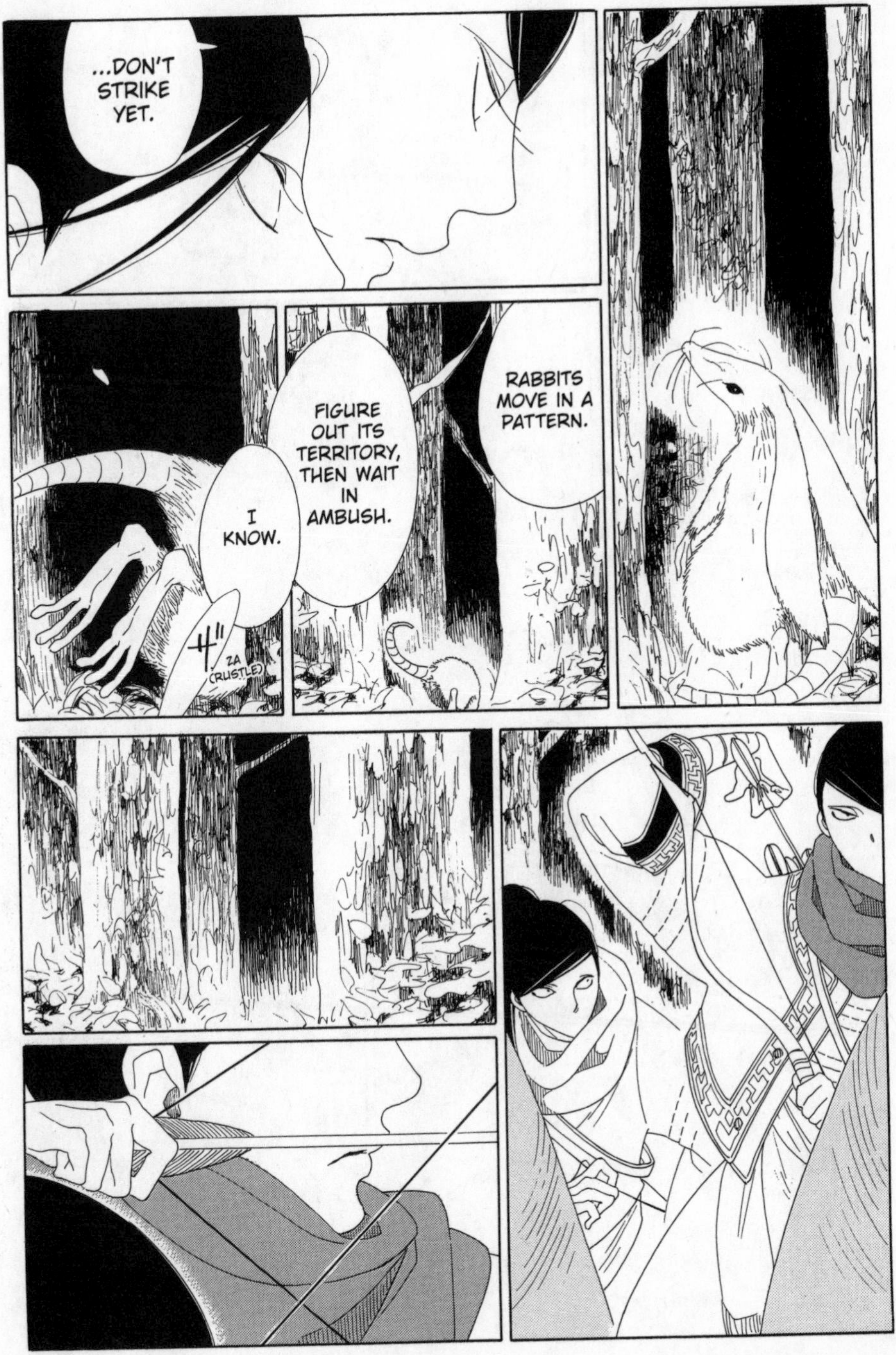
...DON'T STRIKE YET.
RABBITS MOVE IN A PATTERN.
FIGURE OUT ITS TERRITORY, THEN WAIT IN AMBUSH.
I KNOW.
ZA (RUSTLE)

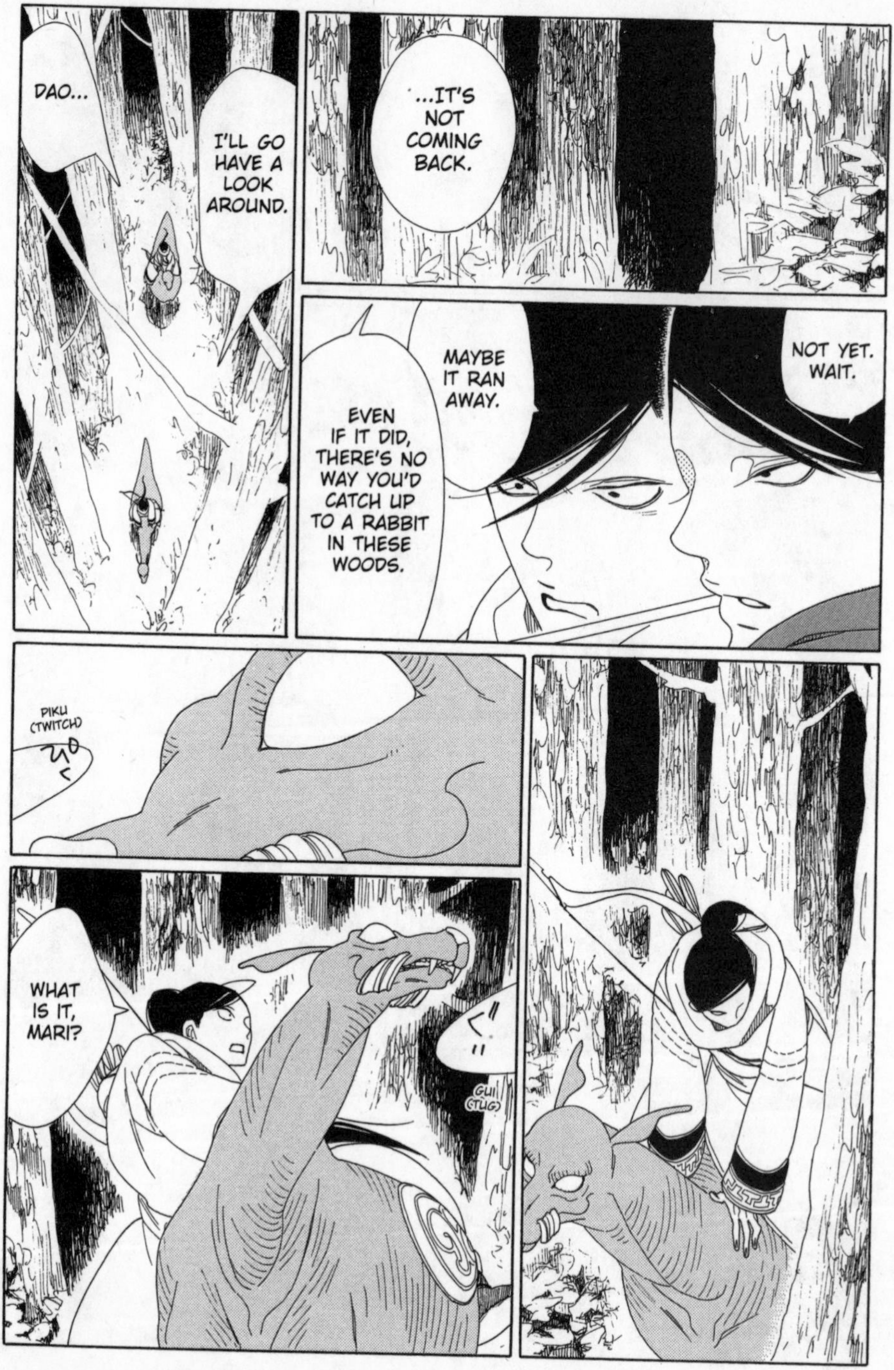
...IT'S NOT COMING BACK.
NOT YET. WAIT.
MAYBE IT RAN AWAY.
EVEN IF IT DID, THERE'S NO WAY YOU'D CATCH UP TO A RABBIT IN THESE WOODS.
DAO...
I'LL GO HAVE A LOOK AROUND.
GUI (TUG)
PIKU (TWITCH)
WHAT IS IT, MARI?

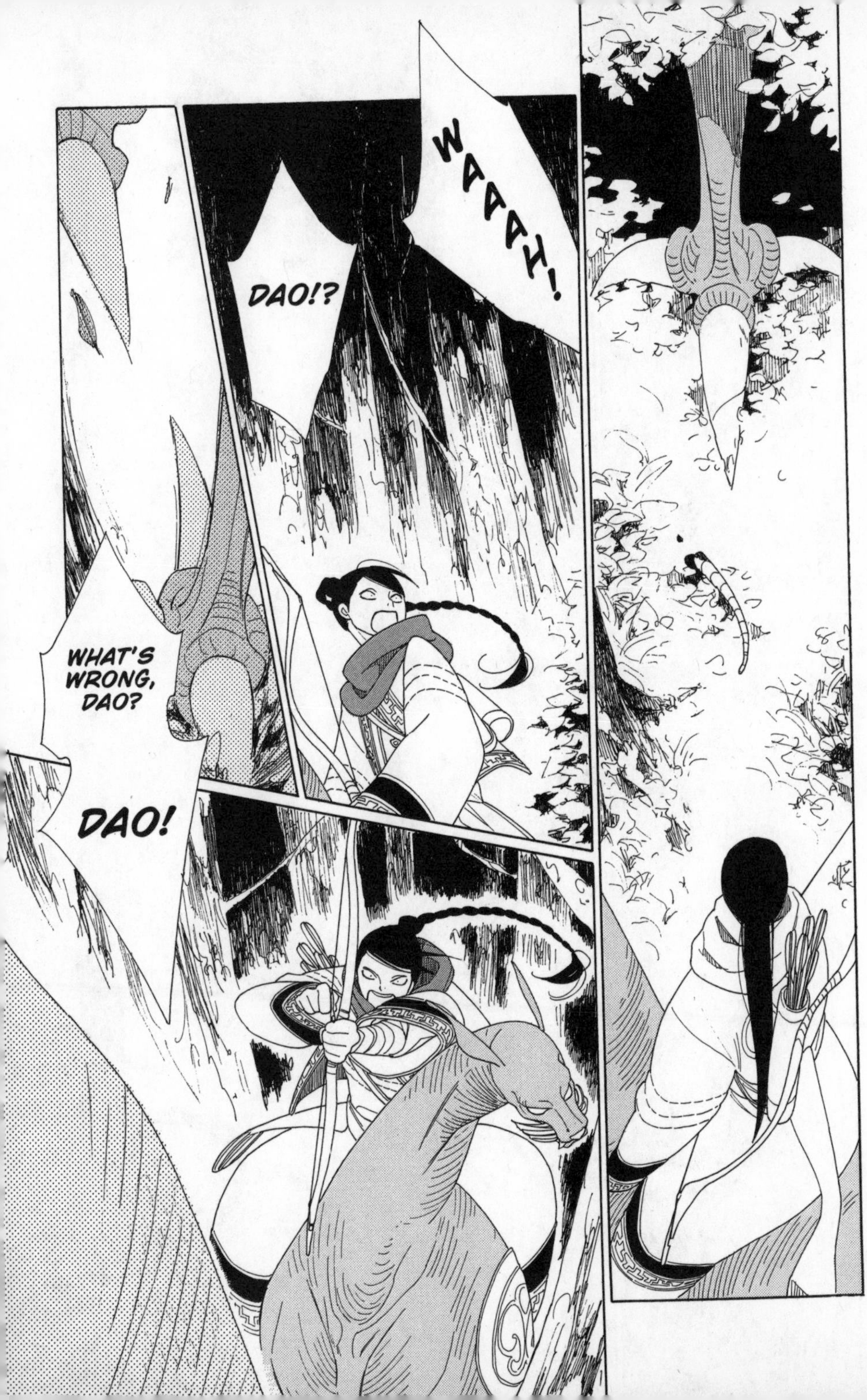
WAAAH!
DAO!?
WHAT'S WRONG, DAO?
DAO!

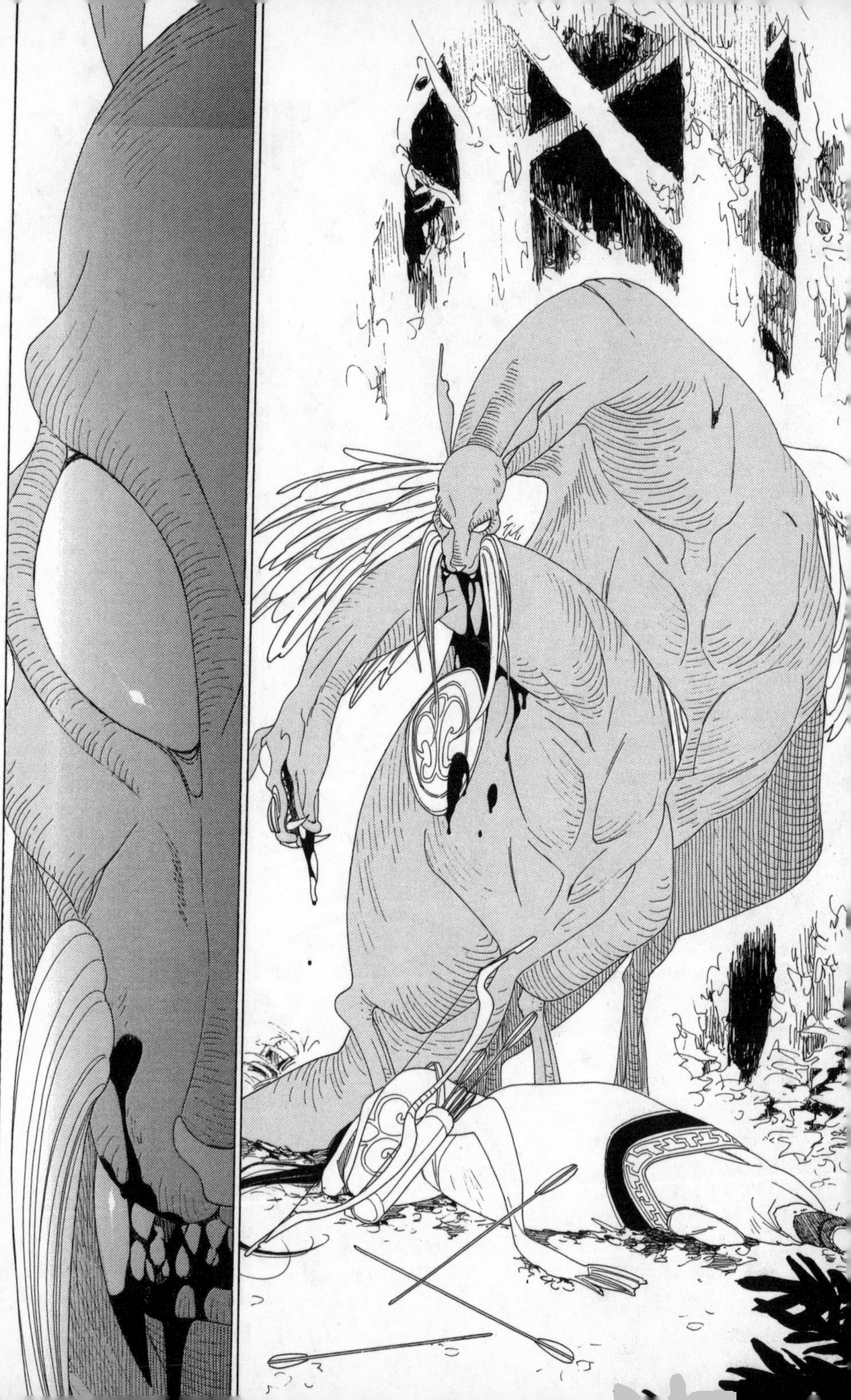

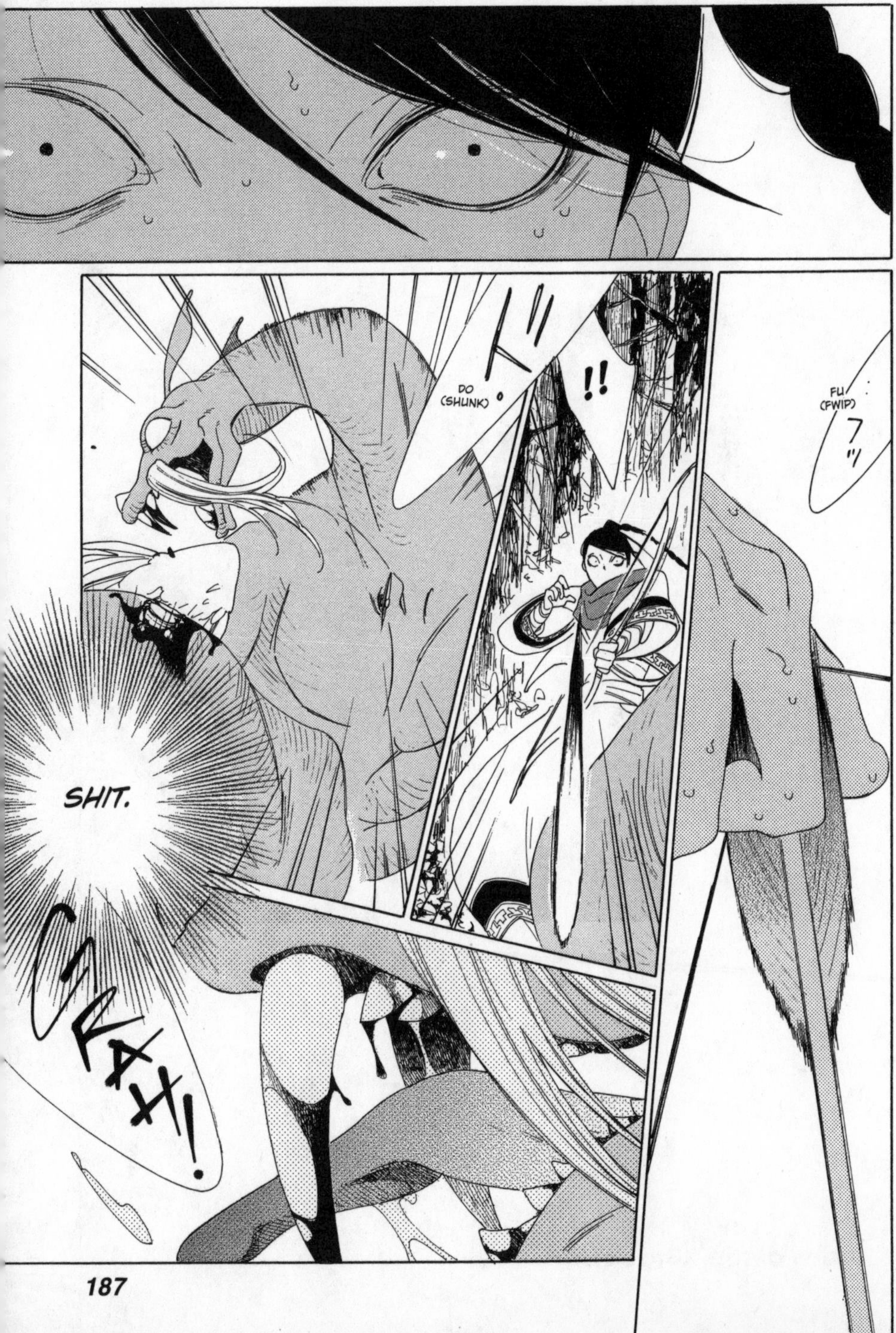
FU (FWIP)
!!
DO (SHUNK)
SHIT.
CRAH!

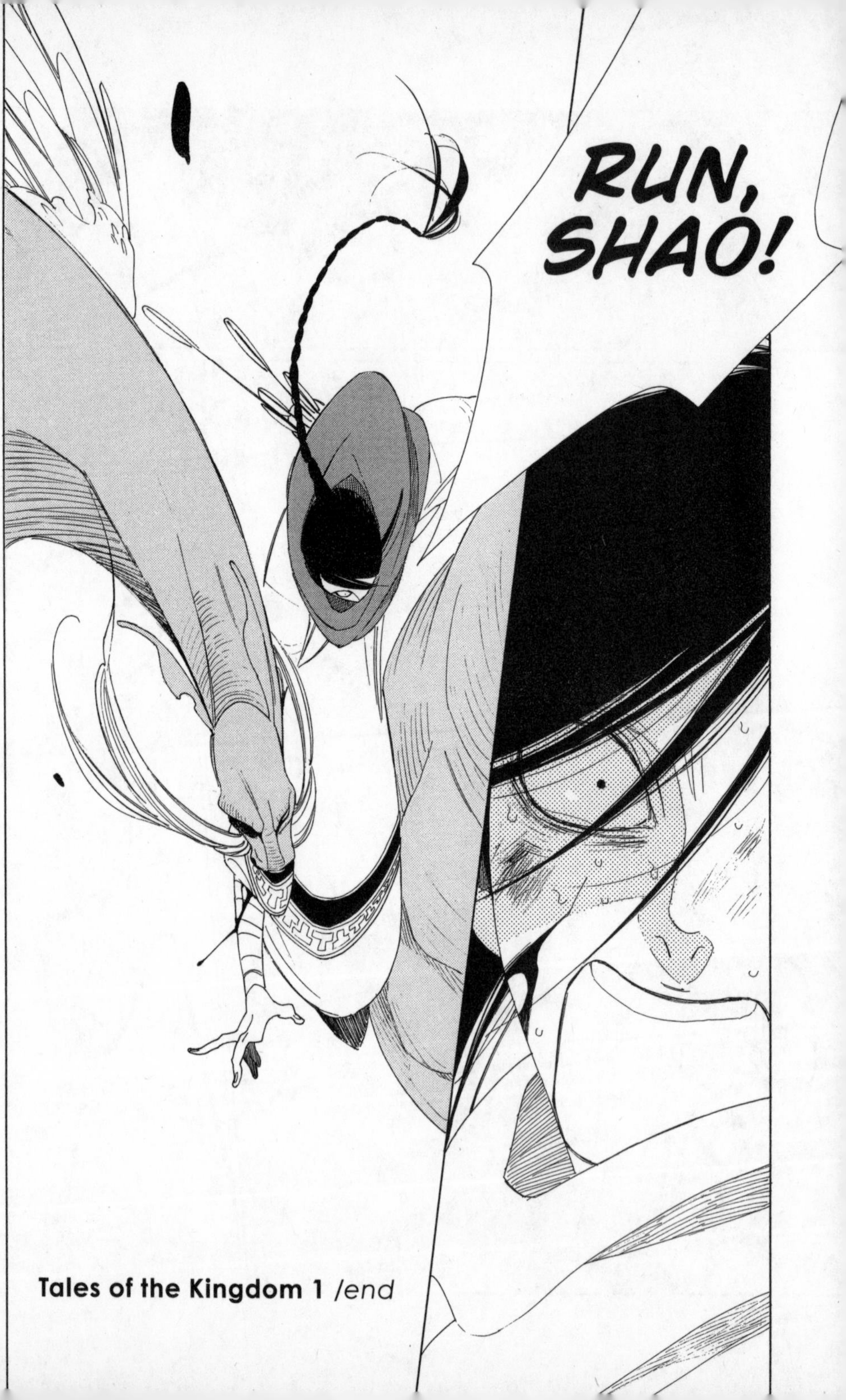
RUN, SHAO!

Tales of the Kingdom 1 /end

First Publication

Chapter 1: Adalte and Adolte ——— Web serialization, *space pocopoco*, April 2011 (Ohta Publishing Co.)

Chapter 2: Adalte and Adolte ————————————————————— *Ultra Jump*, May 2017

Chapter 3: The King and His Aide, Episode 1 ——— *MANGA EROTICS f*, Vol. 71, 2011 (Ohta Publishing Co.)

Chapter 4: The King and His Aide, Episode 2 ———————————————— *Ultra Jump*, June 2017

Chapter 5: The King and His Aide, Episode 3 ——————————— *Ultra Jump*, September 2017

Chapter 6: Shao and Dao, Episode 1 ————————————— *Ultra Jump*, December 2017

Two boys from the plains, attacked by a horse in the forest. Shao, his right arm destroyed in the attack, and Dao, whose heart longs for his twin. The brothers' fates are torn asunder as one of the two is set on the path that will lead him to become a king's aide named Han.

The cruel, fickle trick of fate.

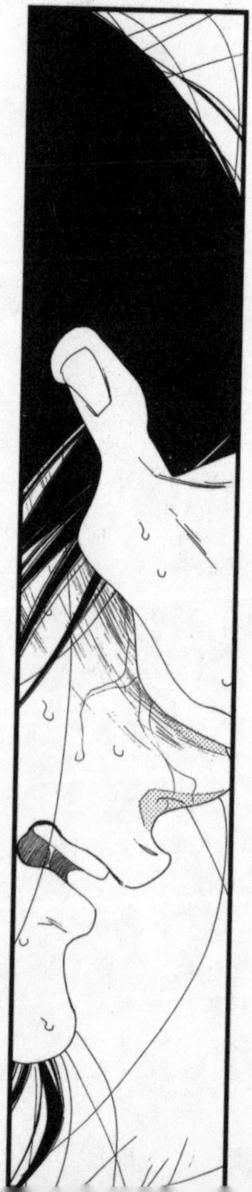

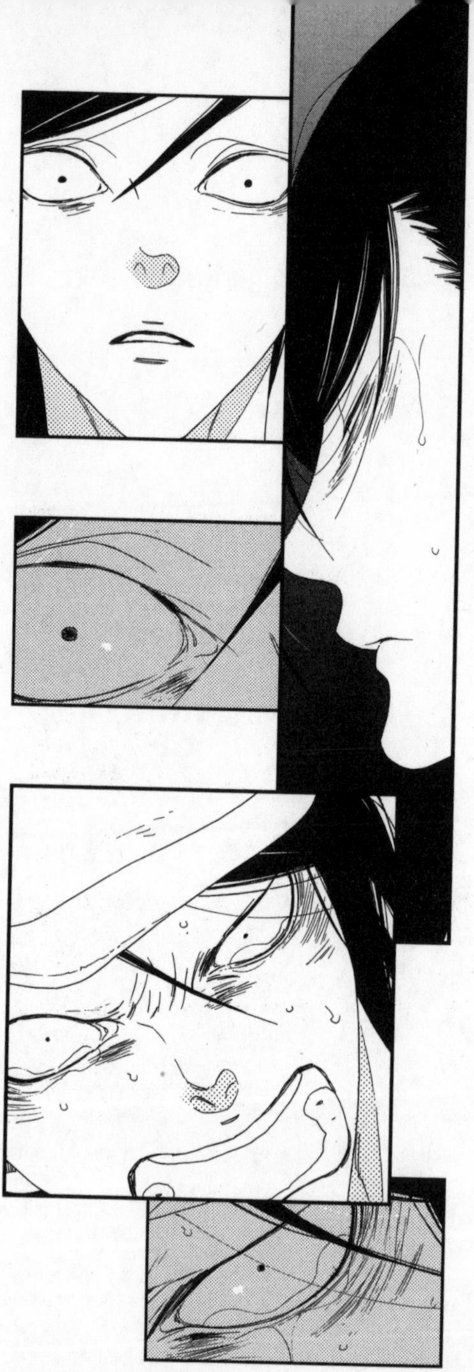

***Tales of the Kingdom*, Volume 2, coming soon.**

Tales *of the* Kingdom

1

Asumiko Nakamura

Translation: LISA COFFMAN ☀ Lettering: ABIGAIL BLACKMAN

OUKOKU MONOGATARI
© 2011 by Asumiko Nakamura
All rights reserved. First published
in Japan in 2011 by SHUEISHA, Inc.
English translation rights arranged with
SHUEISHA, Inc through Tuttle-Mori
Agency, Inc., Tokyo.

English translation © 2022 by Yen Press,
LLC

Yen Press
150 West 30th Street, 19th Floor
New York, NY 10001

Visit us at yenpress.com
facebook.com/yenpress
twitter.com/yenpress
yenpress.tumblr.com
instagram.com/yenpress

First Yen Press Edition: July 2022
Edited by Abigail Blackman &
Yen Press Editorial: Thomas McAlister
Designed by Yen Press Design:
Wendy Chan

Yen Press is an imprint of Yen Press, LLC.
The Yen Press name and logo are trademarks
of Yen Press, LLC.

Library of Congress Control Number:
2022936151

ISBNs: 978-1-9753-4586-0 (hardcover)
978-1-9753-4587-7 (ebook)

10 9 8 7 6 5 4 3 2 1

WOR

Printed in the United States of America

Tales
of the
Kingdom